The Church Teaches

THE REV. GERALD VAN ACKEREN, S.J.,
conceived the idea for this book and interested the
collaborators in the work. Translated and prepared
for publication with his continued encouragement and
counsel, it is now published with his approval. Any
future editions will be prepared at his discretion.

THE

CHURCH TEACHES

*Documents of the Church
in English Translation*

*The selections in this book were translated
and prepared for publication by*

JOHN F. CLARKSON, S.J.

JOHN H. EDWARDS, S.J.

WILLIAM J. KELLY, S.J.

JOHN J. WELCH, S.J.

St. Mary's College, St. Marys, Kansas

B. HERDER BOOK CO.

15 & 17 South Broadway, St. Louis 2, Mo.
AND *2/3 Doughty Mews, London, W.C.1*

Library of Congress Catalog Card Number: 55-10397

IMPRIMI POTEST
    Daniel H. Conway, S.J.
    Provincial, Missouri Province

NIHIL OBSTAT
    Malachi J. Donnelly, S.J.
    Censor Deputatus

IMPRIMATUR
    ✠ Edward J. Hunkeler, D.D.
    Archbishop of Kansas City in Kansas

April 20, 1955

Fourth Printing, 1961

*Printed in the United States of America
by Vail-Ballou Press, Inc., Binghamton, New York*

Rerum Christianarum Antiquarum Studiosissimo
Filio Ignati Insigni
Sacerdoti Patientissimo
Augustino C. Wand, S.J.
Scriptores
Dant Donant Dicant

Preface

In recent years new emphasis has been placed on the religion courses in our Catholic colleges and universities. Programs in religion departments have been reorganized and in some places courses in *theology* have been introduced in an effort to equip the student with a more adequate knowledge and appreciation of the reasonableness, unity, and beauty of his Catholic faith as well as its all-pervading influence in a fully human and fully Christian life.

In developing suitable programs for the intellectual religious training of students engaged in higher education, one of the main problems is the preparation of adequate handbooks for the students. Some new textbooks have already begun to appear, but as yet none has found anything like whole-hearted acceptance. Such textbooks are usually based on different conceptions of the objectives in religious intellectual training at this level of education.

In any course on the college level, however, the teacher must at least begin to acquaint his students with the fundamental sources of his knowledge. In the study of theology the primary sources are the Scriptures and tradition. But as our Holy Father Pius XII in the encyclical *Humani generis* reminds us:

> . . . Together with the sources of positive theology [*Scripture and tradition*] God has given to his Church a living teaching authority to elucidate and explain what is contained only obscurely and implicitly in the deposit of faith. The authentic interpretation of this deposit of faith has been entrusted by our divine Redeemer not to the individual members of the faithful, nor even to theologians, but solely to the teaching authority of the Church. If then the Church exercises this authority, as she has done frequently in the course of the centuries, either in the ordinary or extraordinary way, it is obvious how false that method is which would explain what is clear by what

Preface

is obscure. Indeed, the opposite procedure must be used. Hence, our predecessor of immortal memory, Pius X, when teaching that the most noble function of theology is to show how doctrine defined by the Church is contained in the sources of revelation, with very good reason added these words: "in the sense in which it has been defined by the Church."

It is clear, then, that the ultimate and infallible criterion given to man for the interpretation and understanding of God's revelation is the teaching authority of His Church. Apart from this infallible guide to the meaning of revelation, no sound theology can be developed.

The student of theology, therefore, must be given a first-hand acquaintance with the pronouncements of this teaching authority, if he is to take even the first steps in theological learning. However, all these documents were composed originally either in Latin or Greek—languages difficult to learn and not easily mastered in a way which gives ready access to the treasures of knowledge which they contain. Even seminarians who have had several years of training in Latin still find the stately language of the Church difficult, and eagerly search for translations in their native tongue.

The urgent need for a collection of the more important of these documents in English translation was the reason for initiating the project which has now culminated in the publication of this volume. The translators invited to do the work are competent Latin and Greek scholars who have also manifested their proficiency in theological learning. Although the work has been checked and re-checked, we would be very grateful for any forthcoming suggestions for improving either the translations themselves or the selection of the documents used. Helped in this way, we hope eventually to provide a truly valuable vade mecum for the American student of theology.

GERALD VAN ACKEREN, S.J.

Foreword

This book aims to present to the student of dogmatic theology a translation of some documents of the Church that are most frequently used and are most important for the ordinary courses of theology. In the first place a series of creeds is presented, for the creeds are usually quite general in their dogmatic content. The other documents follow, grouped according to treatises that are now commonly used in the presentation of dogmatic theology. Within each section chronological order is followed.

The introductions to the several divisions of the book and to individual selections do not at all pretend to supplant the work of the teacher in supplying the background necessary for the correct interpretation and evaluation of each document. They are merely intended as helps to give some preliminary orientation for the benefit of the teacher or student, and above all of those persons who may read this book without the guidance of a theologian. Even a competent Church historian or historian of dogma can welcome a handy framework of names and dates. The principal aim was to make the introductory remarks pertinent and accurate, but by no means exhaustive. Usually there is but one fairly complete introduction for each document; if selections from the same document appear elsewhere in the book, a cross reference is made to this principal introduction.

For the convenience of students, there is a topical index that indicates where important theses of each dogmatic treatise can be verified from the sources. There is also a list of the ecumenical councils of the Church with an indication of the main matter treated by each council. A table of reference to Denzinger's *Enchiridion symbolorum* (29th edition) is provided to enable the student to locate easily the English translation in this book corresponding to some of the documents presented in Denzinger. Likewise, the marginal numbers that identify selections in Denzinger's collection, are put in parentheses immediately

Foreword

under the marginal numbers of *The Church Teaches*, to facilitate reference to the Latin or Greek original in Denzinger.

Whenever this book presents the translation of a selection that also appears in Denzinger, the translation has been made from the text as given in Denzinger, unless something else is expressly noted. For the most part, the twenty-fourth edition of Denzinger was used; for more recent documents the enlarged twenty-eighth and twenty-ninth editions were followed.

It is important to notice that, unless some other indication is given, the translation always follows the Greek text when this is given in Denzinger. For translations that are not made from Denzinger, the source of the document is indicated each time the document is presented.

To avoid cumbersome and unnecessary footnotes, this book dispenses with identifying quotations and providing references given in the text of an ecclesiastical document. The reader desiring full information must consult the corresponding number of Denzinger or the source from which the translation has been made. However, references to Sacred Scripture, cross references to other selections in this book, and references to Denzinger are provided in parentheses in the text of the translation.

Our thanks: to the Rev. Gerald Van Ackeren, S.J., professor of dogmatic theology at St. Mary's College, St. Marys, Kansas, who conceived the work and helped us during its preparation with his guidance and encouragement; to Rev. Augustin C. Wand, S.J., whose scholarship and store of learning were always at our disposal, and who patiently read and re-read the manuscript; to Rev. John E. Naus, S.J., without whose generosity the manuscript would not have been prepared; to the members of the faculty and to the students of St. Mary's College for the many impositions on their time.

Feast of St. John
December 27, 1954

John F. Clarkson, S.J.
John H. Edwards, S.J.
William J. Kelly, S.J.
John J. Welch, S.J.

Acknowledgments

The editors of the *Tablet* have given permission for the use of Monsignor Knox's translation of *Humani generis* which appeared in their periodical on September 2, 1950.

America Press has given permission for the use of its edition of *Mystici corporis* prepared by Joseph Bluett, S.J. Some changes, however, were made in the translation.

Except in the few places where our own translation of Scripture has been made, the translations of texts of the Old Testament are from the Douay version; the New Testament texts follow, for the most part, the translation published by St. Anthony Guild Press, Paterson, New Jersey, 1941, under the patronage of the Confraternity of Christian Doctrine.

The Macmillan Company has given permission to use the following quotations from *The New Testament of Our Lord and Savior Jesus Christ* (copyright 1937) translated by the Rev. F. A. Spencer, O.P.: Eph. 4:15 f.; I Cor. 12:27; Phil. 2:7.

Contents

Contents

Professions of Faith

THE APOSTLES' CREED

For many centuries there was no doubt that the apostles themselves had composed and authorized a summary of belief. The first serious questioning as to the authenticity of such a creed seems to have arisen at the Council of Florence (1438–45), and in the light of criticism of the ensuing centuries, it seems rather unlikely that the apostles drafted an official summary of faith. The title *Apostles' Creed* is found for the first time in a letter sent by the synod of Milan (390) to Pope St. Siricius (384–98). Though not written by the apostles, the Apostles' Creed is a faithful summary of the truths taught from the earliest days of the Church.

I believe in God the Father almighty, creator of heaven and earth. And in Jesus Christ, his only Son our Lord, who was conceived by the Holy Spirit, born of the Virgin Mary, suffered under Pontius Pilate, was crucified, died, and was buried; he descended into hell; the third day he rose again from the dead; he ascended into heaven, sits at the right hand of God the Father almighty; from there he shall come to judge the living and the dead. I believe in the Holy Spirit, the holy Catholic Church, the communion of saints, the forgiveness of sins, the resurrection of the body, and life everlasting.

1
(6)

J. N. D. Kelly, - Early Xtian Creeds

THE NICENE CREED, 325

According to Eusebius, the creed promulgated at Nicaea in the first ecumenical council (325) was based on the baptismal creed of Caesarea. However, the council modified and amplified it to protect the Catholic faith against the Arians. Although not originally intended to be a baptismal creed, the Nicene Creed nevertheless greatly influenced the revision of the baptismal creeds in use during the fourth century.

We believe in one God, the Father almighty, creator of all things both visible and invisible. And in one Lord Jesus

2
(54)

Christ, the Son of God, the only-begotten born of the Father, that is, of the substance of the Father; God from God, light from light, true God from true God; begotten, not created, consubstantial with the Father; through him all things were made, those in heaven and those on earth as well. For the sake of us men and for our salvation, he came down, was made flesh, and became man; he suffered and on the third day arose; he ascended into heaven and is going to come to judge the living and the dead. And we believe in the Holy Spirit.

As for those who say: "There was a time when he did not exist"; and, "Before he was begotten, he did not exist"; and, "He was made from nothing, or from another hypostasis or essence," alleging that the Son of God is mutable or subject to change—such persons the Catholic and apostolic Church condemns.

THE NICENO-CONSTANTINOPOLITAN CREED, 381

There are various opinions as to the origin of the Niceno-Constantinopolitan Creed. What is certain, is that after the Councils of Ephesus (431) and Chalcedon (451), this creed made its way into the liturgy of the Eastern Church and soon became the baptismal creed. It was introduced into the Western liturgy towards the end of the eighth century.

3
(86) We believe in one God, the Father almighty, creator of heaven and earth, of all things both visible and invisible. And in one Lord Jesus Christ, the only-begotten Son of God, born of the Father before all time; light from light, true God from true God; begotten, not created, consubstantial with the Father; through him all things were made. For the sake of us men and for our salvation, he came down from heaven, was made flesh by the Holy Spirit from the Virgin Mary, and became man; and he was crucified for our sake under Pontius Pilate, suffered, and was buried. And on the third day he arose according to the Scriptures; he ascended into heaven, sits at the right hand of the Father, and is going to come again in glory to judge the living and the dead. His reign will have no end. We believe in the Holy Spirit, the Lord, the giver of life; he proceeds from the Father, is adored and honored together with the Father and the Son; he spoke through the prophets. We believe in one, holy, Catholic, and apostolic

Church. We profess one baptism for the forgiveness of sins. We expect the resurrection of the dead and the life of the world to come. Amen.

THE LONG FORM OF THE CREED OF
EPIPHANIUS, *cir.* 374

There are two forms of the Creed of Epiphanius, the long and the short. Epiphanius (315?–403) himself proposed both forms in answer to numerous requests for a clear and exact explanation of Catholic doctrine. The requests were prompted by the controversy then being carried on about the Trinity and especially about the Holy Spirit. The long form was to refute the errors of unbelievers; the short form served as an instruction for catechumens before they were admitted to baptism.

We believe in one God, the Father almighty, creator of all things both invisible and visible; and in one Lord Jesus Christ, the Son of God, only-begotten, born of God the Father; born, that is, of the substance of the Father; God from God, light from light, true God from true God; begotten, not created, consubstantial with the Father. Through him all things were made, both those in heaven and those on earth, visible and invisible. He came down and was made flesh for us men and for our salvation; that is, he was in the full sense of the word born of the holy, ever-Virgin Mary by the power of the Holy Spirit. He was made man, that is, he assumed full humanity: soul, body, mind, and whatever constitutes man, excepting sin. He was not born of male seed nor was he *within* a man; but he fashioned human flesh into himself in a single holy unity—not in the way he breathed upon the prophets and spoke and worked in them, but in the full sense of the word he became man (for "the Word was made flesh" without undergoing any change or turning his divinity into humanity). He united his divinity and his humanity in the single holy perfection of his divinity (for the Lord Jesus Christ is one and not two, the same person being God and lord and king). The same Christ also suffered in his flesh; and he arose and ascended into heaven in that very body, and took his seat in glory at the right hand of the Father. He is going to come in glory in that very body to judge the living and the dead. His reign will have no end. And we believe in

4
(13)

the Holy Spirit who spoke by the Law, who preached through the prophets, and who descended on the Jordan; he speaks in the apostles and dwells in the saints. What we believe about him is this: that he is the Holy Spirit, the Spirit of God, a perfect spirit, a spirit of consolation, uncreated, who proceeds from the Father and receives from the Son; in him we believe.

We believe in one Catholic and apostolic Church, in one baptism of repentance, in the resurrection of the dead, in the just judgment of souls with their bodies, in the kingdom of heaven, and in life everlasting.

And the Catholic and apostolic Church, your mother and our mother, condemns those who say that "there was a time when the Son did not exist, nor the Holy Spirit"; or that [*either*] was made out of nothing or out of a pre-existing substance or being; and who say that the Son of God or the Holy Spirit is mutable or subject to change. Further, we condemn all those who do not admit the resurrection of the dead; and we condemn all heresies, which are alien to this orthodox faith.

THE ATHANASIAN CREED

The exact date of this creed is not certain. It was probably written in the fifth or sixth century. Its author was almost certainly not Athanasius. Long usage has given the *Quicumque* Creed great authority as a source of Catholic belief.

6
(39) Whoever wishes to be saved must, above all, keep the Catholic faith; for unless a person keeps this faith whole and entire he will undoubtedly be lost forever.

This is what the Catholic faith teaches. We worship one God in the Trinity and the Trinity in unity; we distinguish among the persons, but we do not divide the substance. For the Father is a distinct person; the Son is a distinct person; and the Holy Spirit is a distinct person. Still, the Father and the Son and the Holy Spirit have one divinity, equal glory, and coeternal majesty. What the Father is, the Son is, and the Holy Spirit is. The Father is uncreated, the Son is uncreated, and the Holy Spirit is uncreated. The Father has immensity, the Son has immensity, and the Holy Spirit has immensity. The Father is eternal, the Son is eternal, and the

4

Holy Spirit is eternal. Nevertheless, there are not three eternal beings, but one eternal being. Thus there are not three uncreated beings, nor three beings having immensity, but one uncreated being and one being that has immensity.

Likewise, the Father is omnipotent, the Son is omnipotent, and the Holy Spirit is omnipotent. Yet there are not three omnipotent beings, but one omnipotent being. Thus the Father is God, the Son is God, and the Holy Spirit is God. But there are not three gods, but one God. The Father is lord, the Son is lord, and the Holy Spirit is lord. There are not three lords, but one Lord. For according to Christian truth, we must profess that each of the persons individually is God; and according to the Christian religion we are forbidden to say that there are three gods or three lords. The Father is not made by anyone, nor created by anyone, nor generated by anyone. The Son is not made nor created, but he is generated by the Father alone. The Holy Spirit is not made nor created nor generated, but proceeds from the Father and the Son.

There is, then, one Father, not three fathers; one Son, not three sons; one Holy Spirit, not three holy spirits. In this Trinity, there is nothing that precedes, nothing subsequent to anything else. There is nothing greater, nothing lesser than anything else. But the entire three persons are coeternal and coequal with one another, so that, as we have said, we worship complete unity in the Trinity and the Trinity in unity. This, then, is what he who wishes to be saved must believe about the Trinity.

It is also necessary for eternal salvation that he believe steadfastly in the Incarnation of our Lord Jesus Christ. The true faith is: we believe and profess that our Lord Jesus Christ, the Son of God, is both God and man. As God he was begotten of the substance of the Father before time; as man he was born in time of the substance of his Mother. He is perfect God; and he is perfect man, with a rational soul and human flesh. He is equal to the Father in his divinity but he is inferior to the Father in his humanity. Although he is God and man, he is not two but one Christ. And he is one, not because his divinity was changed into flesh, but because his

7

(40)

humanity was assumed to God. He is one, not at all because of a mingling of substances, but because he is one person. As a rational soul and flesh are one man, so God and man are one Christ. He died for our salvation, descended to hell, arose from the dead on the third day, ascended into heaven, sits at the right hand of God the Father almighty, and from there he shall come to judge the living and the dead. At his coming, all men are to arise with their own bodies; and they are to give an account of their lives. Those who have done good deeds will go into eternal life; those who have done evil will go into everlasting fire.

This is the Catholic faith. Everyone must believe it, firmly and steadfastly; otherwise, he cannot be saved.

THE CREED OF THE ELEVENTH
COUNCIL OF TOLEDO, 675

This long creed is an explanation of the Catholic faith against the Priscillianists. The creed was proposed by Archbishop Quiricius to the bishops assembled at Toledo on November 7, 675, and it was adopted by the assembly (*see introd. to 299*). For the text of this creed, *see 299–305, 446–50, 879.*

THE CREED OF THE FOURTH
LATERAN COUNCIL, 1215

The first chapter of this council contains a profession of belief in the principal Catholic doctrines (*see introd. to 306*). For the text of this creed, *see 306, 455, 881, 151, 659.*

THE SECOND COUNCIL OF LYONS, 1274

A profession of faith was proposed in 1267 by Clement IV (1265–68) to Michael Palaeologus, the emperor of the East. The emperor, the clergy, and the people had to make this profession of faith to re-enter the Catholic Church. The proposed profession was finally made in 1274 at the Council of Lyons (*see introd. to 152*). For the text of this profession, *see 308, 456, 884, 660, 152.*

THE CREED OF THE COUNCIL OF TRENT, 1564

The bull *Injunctum nobis* was issued by Pope Pius IV (1559–65) on November 13, 1564. The profession of faith contained in this creed summarizes the doctrines which Catholics are to believe.

I, N., with firm faith believe and profess each and every **8**
article contained in the Symbol of faith which the holy Ro- **(994)**
man Church uses; namely: I believe in one God, the Father
almighty, maker of heaven and earth, and of all things visible
and invisible; and in one Lord Jesus Christ, the only-begotten
Son of God, born of the Father before all ages; God from God,
light from light, true God from true God; begotten not made,
of one substance with the Father; through whom all things
were made; who for us men and for our salvation came down
from heaven, and was made incarnate by the Holy Spirit of
the Virgin Mary, and was made man. He was crucified also
for us under Pontius Pilate, died, and was buried; and he rose
again the third day according to the Scriptures, and ascended
into heaven; he sits at the right hand of the Father, and he
shall come again in glory to judge the living and the dead,
and of his kingdom there will be no end. And I believe in
the Holy Spirit, the Lord, and giver of life, who proceeds
from the Father and the Son; who equally with the Father
and the Son is adored and glorified; who spoke through the
prophets. And I believe that there is one, holy, Catholic, and
apostolic Church. I confess one baptism for the remission of
sins; and I hope for the resurrection of the dead, and the life
of the world to come. Amen.

I resolutely accept and embrace the apostolic and eccle- **9**
siastical traditions and the other practices and regulations of **(995)**
that same Church. In like manner I accept Sacred Scripture
according to the meaning which has been held by holy Mother
Church and which she now holds. It is her prerogative to
pass judgment on the true meaning and interpretation of
Sacred Scripture. And I will never accept or interpret it in a
manner different from the unanimous agreement of the
Fathers.

I also acknowledge that there are truly and properly seven **10**
sacraments of the New Law, instituted by Jesus Christ our **(996)**
Lord, and that they are necessary for the salvation of the
human race, although it is not necessary for each individual
to receive them all. I acknowledge that the seven sacraments
are: baptism, confirmation, Eucharist, penance, extreme unction, holy orders, and matrimony; and that they confer grace;

and that of the seven, baptism, confirmation, and holy orders cannot be repeated without committing a sacrilege. I also accept and acknowledge the customary and approved rites of the Catholic Church in the solemn administration of these sacraments. I embrace and accept each and every article on original sin and justification declared and defined in the most holy Council of Trent.

11
(997) I likewise profess that in the Mass a true, proper, and propitiatory sacrifice is offered to God on behalf of the living and the dead, and that the body and blood together with the soul and divinity of our Lord Jesus Christ is truly, really, and substantially present in the most holy sacrament of the Eucharist, and that there is a change of the whole substance of the bread into the body, and of the whole substance of the wine into blood; and this change the Catholic Church calls transubstantiation. I also profess that the whole and entire Christ and a true sacrament is received under each separate species.

12
(998) I firmly hold that there is a purgatory, and that the souls detained there are helped by the prayers of the faithful. I likewise hold that the saints reigning together with Christ should be honored and invoked, that they offer prayers to God on our behalf, and that their relics should be venerated. I firmly assert that images of Christ, of the Mother of God ever Virgin, and of the other saints should be owned and kept, and that due honor and veneration should be given to them. I affirm that the power of indulgences was left in the keeping of the Church by Christ, and that the use of indulgences is very beneficial to Christians.

13
(999) I acknowledge the holy, Catholic, and apostolic Roman Church as the mother and teacher of all churches; and I promise and swear true obedience to the Roman Pontiff, vicar of Christ and successor of Blessed Peter, Prince of the Apostles.

14
(1000) I unhesitatingly accept and profess all the doctrines (especially those concerning the primacy of the Roman Pontiff and his infallible teaching authority) handed down, defined, and explained by the sacred canons and ecumenical councils

and especially those of this most holy Council of Trent (and by the ecumenical Vatican Council). And at the same time I condemn, reject, and anathematize everything that is contrary to those propositions, and all heresies without exception that have been condemned, rejected, and anathematized by the Church. I, N., promise, vow, and swear that, with God's help, I shall most constantly hold and profess this true Catholic faith, outside which no one can be saved and which I now freely profess and truly hold. With the help of God, I shall profess it whole and unblemished to my dying breath; and, to the best of my ability, I shall see to it that my subjects or those entrusted to me by virtue of my office hold it, teach it, and preach it. So help me God and his holy Gospel. [*The words in parentheses in this paragraph are now inserted into the Tridentine profession of faith by order of Pope Pius IX in a decree issued by the Holy Office, January 20, 1877* (Acta Sanctae Sedis, X [1877], 71 ff.).]

Revelation, Faith, and Reason

The Catholic religion is a revealed religion. Its existence, therefore, depends on two acts, the one of the Creator, the other of the creature. There must be a positive act of communication, by which the Creator makes known to the creature the religious truth he intends to reveal. This act is divine revelation. There must be a corresponding act of acceptance by which the creature receives and holds as true the revelation of the Creator on the latter's authority. This act is faith.

The divine communication is something supernatural, not merely as an event that takes place outside of the ordinary, natural course of events, but also in its contents; because the principal revealed truths so far exceed the ability of natural reason that the latter cannot discover or fully understand them. Corresponding to the supernaturalness of revelation, there is a need for the interior supernatural help of grace if men are to believe the revelation.

The Church has always found it necessary to insist on the supernaturalness of revelation and of faith. This has been especially true since the nineteenth century when rationalism and naturalism have threatened to distort the true idea of revealed religion. Yet in these same modern times the Church has been obliged to denounce the almost opposite error. Against the mistaken zeal of those who tried to safeguard revealed religion by a blind kind of faith, emotional rather than intellectual, the Church has had to insist on the reasonableness of faith. It has, therefore, upheld the ability of the human mind to know objective truth in general and, specifically, to know the truths of God's existence and of his dominion over the moral lives of *men. And the Church teaches unhesitatingly that man can recognize the divine signs, notably miracles and prophecies, that God uses as testimonies that he has spoken to men.*

BAUTAIN'S REJECTION OF FIDEISM, 1840

Personal religious experience and a tincture of Kantian philosophy, along with a strong repugnance for contemporary rationalism, influenced Père Louis Bautain (1796–1867), professor at Strasbourg, to exaggerate the role of divine revelation to the point of excluding human reason as a source of religious knowledge. This theory of the relation of faith to reason, known as fideism, counts Bautain as its principal representative. After an examination of Bautain's principal work, *The Philosophy of Christianity,* had been made at Rome at the direction of Pope Gregory XVI (1831–46), Père Bautain rejected his errors by signing the following propositions September 8, 1840. It should be noted, however, that the author of these propositions appears to be, not the Holy See, but Monsignor Roess, the coadjutor of Strasbourg.

Relation of faith and reason

15
(1622)
1. The reasoning process can prove with certitude the existence of God and the infiniteness of his perfections. Faith, a heavenly gift, is posterior to revelation; hence, faith cannot be employed against an atheist to prove the existence of God (*see 32*).

16
(1623)
2. The divine origin of the Mosaic revelation is proved with certitude both by the oral and the written traditions of the Jewish religion and by those of the Christian religion.

17
(1624)
3. The proof based on the miracles of Jesus Christ, sensible and striking for the eyewitnesses, has by no means lost its force and clarity for subsequent generations. We find this proof with all its certitude in the authenticity of the New Testament and in the written and oral tradition of all Christians. By this twofold tradition, we must point out the proof for the divine origin of revelation to those who either reject it or who have not yet accepted it but are seeking it.

18
(1625)
4. We have no right to demand that the unbeliever admit the Resurrection of our divine Savior before we have proposed to him arguments that are certain. These arguments

are deduced by a reasoning process from the aforesaid tradition.

5. In these various questions reason precedes faith and must lead us to it (*see 33*).

19
(1626)

6. Even though reason was rendered weak and clouded by original sin, it still has a sufficiently clear power of perception to lead us with certitude to the knowledge of the existence of God and to the revelation given to the Jews through Moses and to the Christians through our adorable God-man.

20
(1627)

THE ENCYCLICAL *QUI PLURIBUS,* 1846

In the midst of a great political unrest in Europe and in his own Papal States, Pope Pius IX (1846–78) found the time to protect the Catholic faith from the inroads of a new spirit of rationalism and liberalism in philosophical and theological thought. A reaction against the fideism of Bautain (1796–1867) and the traditionalism of de Lamennais (1782–1854) gave rise to the "false freedom of science" of James Frohschammer (*see 42–50, 176 f.*). Previous to the condemnation of Frohschammer, the pope had vigorously condemned Günther (*see DB 1656*) who also exalted human reason over faith. In the encyclical, November 9, 1846, the pope outlined the correct relation between faith and reason and thereby guarded against the errors that threatened the very essence of religion.

(For) you are well aware, Venerable Brethren, that (these) deadly enemies of Christianity have been carried along, sad to say, by the blind impulse of their irreligious madness to so rash an expression of their opinions that, opening their mouths to blaspheme God (*see Apoc. 13:6*) with an utterly new kind of boldness, they do not hesitate to teach quite openly that the sacred mysteries of our religion are fictions and human inventions; that the doctrine of the Catholic Church is opposed to the welfare of human society. Indeed, they do not fear to renounce even Christ himself and God. In addition to this, they pretend that they alone know the road to happiness so that they may with greater ease ensnare and deceive people, especially the unwary and the unlearned, and lead them along their own erroneous ways. For the same purpose they are quite ready to usurp the name of philosophers, with the

21
(1634)

implication that philosophy, which is wholly engaged in investigating natural truths, ought to reject those truths which the supreme and most merciful God—himself the author of nature in its entirety—has deigned in his unparalleled generosity and mercy to reveal to men that they may attain the true happiness of salvation.

22
(1635) Hence, by an utterly absurd and most fallacious type of argumentation, they continually appeal to the power and excellence of human reason, and extol it in opposition to the most holy Christian faith; and with the greatest boldness they assert that faith is opposed to human reason (*see 54*). It is impossible to imagine or devise any opinion more foolish than this, or more vicious, or more repugnant to reason itself. For although faith is above reason, still there can never be found a real opposition or disagreement between them, since both take their origin from one and the same source of unchangeable and eternal truth, the great and good God; and thus they are mutually helpful. As a result, right reason demonstrates, safeguards, and defends the truth of faith, while faith frees reason from all errors and wonderfully enlightens it, strengthens it, and perfects it with a knowledge of divine things (*see 79*).

23
(1636) In truth, it is with the same deceitfulness, Venerable Brethren, that those enemies of divine revelation, while heaping the highest praises upon human progress, would like to use it as an argument in their wholly rash and sacrilegious attack upon the Catholic religion, just as if religion itself were not the work of God, but of men, or as if it were some philosophical discovery that could be brought to completion by human means (*see 53*). To those who so deplorably wander from the truth, the reproach can most fittingly be applied that Tertullian rightly cast upon philosophers of his own day, "who begot a Christian religion that was Stoic, or Platonic, or dialectical." And, truly, since our most holy religion was not discovered by human reason, but was most mercifully revealed to men by God, anyone, then, can very easily see that this religion itself gets all its power from the authority of the God who has spoken and that it can never be deduced or brought to completion by human reason.

To guard against any deception and error in so important **24** a matter, human reason should undoubtedly inquire with **(1637)** all diligence into the fact of divine revelation to make sure that God has spoken and to be able to pay him a reasonable service, as the Apostle so wisely teaches (*see Rom. 12:1*). For everyone knows, in fact, it is impossible not to know that, when God speaks, he is to be believed entirely, and that nothing is more in conformity with reason itself than to be satisfied with, and hold firmly to, whatever is known to have been revealed by God, who can neither deceive nor be deceived.

But how many wonderful, lucid arguments are at hand by **25** which human reason should be thoroughly convinced that **(1638)** the religion of Christ is divine and that "the source of our dogmas is entirely from above, from the Lord of heaven," and that, therefore, there is nothing that stands out as more certain, more secure, or more holy than our faith, nothing that rests upon firmer principles. Actually it is the faith that drives out all vice; it is the teacher of life, the guide to salvation, and the mother and nurse of all virtues; it is confirmed by the birth, life, death, resurrection, wisdom, prodigies, and prophecies of its divine author Christ Jesus who brings it to perfection; it is everywhere refulgent with the light of heavenly doctrine and enriched with the treasures of heavenly wealth; it is most brilliant and remarkable in the predictions of so many prophets, the splendor of so many miracles, the constancy of so many martyrs, and the glory of so many saints; it promulgates the saving laws of Christ and daily acquires greater strength from even the most cruel persecutions. With the cross as its only standard it has spread over the whole earth, on land and sea, from east to west; it has stamped out the base error of idolatry; it has dissipated the clouds of error; it has triumphed over enemies of every kind; it has enlightened with the light of divine knowledge and subjected to the most sweet yoke of Christ all peoples, nations, and tribes, no matter how barbarous and cruel, and no matter how diverse in natural disposition, customs, laws, and institutions —announcing peace and good tidings to all men (*see Isa. 52:7*). Surely all these things are so resplendent with the divine power and wisdom that any reflecting mind may easily come to understand that the Christian faith is the work of God.

26
(1639)
Consequently, when human reason clearly and manifestly sees from these arguments, which are as solid as they are sublime, that God is the author of this faith, it can go no further. Completely casting aside and rejecting every doubt and difficulty, it must make its total submission to that faith because it is certain that God is the author of everything that faith itself prescribes for men to believe and do.

ALLOCUTION *SINGULARI QUADAM*, 1854

In a secret consistory, December 9, 1854, the pope condemns those who claim that human reason is so exalted a gift of God that no limits can be imposed upon it by faith or religion.

27
(1642)
There are, furthermore, Venerable Brethren, certain men of outstanding learning, who admit that religion is by far the most remarkable gift given to men by God and who, nevertheless, greatly exalt human reason and consider it of such great worth that they foolishly think it is equal in value to religion itself. Hence, in their vain opinion, the theological disciplines are to be handled in the same way as the philosophical (*see 56*). But the former studies rest upon the dogmas of faith, and there is nothing more sure and more stable than faith—whereas the latter are evolved and explained by human reason, and there is nothing more uncertain than reason, seeing that it varies according to different mental capacities and is exposed to innumerable fallacies and inaccuracies. And so when the authority of the Church was rejected, there was thrown open a wide field of very abstruse, tangled questions; and human reason, trusting in its weak powers and rushing along without due restraint, fell into the most shameful errors. At this point, we have not the time or the desire to enumerate these errors since they are well known to you and thoroughly understood. These errors have proved quite harmful both in religious and in civil affairs. And, on account of this, these men who give human reason more credit for power than it merits must be shown that this is altogether contrary to that most true saying of the teacher

of the Gentiles: "If anyone thinks himself to be something, whereas he is nothing, he deceives himself" (*see Gal. 6:3*). They must be shown how arrogant it is to dissect the mysteries that the most merciful God has deigned to reveal to us, and to presume to discover and comprehend them with the weakness and limitation of the human mind since they far exceed the powers of our intellect, which on the word of the same Apostle must be brought into the captivity of obedience to faith (*see II Cor. 10:5*).

And such clients, or rather devotees, of human reason, who set it up as their unerring teacher and promise themselves every success under its guidance, have surely forgotten what a deep and severe wound was inflicted on human nature through the sin of our first parent; for darkness has clouded the mind and the will has been made prone to evil. This is the reason why the most famous philosophers of antiquity, in spite of their many splendid writings, have contaminated their doctrines with very serious errors; this is the reason for that ceaseless struggle that we are conscious of within ourselves and about which the Apostle speaks: "I see a law in my members, warring against the law of my mind" (*see Rom. 7:23*). **28** **(1643)**

In reality, since it is certain that the light of reason has been dimmed and that the human race has fallen miserably from its former state of justice and innocence because of original sin, which is communicated to all the descendants of Adam, can anyone still think that reason by itself is sufficient for the attainment of truth? If one is to avoid slipping and falling in the midst of such great dangers and in the face of such weakness, dare he deny that divine religion and heavenly grace are necessary for salvation? To be sure, God most generously gives these helps to those who humbly and prayerfully request them—for it is written: "God resists the proud, but gives grace to the humble" (*Jas. 4:6*). And for that very reason Christ our Lord turned to his Father on one occasion and declared that the deepest secrets of truth are not manifested to the prudent and wise men of this world, who are proud of their own talent and learning and are unwilling to render the submission implied in faith, but rather **29** **(1644)** to the humble and simple men, who rely upon the revelation of divine faith for their strength and conviction (*see Matt. 11:25; Luke 10:21*).

30
(1645) You ought to impress this salutary warning on the minds of those who rate the power of human reason so highly that with it they boldly attempt to examine critically and explain even mysteries themselves. This is the height of folly and madness. Strive to call them back from such intellectual perversity. Take care to explain that God's providence has given to men no more excellent gift than the authority of divine faith; that this faith is like a guiding beacon in the darkness for us to follow towards life; that it is absolutely necessary for salvation, since "without faith it is impossible to please God" (*Heb. 11:6*), and "he who does not believe shall be condemned" (*Mark 16:16*).

BONNETTY'S REJECTION OF TRADITIONALISM, 1855

Like the fideism of Bautain, a doctrine known as traditionalism won acceptance among certain Catholics who went to extremes in their reaction to Kantian rationalism. Abbé de Lamennais (1782–1854) had asserted in his *Essay on Indifference* that the agreement of mankind is the sole guarantee of truth in religious matters; the publicist-philosopher Louis Bonald (1754–1840) had thought that human language itself was the result of a primitive revelation, transmitted by *tradition*. In June, 1855, the French philosopher Augustin Bonnetty (1798–1879), who had been spreading similar errors, was called upon by the Sacred Congregation of the Index to subscribe to the following propositions vindicating the rights of human reason. Approval of the propositions had been given by Pope Pius IX (1846–78).

31
(1649) 1. "Although faith is above reason, still there never can be found a real opposition or disagreement between them, since both take their origin from one and the same unchangeable source of truth, the great and good God; and thus they are mutually helpful" (*see 22, 79*).

32
(1650) 2. The reasoning process can prove with certitude the existence of God, the spirituality of the soul, and the freedom of man. Faith is subsequent to revelation and, therefore, one cannot properly appeal to it against an atheist to prove the existence of God nor against a disciple of naturalism and

fatalism to prove the spirituality and the freedom of the rational soul (*see 15, 18*).

3. The use of reason precedes faith and with the help of revelation and grace leads man to it (*see 19*).

33
(*1651*)

4. The method used by St. Thomas and St. Bonaventure and other scholastics after them does not lead to rationalism nor has it been the reason why philosophy in the present-day schools issues in naturalism and pantheism. These doctors and teachers are not to be blamed for using this method, especially since they used it with the approbation or at least with the silent approval of the Church.

34
(*1652*)

CONDEMNATION OF ERRORS OF ONTOLOGISM, 1861

Ontologism is a system of philosophy which, in the attempt to explain man's natural knowledge of God, maintains that God and divine ideas are the first objects of natural knowledge and that the first act of knowledge is really a natural intuition of God. The order of knowledge is held to be the same as the order of existence; and, therefore, since all things that exist have their existence from God, so all things we know, we know by knowing their ideas which are identified with God. In our abstract idea of anything we attain the notion of being in general, the ontologists claimed, and the knowledge of being in general is not abstract but rather is knowledge of infinite subsistent being itself.

First proposed by Malebranche (1638–1715), the doctrine of ontologism, condemned in the following selections, was proposed by Vincenzio Gioberti (1801–52) who claimed that our first intellectual perception was an intuition of God. Some Catholics like Gerhard C. Ubaghs (1800–75), of the University of Louvain, taught a modified ontologism. Later on Pope Leo XIII (1878–1903) condemned some propositions of Rosmini-Serbati (1797–1855) because of the ontologism underlying his whole thought.

Ontologism tended to pantheism, and this was the main danger it presented to Catholicism. But ontologism also directly tended to overestimate the natural power of the intellect to know God, thereby jeopardizing the role of faith. On September 18, 1861, a decree of the Congregation of the Inquisition listed the following propositions and declared that they cannot safely be taught.

35
(1659)
1. An immediate knowledge of God, which is at least habitual, is so essential to the human intellect that without that knowledge it can know nothing. It is the light of the intellect itself.

36
(1660)
2. That *being* which we understand in all things and without which we understand nothing is the divine being.

37
(1661)
3. Universals considered objectively are not really distinct from God.

38
(1662)
4. The innate notion of God as unmodified being embraces every other knowledge in an eminent way, so that through that notion we implicitly have knowledge of every being under whatever aspect it is knowable.

39
(1663)
5. All other ideas are merely modifications of the idea by which God is understood as unmodified being.

40
(1664)
6. Created things are in God as the part in the whole, not indeed in a formal whole, but in an infinite, absolutely simple whole, which posits its quasi parts outside itself without any division or lessening of itself.

41
(1665)
7. Creation can thus be explained: by means of the special act itself by which God understands and wills himself as distinct from a certain creature, he produces the creature, for example, man.

LETTER TO THE ARCHBISHOP OF MUNICH, 1862

James Frohschammer (1821–93), a Catholic priest, taught in the University of Munich. In the letter *Gravissimas inter* to the archbishop of Munich, December 11, 1862, Pope Pius IX (1846–78) expressed his great distress at the trouble that Frohschammer's books were causing. The pope told the archbishop that the Congregation of the Index declared that the doctrine contained in Frohschammer's books was erroneous and opposed to Catholic truth. With a typical rationalist's bias, Frohschammer asserted the complete independence of the human reason from any superior authority. Frohschammer is condemned for rejecting the role of faith in the knowledge of the truths of the Catholic faith. And in the same letter the pope clearly indicates the role of philosophy in relation to the truths of faith.

Revelation, Faith, and Reason

Rejection of rationalism

During these days of great disturbance and unrest and among
other most serious calamities which surround Us, We are
especially sad to be informed that there are to be found in
various parts of Germany some—even Catholics—who, in
teaching sacred theology and philosophy, have no hesitation
about introducing a type of freedom in teaching and writing previously unheard of in the Church. They are openly and
publicly professing and spreading about among the people
new opinions worthy of the utmost censure.

42
(1666)

Because of this, We were considerably saddened, Venerable Brother, when the distressing report reached Us that the
priest James Frohschammer, a teacher of philosophy at your
Academy of Munich, was displaying worse than all the rest
the aforesaid freedom in teaching and in writing, and that he
was upholding very dangerous errors in his published works.
Without delay We ordered Our Congregation of the Index
to examine very thoroughly the chief works which were being circulated under the authorship of this priest Frohschammer and to bring a report on the matter to Us. These books
written in German have for their titles: *An Introduction to
Philosophy* [*Einleitung in die Philosophie*], *The Freedom of
Science* [*Über die Freiheit der Wissenschaft*], and *Athenaeum*.
They were published there in Munich, the first in 1858, the
second in 1861, the third in the course of this year, 1862. Accordingly, this Congregation . . . judged that the author was
not thinking correctly along many lines and that his doctrine wandered far from Catholic truth.

43
(1667)

His errors are chiefly of two kinds. First, the author attributes certain powers to human reason which by no means
belong to it. Secondly, he concedes to human reason such an
unlimited freedom of thought and scope of operation that
the Church's own rights and her position of authority are
completely set aside.

44
(1668)

In the first place, the author teaches that philosophy, if
one has a correct understanding of it, can perceive and
understand not only those Christian dogmas which natural
reason has in common with faith (since they are a common

45
(1669)

object of perception), but also those dogmas which chiefly and properly constitute the Christian religion and faith. He teaches, for example, that the supernatural destiny of man, with all the truths pertinent to it, and the most holy mystery of the Incarnation of our Lord lie within the province of human reason and philosophy. He claims that human reason, given these objects, can come to a scientific knowledge about them by its own proper principles. Even though the author makes some distinction between the latter and the former kind of dogmas [*i.e., between truths common to faith and reason and those known by faith alone*] and acknowledges that reason has a lesser claim upon the latter, nevertheless, he teaches quite clearly that even the latter dogmas are to be included among those which constitute a true and proper object of science or philosophy. Hence, in this author's opinion, the conclusion definitely can and must be drawn that reason, once given the object of revelation, is able of itself to arrive at a scientific knowledge or a certitude about the most hidden mysteries of the wisdom and goodness of God and even of his free will; and this, starting not from divine authority, but from its own natural principles and power. And anyone even slightly acquainted with the rudiments of Christian doctrine immediately and clearly understands the falsity and the error contained in this opinion of the author.

46
(1670)

For if those philosophers were only safeguarding the true and rightful principles of reason and philosophy, they would certainly deserve due praise. For true and sound philosophy rightfully occupies a distinguished position, since philosophy should diligently seek truth and correctly and thoroughly cultivate and enlighten human reason which, though darkened by the sin of the first man, has by no means been destroyed. Moreover, philosophy's task is to ascertain the object of rational knowledge and many truths, to understand them well, and to look to their progress. By means of arguments sought from reason's own principles, philosophy should demonstrate, vindicate, and defend a large number of these truths which faith also proposes for belief; such as, the existence of God, his nature, and his attributes. In this fashion, philosophy must prepare the way for a more correct grasp of these dogmas by faith and also for some sort of rational understanding of those more hidden dogmas which can be known originally only by faith. The strict, yet very beautiful, science of true philosophy ought to do these tasks and concern itself with them. If the learned men in the academies of Germany, with the peculiar inclination of that renowned nation for the cultivation of deep and serious studies, would strive to perform these services, then their zeal has Our approval and commendation; for thus they will make the discoveries they have made for their own purposes serve for the profit and progress of religion.

However, in a very serious matter like this, We can never allow a disregard of all right order. We cannot allow reason to trespass on the domain of faith and cause confusion; for the limits beyond which reason of itself never has gone or can go are quite certain and well known by everybody. Now among those dogmas of faith belong especially and obviously all those truths that concern the elevation of man to the supernatural order and his supernatural dealings with God and that are known to be revealed for this purpose. And, indeed, since these dogmas are above nature, they cannot, therefore, be attained by mere natural reason and natural principles. Moreover, reason by its own natural principles can never be made capable of dealing with dogmas of this kind with scientific knowledge. But if these men dare to assert these errors rashly, let them know that they are departing from the common and unchanged teaching of the Church, and not from the opinion of just some teachers.

47
(1671)

It is clear from the Sacred Scriptures and from the tradition of the holy Fathers that the existence of God and many other truths are known in the light of natural reason by those also who have not yet embraced the faith (*see Rom. 1*); but it is also clear that those more hidden dogmas were manifested by God alone when he wished to make known "the mystery which has been hidden for ages and generations" (*Col. 1:26*). And he did it in such a way that after he had "at sundry times and in divers manners spoken in times past to the fathers by the prophets, last of all he has spoken to us by his Son . . .

48
(1672)

by whom also he made the world" (*Heb. 1:1 f.*). For "no one has at any time seen God. The only-begotten Son, who is in the bosom of the Father, he has revealed him" (*John 1:18*). Accordingly, the Apostle, who testifies that the Gentiles had known God through the created world, when he is discoursing about the grace and truth, which came through Jesus Christ (*see John 1:17*), says: "But we speak the wisdom of God, mysterious, hidden . . . a wisdom which none of the rulers of this world has known. . . . But to us God has revealed them through his Spirit. For the Spirit searches all things, even the deep things of God. For who among men knows the things of a man save the spirit of man which is in him? Even so, the things of God no one knows but the Spirit of God" (*I Cor. 2:7 ff.*).

49
(1673) Following these and almost countless other divine utterances, the holy Fathers in teaching the doctrine of the Church have always carefully observed a distinction between the knowledge of divine matters which, by the power of natural intelligence, is common to all, and the knowledge of those matters which is had by faith through the Holy Spirit. The Fathers have constantly taught that, by the knowledge of faith, there are revealed to us in Christ those mysteries which transcend not only human philosophy but even the natural intelligence of the angels; and, even though these mysteries have become known by a divine revelation and it is by faith that they have been received, nevertheless, they still remain covered with the sacred veil of faith itself and enveloped in its obscure darkness, as long as we wander exiled from the Lord in this mortal life. From all that precedes, it is clear that the opinion which Frohschammer unhesitatingly asserts is entirely at variance with the doctrine of the Church: namely, that all dogmas of the Christian religion are indiscriminately the objects of natural knowledge or philosophy; and that the human reason, though trained merely in the historical method, can arrive at a true scientific understanding of all dogmas, even the more hidden ones, from its own natural strength and starting point, provided only that these dogmas have been placed before that reason as its object (*see 57*).

But there is, indeed, another opinion which plays a pre-   **50**
dominant part in the previously mentioned works of this   (*1674*)
author and which is clearly opposed to the doctrine and to
the mind of the Catholic Church. For he grants to philosophy
a liberty that is not the freedom of science but must rather
be labeled a thoroughly reprehensible and intolerable license
in favor of philosophy. After setting up a distinction between
the philosopher and philosophy, he concedes to the philosopher the right and the duty of submitting himself to that
authority which he has found for himself to be true; but to
philosophy he denies both the right and the duty of so
submitting; and, as a result, he asserts in utter disregard for
revealed doctrine that philosophy never should and never
can submit itself to authority. Now this assertion could be
allowed and perhaps even admitted if it were applied only
to the right that philosophy has in common with the other
sciences; namely, of using its own principles, method, and
conclusions; and if its liberty consisted in so using the right
that philosophy would not accept anything outside its boundaries and not acquired by itself on its own conditions. But
this sort of true philosophical freedom must know and realize
its own limitations. For not only the philosopher but even
philosophy will never be permitted either to say anything
against those truths which divine revelation and the Church
teaches, or to call into question some particular truth because
philosophy does not understand it, or not to accept a decision which the authority of the Church has pronounced
concerning some conclusion of philosophy which was previously free.

COLLECTION OF MODERN ERRORS, 1864

Along with the bull *Quanta cura*, condemning naturalism, com-
munism, and socialism, Pius IX (1846–78) published on December 8, 1864, a list of eighty propositions embracing the
chief contemporary errors which the pope had himself denounced in previous utterances. Among these propositions
appear the most virulent errors of complete rationalism (*see*
51–55) as well as expressions of the semi-rationalism that had
infected some Catholic theological quarters (*see 56 f.*).

No precise doctrinal censure is attached by the Syllabus to
the errors which it lists. Hence, to interpret the sense in which

each error is condemned, it is necessary to refer to the document of Pius IX in which the error was first denounced (*see* DB 1700 ff.).

51
(1703)
3. Human reason, in complete independence of God, is the sole judge of truth and falsity, good and evil. It is autonomous, and by its own natural powers it is adequate to care for the good of men and nations.

52
(1704)
4. All religious truths originate from the natural power of human reason; therefore, reason is the principal norm by which man can and should reach the knowledge of all truths of every sort.

53
(1705)
5. Divine revelation is incomplete and, therefore, is subject to a continual and indefinite development in order to correspond to the progress of human reason (*see* 23).

54
(1706)
6. The Christian faith is opposed to human reason; and divine revelation is not only useless but even harmful for human perfection (*see* 22).

55
(1707)
7. The prophecies and miracles that are set forth and narrated in the Sacred Scriptures are poetical fictions; the mysteries of the Christian faith are a summary of philosophical investigations; mythical fancies are contained in the books of both Testaments; and Jesus Christ himself is a mythical fiction.

56
(1708)
8. Since human reason is equal in value to religion itself, theological disciplines are to be handled in the same way as the philosophical (*see* 27).

57
(1709)
9. All the dogmas of the Christian religion are, without exception, the object of natural science or philosophy. Human reason, with only historical training, can, by its own powers and principles, acquire true scientific knowledge even of the more difficult dogmas, if only these dogmas are proposed to reason as its object (*see* DB 1682).

THE VATICAN COUNCIL, 1869-70

To meet the rising tide of error, Pope Pius IX had, in the year 1868, summoned the twentieth ecumenical council of the

Church. It met at the Vatican from December, 1869, to September, 1870. Cut short by the outbreak of the Franco-Prussian War, the council had promulgated only two dogmatic pronouncements out of the ambitious program that lay before it. These were the Constitution on the Catholic Faith and the part of the Constitution on the Church of Christ that dealt with papal infallibility. In the Constitution on Faith, April 24, 1870, after a first chapter on God as creator (*see 354–57; 358–62, cans. 1–5*) the council devotes the last three chapters and the corresponding canons to an exposition of the Church's position on the faith-reason relationship. The second chapter vindicates the power of the human reason to know God without revelation (against the fideists and traditionalists), and goes on to explain (against the naturalists and rationalists) in what sense revelation is, nevertheless, necessary. The council also indicates where the revelation that has been made is to be found and gives norms for the interpretation of Sacred Scriptures.

The third chapter deals with the virtue of faith itself, its nature, its reasonableness yet supernaturalness, its object, its necessity, and its conditions.

In the fourth chapter the council clarifies the distinct but complementary roles of faith and reason. It sets aside the bold rationalism that claimed for natural reason an absolute autonomy; it rebukes also the semirationalism of Hermes that diminished the supernaturalness of revealed mysteries. And it confidently asserts the impossibility of a real clash between the natural and supernatural orders of knowledge.

Chapter 2. Revelation

The fact of positive, supernatural revelation

The same holy Mother Church holds and teaches that God, the origin and end of all things, can be known with certainty by the natural light of human reason from the things that he created; "for since the creation of the world his invisible attributes are clearly seen, being understood through the things that are made" (*Rom. 1:20*); and she teaches that it was nevertheless, the good pleasure of his wisdom and goodness to reveal himself and the eternal decrees of his will to the human race in another and supernatural way, as the Apostle says: "God, who at sundry times and in divers manners spoke in times past to the fathers by the prophets, last of all in these days has spoken to us by his Son" (*Heb. 1:1 f.; see 60, can. 1*).

58
(1785)

27

The need for revelation

59
(1786)
It is owing to this divine revelation, assuredly, that even in the present condition of the human race, those religious truths which are by their nature accessible to human reason can easily be known by all men with solid certitude and with no trace of error. Nevertheless, it must not be argued that revelation is, for that reason, absolutely necessary. It is necessary only because God, out of his infinite goodness, destined man to a supernatural end, that is, to a participation in the good things of God, which altogether exceed the human mental grasp; for "eye has not seen nor ear heard, nor has it entered into the heart of man, what things God has prepared for those who love him" (*I Cor. 2:9; see 61 f., cans. 2 and 3*).

Canons on Chapter 2

Against those who deny natural theology

60
(1806)
1. If anyone says that the one and true God, our creator and lord, cannot be known with certainty with the natural light of human reason by means of the things that have been made: let him be anathema.

Against the deists

61
(1807)
2. If anyone says that it is impossible or useless for man to be taught through divine revelation about God and the service to be rendered to him: let him be anathema.

Against the progressionists

62
(1808)
3. If anyone says that man cannot be elevated by the divine power to a knowledge and perfection that surpasses natural knowledge and perfection, but that he can and should by his own efforts and by continual progress eventually arrive at the possession of every truth and good: let him be anathema.

Chapter 3. Faith

The definition of faith

63
(1789)
Because man depends entirely on God as his creator and lord and because created reason is wholly subordinate to uncreated Truth, we are obliged to render by faith a full submission of intellect and will to God when he makes a revelation (*see 69, can. 1*). This faith, however, which is

the beginning of human salvation, the Catholic Church asserts to be a supernatural virtue (*see 565*). By that faith, with the inspiration and help of God's grace, we believe that what he has revealed is true—not because its intrinsic truth is seen with the natural light of reason—but because of the authority of God who reveals it, of God who can neither deceive nor be deceived (*see 70, can. 2*). For, on the word of the Apostle: "Faith is the substance of things to be hoped for, the evidence of things that are not seen" (*Heb. 11:1*).

Faith and reason are in harmony

Nevertheless, in order that the submission of our faith might be consonant with reason (*see Rom. 12:1*), God has willed that external proofs of his revelation, namely divine acts and especially miracles and prophecies, should be added to the internal aids given by the Holy Spirit. Since these proofs so excellently display God's omnipotence and limitless knowledge, they constitute the surest signs of divine revelation, signs that are suitable to everyone's understanding (*see 71 f., cans. 3–4*). Therefore, not only Moses and the prophets but also and pre-eminently Christ our Lord performed many evident miracles and made clear-cut prophecies. Moreover, we read of the apostles: "But they went forth and preached everywhere, while the Lord worked with them and confirmed the preaching by the signs that followed" (*Mark 16:20*). And likewise it is written: "We have the word of prophecy, surer still, to which you do well to attend, as to a lamp shining in a dark place" (*II Pet. 1:19*).

64
(1790)

Faith is essentially a gift of God

However, even though the assent of faith is by no means a blind impulse, still, no one can "assent to the gospel preaching" as he must in order to be saved "without the enlightenment and inspiration of the Holy Spirit, who gives all men their joy in assenting to and believing the truth." Hence, faith itself is essentially a gift of God, even should it not work through charity (*see Gal. 5:6*); and the act of faith is a work that has a bearing upon salvation. By this act man offers to God himself a free obedience inasmuch as he concurs and cooperates with God's grace, when he could resist it (*see 561 f.; 73, can. 5*).

65
(1791)

Revelation, Faith, and Reason

The object of faith

66
(1792)
Moreover, by divine and Catholic faith everything must be believed that is contained in the written word of God or in tradition, and that is proposed by the Church as a divinely revealed object of belief either in a solemn decree or in her ordinary, universal teaching (*see 180*).

The need for embracing and keeping the faith

67
(1793)
Yet, since "without faith it is impossible to please God" (*Heb. 11:6*) and to enter the company of his sons, no one has ever obtained justification without faith and no one will reach eternal life, unless "he has persevered to the end" in faith (*Matt. 10:22; 24:13*). However, in order to enable us to fulfill our obligation of embracing the true faith and steadfastly persevering in it, God established the Church through his only-begotten Son and endowed it with unmistakable marks of its foundation, so that it could be recognized by all as the guardian and teacher of the revealed word.

External graces for fulfilling the obligation to believe

68
(1794)
For all the many marvelous proofs that God has provided to make the credibility of the Christian faith evident point to the Catholic Church alone. Indeed, the Church itself, because of its marvelous propagation, its exalted sanctity, and its inexhaustible fruitfulness in all that is good, because of its catholic unity and its unshaken stability, is a great and perpetual motive of credibility and an irrefutable proof of its own divine mission.

Internal graces for fulfilling the same obligation

Consequently, the Church, like a standard lifted up for the nations (*see Isa. 11:12*), not only calls to herself those who have not yet believed, but also she proves to her own children that the faith they profess rests on a most solid foundation. To this testimony is added the efficacious help of supernatural power. For the most merciful Lord stirs up and helps with his grace those who are wandering astray, so that they can "come to the knowledge of the truth" (*I Tim. 2:4*); and, never abandoning anyone, unless he is abandoned (*see 568*), he strengthens with his grace those whom he has brought out of darkness into his marvelous light (*see I Pet. 2:9*), so that

they may remain in this light. Therefore, the position of those
who have embraced the Catholic truth by the heavenly gift
of faith and of those who have been misled by human opinions and follow a false religion is by no means the same, for the
former, who have accepted the faith under the teaching authority of the Church, can never have any just reason for
changing that faith or calling it into question (*see 74, can. 6*).
In view of all this, let us give thanks to God the Father, "who
has made us worthy to share the lot of the saints in light"
(*Col. 1:12*), and let us not neglect so great a salvation, but
"looking towards the author and finisher of faith, Jesus"
(*Heb. 12:2*), "let us hold fast the confession of our hope without wavering" (*Heb. 10:23*).

Canons on Chapter 3

Against false freedom of reason

1. If anyone says that human reason is so independent that
it cannot be commanded by God to believe: let him be
anathema (*see 63*).

69
(*1810*)

There are some truths that reason left to itself cannot know

2. If anyone says that there is no distinction between divine
faith and natural knowledge about God and morals and, therefore, that for divine faith it is not necessary that revealed
truths be believed on the authority of God who reveals them:
let him be anathema (*see 63*).

70
(*1811*)

The reasonableness of faith

3. If anyone says that it is impossible for external signs to
render divine revelation credible and that, therefore, men
ought to be impelled towards faith only by each one's internal
experience or private inspiration: let him be anathema (*see
64*).

71
(*1812*)

The demonstrability of revelation

4. If anyone says that all miracles are impossible and,
hence, that all accounts of them, even though contained in
Sacred Scripture, should be classed with fables and myths; or
that miracles can never be recognized with certainty and that
the divine origin of the Christian religion cannot be success-
fully proved by them: let him be anathema (*see 64*).

72
(*1813*)

The freedom of faith and the necessity of grace; against Hermes (see DB 1618 ff.)

73
(1814)
5. If anyone says that the assent of Christian faith is not free, but necessarily results from arguments of human reason; or that the grace of God is only necessary for living faith, which works through charity (*see Gal. 5:6*): let him be anathema (*see 65*).

Against the positive doubt of Hermes (see DB 1619)

74
(1815)
6. If anyone says that the position of the faithful and of those who have not yet reached the only true faith is the same, so that Catholics could have good reason for suspending their assent and calling into question the faith that they have already accepted under the teaching authority of the Church, until they have completed a scientific demonstration of the credibility and truth of their faith: let him be anathema (*see 68*).

Chapter 4. Faith and Reason

The two kinds of knowledge

75
(1795)
Furthermore, the perpetual universal belief of the Catholic Church has held and now holds that there are two orders of knowledge, distinct not only in origin but also in object. They are distinct in origin, because in one we know by means of natural reason; in the other, by means of divine faith. And they are distinct in object, because in addition to what natural reason can attain, we have proposed to us as objects of belief mysteries that are hidden in God and which, unless divinely revealed, can never be known (*see 81, can. 1*). This is why the Apostle asserts that God is known by the Gentiles "through the things that are made" (*Rom. 1:20*); yet, when he is discoursing about the grace and truth that "came through Jesus Christ" (*John 1:17*), he declares: "We speak the wisdom of God, mysterious, hidden, which God foreordained before the world unto our glory, a wisdom which none of the rulers of this world has known. . . . But to us God has revealed them through his Spirit. For the Spirit searches all things, even the deep things of God" (*I Cor. 2:7 ff.*). And the Only-begotten himself praises the Father for having hidden these things from the wise and prudent, and having revealed them to little ones (*see Matt. 11:25*).

Revelation, Faith, and Reason

Reason's part in the study of supernatural truth

It is, nevertheless, true that if human reason, with faith as **76**
its guiding light, inquires earnestly, devoutly, and circum- **(1796)**
spectly, it does reach, by God's generosity, some understanding of mysteries, and that a most profitable one. It achieves
this by the similarity with truths which it knows naturally
and also from the interrelationship of mysteries with one another and with the final end of man. Reason, however, never
becomes capable of understanding them the way it does
truths which are its own proper object. For divine mysteries
of their very nature so excel the created intellect that even
when they have been given in revelation and accepted by
faith, that very faith still keeps them veiled in a sort of ob-
scurity, as long as "we are exiled from the Lord" in this mortal life, "for we walk by faith and not by sight" (*II Cor.*
5:6 f.).

No disagreement between faith and reason

Nevertheless, although faith is above reason, yet there can **77**
never be any real disagreement between faith and reason, **(1797)**
because it is the same God who reveals mysteries and infuses
faith and has put the light of reason into the human soul. Now
God cannot deny himself any more than the truth can ever
contradict the truth. However, the chief source of this merely
apparent contradiction lies in the fact that dogmas of faith
have not been understood and explained according to the
mind of the Church or that deceptive assertions of opinions
are accepted as axioms of reason. Therefore, "We define that
every assertion opposed to the enlightened truth of faith is
entirely false" (*see* 345).

Moreover, the Church, which received the office of safe- **78**
guarding the deposit of faith along with the apostolic duty of **(1798)**
teaching, likewise possesses, according to the divine will,
the right and duty of proscribing so-called knowledge (*see*
I Tim. 6:20) so that none may be deceived by philosophy and
vain deceit (*see Col. 2:8; and 82, can. 2*). Hence, all faithful
Christians are forbidden to defend as legitimate conclusions
of science such opinions that are known to be opposed to the
doctrine of faith, especially if they have been censured by the

Church; rather, they are absolutely bound to regard them as errors that treacherously wear the appearance of truth.

Faith and reason aid each other; and human knowledge is free in its own domain

79
(1799)
Faith and reason can never disagree; but more than that, they are even mutually advantageous. For right reason demonstrates the foundations of faith and, enlightened by the light of faith, it pursues the science of divine things; faith, on the other hand, sets reason free and guards it from errors and furnishes it with extensive knowledge. Hence, far from opposing the study of human arts and sciences, the Church helps and furthers this study in many ways. For it is neither ignorant nor scornful of the advantages for human living that result from those pursuits. Indeed, it asserts that just as they have their source in God, the lord of all knowledge (*see I Kings 2:3*), so too, if properly pursued, they lead men back to God with the help of his grace. And it certainly does not forbid these sciences to use their own principles and method within their own field. But while recognizing this due liberty, it is carefully on the watch to see that they do not admit errors by going contrary to divine doctrine, or step beyond their own boundaries and cause confusion by assuming authority in the domain of faith.

Genuine progress in natural and revealed knowledge

80
(1800)
For the doctrine of faith as revealed by God has not been presented to men as a philosophical system to be perfected by human ingenuity; it was presented as a divine trust given to the bride of Christ to be faithfully kept and infallibly interpreted. It also follows that any meaning of the sacred dogmas that has once been declared by holy Mother Church, must always be retained; and there must never be any deviation from that meaning on the specious grounds of a more profound understanding (*see 83, can. 3*). "Therefore, let there be growth . . . and all possible progress in understanding, knowledge, and wisdom whether in single individuals or in the whole body, in each man as well as in the entire Church, according to the stage of their development; but only within proper limits, that is, in the same doctrine, in the same meaning, and in the same purport."

Canons on Chapter 4

1. If anyone says that in divine revelation there are no true mysteries properly so called, but that all the dogmas of faith can be understood and demonstrated from natural principles by a well-trained mind: let him be anathema (*see 75 f.*).

81
(*1816*)

2. If anyone says that human sciences can be pursued with such liberty that their assertions may be held as true, even though they are opposed to revealed doctrine, and that they cannot be condemned by the Church: let him be anathema (*see 77–79*).

82
(*1817*)

3. If anyone says that as science progresses it is sometimes possible for dogmas that have been proposed by the Church to receive a different meaning from the one which the Church understood and understands: let him be anathema (*see 80*).

83
(*1818*)

Concluding exhortation

Therefore, exercising the duty of Our supreme pastoral office, through the heart of Jesus Christ We beseech all the Christian faithful and especially those who hold authority or who have the duty of teaching, and We command by the authority of the same God and our Savior, that they unite their zealous endeavors in order to repel and eliminate these errors from the holy Church and to spread abroad the light of purest faith.

84
(*1819*)

However, since it is not enough to shun the malice of heresy if those errors that more or less approach it are not also carefully avoided, We admonish all of their further duty of observing the constitutions and decrees by which suchlike perverse opinions, which are not expressly specified here, have been condemned by this Holy See.

85
(*1820*)

CONDEMNATION OF ERRORS OF ROSMINI-SERBATI, 1887

The saintly philosopher-priest Antonio Rosmini-Serbati (1797–1855) drew considerable attention during his lifetime by reason of the novel speculations that appeared in his voluminous writings. Although in the year 1854 the Congregation of the Index had dismissed his writings without any censure, thirty-three years later, December 14, 1887, the Holy Office issued a condemnation of forty propositions gathered for the most part from posthumous works which Rosmini himself had left in manuscript and never revised or completed for publication. Pope Leo XIII (1878–1903), in a letter to the archbishop of Milan, stated plainly that he approved and confirmed the decree. The fundamental ontologism of Rosmini-Serbati is manifested in the two following propositions taken from his posthumously published *Teosofia*. It hardly differs from the ontologist errors condemned in the year 1861 (*see 35–41*).

86
(1891)
1. In the created universe there is immediately manifest to the human intellect something that is divine in itself, something, namely, that belongs to the divine nature.

87
(1895)
5. The being which man knows intuitively must necessarily be that of some eternal, necessary being, a creating cause, determining and terminating all contingent beings: and this is God.

THE OATH AGAINST MODERNISM, 1910

With the decree *Lamentabili* (1907) and the encyclical *Pascendi* (1907), the dangers of the modernist interpretation of Catholic truth had been exposed and fully expounded. Nevertheless, efforts to promote the modernist cause were continued in various countries. To eliminate the possibility of modernist error spreading through the clergy, St. Pius X (1903–14) drew up and published on September 1, 1910, the following oath against modernism and imposed it on all clergy to be advanced to major orders, on pastors, confessors, preachers, religious superiors, and on professors in philosophical and theological seminaries.

The first part of the oath is a strong affirmation of the basic Catholic truths opposed to modernism: the demonstrability of God's existence by human reason; the value and suitability of miracles and prophecies as criteria of revelation; the historical institution of the Church by Christ; the invariable character of Catholic tradition; the reasonableness and supernaturalness of faith.

The second part of the oath is an expression of interior assent to the decree *Lamentabili* and the encyclical *Pascendi* with their contents. Particular modernist errors are singled out for censure and rejection.

88
(2145)
I . . . firmly embrace and accept each and every definition that has been set forth and declared by the unerring teaching authority of the Church, especially those principal

truths which are directly opposed to the errors of this day.
And first of all, I profess that God, the origin and end of all
things, can be known with certainty by the natural light of
reason from the created world (*see Rom. 1:20*), that is, from
the visible works of creation, as a cause from its effects, and
that, therefore, his existence can also be demonstrated. Secondly, I accept and acknowledge the external proofs of revelation, that is, divine acts and especially miracles and prophecies as the surest signs of the divine origin of the Christian
religion and I hold that these same proofs are well adapted
to the understanding of all eras and all men, even of this time.
Thirdly, I believe with equally firm faith that the Church, the
guardian and teacher of the revealed word, was personally
instituted by the real and historical Christ, when he lived
among us, and that the Church was built upon Peter, the
prince of the apostolic hierarchy, and his successors for the
duration of time. Fourthly, I sincerely hold that the doctrine
of faith was handed down to us from the apostles through
the orthodox Fathers in exactly the same meaning and always
in the same purport. Therefore, I entirely reject the heretical
misrepresentation that dogmas evolve and change from one
meaning to another different from the one which the Church
held previously. I also condemn every error according to
which, in place of the divine deposit which has been given to
the spouse of Christ to be carefully guarded by her, there is
put a philosophical figment or product of a human conscience
that has gradually been developed by human effort and will
continue to develop indefinitely. Fifthly, I hold with certainty
and sincerely confess that faith is not a blind sentiment of
religion welling up from the depths of the subconscious under the impulse of the heart and the motion of a will trained
to morality; but faith is a genuine assent of the intellect to
truth received by hearing from an external source. By this assent, because of the authority of the supremely truthful God,
we believe to be true that which has been revealed and attested to by a personal God, our creator and lord.

Furthermore, with due reverence, I submit and adhere with
my whole heart to the condemnations, declarations, and all
the prescripts contained in the encyclical *Pascendi* and in the

89
(2146)

decree *Lamentabili*, especially those concerning what is known as the history of dogmas. I also reject the error of those who say that the faith held by the Church can contradict history, and that Catholic dogmas, in the sense in which they are now understood, are irreconcilable with a more realistic view of the origins of the Christian religion. I also condemn and reject the opinion of those who say that a well-educated Christian assumes a dual personality—that of a believer and at the same time of a historian; as if it were permissible for a historian to hold things that contradict the faith of the believer, or to establish premises which, provided there be no direct denial of dogmas, would lead to the conclusion that dogmas are either false or doubtful. Likewise, I reject that method of judging and interpreting Sacred Scripture which, departing from the tradition of the Church, the analogy of faith, and the norms of the Apostolic See, embraces the misrepresentations of the rationalists and with no prudence or restraint adopts textual criticism as the one and supreme norm. Furthermore, I reject the opinion of those who hold that a professor lecturing or writing on a historico-theological subject should first put aside any preconceived opinion about the supernatural origin of Catholic tradition or about the divine promise of help to preserve all revealed truth forever; and that they should then interpret the writings of each of the Fathers solely by scientific principles, excluding all sacred authority, and with the same liberty of judgment that is common in the investigation of all ordinary historical documents.

90
(2147) Finally, I declare that I am completely opposed to the error of the modernists who hold that there is nothing divine in sacred tradition; or what is far worse, say that there is, but in a pantheistic sense, with the result that there would remain nothing but this plain simple fact—one to be put on a par with the ordinary facts of history—the fact, namely, that a group of men by their own labor, skill, and talent have continued through subsequent ages a school begun by Christ and his apostles. I firmly hold, then, and shall hold to my dying breath the belief of the Fathers in the charism of truth, which certainly is, was, and always will be in the suc-

cession of the episcopacy from the apostles. The purpose of this is, then, not that dogma may be tailored according to what seems better and more suited to the culture of each age; rather, that the absolute and immutable truth preached by the apostles from the beginning may never be believed to be different, may never be understood in any other way.

I promise that I shall keep all these articles faithfully, entirely, and sincerely, and guard them inviolate, in no way deviating from them in teaching or in any way in word or in writing. Thus I promise, thus I swear, so help me God. . . .

Tradition and Holy Scripture

The Council of Trent teaches that the revealed truths of faith and morals are contained in "written books and in unwritten traditions that the apostles received from Christ himself or that were handed on . . . from the apostles under the inspiration of the Holy Spirit. . . ."

Tradition is the communication by the teaching Church of the revelation made by Christ and his Spirit to the apostles. Theologians distinguish three elements in the notion of tradition. First there is *objective* (or *passive*) tradition: the doctrine revealed to the apostles by God. This doctrine, composed of truths to be believed, norms of morality to be observed, institutions, and practices, is always the same. Secondly, there is *active* tradition: that is, the act of teaching this revealed doctrine that has to be believed. Thirdly, there is the *teacher* of the doctrine: that is, the body of men who, as successors of the apostles in each succeeding age, constitute the authorized teaching authority within the Church.

The concept of "Catholic tradition," as ordinarily used, unites the first two elements: the doctrine taught and the act of teaching. It implies the third element, the teaching authority in the Church, as the agent of the act of teaching.

Between present and past tradition there can be no difference as regards the doctrine taught. But with regard to the act of teaching there can be growth and progress precisely because of the continuous and vital character of both the teacher and the actual teaching. The body of men who make up the teaching authority changes with the successive generations. The acts by which these men communicate the revealed truth in various

*ways in every age are vital expressions of a present conscious-
ness and understanding of the revealed doctrine that is preserved and nourished in them by the Holy Spirit. The growth
in the Church's consciousness of the doctrine she has to teach
and the improvement in her presentation of it are the measure
of the growth and progress possible in tradition.*

*Because tradition is a living thing—the communication here
and now of revealed truths—it follows that it does not need to
be discovered in the past. Positive theologians may very well
study Catholic tradition of the third or thirteenth centuries and
demonstrate its conformity with tradition in the twentieth
century. But Catholic tradition in the twentieth century is not
the mere repetition of ancient or medieval formulas, but the
present manifestation of the revealed truth that the Church's
teaching authority holds fresh in its consciousness.*

*Another way in which certain of the revealed truths have
come down to us is the written documents of Sacred Scripture.
The Church has always taught that God is the author of Sacred
Scripture and that the inspired writers wrote their works at the
dictation of the Holy Spirit. Consequently, just as it is impossible for God to err, so it is impossible for the Sacred Scriptures
to err. The books of the Bible have been entrusted to the
Church and it is the duty of the Church's teaching authority
to guard the Bible, to determine the authentic canonical books,
to lay down norms of interpretation, to pronounce the last
word on the sense of controverted texts.*

*After the Reformers had divorced Scripture from the living
tradition of the Church, rationalists later began to treat the
Scriptures as purely human documents and to judge and interpret them by historical and scientific norms alone. In the nineteenth and twentieth centuries, the Church has had to protest
vigorously against this rash mishandling of the word of God.
At the same time it has assigned to modern techniques of
exegesis their proper role in the interpretation of Scripture.
They are subordinate to the Church's official teaching and must
not replace it as the ultimate norm of interpretation; yet they*

must be diligently cultivated, precisely because they are aids to arriving at the true meaning of the inspired word.

Formal dogmatic pronouncements on the nature of tradition are hardly to be found in the documents of the early Church. Frequently, however, there occur expressions that show how vividly the early Church was aware that its divinely safe-guarded apostolic tradition preserved undiminished the purity of the original revelation. A few examples are given to illustrate this fact.

THE SECOND COUNCIL OF CONSTANTINOPLE, 553

We profess to hold and to preach the faith originally revealed by our great God and Savior Jesus Christ to his holy apostles and preached by them in the entire world. This faith the holy Fathers, especially those who assembled in the four holy councils, professed and explained and handed down in sacred assemblies. These Fathers we follow and accept throughout and in everything. . . . But everything that does not agree with what has been defined by the same four holy councils as belonging to the true faith: . . . we judge to be foreign to piety and condemn and declare anathema.

91
(212)

THE LATERAN COUNCIL, 649

If anyone does not profess, in accordance with the holy Fathers, properly and truthfully all that has been handed down and taught publicly to the holy, Catholic, and apostolic Church of God, both by the same holy Fathers and the five approved universal councils, to the last detail in word and intention: let him be condemned.

92
(270)

THE SECOND COUNCIL OF NICAEA, 787

If anyone rejects all ecclesiastical tradition, either written or unwritten: let him be anathema. . . .

93
(308)

THE COUNCIL OF FLORENCE, 1438-45

After achieving a successful but, unhappily, short-lived union with the Greek schismatics in 1439, the Council of Florence, the seventeenth ecumenical council, likewise received the submission of two other schismatic groups, the Armenians and the Jacobites. On each occasion it promulgated a pronouncement on matters of faith and practice. The decree for

the Jacobites is of interest here for its list of the canonical, inspired books of the Old and New Testaments. It was this list
that the Council of Trent later adopted and reaffirmed.

94
(706)
    The holy Roman Church firmly believes, professes, and
preaches that the one true God, Father, Son, and Holy Spirit,
is the creator of all things visible and invisible. When God
willed, in his goodness he created all creatures both spiritual
and corporeal. These creatures are good because they were
made by the Supreme Good, but they are changeable because
they were made from nothing. The Church asserts that there is
no such thing as a nature of evil, because every nature insofar
as it is a nature is good. It professes that one and the same
God is the author of the Old and the New Testament, that is,
of the Law, of the Prophets, and of the Gospel because the
holy men of both Testaments have spoken under the inspiration
of the same Holy Spirit. It accepts and reverences their books
as here listed. [*There follows the canon of books (see 96).*]

THE COUNCIL OF TRENT, 1545-63

The first action of the nineteenth ecumenical council, the Council of Trent (*see introd. to 371*), was to reaffirm the ancient
faith of the Nicene Creed. Its very next step was to lay down
the sources of revealed truth that would provide the foundation for all its subsequent actions. These two sources are the
inspired writings of Sacred Scripture and the unwritten tradition handed down from the apostles. The Reformers had maintained that a personal interpretation of Sacred Scripture was a
sufficient rule of faith, and they had denied the canonicity of
certain books in each Testament. To refute these errors the
council affirms that tradition is a source of evangelical truth
that is as worthy of respect as the inspired writings themselves;
and it reaffirms the listing of the canonical books given by the
Council of Florence—a listing that agrees exactly with the list
given as early as the year 382 in the Council of Rome under
Pope St. Damasus I (*see DB 84*). In a concluding section the
council accepts the old Latin Vulgate text as having official,
recognized, decisive authority among various Latin texts and
lays down certain norms for interpretation of Holy Scripture.

95
(783)
    The holy, ecumenical, and general Council of Trent, which
has lawfully assembled in the Holy Spirit and is presided

over by the same three legates of the Apostolic See, has always as its purpose to remove error and preserve in the Church the purity of the gospel that was originally promised by the prophets in Sacred Scripture and first promulgated by the Son of God himself, our Lord Jesus Christ. He, in turn, ordered his apostles, who are the source of all saving truth and moral teaching, to preach it to every creature (*see Matt. 28:19 f.; Mark 16:15*). The council is aware that this truth and teaching are contained in written books and in the unwritten traditions that the apostles received from Christ himself or that were handed on, as it were from hand to hand, from the apostles under the inspiration of the Holy Spirit, and so have come down to us. The council follows the example of the orthodox Fathers and with the same sense of devotion and reverence with which it accepts and venerates all the books both of the Old and the New Testament, since one God is the author of both, it also accepts and venerates traditions concerned with faith and morals as having been received orally from Christ or inspired by the Holy Spirit and continuously preserved in the Catholic Church. It judged, however, that a list of the Sacred Books should be written into this decree so that no one may doubt which books the council accepts. The list is as follows.

The Old Testament: five books of Moses, that is, Genesis, Exodus, Leviticus, Numbers, Deuteronomy; Josue, Judges, Ruth, four books of Kings, two of Paralipomenon; the first book of Esdras and the second, which is called Nehemias; Tobias, Judith, Esther, Job, David's Psalter of one hundred and fifty psalms, Proverbs, Ecclesiastes, the Canticle of Canticles, Wisdom, Ecclesiasticus, Isaias, Jeremias with Baruch, Ezechiel, Daniel; the twelve minor prophets, that is, Osee, Joel, Amos, Abdias, Jonas, Micheas, Nahum, Habacuc, Sophonias, Aggeus, Zacharias, Malachias; two books of Machabees, the first and the second.

96
(784)

The New Testament: the four Gospels, according to Matthew, Mark, Luke, and John; the Acts of the Apostles, written by the Evangelist Luke; fourteen epistles of the Apostle Paul: to the Romans, two to the Corinthians, to the Galatians, to the Ephesians, to the Philippians, to the Colossians, two to the Thessalonians, two to Timothy, to Titus, to Philemon, to the Hebrews; two epistles of the Apostle Peter, three of the Apostle John, one of the Apostle James, one of the Apostle Jude; and the Apocalypse of the Apostle John. Moreover, if anyone does not accept these books as sacred and canonical in their entirety, with all their parts, according to the text usually read in the Catholic Church and as they are in the ancient Latin Vulgate, but knowingly and willfully contemns the traditions previously mentioned: let him be anathema. And so, let all understand the order and the procedure the council itself will follow after placing this foundation of profession of faith, and what sources and arguments it will especially rely upon in strengthening dogmas and restoring morals in the Church.

97
(785) Moreover, since the same sacred council has thought that it would be very useful for the Church of God if it were known which one of all the Latin editions that are in circulation is the authentic edition, it determines and decrees that the ancient Vulgate, which has been approved in the Church by the use of many centuries, should be considered the authentic edition in public readings, disputations, preaching, and explanations; and that no one should presume or dare to reject it under any pretext whatever.

98
(786) Furthermore, to keep undisciplined minds under proper control, the council decrees that no one should dare to rely on his own judgment in matters of faith and morals affecting the structure of Christian doctrine and to distort Sacred Scripture to fit meanings of his own that are contrary to the meaning that holy Mother Church has held and now holds; for it is her office to judge about the true sense and interpretation of Sacred Scripture. Nor should anyone dare to interpret Sacred Scripture contrary to the unanimous agreement of the Fathers, even though such interpretations are never going to be published (*see 133*).

THE VATICAN COUNCIL, 1869-70

While treating of revelation in the second chapter of the Dogmatic Constitution on Catholic Faith, April 24, 1870, the Vatican Council, the twentieth ecumenical council, repeated the teaching of the Council of Trent on the two sources of revelation, Scripture and tradition. It approved the canon of Holy Scripture that the Council of Trent had prescribed, and again vindicated the right of official interpretation to the Church alone.

The source of revelation

Furthermore, according to the faith of the universal Church, declared by the holy Council of Trent, this supernatural revelation is "contained in written books and in the unwritten traditions that the apostles received from Christ himself or that was handed on, as it were from hand to hand, from the apostles under the inspiration of the Holy Spirit, and so have come down to us" (*see 95*). Those books of the Old and the New Testament must be accepted as sacred and canonical in their entirety, with all their parts, just as they are listed in the decree of that Council and are contained in the ancient Latin Vulgate. Those books, however, are held to be sacred and canonical by the Church, not on the grounds that they were produced by mere human ingenuity and afterwards approved by her authority; nor on the mere score that they contain revelation without error. But they are held to be sacred and canonical because they were written as a result of the prompting of the Holy Spirit, they have God for their author, and as such they were entrusted to the Church (*see 101, can. 4*).

99
(1787)

The interpretation of Sacred Scripture

However, the norms for the interpretation of divine Scripture which, to good purpose, were decreed by the holy Council of Trent with a view to restraining undisciplined minds are being explained in a distorted sense by certain men. Therefore, We renew the same decree and declare that this is its meaning: in matters of faith and morals affecting the structure of Christian doctrine, that sense of Sacred Scripture is to be considered as true which holy Mother Church has held and now holds; for it is her office to judge about the true sense and interpretation of Sacred Scripture; and, therefore, no one is allowed to interpret Sacred Scripture contrary to this sense nor contrary to the unanimous agreement of the Fathers.

100
(1788)

Canon on Chapter 2

101
(1809)
4. If anyone does not admit as sacred and canonical the complete books of Sacred Scripture with all their parts, as the holy Council of Trent enumerated them (*see 95*), or denies that they were divinely inspired: let him be anathema.

THE ENCYCLICAL *PROVIDENTISSIMUS DEUS,* 1893

The rationalistic spirit had so affected biblical exegesis during the nineteenth century that liberal scholars were interpreting the Holy Scriptures as though the books were of merely human authorship and needed to be judged by no criterion other than that provided by human science. In this encyclical, published November 18, 1893, the Church for the first time shows its attitude to the new exegesis. It is grateful for the services that modern historical science has rendered in the attempt to understand Scripture better. Yet it emphasizes that the sacred character of the Bible makes it impossible for an exegete to follow merely scientific norms in its interpretation.

The inerrancy of the sacred writers, due to the fact that God himself is the author of all the books of Scripture, precludes the possibility of internal contradictions within the Bible. Catholic exegetes should follow the clear teaching of the Church, Catholic tradition as mirrored in the Fathers' writings, and the analogy of faith in their work of elucidating the Scriptures. A spirit of independence from Catholic ecclesiastical and scholarly tradition is not safe in scriptural exegesis.

Pope Leo XIII (1878–1903) warns that a purely scientific exegesis which neglects the norms established by faith leads naturally to the most biased type of interpretation. In reality, Catholic exegetes who dutifully follow Catholic tradition need never fear a clash between historically demonstrated truth and the contents of Holy Scripture; for God, the author of all truth, does not contradict himself. The pope goes on to offer some detailed rules for interpretation and to give the principles for solving difficulties and objections.

Norms for exegesis of Holy Scripture

102
(1943)
In other things, the analogy of faith and the Catholic teaching just as received from the authority of the Church should be followed as the supreme norm. . . . Hence it is clear that an interpretation should be rejected as wrong and erroneous if it pictures the inspired writers as somehow dis-

agreeing among themselves, or if it opposes the teaching of the Church. . . .

But the Fathers have supreme authority whenever they all explain in one and the same way any passage in the Bible as pertaining to the teaching of faith or morals. For the holy Fathers, "who came after the apostles, planted and watered, built, shepherded and nurtured the growing Church." . . .

103
(*1944*)

The other Catholic interpreters have less authority, but since in the Church there has been a certain continuous growth in Scripture studies, their commentaries should also be duly respected. For on occasion it is possible to learn from them many things to refute contrary opinions, and to explain difficult passages. It would be most unsuitable for anyone to ignore or contemn the many outstanding writings which our authors have left and to prefer the books of the heterodox authors. It would not be becoming for a person to seek in those books, at the imminent risk of sound doctrine and sometimes with danger to faith, an explanation of passages on which Catholics have already well spent much talent and time. . . .

104
(*1945*)

The primary [aids to interpretation] are the critical method and the study of ancient Oriental languages. . . . Therefore, it is necessary for teachers of Sacred Scripture and very proper for theologians to know thoroughly the languages in which the canonical books were first written by the holy writers. . . . And for the same reason these men should be well instructed and well trained in sound principles of criticism. For without foundation and with harmful effect to religion, the method known as *higher criticism* has been introduced. This is a euphemism for the system in which the origin, integrity, and authority of any book can be judged by what they call internal criteria. On the contrary, it is obvious that in questions of an historical nature, such as the origin and the preservation of books, historical testimonies are more important than anything else and should be collected and weighed with the greatest care. On the other hand, internal criteria are generally not important enough to be admitted except as a sort of confirmatory evidence. . . . In the final

105
(*1946*)

analysis, that very type of higher criticism that is so highly praised will come down to this: in his interpretation each one will follow his own prejudice and partisan interest. . . .

106
(1947)
A knowledge of natural sciences will considerably help a professor of Sacred Scripture more easily to detect and refute fallacies which are taken from science and are proposed against the divine books. There is no real disagreement between theologians and scientists, as long as each stays in his own field and follows the advice of St. Augustine "not to assert rashly anything unknown as if it were known." But if they do disagree, the same author sums up the rules the theologian should follow: "If they ever succeed in demonstrating any scientific truth with irrefutable evidence, let us show that that truth is not opposed to our Scripture; but if they ever cite anything from their works as opposed to our Scripture, that is, to the Catholic faith, let us either show that it is false from our own sources or else hold with unhesitating faith that it is erroneous." The first thing to note in considering the fairness of this rule is that the sacred authors, or rather "the spirit of God who spoke through them, did not intend to teach men such things as the inner structure of sensible objects, for they would not be conducive to anyone's salvation"; and so, rather than give a strictly scientific exposition of nature in their description and treatment, they have occasionally spoken in somewhat figurative language or in the common parlance of those times; and today even good scientists follow the same practice. Since common language is best adapted to describing sensible objects, hence it is (as the Angelic Doctor has told us) that a sacred writer "looks to the sensible appearances of things," that is, to the human way in which God himself adapted his revelation to men for their understanding. . . .

107
(1949)
These same principles can be usefully applied to related branches of knowledge, especially to history. It is regrettable that there are many who with great effort investigate and bring to light the monuments of antiquity, the customs and institutions of peoples, and similar evidence, but frequently with the intention of finding some taint of error in the Sacred Books so that their authority may be continually weakened

and lose its credibility. That is what some do with overly hostile intent and without sufficiently balanced judgment. These persons trust profane books and documents of early date with such confidence that they cannot even suspect the presence of any error in them; but at the mere appearance of error and without proper investigation into it, they refuse to place a like trust in the books of Sacred Scripture.

It could well be that in the copying of codices some mistakes were made by copyists. This possibility should be carefully weighed and should not be readily admitted except in those passages where it has been duly proved. It is also possible that the true meaning of a passage may remain ambiguous; in clarifying such a passage the best rules of interpretation will be very useful. It would, however, be altogether wrong either to limit inspiration to certain parts only of Sacred Scripture or to concede that the sacred author himself has erred. For it is impossible to tolerate the mentality of those who evade these difficulties by going so far as to admit that divine inspiration extends to matters of faith and morals, but to nothing else . . .

108
(1950)

All of the books that the Church accepts as sacred and canonical, in their entirety, and together with all their parts, were written under the inspiration of the Holy Spirit. Moreover, it is utterly impossible for the least error to be divinely inspired. In fact, by its very nature inspiration not only excludes all error, but makes its presence as utterly impossible as it is for God, the supreme truth, to be the author of any error whatever.

109
(1951)

The Vatican Council made the unqualified statement that the "books of the Old and the New Testament . . . have God for their author" (*see 99*). This is the ancient and continuous belief of the Church; a belief, too, that was solemnly defined in the Councils of Florence (*see 94*) and Trent (*see 95–98*), and finally reaffirmed and more fully explained in the Vatican Council. Therefore, it is now useless to say that the Holy Spirit used men as his instruments in writing and mean that, although the primary Author could, of course, have made no mistake, still, the inspired writers could have done so. For with

110
(1952)

his supernatural power, God so stimulated and moved men to write and so assisted them in their writing that they properly understood and willed to write faithfully and express suitably with infallible truthfulness all that he ordered, but nothing more. Otherwise, God would not be the author of Sacred Scripture in its entirety. . . . For this reason the Fathers and Doctors were convinced that the divine writings, precisely as written by the sacred writers, were free from all error. They therefore tried with ingenuity no less than with reverence to reconcile the many passages which seemed to differ from one another or even to be contradictory—these are almost exactly the same passages which are brought up now in the name of modern science. They were in complete accord in claiming that those books, both as a whole and in their single parts, were divinely inspired, and that God himself, speaking through the sacred authors, could not put down the slightest statement which was not true.

What Augustine wrote to Jerome should be a rule of universal application: ". . . if I come upon anything in the Scripture which appears contrary to the truth, it must be that the codex is in error, or the translator did not understand what was said, or I did not grasp its meaning. . . ."

111
(1953)
Many objections from every branch of learning have repeatedly been brought against Scripture but, being without solid foundation, they have now lost all their force. Moreover, quite a number of interpretations were once proposed for certain scriptural passages that have been better understood by the more penetrating type of investigation of a later date—the passages in question had no strict connection with the rule of faith and morals. For time blots out the vagaries of mere opinions, but "truth stands and prevails forever."

CONDEMNATION OF THE ERRORS OF THE MODERNISTS, 1907

The decree *Lamentabili* containing the errors listed below was issued by the Holy Office, July 3, 1907. Since 1903, Cardinals Richard and Peraud and others had been taking note of errors from the writings of the modernists and gathering them into a list to present to Pope St. Pius X (1903–14) for condemnation.

Although the sources of these errors are not indicated, either by book or by author, the doctrines condemned have been identified as errors in the writings of Loisy, Tyrrell, Le Roy, Dimnet, and Houtin. The condemnation is impersonal, universal, without a precise and definite theological censure. Undoubtedly, though, some of the condemned propositions are heretical. Because of the *motu proprio Praestantia,* November 18, 1907 (*see DB 2114*), in which St. Pius X strongly confirms the decree *Lamentabili* together with the encyclical *Pascendi,* some theologians consider its dogmatic value greatly increased.

The following propositions contain errors concerning the the authority of the Church in biblical matters (112–15); interpretation and the historical worth particularly of the Gospels (116–26); and the traditional concepts of revelation, dogma, and faith (127–28).

1. The ecclesiastical law which prescribes that books treating of divine Scripture be submitted to previous censorship does not apply to men who are making critical investigation or scientific exegesis of the books of the Old and New Testament.
112
(*2001*)

2. The Church's interpretation of the Sacred Books is certainly not to be despised, but it is subject to the more painstaking judgment and correction of the exegetes.
113
(*2002*)

3. From ecclesiastical judgments and censures that have been passed against a free and advanced exegesis, one can infer that the faith proposed by the Church contradicts history, and that Catholic dogmas are actually irreconcilable with a more realistic view of the origins of the Christian religion.
114
(*2003*)

4. The teaching authority of the Church cannot determine the true meaning of the Sacred Scriptures even through dogmatic definitions.
115
(*2004*)

9. They who believe that God is truly the author of Sacred Scripture manifest excessive simplicity or ignorance.
116
(*2009*)

10. The inspiration of the books of the Old Testament consists in this: the Israelite writers handed on their religious teaching under a special form which was largely or entirely unknown to the Gentiles.
117
(*2010*)

118
(2011)   11. Divine inspiration does not extend to the whole of Sacred Scripture in such a way that it protects each and every part of it from all error.

119
(2012)   12. If an exegete wishes to apply himself profitably to biblical studies, he must first put aside any preconceived opinion about the supernatural origin of Sacred Scripture and interpret it the same way as other merely human documents.

120
(2013)   13. The Evangelists themselves and the Christians of the second and third generations ingeniously arranged the parables of the Gospels and thus accounted for the little success of Christ's preaching among the Jews.

121
(2014)   14. In a number of their narrations, the Evangelists did not so much recount what was true as what they thought would be more profitable to their readers, even though false.

122
(2015)   15. Continuous additions and corrections were made in the Gospels until a definite canon was established; hence, nothing but a slight uncertain trace of Christ's own teaching remains in the Gospels.

123
(2016)   16. The narrations of John are not history in the strict sense but mystical contemplation on the Gospel; the discourses in his Gospel are theological meditations about the mystery of salvation and are devoid of historical truth.

124
(2017)   17. The fourth Gospel exaggerated the miracles not only to make the extraordinary stand out more clearly but also that they might be more suited to show the work and glory of the Incarnate Word.

125
(2018)   18. John claims for himself the office of witness to Christ; but in reality he is nothing more than an outstanding witness of Christian life, that is, of the life of Christ in the Church at the end of the first century.

126
(2019)   19. Heterodox exegetes have expressed the true sense of Scripture more faithfully than Catholic exegetes.

127
(2023)   23. There can be and in fact there is contradiction between the facts narrated in Sacred Scripture and the dogmas of

the Church based on them; hence, a critic can reject as false facts that the Church believes to be most certain.

24. An exegete must not be censured for establishing premises from which it follows that dogmas are historically false or doubtful, provided only he does not directly deny the dogmas themselves.

128
(2024)

THE ENCYCLICAL *SPIRITUS PARACLITUS,* 1920

As Catholic scholars became more interested in applying modern criticism to scriptural exegesis, some dangerous tendencies appeared in the norms of interpretation that were employed. On September 15, 1920, Pope Benedict XV (1914–22) took the occasion of the fifteenth centenary of the death of St. Jerome, the great Catholic Scripture scholar, to warn against these errors. He shows that it is wrong to restrict arbitrarily the extent of scriptural inerrancy to purely religious matters. He declares further that the distinction between an "absolute" and a "relative" truth in historical matters is unacceptable. And he emphasizes that it is a violent misinterpretation of Leo XIII's meaning (*see 107*) to say that such a distinction had been proposed in *Providentissimus Deus*.

The teaching of Jerome strongly corroborates and illustrates what Our predecessor of blessed memory Leo XIII solemnly declared to be the ancient and constant faith of the Church about the complete immunity of Scriptures from error of any kind: "It is utterly impossible for the least error to be divinely inspired. In fact, by its very nature inspiration not only excludes all error, but makes its presence as utterly impossible as it is for God, the supreme truth, to be the author of any error whatever" (*see 109*). Citing the definitions of the Councils of Florence and of Trent, which were upheld in the Vatican Council, he also has the following: "Therefore, it is now useless to say that the Holy Spirit used men as his instruments in writing and mean that, although the primary Author could, of course, have made no mistake, still, the inspired writers could have done so. For with his supernatural power, God stimulated and moved men to write and so assisted them in their writing that they properly understood and willed to write faithfully and express suitably with infal-

129
(2186)

lible truthfulness all that he ordered, but nothing more. Otherwise, God would not be the author of Sacred Scripture in its entirety" (*see 110*).

These words of Our predecessor leave no room for doubt or hesitation. And yet We regret, Venerable Brethren, that not only among those who are outside the Church, but also among the sons of the Catholic Church, and even (and this is what especially grieves Our heart) among clerics and teachers of sacred sciences, there are some who proudly rely on their own judgment and openly reject the teaching authority of the Church in this matter or secretly impugn it. We fully approve of the procedure of those who, intending to free themselves and others from difficulties arising from the sacred text, use all the tools of research and of the critical method and look for new ways and means of solving those difficulties. But they will fail sadly in accomplishing their purpose, if they neglect the directive norms of Our predecessor and overstep the definite limits and bounds set by the Fathers (*see Prov. 22:28*). There is a recent opinion that certainly does not conform to those directive norms and limits. Its advocates distinguish between the primary or religious content of Scripture and the secondary or profane content. While admitting that inspiration proper surely extends to every sentence, even to individual words of the Bible, they strictly confine to the primary or religious content the effects of inspiration, especially absolute truth and freedom from error. For they say that in the Scripture God intends and teaches only what is concerned with religion. Everything else, since it deals with profane subjects and serves divine revelation as a sort of cloak for divine truth, was merely permitted and was left to the fallibility of the writers. Consequently, it is not surprising if there are a good number of things in the Bible about scientific and historical matters and the like that are completely irreconcilable with present-day advances in knowledge. There are some who contend that these opinions contain no misrepresentations inconsistent with the directive norms of Our predecessor since he declared that the sacred writer spoke of natural things according to their external appearance which certainly can be deceptive (*see 106*). How rash and false is their claim, is evident from the very words of the Pontiff. . . .

They also depart from the teaching of the Church . . . who think that the historical passages of Scripture are not based on the *absolute* truth of facts, but only on what they call *relative* truth and the common belief of ordinary people. They do not hesitate to deduce this teaching from the words of Pope Leo since he has said that the principles laid down concerning the natural sciences can be transferred to the historical sciences (*see 107*). And so they maintain that, just as the sacred writers spoke about physical nature according to the way it appears, so also the sacred writers, in ignorance of what actually happened, reported events as they seemed to rest upon the common opinion of men or upon the false testimony of others without giving any indication of the source of their information but without adopting as their own the accounts of others. Why need We refute in great detail an opinion which is so completely false and very injurious to Our predecessor? What parallel is there between history and natural science? Natural science is concerned with "the sensible appearances" of things and must, therefore, correspond to phenomena. The basic law of history, on the contrary, is this: what is written should agree with past events precisely as they took place. If the false opinion just mentioned were once accepted, how would the truth of the sacred narration still be free from all error, as Our predecessor in the whole context of his letter declared we must believe? As for his statement that the same principles which have application in scientific matters can be usefully applied to history and to related subjects, he certainly does not mean that those principles should be transferred without qualification, but all he intends to say is that our method should be similar when our purpose is to refute the fallacies of the adversaries and to protect the historical reliability of Sacred Scripture from their attacks.

130
(2187)

THE ENCYCLICAL *DIVINO AFFLANTE SPIRITU,* 1943

On September 30, 1943, this important document was issued by Pope Pius XII (1939–58). Its purpose was to enforce the directives given by Leo XIII in *Providentissimus Deus,* to give approbation and encouragement to biblical scholarship, and to perfect Leo's work by giving appropriate directives for scientific Scripture studies.

Pope Pius again encourages a knowledge and a mastery of biblical and Oriental languages; he asks for a renewal of interest in the art and science of textual criticism; he clarifies the position of the Church with regard to the Vulgate edition of Holy Scripture and its authority. This encyclical marks an important advance in Catholic biblical studies. The following passages were selected to indicate what Pius XII added to the directives of the *Providentissimus Deus.* (The translation is made from the text of the encyclical in *Acta Apostolicae Sedis,* XXXV [1943], 297–325. At the end of each of the selections the page reference is indicated in brackets.)

Study of the original text

131   The Fathers of the Church, and especially St. Augustine strongly recommended that Catholic scholars who undertook to understand and explain Holy Scripture should study ancient languages and consult the original texts. . . . In modern times there is such an abundance of helps available to learn these languages that biblical scholars who neglect languages and as a result cannot work with the original texts must either be superficial or careless. For to understand more completely and fully the mind of the sacred writers, an exegete must study with supreme care and reverence even the most minute details that the sacred writers have produced under divine inspiration. And so, he should carefully work to gain day by day greater mastery over the biblical languages and other Oriental languages as well; and his interpretation should be supported by all the helps which any branch of philology can provide. This was what St. Jerome seriously ambitioned, in accord with the studies of his time. This was also the continual ambition of the great exegetes of the sixteenth and seventeenth centuries, and they realized their ambition to a certain extent even though the study of languages was then far less advanced than it is now. The exegete should also explain the original text which, since it was written by the sacred writer himself, has more authority and is of greater consequence than even the best translation, ancient or mod-

ern. All this can be done more easily and will result in greater good if a knowledge of languages and a real skill in literary criticism are brought to bear on the same text [306–7].

The place of textual criticism

In our times it is praiseworthy to use the art known as **132** *textual criticism* in editing secular writings, and this art finds its most proper use when exercised on the sacred writings; for these writings deserve the respect due to the divine word. The purpose of this art is to restore the original text as perfectly as possible, to remove the corruptions which the fallibility of copyists has caused, and, as far as it can, to do away with the glosses and omissions, the inversions and repetitions of words, and all the other kinds of mistakes that invariably slip into texts handed down through many centuries. . . . And all should well realize that this lengthy task is necessary to understand correctly the divinely inspired texts. This task is demanded of us by love since we should certainly be grateful to the providence of God who, from his throne of majesty, has given these writings to his children [307–8].

The authority of the Vulgate

No one should imagine that using the original texts ac- **133** cording to critical norms is opposed to the decrees which the **(2292)** Council of Trent wisely enacted about the Latin Vulgate. . . . The Council of Trent desired that the Vulgate be the Latin translation, "which all are to use as authentic." It is common knowledge that this concerned only the Latin Church and its public use of the Scriptures. It did not in any way detract from the authority and importance of the original texts. For they did not at that time raise the question about the original texts, but about the Latin texts that were then in circulation. The council correctly decreed that the Vulgate was to be preferred since "it has been approved by long use for many centuries in the Church." This special authority or *authenticity*, as is sometimes said, which the council gave the Vulgate was not given because of any special critical reasons, but rather was given because of the lawful use the Vulgate had seen in the Church for many centuries. This long use proves that the Vulgate, as the Church has understood and does now understand, is free from all error in matters of faith and morals. Consequently, as the Church herself testifies, it can be safely quoted, without the least fear of erring, in disputations, public readings, and sermons. Its *authenticity* should not be called *critical,* but *juridical.* The authority the Vulgate enjoys in doctrinal matters does not by any means proscribe—and in modern times it fairly demands —that this same doctrine be corroborated by the original texts. Nor does it mean that the original texts cannot be continually used to help clarify and explain more and more the proper meaning of Sacred Scripture. Nor does the decree of the Council of Trent forbid that translations be made into the vernacular so that the faithful may use them and profit by them and understand more readily the meaning of the divine message. These translations may be made from the original texts; and We have learned that with the Church's approval this has already been well done in many places [*308–10*].

The method to be followed

134
(2293)
Equipped with knowledge of languages and skill in the critical art, the Catholic exegete should undertake, as his most important task, to ascertain and to explain the true meaning of the Sacred Books. In carrying out this task, the scholar should keep in mind that his main purpose is to determine and define precisely the *literal* meaning of the words of the Bible. Scholars should diligently search for this literal meaning with their knowledge of languages, making use of the context and of comparisons with similar passages. These are the helps that are used to discover the mind of the author in interpreting secular literature. Exegetes of the sacred writings should remember that they are dealing with a divinely revealed message that has been given by God to the Church to preserve and to interpret. Consequently, they should carefully take into account the explanations and decrees of the teaching authority of the Church, the explanation given by the holy Fathers, and the *analogy of faith,* as Leo XIII wisely pointed out in the encyclical *Providentissimus Deus.* These exegetes should make a special effort not to limit themselves to an explanation of matters that belong to history, archae-

ology, philology, and similar sciences, as we have noticed, to our regret, happens in some commentaries. They should give these matters as much space as exegesis requires, and then go on to show above all the theological doctrine of faith or morals in each of the books or texts. Their explanation will thus help teachers of theology in explaining and proving the dogmas of faith; it will help priests to clarify Christian doctrine to their people; finally, it will help all the faithful to lead a holy life worthy of a Christian [*310*].

Spiritual meaning and transferred meaning

Of course, not all the spiritual meaning of Sacred Scripture is excluded. For the things that were said and done in the Old Testament were wisely ordained and disposed by God so that past happenings might be a spiritual type of what would happen in the new covenant of grace. The exegete, therefore, in ascertaining and explaining the literal meaning of the words as the holy writer intended them, should do the same for the spiritual meaning, provided this meaning is duly proven to have been given by God. Only God could know this spiritual meaning and reveal it to us. This type of meaning our divine Savior points out and teaches to us in the holy Gospels. The apostles follow his example and profess this meaning in their teaching and writing. The teaching always handed down by the Church shows this meaning. Finally, the ancient practice of the liturgy bears out this meaning wherever that well-known saying can be used in truth: "A law of prayer is a law of belief." Catholic exegetes should bring this divinely intended spiritual meaning to light and propound it with the carefulness that the dignity of the divine word of God demands. They should be scrupulously careful not to propose other transferred meanings as the real sense of Sacred Scripture. To exemplify matters of faith and morals and to make them acceptable, it may be useful, especially in preaching, to make a broader use of the sacred text in the transferred sense, provided it is done in moderation and with good judgment; but it must always be remembered that this use of the words of Sacred Scripture is in the nature of an external adjunct. In modern times, such a use of Scripture can be dangerous since the faithful, especially

135
(2293)

those who are educated in sacred and profane sciences, are looking for what message God himself gives us in Scripture rather than for what is propounded by a facile preacher or writer who makes free use of the words of the Bible. "The word of God is living and efficient and keener than any two-edged sword, and extending even to the division of soul and spirit, of joints also and of marrow, and a discerner of the thoughts and intentions of the heart" (*Heb. 4:12*); and it does not need any oratorical flourish or adaptation by men to move and inspire hearts. The sacred pages have been written under the inspiration of the Spirit of God and they themselves are rich with their own value; God has made them beautiful so that they radiate light and splendor. The only condition is that scholars explain these sacred pages fully and exactly so as to reveal all the treasures of wisdom and prudence that are hidden in them [*311–12*].

Study of the sacred writer and his circumstances

136
(2294)
The scholar should use all care and everything which recent investigations have brought to light to try to learn about the character of the sacred writer, the circumstances of his life, when he lived, what written or oral sources he used, and the forms of expression that he used. In this way he will have a more satisfactory knowledge of who the sacred writer was and what he wanted to say in writing [*314*].

The exegete should determine literary types

137
(2294)
It is not as easy to determine the *literal* meaning of the sayings and writings of ancient Oriental writers as it is of contemporary authors. The meaning they wished to convey by their words is determined not only by the laws of grammar, or philology, nor merely by the context of the words. The scholar should return in mind to the long past ages of the Orient and he should make good use of the help of history, archaeology, ethnology, and other sciences to determine what literary types those ancient writers made a policy of using, and which ones they did in fact use. The ancient Orientals did not always use the same forms and types of expression to convey their ideas that we use today. Rather, they used the types that were in common use among the men of their time

and locale. The exegete cannot determine what these types were by a preconceived judgment, but only by a careful investigation of ancient Oriental literature. This investigation has been carried out in recent decades with greater care and exactness than ever before and has yielded rather clear information as to what forms of expression were used in those ancient times in poetry, in ethical and legislative writings, and in historical accounts. This same investigation has also clearly proven that the Israelites were outstanding among the other ancient nations of the Orient in their exact recording of history. Their recording of history is outstanding because it goes back so far and is so very faithful to events. This is undoubtedly due to the charism of divine inspiration and to the peculiar religious purpose of biblical history. Certain arts of exposition and narration, certain idioms, especially the ones peculiar to Semitic languages known as *approximations*, certain hyperbolic ways of speaking, and sometimes paradoxes intended to impress the subject matter on the mind, are found in the sacred writers as they are in other ancient authors. But this should not surprise anyone who has the correct notion about biblical inspiration. None of the ways of expression which human language used to express thought among the ancient nations, particularly among the Orientals, is excluded from the Sacred Books, provided that the manner of expression offers no contradiction to the sanctity and veracity of God. This is what the Angelic Doctor with his usual wisdom writes: "Scripture gives us divine things in a way that men are accustomed to." As the substantial Word of God became like man in everything "except sin" (*see Heb. 4:15*), so the words of God, expressed in human language, are like human expression in every respect except error. This is the συγκατάβασις or condescension of God's providence which St. John Chrysostom praises so highly and which he time and again asserted is to be found in the Sacred Books.

To satisfy the needs of modern biblical studies, the Catholic exegete, when he explains Sacred Scripture and shows that it is free from all error, should make a prudent use of the help he can get from an investigation of the extent to which

**138
(2294)**

the form of expression or the literary type used by the sacred writer can contribute to correct and genuine interpretation. He should realize that he cannot neglect this part of his task without great loss to the cause of Catholic exegesis [*314–16*].

Esteem for Sacred Scripture

139   If a person considers the amount of work carried out by Catholic exegesis for almost two thousand years in order to give men the opportunity of constantly growing in a fuller and more perfect understanding and more ardent love of the word of God as given to men in Holy Scripture, he will easily be convinced that the faithful and particularly priests have a serious duty to make continual and holy use of this treasure which brilliant men have accumulated for centuries. God did not give the Sacred Books to men to satisfy their curiosity or to give them material for study and research. As the Apostle says, these divine words are able "to instruct unto salvation by the faith which is in Christ Jesus," and "that the man of God may be perfect, equipped for every good work" (*II Tim. 3:15, 17*). Priests, who are charged with winning the eternal salvation of the faithful, should diligently study the sacred pages; they should assimilate them by prayer and meditation; and then they should zealously dispense the supernatural power of the divine word in their sermons, homilies, and exhortations. They should support Christian doctrine with passages taken from the Sacred Books, with outstanding examples from sacred history, particularly from the Gospel of Christ our Lord. They should meticulously avoid accommodations which are purely arbitrary and far-fetched, which are a misuse rather than a use of the divine word. Their use of Scripture should be eloquent, orderly, and clear. It should move the faithful to lead a good life and inspire in them a deep reverence for Sacred Scripture [*320–21*].

LETTER OF THE BIBLICAL COMMISSION TO CARDINAL SUHARD, ARCHBISHOP OF PARIS, 1948

In a letter written to Cardinal Suhard, archbishop of Paris, and approved by Pope Pius XII, January 16, 1948, Father J. M. Vosté, O.P., secretary of the Biblical Commission, encouraged Catholic scholars to investigate scriptural problems with the full liberty enjoyed within the limits of Catholic doctrine and tradition. Of particular importance in this letter are the secretary's remarks concerning the literary genre of the first eleven chapters of Genesis and the necessary caution in interpreting them.

. . . To declare a priori that these narratives do not contain history in the modern sense of the word might easily be understood to mean that they do not contain history in any sense, whereas they do actually relate in simple and figurative language, adapted to the intelligence of less educated men, the fundamental truths underlying the divine plan of salvation. And they are a popular description of the origins of the human race and of the chosen people.   **140** *(2302)*

THE ENCYCLICAL *HUMANI GENERIS,* 1950

Pope Pius XII (1939–58) published this encyclical on August 12, 1950, to warn the whole Church of many contemporary errors. Outside the Church, existentialist philosophy, historicism, anti-intellectual and anti-ecclesiastical religions, are some of the erroneous opinions of the day that are censured. Within the Church, an eagerness for novelty, a dangerous spirit of compromise, and a scorn of scholastic thought also are censured by the pope. In the selection from the encyclical that follows, the historical nature of the first eleven chapters of Genesis is clearly vindicated; however, Catholic exegetes are invited to determine in what exact sense these chapters come under the heading of history.

As with biology and anthropology, so with history; there are some who make bold to overstep the warning landmarks which the Church has laid down. One especially regrettable tendency is to interpret the historical books of the Old Testament with overmuch freedom. In vain do the exponents of this method appeal, for their defence, to the letter recently received by the archbishop of Paris from the Pontifical Commission on Biblical Studies (*see 140*). It was clearly laid down in that letter that the first eleven chapters of Genesis, although it is not right to judge them by modern standards of historical composition, such as would be applied to the great classical authors, or to the learned of our own day, do nevertheless come under the heading of history; in what exact sense, it is for the further labors of the exegete to deter-   **141** *(2329)* mine. These chapters have a naif, symbolical way of talking, well suited to the understanding of a primitive people. But they do disclose to us certain important truths, upon which the attainment of our eternal salvation depends; and they do also give a popularly written description of how the human race, and the chosen people in particular, came to be. It may be true that these old writers of sacred history drew some of their material from the stories current among the people of their day. So much may be granted; but it must be remembered on the other side that they did so under the impulse of divine inspiration, which preserved them from all error in selecting and assessing the material they used.

142
(2330) These excerpts from current stories, which are found in the sacred books, must not be put on a level with mere myths, or with legend in general. Myths arise from the untrammelled exercise of the imagination; whereas in our sacred books, even in the Old Testament, a love of truth and a cult of simplicity shine out, in such a way as to put these writers on a demonstrably different level from their profane contemporaries.

The Church

"The word of the Lord endures forever" (see I Pet. 1:25). *The stupendous revelation made to men in the words and life of Jesus Christ was destined to be spirit and life to men of all generations. As his own earthly life was limited to a definite period of history and a small geographical locality, Christ instituted a divine society through which he could prolong and extend his life-giving contact with all men of all times.*

Because the Church is a continuation of the Incarnation of Christ, it shares in the characteristics of the Incarnation. It has, therefore, a human and a divine element, a visible and an invisible element. It is so closely associated with Christ that it can truly be called the bride of Christ, and his mystical body.

The Holy Spirit animates the body of the Church invisibly with the divine life that is the life of grace, imparted to the members of the Church through their head, Jesus Christ. Yet in the Church this invisible life is not independent of the visible and exterior structure of the Church as a society made up of men. It was Christ's will and institution that the Church carry on his work as a visible organized society, like a city set on a mountain, since it was to be a necessary means for salvation for all men. For this reason, he gave it a visible supreme head and hierarchical government (in the persons of St. Peter and the apostles, and their successors: the Roman Pontiff and the bishops throughout the world). Moreover, Christ promised these rulers his efficacious and perpetual assistance in carrying out his work of teaching the revealed truth unerringly, of ruling wisely, and of sanctifying effectively.

Such is the Church of Christ which endures through all the ages one, holy, Catholic, and apostolic. It is always unchanged in its essence; yet it always accommodates itself to the variety of times and conditions in which it lives, so that it can effectively be what it truly is, the unique and necessary ark of salvation for all. It is itself a "great and perpetual motive of credibility and an irrefutable proof of its own divine mission" (see 68).

LETTER TO THE ORIENTALS, 341

Indicative of the Roman sureness that its supreme authority is of apostolic origin is this letter in which Pope St. Julius (337–52) rebukes the Eastern Arian bishops, led by Eusebius, who had intrigued against St. Athanasius, bishop of Alexandria.

143
(57a) Why was nothing written to us about the Church of Alexandria especially? Did you not know that the custom was this: to write to us first, and thus from here justice would be determined? Therefore, if any such suspicion fell upon the bishop of Alexandria, the thing to do was to write to this Church.

LETTER TO THE AFRICAN BISHOPS, 417

In commending the bishops of Africa for referring their action against the Pelagians to him for his approval, St. Innocent I (401–17) gives another indirect but very clear indication of the position of primacy with which the Roman See was everywhere credited.

144
(100) (1) Following the examples of ancient tradition . . . in your pursuit of the things of God, . . . you have made manifest by your proper course of action the vitality of your religion . . . when you agreed to refer to our judgment. For you knew what was due to the Apostolic See, since all of us who are here desire to follow the apostle from whom have come this episcopate and all the authority belonging to this name. By following him we know how to condemn what is wrong and to approve of what is praiseworthy. Moreover, in safeguarding the ordinances of the Fathers with your priestly zeal, you certainly believe they must not be trodden under foot. They decreed, not with human, but with divine judg-

ment that no decision (even though it concerned the most remote provinces) was to be considered final unless this See were to hear of it, so that all the authority of this See might back up whatever just decision was reached.

LETTER TO THE BISHOP OF THESSALONICA, 422

Writing to Rufus, bishop of Thessalonica and papal vicar for Illyricum, Pope St. Boniface I (418–22) refers to an illicit council that had been held at Corinth. His words imply the universal recognition of Rome's supreme authority and the finality of its judgments.

(2) . . . We have sent a letter . . . to the Synod [at   **145** Corinth] and from this letter all the brethren may realize . . .   **(110)** that Our judgment is not to be reviewed. For it has never been permitted to go over anything once it has been decided by the Apostolic See.

THE COUNCIL OF EPHESUS, 431

Famous for its Christological doctrine (*see introd. to 399*), the Council of Ephesus, the third ecumenical council, also demonstrates the esteem in which the entire Church, Eastern and Western, held the Roman Pontiff. The following excerpt is from the address of the priest Philip, papal legate, to the assembled bishops exhorting them to execute the decisions of Pope St. Celestine I (422–32) with regard to Nestorius—which the council subsequently did.

No one doubts, in fact, it is obvious to all ages that the   **146** holy and most Blessed Peter, head and Prince of the Apostles,   **(112)** the pillar of faith, and the foundation of the Catholic Church, received the keys of the kingdom from our Lord Jesus Christ, the savior and the redeemer of the human race. Nor does anyone doubt that the power of forgiving and retaining sins was also given to this same Peter who, in his successors, lives and exercises judgment even to this time and forever (*see* 204).

THE FORMULA OF POPE ST. HORMISDAS, 517

During the pontificate of Pope St. Hormisdas (514–23), the accession of Justinian, a Catholic and a Latin, to the imperial throne at Constantinople provided an opportunity to heal the thirty-five-year-old Acacian schism. The document which Justinian ordered the Eastern bishops to sign is a profession of faith which had been added to a letter that the pope had sent to the bishops of Spain in the year 517. Its acceptance by later councils gives it the value of a definition.

147
(171)
The first condition of salvation is to keep the norm of the true faith and in no way to deviate from the established doctrine of the Fathers. For it is impossible that the words of our Lord Jesus Christ who said, "Thou art Peter, and upon this rock I will build my Church" (*Matt. 16:18*), should not be verified. And their truth has been proved by the course of history, for in the Apostolic See the Catholic religion has always been kept unsullied. From this hope and faith we by no means desire to be separated and, following the doctrine of the Fathers, we declare anathema all heresies, and especially the heretic Nestorius, former bishop of Constantinople, who was condemned in the Council of Ephesus by Blessed Celestine, bishop of Rome, and by the venerable Cyril, bishop of Alexandria. We likewise condemn and declare to be anathema Eutyches and Dioscorus of Alexandria, who were condemned in the holy Council of Chalcedon (*see 414*), which we follow and endorse. This council followed the holy Council of Nicaea and preached the apostolic faith. And we condemn the assassin Timothy, surnamed Aelurus, and also Peter of Alexandria, his disciple and follower in everything. We also declare anathema their helper and follower, Acacius of Constantinople, a bishop once condemned by the Apostolic See, and all those who remain in contact and company with them. Because this Acacius joined himself to their communion, he deserved to receive a judgment of condemnation similar to theirs. Furthermore, we condemn Peter of Antioch with all his followers together with the followers of all those mentioned above.

148
(172)
Following, as we have said before, the Apostolic See in all things and proclaiming all its decisions, we endorse and approve all the letters which Pope St. Leo wrote concerning the Christian religion. And so I hope I may deserve to be associated with you in the one communion which the Apostolic See proclaims, in which the whole, true, and perfect security of the Christian religion resides. I promise that from now on

those who are separated from the communion of the Catholic Church, that is, who are not in agreement with the Apostolic See, will not have their names read during the sacred mysteries. But if I attempt even the least deviation from my profession, I admit that, according to my own declaration, I am an accomplice to those whom I have condemned. I have signed this my profession with my own hand and have directed it to you, Hormisdas, the holy and venerable pope of Rome.

LETTER TO MICHAEL CAERULARIUS, 1053

Fearing the Latinization of Byzantine churches in Italy if a proposed reunion of the Eastern and Western Church were successful, the Patriarch Michael Caerularius of Constantinople had raised a storm over certain Latin usages, such as that of unleavened bread in the Eucharistic Sacrifice. The following excerpt is from a reply to Michael written by Cardinal Humbert and signed by Pope St. Leo IX (1049–54). It is noteworthy in that its emphasis is not upon the minutiae of ritual differences but on the essential point of Roman authority and infallibility. There is doubt that this letter, dated September 2, 1053, was ever actually transmitted to Michael Caerularius.

Chapter 7. . . . The holy Church has been built upon a rock, that is, upon Christ, and upon Peter or Cephas, the son of John, who was first called Simon. It was so built because it never was to be conquered by the gates of hell, that is, by heretical opinions which lead the unwary to destruction. This is the promise of Truth itself who is the cause of all that is true: "The gates of hell shall not prevail against it" (*Matt. 16:18*). The same Son of God bears witness that by his prayers he obtained the fulfillment of this promise from the Father, for he said to Peter, "Simon, Simon, behold, Satan has desired to have you . . . but I have prayed for thee, that thy faith may not fail" (*Luke 22:31 f.*). Will there be anyone, then, so foolish as to dare think that the prayer of the person whose will is power to do, can be devoid of effect? Is it not by the See of the Prince of the Apostles, namely, by this Roman Church, both by this same Peter and by his successors, that all the inventions of heretics stand condemned, exposed, and overcome? Are not the hearts of the brethren strengthened in

149
(351)

71

the faith of Peter which has not failed thus far and will not fail till the end of time?

PROFESSION OF FAITH PRESCRIBED FOR DURANDUS OF OSCA AND FOLLOWERS, 1208

Durandus of Osca, a follower of Peter Waldes, converted by St. Dominic, was asked by Innocent III (1198–1216) to make a profession of faith. It included the following proposition on the unity of the Church and its necessity for salvation.

150
(423)
We believe in our heart and profess with our lips one Church, not a church of heretics, but the holy, Roman, Catholic, apostolic Church. We believe that outside this Church no one is saved.

THE FOURTH LATERAN COUNCIL, 1215

Innocent III also organized the resistance to the Albigensian heresy, a reincarnation of Manichaeanism and Docetism. At the Fourth Council of the Lateran, the twelfth ecumenical council, among the doctrines defined against the Albigenses, a profession of faith in the one true Church was included (*see introd. to 306*).

151
(430)
Indeed, there is but one universal Church of the faithful outside which no one at all is saved and in which the priest himself, Jesus Christ, is the victim . . .

THE SECOND COUNCIL OF LYONS, 1274

In the Second Council of Lyons, the fourteenth ecumenical council, Gregory X (1271–76) was concerned with reuniting the Greek Church, in schism since the Photian scandal in the ninth century. The emperor in the East, Michael Palaeologus, subscribed to this creed through his ambassadors at Lyons. Besides the famous *Filioque*, the creed contains a profession of faith in the one, holy, Catholic, and apostolic Church as the only true Church and acknowledges its primacy.

152
(466)
The same holy Roman Church also has supreme and full primacy and jurisdiction over the whole Catholic Church. This it truly and humbly recognizes as received from the Lord himself in the person of St. Peter, the Prince or head of the Apostles, whose successor in the fullness of power is the Roman Pontiff. And just as the holy Roman Church is

bound more than all the others to defend the truth of faith, so, if there arise any questions concerning the faith, they must be decided by its judgment. Anyone who is aggrieved may appeal to it in matters pertaining to the ecclesiastical court; and in all cases that require ecclesiastical investigation, one may have recourse to its judgment. Also, all churches are subject to it, and their prelates render it obedience and reverence. There is such a fullness of power vested in this Church that it admits other churches to a share in its responsibility; and many of these, especially the patriarchal churches, the same Roman Church has honored with various privileges. Yet always its special position has remained intact, both in general councils and in some others.

THE BULL UNAM SANCTAM, 1302

Out of an unfortunate and turbulent period of Church history comes this very clear definition of the unity of the Church, its necessity for salvation, its divine origin, and the foundation of the authority of the Roman Pontiff. This bull of Boniface VIII (1294–1303) also contains the well-known reference to the two swords, the spiritual and the temporal. At this time the hierocratic theory, that is, that the temporal power was bestowed by God through the mediation of the pope, was a common, though by no means universal, theory among the canonists. The theologians, men such as St. Thomas and John Quidort (John of Paris), did not generally hold with the canonists. Boniface states the hierocratic theory in its extreme form, but as a theory, not as a dogmatic definition.

The theologians (and some canonists) held that the temporal society is autonomous, though its end is inferior in dignity to the end of the spiritual society, the Church. The difficulty arose from the need of safeguarding the distinct finality of the temporal society and the pre-eminence of the spiritual society. God is the source of both powers; the two theories differed in explaining how that power is conferred.

We are compelled in virtue of our faith to believe and maintain that there is only one Catholic Church, and that one apostolic. This we firmly believe and profess without qualification. Outside this Church there is no salvation and no remission of sins. Thus the spouse proclaims in the Canticle, "One is my dove: my perfect one is but one. She is the only

153
(468)

one of her mother, the chosen of her that bore her" (*Cant. 6:8*). Now this chosen one represents the one mystical body whose head is Christ, and Christ's head is God. In her there is "one Lord, one faith, one baptism" (*Eph. 4:5*). For at the time of the deluge there existed only one ark, the figure of the one Church. This ark received its final touch by one cubit's provision and had but one pilot and captain, that is, Noe. And we read that all things existing upon the earth outside this ark perished. We honor this Church as the one and only Church, as the Lord says by his prophet, "Deliver, O God, my soul from the sword: my only one from the hand of the dog" (*Ps. 21:21*). The Lord was praying for his soul, that is, for himself as head, and at the same time for his body which he called his only one, that is, his Church, because of the oneness of his spouse, the Church, in faith, in the sacraments, and in charity. This Church is the seamless robe of the Lord (*see John 19:23*), which was not cut but for which lots were cast. Therefore, the one and only Church has one body, one head (not two heads, like a monster); namely, Christ and his Vicar Peter, and the successor of Peter; for the Lord said to Peter himself, "Feed my sheep" (*John 21:17*). *My*, says Christ, and this universally, not singling out "these" or "those." By this expression it is clearly understood that He entrusted to him all without exception. If, therefore, the Greeks or others say that they are not committed to Peter and to his successors, they necessarily say that they are not of the sheep of Christ, as the Lord says in John that there is one fold and one shepherd (*see John 10:16*).

154
(469) We are taught by the words of the Gospel that in this Church and under its control there are two swords, the spiritual and the temporal. . . . Both of these, that is, the spiritual and the temporal swords, are under the control of the Church. The first is wielded by the Church; the second is wielded on behalf of the Church. The first is wielded by the hand of the priest, the second by the hand of kings and soldiers but at the wish and by the permission of the priests. Sword must be subordinated to sword, and it is only fitting that the temporal authority should be subject to the spiritual. . . . We must be all the more explicit in declaring that the

spiritual power is as far superior to any earthly power both in dignity and nobility as spiritual things are superior to temporal. . . . For, as Truth witnesses, the spiritual power can both establish the earthly power and judge it, if it proves to be no good. . . . Therefore, if the earthly power goes astray, it will be judged by the spiritual power; and if the lesser spiritual power goes astray, it will be judged by its superior; but if the supreme power goes astray, it will not be judged by men, but only by God, as the Apostle says, "The spiritual man judges all things, and he himself is judged by no man" (*I Cor. 2:15*). This authority, moreover, although given to man and exercised by man, is not human, but divine, given by the divine lips to Peter and, as far as he and his successors were concerned, grounded upon Him, whom the Rock [*Peter*] had confessed. For to Peter himself the Lord said, "Whatever thou shalt bind on earth shall be bound in heaven" (*Matt. 16:19*). Whoever, therefore, resists this authority thus ordered by God, resists the command of God (*see Rom. 13:2*); unless, like a Manichaean, he supposes that there are two sources of power; and this we judge to be false and heretical because, as Moses testifies, God created heaven and earth not by several powers, but by one power (*see Gen. 1:1*). Further, We declare, say, define, and pronounce that it is absolutely necessary for the salvation of every human creature to be subject to the Roman Pontiff. [*There is a word play in the Latin that the English cannot reproduce. The first verse of Genesis begins with the words* in principio *in Latin. Our English Douay version reads* in the beginning. *But the Latin words can also mean* by the power *or* by one power. *Pope Boniface takes them in this last sense to point the contrast between the Catholic doctrine according to which there is but one omnipotent source of all power, and the Manichaean doctrine, according to which there are two absolute sources of power, a good and an evil one.*]

CONDEMNATION OF ERRORS OF
MARSILIUS OF PADUA AND JOHN OF JANDUN, 1327

Marsilius of Padua (1280?–1343) and John of Jandun (d. 1328), his pupil and collaborator in the work *Defensor pacis*, were defenders of the imperial party of Louis of Bavaria against Pope John XXII. On October 23, 1327, both were condemned by name as heretics in the bull *Licet juxta doctrinam*. The condemned errors of these men indicate the beginnings of a false notion of the constitution of the Church—that it is a democratic not a monarchical society; and they undoubtedly influenced Wyclif and Hus and the theologians of the Reformation.

155
(496) (2) The Apostle St. Peter had no more authority than the other apostles had, and he was not their head. Again, Christ did not bequeath any head for his Church, nor did he appoint anyone his vicar.

156
(497) (3) It is the emperor's duty to correct the pope, to appoint and depose him, and to punish him.

157
(498) (4) According to the institution of Christ, every priest, whether he be pope, archbishop, or simple priest has equal authority and jurisdiction.

THE COUNCIL OF CONSTANCE, 1414-18

John Wyclif (1324–84), heir to the spirit of Occam, Marsilius, and John of Jandun, began with an exaggerated notion of evangelical poverty which led him to a hatred of Church property and government. This led him to deny that the authority of the Church and of the pope is of divine origin and, consequently, to stress the Bible as the sole norm of orthodoxy. His spiritual heir was John Hus (1369–1415). Hus translated Wyclif's heretical writings into Bohemian and defended them in spite of warnings from Pope Gregory XII. In 1412 Hus wrote his *De Ecclesia;* and in 1414 he was summoned to the Council of Constance, the sixteenth ecumenical council, where he was tried and condemned; he was then burnt at the stake by the secular authorities on July 6, 1415. The following errors of these men were condemned in the council.

Errors of Wyclif

158
(588) 8. If the pope be a reprobate and an evil man, and, consequently, a member of the devil, he has no power over the faithful given to him by anyone, except perhaps by the state.

159
(617) 37. The Roman Church is the synagogue of Satan, and the pope is not the proximate and immediate vicar of Christ and of the apostles.

The Church

Errors of Hus

3. The reprobates are not parts of the Church, since no part of the Church will ultimately fall away from it; for the charity of predestination, which keeps it together, will not fail.

160
(629)

5. Even if sometimes the reprobate is in grace according to his actual state of justice, he is nonetheless, never a part of the holy Church; and the predestined always remains a member of the Church even though sometimes he may fall from temporary grace, but not from the grace of predestination.

161
(631)

6. The Church is an article of faith only if by *Church* is meant the gathering of the predestined, whether they are in grace according to their actual state of justice or not.

162
(632)

10. It would be unreasonable for anyone without a revelation to make the claim for himself or for another that he is the head of a particular Church; and not even the Roman Pontiff is the head of the particular Roman Church.

163
(636)

THE COUNCIL OF FLORENCE, 1438-45

The heretical doctrines of Wyclif and Hus were preparing the way for the Protestant Revolt and the rejection of a divinely established, monarchical society. In the meantime the Church was occupying itself with another attempt to bring the Churches of the East into union with Rome. There are three decrees: one for the Greeks and one for two other groups of schismatics, the Jacobites and the Armenians. A profession of faith was set down in the acts of the Council of Florence, the seventeenth ecumenical council, in which the primacy of the Roman Pontiff, the unity of the Church, and its necessity for salvation were proposed to these schismatics.

Decree for the Greeks

Likewise, we define that the holy Apostolic See and the Roman Pontiff have the primacy over the whole world, and that the same Roman Pontiff is the successor of St. Peter, the Prince of the Apostles, and the true vicar of Christ, the head of the whole Church, the father and teacher of all Christians; and that to him, in the person of St. Peter, was given by our Lord Jesus Christ the full power of feeding, ruling, and gov-

164
(694)

erning the whole Church; as is also contained in the proceedings of the ecumenical councils and in the sacred canons.

Decree for the Jacobites

165
(714)
The holy Roman Church believes, professes, and preaches that "no one remaining outside the Catholic Church, not just pagans, but also Jews or heretics or schismatics, can become partakers of eternal life; but they will go to the 'everlasting fire which was prepared for the devil and his angels' (*Matt. 25:41*), unless before the end of life they are joined to the Church. For union with the body of the Church is of such importance that the sacraments of the Church are helpful to salvation only for those remaining in it; and fasts, almsgiving, other works of piety, and the exercise of Christian warfare bear eternal rewards for them alone. And no one can be saved, no matter how much alms he has given, even if he sheds his blood for the name of Christ, unless he remains in the bosom and the unity of the Catholic Church."

CONDEMNATION OF ERRORS OF LUTHER, 1520
On June 15, 1520, Leo X (1513–21) condemned the errors of Martin Luther in the bull *Exsurge Domine*. The errors of Occam and Marsilius, of Wyclif and Hus, had been taken up by Luther in his revolt from Rome and the authority of the Roman Pontiff.

166
(765)
25. The Roman Pontiff, the successor of Peter, was not, in the person of St. Peter, appointed by Christ as his vicar over all the churches of the entire world.

167
(766)
26. The words of Christ to Peter: "Whatever thou shalt loose on earth" (*Matt. 16:19*), are applicable only to what was bound by Peter himself.

168
(767)
27. It is certain that it is not at all within the power of the Church or the pope to lay down articles of faith, or even to pass laws concerning morals or good works.

169
(768)
28. If the pope would agree with a large part of the Church in holding an opinion one way or another, he would not go wrong; but even so it would not be sinful or heretical to hold the opposite opinion—especially in a matter that is not necessary for salvation—until one side of the question has

been condemned and the other side approved by a general council.

DECREE OF THE HOLY OFFICE, 1647

On January 24, 1647, the following decree was issued. Innocent X (1644–55) condemned as heretical the propositions of Martin de Barcos, an abbot of St. Cyran. De Barcos, who had studied under Jansen, maintained that the Apostles Peter and Paul were two heads of the Church, thus implying an equality of the two apostles.

"There are two princes of the Church, SS. Peter and Paul, who together make one prince." "They are two heads of the Catholic Church and two supreme rulers joined in perfect unity." "They are two leaders of the universal Church who have coalesced into one under God." "They are two supreme pastors and rulers who make but one head." His Holiness . . . has judged and declared the above propositions heretical if they are explained so as to establish complete equality between St. Peter and St. Paul, without subordinating and subjecting St. Paul to St. Peter in the supreme power and government of the universal Church. **170** *(1091)*

CONDEMNATION OF THE ERRORS OF THE SYNOD OF PISTOIA, 1794

The Synod of Pistoia was held in 1786. Some of the proposals of this synod were condemned in the constitution *Auctorem fidei*, issued on August 28, 1794, by Pius VI (1775–99).

Moreover, it is heretical to propose that the Roman Pontiff is ministerial head, if this is explained to mean that the Roman Pontiff received, not from Christ in the person of St. Peter, but from the Church, the power of his office by which, as the successor of Peter, the true vicar of Christ, and the head of the entire Church, he has power over the universal Church. **171** *(1503)*

The following doctrine is heretical if it is understood to mean that the body of the Church is made up only of the faithful who are perfect adorers in spirit and in truth: The Church is to be considered as one mystical body made up of Christ, the head, and of the faithful who are members of Christ by an indescribable union. By this union we become **172** *(1515)* with Christ, in some wonderful way, the one and only priest, the one and only victim, the one and only perfect adorer of God the Father in spirit and in truth.

THE ALLOCUTION *SINGULARI QUADAM*, 1854

A natural corollary of the nineteenth century's rationalistic attitude to revelation was the erroneous opinion that all religions were of equal value. In his allocution *Singulari quadam,* December 9, 1854, Pius IX (1846–78) repudiates this opinion but at the same time makes it clear that, though the Church is necessary for salvation, it is not for us to judge about the state of those who are invincibly ignorant of the true religion.

173
(1646)   Another error, equally destructive, has taken hold of some parts of the Catholic world, as we see to our sorrow. It has sunk deep into the minds of those Catholics principally who think there is good hope for the eternal salvation of all those who in no wise live in the true Church of Christ. Therefore, they are in the habit of frequently asking what will be the future lot and condition after death of those who in no way have given adherence to the Catholic faith. Advancing the flimsiest of arguments, they expect a reply that will support this erroneous opinion. Far be it from Us, Venerable Brethren, to dare set limits to the divine mercy, which is infinite. Far be it from Us to want to penetrate the secret plans and judgments of God, which are a great abyss (*see Ps. 35:7*), impenetrable to human thought. But according to Our apostolic office, We want your episcopal care and vigilance to be on the alert to keep away from men's minds, with all possible effort, that opinion which is as unholy as it is deadly. We mean the opinion that a way of eternal salvation can be found in any religion whatever. With all the learning and ingenuity that is yours, teach the people entrusted to your care that the dogmas of the Catholic faith are not in the slightest opposed to the mercy and justice of God.

174
(1647)   It must, of course, be held as a matter of faith that outside the apostolic Roman Church no one can be saved, that the Church is the only ark of salvation, and that whoever does not enter it will perish in the flood. On the other hand, it

must likewise be held as certain that those who are affected by ignorance of the true religion, if it is invincible ignorance, are not subject to any guilt in this matter before the eyes of the Lord. Now, then, who could presume in himself an ability to set the boundaries of such ignorance, taking into consideration the natural differences of peoples, lands, native talents, and so many other factors? Only when we have been released from the bonds of this body and see God just as he is (*see I John 3:2*) shall we really understand how close and beautiful a bond joins divine mercy with divine justice. But as long as we dwell on earth, encumbered with this soul-dulling, mortal body, let us tenaciously cling to the Catholic doctrine that there is one God, one faith, one baptism (*see Eph. 4:5*). To proceed with further investigation is wrong.

Nevertheless, as charity demands, let us pray continually for the conversion to Christ of all nations everywhere. Let us devote ourselves to the salvation of all men as far as we can, for the hand of the Lord is not shortened (*see Isa. 59:1*). The gifts of heavenly grace will assuredly not be denied to those who sincerely want and pray for refreshment by the divine light. These truths need to be fixed deeply in the minds of the faithful so that they cannot be infected with doctrines tending to foster the religious indifferentism which We see spreading widely, with growing strength, and with destructive effect upon souls.

175
(1648)

LETTER TO ARCHBISHOP SCHERR OF MUNICH, 1862

In a spirit of independence, Frohschammer (*see introd. to 42*) had sought to emancipate philosophical speculation from all subjection to ecclesiastic authority. Writing to Frohschammer's archbishop, Pius IX points out that the Church's duty to teach gives it competence to speak out in every field where error can endanger the salvation of souls. In the same letter he again denounces the error of religious indifferentism and explains the Church's position.

And what is more, the same author imprudently and passionately defends liberty or, rather, ungoverned license in philosophy. And as a result of this, he unhesitatingly asserts that the Church should not only never take measures against

176
(1675)

philosophy, but should even allow the errors of philosophy and leave it free to correct itself. Consequently, the inevitable result is that philosophers share in this liberty of philosophy, and so they themselves are set free from every law. Who does not see that this opinion and the doctrine of Frohschammer should be forcefully rejected and disapproved and altogether condemned? For, by reason of its divine establishment, the Church must diligently watch over the deposit of divine faith, keep it whole and unsullied, and, with the greatest zeal, continually watch out for the salvation of souls. The Church must remove and eliminate with the greatest possible care everything that can either oppose the faith or in any way endanger the salvation of souls.

177
(1676) Therefore, by the power entrusted to it by its divine founder, the Church has not only the right but above all the duty of not allowing, but of proscribing and condemning all errors, if the integrity of the faith and the salvation of souls demand it. Upon every philosopher who wishes to be a son of the Church, and even upon philosophy, there is incumbent an obligation of never saying anything contrary to the teachings of the Church, and of retracting those statements about which the Church has admonished them. And We state and declare that the opinion which teaches the contrary is thoroughly false and very injurious to faith itself, to the Church, and to its authority.

ENCYCLICAL TO THE BISHOPS OF ITALY, 1863

The following encyclical, *Quanto conficiamur moerore,* was addressed to the bishops of Italy on August 10, 1863. Once more Pope Pius IX (1846–78) gives a warning that liberal indifferentism is a serious error opposed to Catholic truth.

178
(1677) And here, Beloved Sons and Venerable Brethren, it is necessary once more to mention and censure the serious error into which some Catholics have unfortunately fallen. For they are of the opinion that men who live in errors, estranged from the true faith and from Catholic unity, can attain eternal life (*see 187*). This is in direct opposition to Catholic teaching. We all know that those who are afflicted with invincible ignorance with regard to our holy religion, if they carefully

keep the precepts of the natural law that have been written by God in the hearts of all men, if they are prepared to obey God, and if they lead a virtuous and dutiful life, can attain eternal life by the power of divine light and grace. For God, who reads comprehensively in every detail the minds and souls, the thoughts and habits of all men, will not permit, in accordance with his infinite goodness and mercy, anyone who is not guilty of a voluntary fault to suffer eternal punishment. However, also well-known is the Catholic dogma that no one can be saved outside the Catholic Church, and that those who obstinately oppose the authority and definitions of that Church, and who stubbornly remain separated from the unity of the Church and from the successor of Peter, the Roman Pontiff (to whom the Savior has entrusted the care of his vineyard), cannot obtain salvation.

LETTER TO ARCHBISHOP SCHERR OF MUNICH, 1863

The Congress of German Catholic theologians at Munich in September, 1863, occasioned some disquiet in ecclesiastical circles owing to the tone of Döllinger's discourses at the Congress and the irregular procedure followed by its organizers. After the Congress, on December 21, 1863, Pius IX addressed a letter to the archbishop of Munich in which, among other matters, he calls attention to the fact that not only the Church's dogmatic definitions but also its ordinary teaching infallibly proposes revealed truth. The Vatican Council (*see 66*) reiterates this teaching.

[*The members of the Congress*] recognized and asserted that all Catholics in their scholarly writings are obliged in conscience to obey the dogmatic decrees of the infallible Catholic Church.

179
(1682)

We certainly give them their due praise for professing that truth which necessarily springs from an obligation imposed by the Catholic faith; yet, We desire to reassure ourselves that they did not mean to limit the obligation, which strictly binds Catholic teachers and writers, to those things only which are proposed by the infallible judgment of the Church as dogmas of faith to be believed by everybody. In a like manner, We are convinced that it was not their intention to state that the perfect adherence to revealed truths (which they

180
(1683)

regard as absolutely necessary for true progress in science and for refuting errors) can be maintained, if the submission of faith is given only to those dogmas expressly defined by the Church. The reason for this is the following: even supposing that we are treating of that subjection which is to be made by an explicit act of divine faith, this must not be limited to those things which have been defined in the express decrees of the ecumenical councils or of the Roman Pontiffs of this See; but it must also be extended to those things which, through the ordinary teaching of the whole Church throughout the world, are proposed as divinely revealed and, as a result, by universal and constant consent of Catholic theologians are held to be matters of faith.

LETTER OF THE HOLY OFFICE TO THE BISHOPS OF ENGLAND, 1864

Since 1857 the Association for the Promotion of the Reunion of Christendom had enjoyed the membership of both Catholics and Anglicans. The Holy Office finally condemned the association in this letter of September 16, 1864, because it rested on the false Branch Theory of the Church, favored indifferentism, and was directed by heretics. In the document there is an important pronouncement on the four notes of the Church.

181
(1686) . . . The true Church of Jesus Christ is constituted by divine authority and is known by four notes. We lay down these notes as matters of faith in the Creed. And any one of these notes is so joined to the others that it cannot be separated from them. Hence it is that the Church that really is catholic, and is called Catholic, must, at the same time, shine with the prerogatives of unity, sanctity, and apostolic succession. Therefore, the Catholic Church is one by a conspicuous and perfect unity of the whole world and of all peoples, by that unity, indeed, whose principle, root, and never-failing source is in the supreme authority and "greater sovereignty" of St. Peter, the Prince of the Apostles, and of his successors in the Roman Chair. Nor is any other church catholic except that which has been built upon Peter alone and which rises into one body closely joined and knit together (*see Eph. 4:16*) in the unity of faith and love. . . .

The Church

THE ENCYCLICAL QUANTA CURA, 1864

In a forcible dogmatic letter, issued the same day as his Collection of Errors, December 8, 1864, Pius IX reviews some of the errors of his time on the relationship of Church and state. He stresses the Church's full independence from temporal powers and the divine origin of its authority.

But others have revived the evil mistakes of the Reformers which have been condemned very often. Acting with extraordinary boldness they dare to subordinate to the judgment of civil authority the supreme authority of the Church and of this Apostolic See—an authority which was received from Christ our Lord. And they deny the Church and this See any rights in matters belonging to external order.

182
(1696)

They do not hesitate to maintain that, "the legislation of the Church does not bind in conscience unless it is promulgated by civil authority. The acts and decrees of the Roman Pontiffs in matters pertaining to religion and to the Church require the sanction and the approval, or at least the consent, of the civil authority. The apostolic constitutions condemning secret societies (regardless of whether or not those societies require an oath of secrecy), and anathematizing the followers and patrons of those societies, are void in those sections of the world where the civil government allows such secret societies. The excommunication that the Council of Trent and the Roman Pontiffs have pronounced against those who violate and usurp the rights and possessions of the Church, are intended to achieve a purely worldly end, and are based upon a confusion of the spiritual order with the civil and political order. . . ."

183
(1697)

They do not hesitate to profess openly and publicly an heretical principle that has led to very many errors and wrong ideas. For they say: "It is not the divine law that the power of the Church be distinct and independent from the civil power. Indeed, it is impossible to keep such independence and distinction without having the Church infringe upon and usurp essential rights of the civil power." And we cannot be silent about the arrogant claim of those who, not enduring

184
(1698)

sound doctrine (*see II Tim. 4:3*), maintain: "It is possible, without sinning and without departing in the least bit from the profession of the Catholic faith, to refuse assent and obedience to those decisions and decrees of the Apostolic See, which are declared to have as their object the general good of the Church and its rights and discipline, provided only that such decisions do not touch upon dogmas of faith or morals." No one can fail to see that this doctrine is clearly in direct opposition to the Catholic dogma according to which Christ our Lord with his divine authority gave to the Roman Pontiff the supreme power of shepherding, ruling, and governing the Church.

COLLECTION OF MODERN ERRORS, 1864

The various errors relating to religious indifferentism were brought together for condemnation and were published on December 8, 1864. (For interpretation of this document, see DB 1700 ff.)

185
(1715) Everyone is free to follow and to profess the religion which the light of reason leads him to judge to be the true religion.

186
(1716) Men can find the way to eternal salvation, and they can attain eternal salvation in the practice of any religion whatever.

187
(1717) There is good reason at least to hope for the eternal salvation of all those who are in no way in the true Church of Christ (*see 178*).

188
(1718) Protestantism is simply another form of the same true Christian religion, and it is possible to please God just as much in it as in the Catholic Church.

THE VATICAN COUNCIL, 1869-70

The third session of the Vatican Council on April 24, 1870, dealt primarily with faith and revelation (*see introd. to 58*), but in the same place it dealt with the position of the Church as guardian and teacher of the revealed word (*see 67, 80*) and as a visible proof of its own divine mission (*see 68*). Originally the council, the twentieth ecumenical council of the Church, had planned to define much more on the constitution and nature of the Church; but there was not enough time to

The Church

complete its work. The first draft of the constitution (*see* **Collectio Lacensis, VII, 567 ff.**) contains no official teaching on the part of the Church, since it was never voted upon by the fathers in solemn assembly. However, since it had been carefully prepared by theologians and presented to the fathers of the council, the draft may be said to reflect the mind of the teaching Church at that time. Its theological value is further attested by the conformity evident between it and later papal pronouncements on the nature and properties of the Church.

THE *FIRST DRAFT* OF THE DOGMATIC CONSTITUTION ON THE CHURCH OF CHRIST

Introduction

. . . Therefore, We think it Our duty to explain the more **189** important headings of the true Catholic doctrine on the nature of the Church, its properties, and its power; the growing errors opposed to these, We shall condemn in articles subjoined in the form of canons.

Chapter 1. The Church Is the Mystical Body of Christ

The only-begotten Son of God who enlightens every man **190** who comes into this world (*see John 1:9*) and who has never in any age failed to proffer his help to the wretched sons of Adam, now in the fullness of time, which had been determined in the eternal plan, being made like unto man in a visible way (*see Phil. 2:7*), appeared visibly in the assumed form of our body so that carnal men of this earth might put on the new man, who has been created according to God in justice and holiness of truth (*see Eph. 4:24*), and form a mystical body whose head would be Christ himself. Indeed, to bring about this union of a mystical body, Christ the Lord instituted the holy washing of regeneration and renovation so that the sons of men, divided among themselves for many different reasons, especially because they are sunk in sin, being cleansed from all stain of guilt, might be members of one another (*see Eph. 4:25*); and, being joined to their divine Head by faith, by hope, and by love, they all might be given life in his one spirit, and receive copiously the gifts of heavenly graces and charisms. And this is the magnificent beauty of the Church, whose head is Christ (*see Col. 1:18*), from whom the whole body—fitted together and connected by the aid of every joint with a view to the operation in due measure of each one of its parts—from whom the whole body takes its growth, so as to build itself up in love (*see Eph. 4:16*). And We cannot recommend sufficiently that this idea be presented to the minds of the faithful and there be deeply and firmly rooted.

Chapter 2. The Christian Religion Cannot Be Practiced Except in and Through the Church That Christ Founded

191 The author and perfecter of faith, Jesus himself, founded and instituted this Church, which he purchased for himself with his own blood, and loved it eternally as his only chosen spouse. And he gave the command that it should be gathered from the whole human race, taught, and guided perpetually throughout the whole world until the end of time by his apostles and their successors, that there might be one holy nation, one acceptable people, pursuing good works (*see Titus 2:14*). And it is not the doctrine of the law of the gospel that true worshippers, taken singly and alone, adore the Father in spirit and in truth without any kind of society; but our Redeemer determined his religion to be so much a part of the society he founded that it was to be intimately connected to and, as it were, grown together with his society, and that outside this society there would be no true religion of Christ.

Chapter 3. The Church Is a True, Perfect, Spiritual, and Supernatural Society

192 The Church has all the qualities of a true society. Christ did not leave this society indeterminate and without form. But just as it has its existence from him, so too it has received its form of existence and its constitution according to his will and his law. The Church is not a member or a part of any other society whatsoever, and it does not and cannot coalesce with any other. But it is so perfect in itself that, although it is distinct from all other human societies, it is nevertheless far superior to them. For, having proceeded from the never-failing font of mercy of the divine Father, and established through the ministry and work of the very Word Incarnate, this society rests on the Holy Spirit. This Holy

Spirit, who first was given in such fullness to the apostles, now also is perpetually given in abundance to the sons of adoption so that, shining with his light and with one faith in their minds, they both adhere to God and remain united. Thus, bearing within their hearts the assurance of their inheritance, they can free the desires of the flesh from that corruption of concupiscence which is in the world. And strengthened in one holy and common hope, they may desire the promised eternal glory of God, and as a consequence make their calling and election sure by good works (*see II Pet. 1:10*). Since, however, in the Church men are multiplied by these treasures through the Holy Spirit and held together in unity by these ties of the Holy Spirit, the Church is a spiritual society and entirely of the supernatural order.

Chapter 4. The Church Is a Visible Society

No one should ever believe that the members of the Church **193** are united with merely internal, hidden bonds and that, therefore, they constitute a hidden and completely invisible society. For the eternal wisdom and power of the Godhead willed that, to these spiritual and invisible bonds by which the faithful through the Holy Spirit adhere to the supreme and invisible head of the Church, there should be corresponding external, visible bonds also in order that this spiritual and supernatural society might appear in external form and be conspicuously evident. Consequently, there is a visible teaching authority which publicly proposes dogma that must be interiorly believed and openly professed. There is a visible priestly office which publicly supervises and takes care of the visible mysteries of God by which interior sanctification is conferred on men and due worship is paid to God. There is a visible governing body which orders the union of the members among themselves and which guides and directs the whole external and public life of the faithful in the Church. Finally, the whole body of the Church is visible; and not only the just or the predestined belong to it, but also those who are in sin, but who are linked with it by their common profession of faith. Thus the Church of Christ on earth is neither invisible nor hidden; but it is placed in clear view like a city set upon a mountain, high and brilliant, impossible to hide, and like a lamp on a lampstand (*see Matt. 5:15*) that is illuminated by the sun of justice and shines on the whole world with the light of its truth.

Chapter 5. The Visible Unity of the Church

194   Since this is the nature of the true Church of Christ, We declare that this visible and conspicuous society is that very same Church of the divine promises and mercies, which Christ willed to characterize and adorn with so many prerogatives and privileges. We declare that it has been so plainly determined in its founding that any societies whatsoever that are separated from the unity of faith or from communion with this body cannot in any way be said to be a part or a member of it. And it cannot be said to be diffused and distributed among the various Christian denominations; but it is an integrated unit, entirely coherent; and, in its conspicuous unity, it shows itself an undivided and indivisible body, which is the true mystical body of Christ. The Apostle says of it: "One body, one spirit, even as you were called in one hope of your calling; one Lord, one faith, one baptism; one God and Father of all, who is above all, and throughout all, and in us all" (*Eph. 4:4–6*).

Chapter 6. The Church Is a Society Absolutely Necessary for Salvation

195   Therefore, let all understand how necessary a society the Church of Christ is for obtaining salvation. Indeed, it is just as necessary as participation in, and conjunction with, Christ the head and his mystical body is necessary. Christ himself nourishes and fosters as his Church no communion other than this body. He loved it and delivered himself up for it that he might sanctify it, cleansing it in the washing of water by means of the word of life, so that he might present to himself the Church in all its glory, not having spot or wrinkle or any such thing, but that it might be holy and without blemish (*see Eph. 5:25–28*). Therefore, We teach that the Church is not a free society, as if it were a matter indifferent to salvation whether it were known or ignored, en-

tered or abandoned; but the Church is absolutely necessary, and, indeed, not just with a necessity coming from the precept of the Lord by which the Savior commanded all nations to enter it; but it is also necessary as a means because, in the order of salvation established by Providence, the communication of the Holy Spirit and the participation of truth and life is not had except in the Church and through the Church of which Christ is the head.

Chapter 7. Outside the Church No One Can Be Saved

Furthermore, it is a dogma of faith that no one can be **196** saved outside the Church. Nevertheless, those who are invincibly ignorant of Christ and his Church are not to be judged worthy of eternal punishment because of this ignorance. For they are innocent in the eyes of the Lord of any fault in this matter. God wishes all men to be saved and to come to a knowledge of the truth; and if one does what he can, God does not withhold the grace for him to obtain justification and eternal life. But no one obtains eternal life if he dies separated from the unity of faith or from communion with the Church through his own fault. If anyone is not in this ark while the flood rages, he will perish. Therefore, We reject and detest that irreverent and irrational doctrine of religious indifferentism by which the children of this world, failing to distinguish between truth and error, say that the gate of eternal life is open to anyone, no matter what his religion. Or else they say that, with regard to religious truth, only opinion in varying degrees of probability is possible and certainty cannot be had. Likewise, We condemn the ungodliness of those who shut the door to the kingdom of heaven to their fellow men with the false pretense that to desert the religion in which one was born, or educated and brought up, even if that religion is false, is unbecoming; or that it is not at all necessary for salvation. They blame the Church for professing itself to be the only true religion and for condemning and proscribing all religions and sects separated from communion with it, as if justice could ever have anything in common with iniquity, or light associate with darkness, or Christ meet with Belial.

Chapter 8. The Indefectibility of the Church

197   We declare, moreover, that, whether one considers its existence or its constitution, the Church of Christ is an everlasting and indefectible society, and that, after it, no more complete nor more perfect economy of salvation is to be hoped for in this world. For, to the very end of the world the pilgrims of this earth are to be saved through Christ. Consequently, his Church, the only society of salvation, will last until the end of the world ever unchangeable and unchanged in its constitution. Therefore, although the Church is growing—and We wish that it may always grow in faith and charity for the upbuilding of Christ's body—although it evolves in a variety of ways according to the changing times and circumstances in which it is constantly displaying activity, nevertheless, it remains unchangeable in itself and in the constitution it received from Christ. Therefore, Christ's Church can never lose its properties and its qualities, its sacred teaching authority, priestly office, and governing body, so that through his visible body, Christ may always be the way, the truth, and the life for all men.

Chapter 9. The Infallibility of the Church

198   Furthermore, the Church would lose its immutability and dignity and it would cease being a life-giving society and a necessary means of salvation if it could wander from the safe path of truth in matters of faith and morals and if, in preaching and explaining these matters, it could deceive or be deceived. But it is the pillar and mainstay of the truth (see 1 Tim. 3:15); and therefore it is free and immune from every danger of error and untruth. With the approval of the sacred general council, We teach and declare that the quality of infallibility, which has been revealed as a perpetual prerogative of the Church of Christ, which should not be confused with the charism of inspiration, and which does not look to enriching the Church with new revelations, has been conferred for this reason that the word of God, whether it be written or handed down, may in the whole Church of Christ be proclaimed in its entirety and kept immune from any corruption of novelty and change, according to the command of the Apostle: "O Timothy, guard the trust and keep free

from profane novelties in speech and the contradictions of so-called knowledge, which some have professed and have fallen away from the faith" (*I Tim. 6:20*). And the Apostle again emphasizes this when he writes: "Hold to the form of sound teaching which thou hast heard from me, in the faith and love which are in Christ Jesus. Guard the good trust through the Holy Spirit, who dwells in us" (*II Tim. 1:13 f.*).

We teach, therefore, that the object of infallibility extends **199** as far as the deposit of faith and as far as the office of guarding it demands. And so We teach that the prerogative of infallibility with which Christ's Church is endowed embraces not only the whole revealed word of God but also everything that, although in itself not revealed, is necessary for safeguarding the revealed word, for certainly and definitively proposing and explaining it for belief, or for legitimately asserting and defending it against the errors of men and the contrary oppositions of so-called knowledge. However, this infallibility, the purpose of which is to maintain in the society of the faithful unsullied truth in its teaching of faith and morals, belongs to the teaching authority which Christ instituted in perpetuity in his Church when he said to the apostles: "Go, therefore, and make disciples of all nations, baptizing them in the name of the Father, and of the Son, and of the Holy Spirit, teaching them to observe all that I have commanded you; and behold, I am with you all days, even unto the consummation of the world" (*Matt. 28:19 f.*). And Christ promised them the Spirit of his truth who would dwell with them forever, would be in them, and would teach them all truth (*see John 14:16 f.; 16:13*).

Chapter 10. The Power of the Church

Christ's Church is not a society of equals as if all the faith- **200** ful in it had the same rights; but it is a society in which not all are equal. And this is so not only because some of the faithful are clerics and some laymen, but especially because in the Church there is a power of divine institution, by which some are authorized to sanctify, teach, and govern, and others do not have this authority. Since, however, there is a twofold power in the Church, one called the power of orders and the other called the power of jurisdiction, We teach with regard to this latter power in particular that it is jurisdiction that is absolute and perfectly complete, legislative, judicial, and coercive, and that it pertains not only to the internal and sacramental forum but also to the external and public. The subjects of this power are the pastors and teachers appointed by Christ; and they exercise it freely and independently of any secular control; and, therefore, with all authority (*see Titus 2:15*), they rule the Church of God with laws that are necessary and binding in conscience, with judicial decrees, and, finally, with salutary punishments for offenders even though they are unwilling; and this applies not only in matters of faith and morals, of worship, and of sanctification, but also in those matters which pertain to the external discipline and administration of the Church. Hence, we must believe Christ's Church is a perfect society. This true and highly favored Church of Christ is none other than the one, holy, Catholic, apostolic, and Roman Church.

THE FIRST DOGMATIC CONSTITUTION ON THE CHURCH OF CHRIST

After much discussion and argument, finally on July 18, 1870, the fourth session of the Vatican Council solemnly defined the primacy and the infallible authority of the Roman Pontiff.

The institution and foundation of the Church

201
(1821)
The eternal Shepherd and Guardian of our souls (*see I Pet. 2:25*), in order to render the saving work of redemption lasting, decided to establish his holy Church that in it, as in the house of the living God, all the faithful might be held together by the bond of one faith and one love. For this reason, before he was glorified, he prayed to the Father not for the apostles only, but for those also who would believe in him on their testimony, that all might be one as he, the Son, and the Father are one (*see John 17:20 ff.*). Therefore, just as he sent the apostles, whom he had chosen for himself out of the world, as he himself was sent by the Father (*see John 20:21*), so also he wished shepherds and teachers to be in his Church until the consummation of the world (*see Matt. 28:20*). Indeed, he placed St. Peter at the head of the other apostles that the episcopate might be one and undivided, and that the whole multitude of believers might be preserved in unity of faith and

communion by means of a well-organized priesthood. He made Peter a perpetual principle of this twofold unity and a visible foundation, that on his strength an everlasting temple might be erected and on the firmness of his faith a Church might arise whose pinnacle was to reach into heaven. But the gates of hell, with a hatred that grows greater each day, are rising up everywhere against its divinely established foundation with the intention of overthrowing the Church, if this were possible. We, therefore, judge it necessary for the protection, the safety, and the increase of the Catholic flock to pronounce with the approval of the sacred council the true doctrine concerning the establishment, the perpetuity, and the nature of the sacred apostolic primacy. In this primacy all the efficacy and all the strength of the Church are placed. We judge it necessary to pronounce what all the faithful must believe in its regard and what they must hold according to the ancient and constant belief of the universal Church. Likewise We judge it necessary to proscribe with sentence of condemnation the contrary erroneous opinions so detrimental to the Lord's flock.

Chapter 1. The Establishment of the Apostolic Primacy in St. Peter

Against heretics and schismatics

We teach and declare, therefore, according to the testimony of the Gospel that the primacy of jurisdiction over the whole Church of God was immediately and directly promised to and conferred upon the blessed Apostle Peter by Christ the Lord. For to Simon, Christ had said, "Thou shalt be called Cephas" (*John 1:42*). Then, after Simon had acknowledged Christ with the confession, "Thou art the Christ, the Son of the living God" (*Matt. 16:16*), it was to Simon alone that the solemn words were spoken by the Lord: "Blessed art thou, Simon Bar-Jona, for flesh and blood has not revealed this to thee, but my Father in heaven. And I say to thee, thou art Peter, and upon this rock I will build my Church, and the gates of hell shall not prevail against it. And I will give thee the keys of the kingdom of heaven; and whatever thou shalt bind on earth shall be bound in heaven, and whatever thou shalt loose on earth shall be loosed in heaven" (*Matt.*

202
(1822)

16:17–19). And after his Resurrection, Jesus conferred upon Simon Peter alone the jurisdiction of supreme shepherd and ruler over his whole fold with the words, "Feed my lambs. . . . Feed my sheep" (*John 21:15, 17*). In open opposition to this very clear teaching of the Holy Scriptures, as it has always been understood by the Catholic Church, are the perverse opinions of those who wrongly explain the form of government established by Christ in his Church; either by denying that Peter alone in preference to the other apostles, either singly or as a group, was endowed by Christ with the true and proper primacy of jurisdiction; or by claiming that this same primacy was not given immediately and directly to St. Peter, but to the Church and through the Church to Peter as to an agent of the Church.

Canon

203
(1823)
Therefore, if anyone says that the blessed Apostle Peter was not constituted by Christ the Lord as the Prince of all the Apostles and the visible head of the whole Church militant, or that he received immediately and directly from Jesus Christ our Lord only a primacy of honor and not a true and proper primacy of jurisdiction: let him be anathema.

Chapter 2. The Continuation of St. Peter's Primacy in the Roman Pontiffs

204
(1824)
Now, what Christ the Lord, supreme shepherd and watchful guardian of the flock, established in the person of the blessed Apostle Peter for the perpetual safety and everlasting good of the Church must, by the will of the same, endure without interruption in the Church which was founded on the rock and which will remain firm until the end of the world. Indeed, "no one doubts, in fact, it is obvious to all ages that the holy and most Blessed Peter, Prince and head of the Apostles, the pillar of faith, and the foundation of the Catholic Church, received the keys of the kingdom from our Lord Jesus Christ, the savior and the redeemer of the human race; and even to this time and forever he lives," and governs, "and exercises judgment in his successors," the bishops of the holy Roman See, which he established and consecrated

with his blood (*see 146*). Therefore, whoever succeeds Peter
in this Chair holds Peter's primacy over the whole Church
according to the plan of Christ himself. "Therefore, the dispositions made by Truth endure; and St. Peter still has the rock-
like strength that has been given to him, and he has not surrendered the helm of the Church with which he was entrusted."
For this reason, "because of its greater sovereignty," it was
always "necessary for every church, that is, the faithful who
are everywhere, to be in agreement" with the Roman Church.
The outcome of this will be that in this See, from which "the
bonds of sacred communion" are imparted to all, the members
will be joined as members under one head and thus coalesce
into one compact body.

Canon

Therefore, if anyone says that it is not according to the
institution of Christ our Lord himself, that is, by divine law,
that St. Peter has perpetual successors in the primacy over
the whole Church; or if anyone says that the Roman Pontiff
is not the successor of St. Peter in the same primacy: let
him be anathema.

205
(1825)

Chapter 3. The Power and the Nature of the Primacy of the Roman Pontiff

Declaration of the primacy

Therefore, relying on the clear testimony of the Holy Scriptures and following the express and definite decrees of Our
predecessors, the Roman Pontiffs, and of the general councils, We reaffirm the definition of the ecumenical Council of
Florence. According to this definition all the faithful of Christ
must believe "that the holy Apostolic See and the Roman
Pontiff have the primacy over the whole world, and that the
same Roman Pontiff is the successor of St. Peter, the Prince
of the Apostles, and the true vicar of Christ, the head of the
whole Church, the father and teacher of all Christians; and
that to him, in the person of St. Peter, was given by our Lord
Jesus Christ the full power of feeding, ruling, and governing
the whole Church; as is also contained in the proceedings of
the ecumenical councils and in the sacred canons" (*see 164*).

206
(1826)

The Church

Consequences that the Reformers deny

207
(1827)
And so We teach and declare that, in the disposition of God, the Roman Church holds the pre-eminence of ordinary power over all the other churches; and that this power of jurisdiction of the Roman Pontiff, which is truly episcopal, is immediate. Regarding this jurisdiction, the shepherds of whatever rite and dignity and the faithful, individually and collectively, are bound by a duty of hierarchical subjection and of sincere obedience; and this not only in matters that pertain to faith and morals, but also in matters that pertain to the discipline and government of the Church throughout the whole world. When, therefore, this bond of unity with the Roman Pontiff is guarded both in government and in the profession of the same faith, then the Church of Christ is one flock under one supreme shepherd. This is the doctrine of Catholic truth; and no one can deviate from this without losing his faith and his salvation.

The jurisdiction of the Roman Pontiff and the bishops

208
(1828)
This power of the Supreme Pontiff is far from standing in the way of the power of ordinary and immediate episcopal jurisdiction by which the bishops who, under appointment of the Holy Spirit (see Acts 20:28), succeeded in the place of the apostles, feed and rule individually, as true shepherds, the particular flock assigned to them. Rather this latter power is asserted, confirmed, and vindicated by this same supreme and universal shepherd in the words of St. Gregory the Great: "My honor is the honor of the whole Church. My honor is the solid strength of my brothers. I am truly honored when due honor is paid to each and every one."

The right to deal freely with all the faithful

209
(1829)
Furthermore, from his supreme power of governing the whole Church, the Roman Pontiff has the right of freely communicating with the shepherds and flocks of the whole Church in the exercise of his office so that they can be instructed and guided by him in the way of salvation. Hence, We condemn and disapprove the opinions of those who say that it can be licit to hinder the communication of the supreme head with the shepherds and flocks; or those who make this com-

munication subject to the secular power in such a way that they claim whatever is decreed for the government of the Church by the Apostolic See or by its authority has no binding force unless it is confirmed by the placet of the secular power.

The right of recourse to the Roman Pontiff as supreme judge

And because, by the divine right of apostolic primacy, the Roman Pontiff is at the head of the whole Church, We also teach and declare that he is the supreme judge of the faithful; and that one can have recourse to his judgment (*see 152*) in all cases pertaining to ecclesiastical jurisdiction. We declare that the judgment of the Apostolic See, whose authority is unsurpassed, is not subject to review by anyone; nor is anyone allowed to pass judgment on its decision. Therefore, those who say that it is permitted to appeal to an ecumenical council from the decisions of the Roman Pontiff (as to an authority superior to the Roman Pontiff) are far from the straight path of truth.

210
(1830)

Canon

And so, if anyone says that the Roman Pontiff has only the office of inspection or direction, but not the full and supreme power of jurisdiction over the whole Church, not only in matters that pertain to faith and morals, but also in matters that pertain to the discipline and government of the Church throughout the whole world; or if anyone says that he has only a more important part and not the complete fullness of this supreme power; or if anyone says that this power is not ordinary and immediate either over each and every church or over each and every shepherd and faithful member: let him be anathema.

211
(1831)

Chapter 4. The Infallible Teaching Authority of the Roman Pontiff

Argument based on public documents

Moreover, this Holy See has always held that the supreme power of teaching is also included in this apostolic primacy which the Roman Pontiff, as the successor of St. Peter, the Prince of the Apostles, holds over the whole Church. The per-

212
(1832)

petual practice of the Church confirms this; and the ecumenical councils have declared it, especially those in which the Eastern and Western Churches were united in faith and love.

213
(1833)
For the fathers of the Fourth Council of Constantinople, following closely in the footsteps of their predecessors, made this solemn profession: "The first condition of salvation is to keep the norm of the true faith. For it is impossible that the words of our Lord Jesus Christ who said, 'Thou art Peter, and upon this rock I will build my Church' (*Matt. 16:18*), should not be verified. And their truth has been proved by the course of history, for in the Apostolic See the Catholic religion has always been kept unsullied, and its teaching kept holy. From this faith and doctrine we by no means desire to be separated; and we hope that we may deserve to be associated with you in the one communion which the Apostolic See proclaims, in which the whole, true, and perfect security of the Christian religion resides" (*see 147 f.*).

214
(1834)
Furthermore, with the approval of the Second Council of Lyons, the Greeks professed "that the holy Roman Church has supreme and full primacy and jurisdiction over the whole Catholic Church. This it truly and humbly recognizes as received from the Lord himself in the person of St. Peter, the Prince or head of the Apostles, whose successor in the fullness of power is the Roman Pontiff. And just as the holy Roman Church is bound more than all the others to defend the truth of faith, so, if there arise any questions concerning the faith, they must be decided by its judgment" (*see 152*).

215
(1835)
Finally, the Council of Florence defined "that the Roman Pontiff is the true vicar of Christ, the head of the whole Church, the father and teacher of all Christians; and that to him, in the person of St. Peter, was given by our Lord Jesus Christ the full power of feeding, ruling, and governing the whole Church" (*see 164*).

Argument based on the agreement of the Church

216
(1836)
To satisfy this pastoral duty, Our predecessors have always expended untiring effort to propagate Christ's doctrine of

salvation among all the people of the world. And with similar care they have watched that the doctrine might be preserved genuine and pure wherever it was received. Therefore, the bishops of the whole world, sometimes singly, sometimes assembled in councils, following the long-standing custom of the churches and the form of the ancient rule, reported to this Apostolic See those dangers especially which came up in matters of faith, so that here where the faith can suffer no diminution, the harm suffered by the faith might be repaired. However, the Roman Pontiffs on their part, according as the condition of the times and the circumstances dictated, sometimes calling together ecumenical councils or sounding out the mind of the Church throughout the whole world, sometimes through regional councils, or sometimes by using other helps which divine Providence supplied, have, with the help of God, defined as to be held such matters as they had found consonant with the Holy Scripture and with the apostolic tradition. The reason for this is that the Holy Spirit was promised to the successors of St. Peter not that they might make known new doctrine by his revelation, but rather, that with his assistance they might religiously guard and faithfully explain the revelation or deposit of faith that was handed down through the apostles. Indeed, it was this apostolic doctrine that all the Fathers held, and the holy orthodox Doctors reverenced and followed. For they fully realized that this See of St. Peter always remains untainted by any error, according to the divine promise of our Lord and Savior made to the prince of his disciples, "I have prayed for thee, that thy faith may not fail; and do thou, when once thou hast turned again, strengthen thy brethren" (*Luke 22:32*).

Now this charism of truth and of never-failing faith was conferred upon St. Peter and his successors in this Chair, in order that they might perform their supreme office for the salvation of all; that by them the whole flock of Christ might be kept away from the poison of error and be nourished by the food of heavenly doctrine; that the occasion of schism might be removed, the whole Church preserved as one, and, secure on its foundation, stand firm against the gates of hell.

217
(*1837*)

The Church

The definition of infallibility

218
(1838) But since in this present age, which especially requires the salutary efficacy of the apostolic office, not a few are found who minimize its authority, We think it extremely necessary to assert solemnly the prerogative which the only-begotten Son of God deigned to join to the highest pastoral office.

219
(1839) And so, faithfully keeping to the tradition received from the beginning of the Christian faith, for the glory of God our Savior, for the exaltation of the Catholic religion, and for the salvation of Christian peoples, We, with the approval of the sacred council, teach and define that it is a divinely revealed dogma: that the Roman Pontiff, when he speaks ex cathedra, that is, when, acting in the office of shepherd and teacher of all Christians, he defines, by virtue of his supreme apostolic authority, doctrine concerning faith or morals to be held by the universal Church, possesses through the divine assistance promised to him in the person of St. Peter, the infallibility with which the divine Redeemer willed his Church to be endowed in defining doctrine concerning faith or morals; and that such definitions of the Roman Pontiff are therefore irreformable because of their nature, but not because of the agreement of the Church.

Canon

220
(1840) But if anyone presumes to contradict this Our definition (God forbid that he do so): let him be anathema.

THE ENCYCLICAL SAPIENTIAE CHRISTIANAE, 1890

In this encyclical, Pope Leo XIII (1878-1903) explains the love that a Catholic should have for the Church.

221
(1936a) Undoubtedly, Catholics have more and greater duties in life than those who have little or no knowledge of the Catholic faith. . . . A man who accepts the Christian faith, as he should do, is, by that very fact, subject to the Church since he has been born of it and has become a member of its great and holy society. Over this society, it is the proper duty of the Supreme Pontiff to rule with his supreme authority, under its invisible head, Christ Jesus. Now we are commanded by the natural law to love and to support above all others the state in which we are born and reared in this world; and this

command is so strong that a good citizen does not hesitate even to die for his country. Christians, then, have an even greater duty to bear similar love towards the Church. For the Church is the holy city of the living God, born of him and founded by him. The Church on earth is like a stranger in a foreign country; but it calls to men, instructs them and leads them to everlasting happiness in heaven. We must, therefore, dearly love the fatherland from which we receive the benefit of this mortal life. But we must love even more the Church to which we owe the everlasting life of our souls. For it is right to prefer the good of the soul to the good of the body, and our duties toward God are far more sacred than our duties towards men.

Moreover, correctly speaking, the supernatural love of the Church and the natural charity towards our country are twin loves since both proceed from the same eternal principle, God, who is the source and the cause of both of them. Consequently, it is impossible that the obligations of one of these loves should conflict with the obligations of the other. . . . At times, however, the proper ordering of these duties is upset by the disturbed times, or even more by the wickedness of men. For conditions occur when it seems that the state is demanding one thing of its citizens and religion is demanding something else of them as Christians. The only reason for this is that the officials of the state disregard the sacred power of the Church or wish to subject that power to themselves. . . . If, however, the laws of the state openly disagree with the divine law, or if they do an injustice to the Church, if they go counter to the duties of religion, or if they attack the authority of Jesus Christ in his Supreme Pontiff, then it is a duty to resist these laws, and it is a crime to obey them. And this crime is necessarily harmful even to the state, because any wrong done to religion offends against the state.

222
(1936b)

THE ENCYCLICAL *SATIS COGNITUM,* 1896

In this encyclical, Pope Leo XIII treats of the unity of the Church and of its teaching authority.

. . . There is clear and abundant proof in Sacred Scripture that there is one genuine Church of Jesus Christ. All agree on

223
(1954)

this and no Christian would dare deny it. But in determining the nature of this uniqueness, errors of different kinds have led many men from the truth. The origin of the Church and its whole constitution are matters determined by free will. Therefore, any judgment about them must be based on factual history; and we should investigate, not the ways in which it was possible that there could be only one Church, but how the founder fixed it that there should be but one.

224
(1955)
According to factual history, then, Jesus Christ did not plan and establish a Church made up of a number of organizations that were generically similar, yet separate and without those bonds of unity which make the Church one and indivisible as we profess in the Creed, "I believe in one Church". . . . When Jesus Christ spoke of this mystical structure, he spoke of one Church only which he called his own, "I will build my Church" (*Matt. 16:18*). Since no other church besides this one was founded by Jesus Christ, no other church which could be imagined can be the true Church of Christ. . . . It is the duty of the Church to carry to all men of all ages the salvation won by Jesus Christ and all the blessings that flow from it. It is therefore necessary, in accordance with the will of its founder, that it should be the only Church in the whole world for all time. . . . The Church of Christ, therefore, is the only and ever enduring Church; and all who depart from it, depart from the will and the command of Christ our Lord. They have left the path of salvation and are heading towards destruction.

Another principle of unity, the living teaching authority

225
(1956)
He who founded this one Church also wanted it to have such unity that its future members would be united by the closest ties so as to form one people, one kingdom, one body: ". . . one body and one Spirit, even as you were called in one hope of your calling . . ." (*Eph. 4:4*). . . . The necessary foundation of such great and absolute concord is intimate agreement of minds—which will naturally lead to conformity in will and uniformity in action. . . . Consequently to unify thought, to achieve and to protect agreement of opinion, another principle, besides that of Sacred Scripture, was absolutely necessary.

The Church

This was the reason why Jesus Christ instituted in the Church a living, authentic, and never-failing teaching authority. This teaching authority he endowed with his own power; he endowed it with the Spirit of Truth; he authenticated it by miracles; and it was his will and solemn command that the doctrinal precepts of this Church be accepted as his own. . . . There is no doubt that it is the duty of the Church to preserve and to spread Christian doctrine entire and unadulterated.

226
(1957)

The divine teaching was never entrusted to the interpretation or judgment of private individuals. In the beginning this doctrine was taught by Jesus and then given exclusively into the keeping of that teaching authority about which we have spoken. A like situation holds with regard to consecrating and administering the divine mysteries and with regard to the power of ruling and governing—these divine powers were not given to each individual Christian but to certain chosen ones.

227
(1958)

The Church, a society of divine origin

For this purpose, then, Jesus Christ called all men who were his contemporaries and all posterity to follow him, their leader and savior. They were to follow him not only as individuals, but all were to be closely united in deed and in spirit so that a true society would be formed from the group. This society was to be one in faith, in purpose, and in its use of the same means adapted to the end; and it was to be subject to one and the same jurisdiction. . . . The Church, therefore, is a society divine in its origin, supernatural in its end and in the means immediately leading to its end. However, it is a human association in that it is made up of men.

228
(1959)

An organic society with one head

Since the divine founder of the Church decreed that it was to be one in faith, in government, and in social organization, he chose Peter and his successors to be the source and the center of this unity. . . . The episcopal order is considered to be in proper union with Peter, as Christ commanded, if it is subordinate to Peter and obeys him. Otherwise it necessarily degenerates into a disorganized and confused group.

229
(1960)

The Church

To preserve correct union of faith and communion, it is not enough merely to have a priority of honor nor even to exercise watchfulness. Rather it is absolutely necessary to have true and supreme authority which the whole community obeys. . . . This is the source of those emphatic expressions which men in ancient times used concerning St. Peter and which emphasized so well his position of supreme dignity and power. In different places he is called: the prince of the band of disciples, the Prince of the holy Apostles, the head of that distinguished group, the spokesman of all the apostles, the head of the family, the ruler of the whole earth, the first of the apostles, the pillar of the Church. . . .

The Roman Pontiff is head of this society

**230
(1961)**
It is false, and in obvious contradiction to the divine constitution, to say that the individual bishops, but not the bishops as a whole, should be subject to the jurisdiction of the Roman Pontiffs. . . . This power over the college of bishops, of which we have been treating, is clearly mentioned in Scripture, and the Church has never failed to recognize it and to bear witness to it. . . . Therefore the decree of the Vatican Council (*see 206 ff.*) about the nature and extent of the primacy of the Roman Pontiff is not a newly introduced opinion, but states the ancient and constant faith of all centuries. Nor can it be said that the same men being subject to two powers leads to administrative confusion. In the first place the wisdom of God forbids us even to entertain such suspicions, for it was by his planning that this particular type of government was established. Secondly, it is obvious that good order and mutual relationships are interrupted only when a people has two authorities of the same rank, neither of which is subordinate to the other. But the power of the Roman Pontiff is supreme, universal, and absolutely independent, whereas the power of the bishops is fixed within definite limits and is not absolutely independent. . . .

**231
(1962)**
And the Roman Pontiffs, recognizing their duty, have willed above all to preserve in the Church everything that was divinely established. Consequently, just as they exert proper care and vigilance to protect their own power, so they have always taken care, and will continue to take care that the

106

authority of the bishops be protected. Indeed, they consider as given to themselves all honor and obedience that is given to the bishops.

THE DECREE LAMENTABILI, 1907

Under Pope St. Pius X (1903–14), the Holy Office published the decree *Lamentabili* which condemned the following errors of the modernists about the Church.

The teaching Church and the learning Church so work together in defining truths, that the only function of the teaching Church is to ratify the generally held opinions of the learning Church.

232
(2006)

In proscribing errors the Church cannot exact from the faithful any internal assent by which the judgments that it has decreed are accepted.

233
(2007)

It was far from the mind of Christ to establish a Church as a society that would last on earth for a long succession of centuries; in fact, in the mind of Christ the kingdom of heaven together with the end of the world was imminent.

234
(2052)

The organic constitution of the Church is not unchangeable; rather, the Christian society is just as subject to perpetual evolution as human society is.

235
(2053)

Dogmas, sacraments, hierarchy—both their notion and their reality—are nothing but evolutions and interpretations of Christian thought which caused the tiny seed, hidden in the Gospel, to grow through external accretions and brought it to fruition.

236
(2054)

Simon Peter never even suspected that the primacy in the Church was entrusted to him by Christ.

237
(2055)

The Roman Church became the head of all churches not because of any determination on the part of divine providence but because of political conditions.

238
(2056)

THE ENCYCLICAL MYSTICI CORPORIS, 1943

On June 29, 1943, Pius XII (1939–58) issued an important encyclical about the mystical body of Christ. It is a document extraordinarily rich in doctrinal content. In dealing authoritatively with many widely discussed problems about the nature, the characteristics, and the necessity of the Church, the pope clarifies the traditional doctrine of the mystical body and explains the relationship between the members of this body, the Head of the body, and the Soul of the body. (The translation is made from the text of the encyclical in *Acta Apostolicae Sedis*, XXXV [1943], 193–248. At the end of each of the selections the page reference will be indicated in brackets.)

The Church is the mystical body

239   If we would define and describe this true Church of Jesus Christ—which is the holy, Catholic, apostolic, Roman Church —we shall find no expression more noble, more sublime or more divine than the phrase which calls it "the mystical body of Jesus Christ." This title is derived from and is, as it were, the fair flower of the repeated teaching of Sacred Scripture and the holy Fathers [*p. 199*].

240   That the Church is a body is frequently asserted in Sacred Scripture. "Christ," says the Apostle, "is the head of his body, the Church" (*Col. 1:18*). If the Church is a body, it must be an unbroken unity according to those words of Paul: "We, the many, are one body in Christ" (*Rom. 12:5*). But it is not enough that the body of the Church be an unbroken unity; it must also be something definite and perceptible to the senses, as Our predecessor of happy memory, Leo XIII, in his Encyclical *Satis cognitum* (*see* 223) asserts: "The Church is visible because she is a body." It is an error in a matter of divine truth to imagine the Church is invisible, intangible, a something merely "pneumatological," as they say, by which many Christian communities, though they differ from each other in their profession of faith, are united by a bond that is invisible to the senses [*p. 199*].

241   One must not think, however, that this ordered or "organic" structure of the body of the Church contains only hierarchical elements and with them is complete; or, as an opposite opinion holds, that it is composed only of those who enjoy charismatic gifts—though members gifted with miraculous powers will never be lacking in the Church. It must be maintained uncompromisingly that those who hold sacred power in this body are its first and chief members. It is through them, in accordance with the plan of the divine Redeemer himself, that Christ's apostolate as teacher, king, priest, endures forever [p. 200].

The members of the mystical body

Only those are really to be included as members of the Church who have been baptized and profess the true faith and who have not had the misfortune of withdrawing from the body or for grave faults been cut off by legitimate authority. "For in one Spirit," says the Apostle, "we were all baptized into one body, whether Jews or Gentiles, whether slaves or free (*I Cor. 12:13*). As, therefore, in the true Christian community there is only one body, one Spirit, one Lord and one baptism, so there can be only one faith (*see Eph. 4:5*). And so if a man refuses to listen to the Church, he should be considered, so the Lord commands, as a heathen and a publican (*see Matt. 18:17*). It follows that those who are divided in faith or government cannot be living in one body such as this, and cannot be living the life of its one divine Spirit [p. 202].

242 (2286)

One must not imagine that the body of the Church, just because it bears the name of Christ, is made up during the days of its earthly pilgrimage only of members conspicuous for their holiness, or consists only of the group of those whom God has predestined to eternal happiness. It is the Savior's infinite mercy that allows place in his mystical body here for those whom he did not exclude from the banquet of old (*see Matt. 9:11; Mark 2:16; Luke 15:2*). For not every sin, even though it be serious, is such as to sever a man automatically from the body of the Church, as does schism or heresy or apostasy. Men may lose charity and divine grace through sin and so become incapable of supernatural merit, and yet not be deprived of all life, since they hold on to faith and Christian hope, and illumined from above they are spurred on by the strong promptings of the Holy Spirit to salutary fear and by God are moved to prayer and penance for their sins [p. 203].

243

The beginning of the mystical body

. . . The divine Redeemer began the building of the mystical temple of the Church when by his preaching he announced

244

his precepts; he completed it when he hung glorified on the cross; and he manifested and proclaimed it when he sent the Holy Spirit, the Paraclete, in visible form on his disciples [*p. 204*].

The head of the mystical body

245 . . . It is by the power of the cross that our Savior, although he had been constituted the head of the whole human family in the womb of the Blessed Virgin, exercises fully the office of head in his Church. . . . It was on the tree of the cross, finally, that he entered into possession of his Church, that is, all the members of his mystical body; for they would not have been united to this mystical body through the waters of baptism except by the salutary virtue of the cross, by which they had been already brought under the complete sway of Christ [*p. 206*].

246 That this mystical body which is the Church should be called Christ's, is proved, in the second place, from the fact that he must be universally acknowledged as its actual head. As St. Paul says, "He is the head of his body, the Church" (*Col. 1:18*). He is the head from whom the whole body, perfectly organized, "derives its increase to the building up of itself" (*Eph. 4:16*).

247 . . . First of all, it is clear that the Son of God and of the Blessed Virgin is to be called the head of the Church for his singular pre-eminence. For the head holds the highest position. But who is in a higher position than the divine Christ, who as the Word of the eternal Father must be acknowledged as the "first-born of every creature" (*Col. 1:15*) [*p. 208*]?

248 Because Christ is so exalted, he alone by every right rules and governs the Church; and herein is yet another reason why he must be likened to a head. As the head is the "royal citadel" of the body—to use the words of Ambrose—and all the members, over which it is placed for their good, are naturally guided by it as being endowed with superior powers, so the divine Redeemer guides the course of the entire Christian kingdom. And as a government of human society means merely this, to lead men to the end proposed by means

that are expedient, suitable, and helpful, it is easy to see how our Savior, model and ideal of good shepherds (*see John 10:1–18*), performs all these functions in a most striking way.

For while still on earth, he instructed us by precept, counsel, and warning, in words that shall never pass away, and will be spirit and life to all men of all times (*see John 6:63*). Moreover, he conferred a triple power on his apostles and their successors, to teach, to govern, to lead men to holiness. This triple power, defined by special ordinances, by rights and obligations, he made the fundamental law of the whole Church [*p. 209*].   **249**

. . . Our divine Redeemer also governs his mystical body in a visible and ordinary way through his vicar on earth. You know, Venerable Brothers, that after he himself had ruled the "little flock" in a visible manner during his mortal pilgrimage, when about to leave this world and return to the Father, Christ our Lord entrusted to the Prince of the Apostles the visible government of the entire community He had founded. He was all wise; and it was absolutely necessary for him to provide with a visible head the body of the Church he had founded as a human society. Nor against this may one argue that the primacy of jurisdiction established in the Church gives such a mystical body two heads. For Peter in virtue of his primacy is only Christ's vicar; so that there is only one chief head of this body, namely Christ. He never ceases personally to guide the Church by an unseen hand, though at the same time he rules it externally, visibly through him who is his representative on earth. After his glorious Ascension into heaven, this Church rests not on him alone, but on Peter, too, its visible foundation stone. That Christ and his vicar constitute one only head is the solemn teaching of Our predecessor of immortal memory, Boniface VIII, in the Apostolic Letter *Unam sanctam* (*see 153*); and his successors have never ceased to repeat the same [*p. 210*].   **250**

Therefore, those who believe that they can accept Christ as the head of the Church, without giving their loyal adherence to his vicar on earth, walk the path of dangerous error. They have taken away the visible head, broken the visible bonds   **251** of unity, and they so disfigure the true concept of the mystical body of the Redeemer that it cannot be recognized or found by those who are seeking the haven of eternal salvation [*p. 211*].

252
(2287)
What We have thus far said of the universal Church must be understood also of the individual Christian communities, whether Eastern or Latin, which go to make up the one Catholic Church. For they, too, are ruled by Christ Jesus through the authoritative voice of their own respective bishops. Bishops, then, must be considered as the nobler members of the universal Church, for they are linked in an altogether special way to the divine Head of the whole body and so are rightly called "most excellent among the members of the Lord"; what is more, as far as each one's own diocese is concerned, they each and all as true shepherds feed the flocks entrusted to them and rule them in the name of Christ (*see 208*). Yet in exercising this office they are not altogether independent, but are duly subordinate to the authority of the Roman Pontiff; and although their jurisdiction is inherent in their office, yet they receive it directly from the same supreme pontiff. Hence, they should be revered by the faithful as divinely appointed successors of the apostles. To bishops even more than to the most powerful rulers of this world, can be applied the warning: "Touch not my anointed ones" (*I Par. 16:22; Ps. 104:15*), for bishops have been anointed with the chrism of the Holy Spirit [*p. 211*].

253
To the reasons thus far adduced to show that Christ the Lord should be called the head of the society which is his body, three others may be added here. They are closely related to one another.

254
We begin with the similarity which we see existing between head and body, in that they have the same nature. Our human nature is inferior to angelic nature; and yet, we must note, through God's goodness it has risen above angelic nature: "For Christ," as Aquinas says, "is head of the angels; for even in his humanity he is superior to angels. . . . Secondly, as man he illumines the angels and exerts his influence upon them. But it is not because of a similarity of nature that Christ

is head of the angels, because he has not assumed angelic nature—to quote the Apostle—but the seed of Abraham." And Christ not only took our nature, he became one of our flesh and blood with a frail body that could suffer and die. But if the Word "emptied himself, taking the nature of a slave" (*Phil. 2:7*), it was that he might make his brothers in the flesh partakers of the divine nature—in this earthly exile through sanctifying grace, in heaven through the joys of eternal bliss. The reason why the only-begotten Son of the eternal Father wished to be the Son of man, was that we might be made conformed to the image of the Son of God and be remade according to the image of him who created us (*see Rom. 8:29; Col. 3:10*) [*p. 213*].

Christ must also be acknowledged head of the Church for **255** this reason that, since supernatural gifts have found their supreme fullness and perfection in him, it is from this fullness that his mystical body receives. It is an observation made by a number of Fathers, that as the head of the human body is the seat of all the senses, whereas the other parts of our organism have only the sense of touch, so all the powers that are found in Christian society, all the gifts, all the extraordinary graces, all these are perfectly expressed in Christ, the head. "It has pleased God the Father that in him all his fullness should dwell" (*Col. 1:19*). He is endowed with those supernatural virtues that accompany the hypostatic union. For the Holy Spirit dwells in him with the greatest possible fullness of grace. To him has been given power over all flesh (*see John 17:2*); and he has an abundance of "all the treasures of wisdom and knowledge" (*Col. 2:3*). He also possesses the knowledge which is called vision, and in such fullness that it surpasses the scope and clarity of the similar celestial knowledge that all the saints in heaven have. Finally, he is so full of grace and of truth, that of his inexhaustible fullness we have all received (*see John 1:14-16*).

These words of the disciple whom Jesus especially loved **256** lead us to the last reason why Christ our Lord should be declared in a very particular way head of his mystical body. In us the nerves reach from the head to all parts of the body and give them the power to feel and move; in like manner our Savior communicates power to his Church so that the things of God are understood more clearly and are more eagerly desired by the faithful. From him comes into the body of the Church whatever supernatural light illumines the minds of the faithful; from him comes every grace to make them holy, as he himself is holy [*p. 215*].

The soul of the mystical body

257
(2288)
If we examine closely this divine principle of life and power given by Christ, insofar as it constitutes the very source of every gift and created grace, we easily see that it is nothing else than the Holy Spirit, the Paraclete who proceeds from the Father and the Son, and who is called in a special way the "Spirit of Christ" or the "Spirit of the Son" (*see Rom. 8:9; II Cor. 3:17; Gal. 4:6*). For it was by His Breath of grace and truth that the Son of God adorned his own soul in the immaculate womb of the Blessed Virgin; this Spirit delights to dwell in the dear soul of our Redeemer as in his most cherished shrine; this Spirit Christ merited for us on the cross by shedding his own blood; this Spirit he bestowed on the Church for the remission of sins, when he breathed on the apostles (*see John 20:22*); and while Christ alone received this Spirit without measure (*see John 3:34*), to the members of the mystical body He is imparted only according to the measure of the giving of Christ, from Christ's own fullness (*see Eph. 1:8; 4:7*). But after Christ's glorification on the cross, his Spirit is communicated to the Church in an abundant outpouring, so that the Church and each of its members may become daily more and more like to our Savior. It is the Spirit of Christ that has made us adopted sons of God (*see Gal. 4:6, 7; Rom. 8:14-17*) in order that one day we all with faces unveiled, reflecting as in a mirror the glory of the Lord, may be transformed into his very image from glory to glory (*see II Cor. 3:18*) [*p. 218 f.*].

258
(2288)
To this Spirit of Christ, too, as to an invisible principle, is to be ascribed the fact that all the parts of the body are joined one with the other and with their exalted head; for the whole Spirit of Christ is in the head, the whole Spirit is in the body, and the whole Spirit is in each of the members.

He is present in the members and assists them in proportion to their various tasks and offices and to the degree of spiritual health which they enjoy. It is he who through his heavenly grace is the principle of every truly supernatural act in all parts of the body. It is he who, while he is personally present and divinely active in all the members, also acts in the inferior members through the ministry of the higher members. Finally, while with his grace he provides for the constant growth of the Church, he yet refuses to dwell with sanctifying grace in members that are wholly severed from the body. This presence and activity of the Spirit of Jesus Christ are tersely and vigorously described by Our predecessor of immortal memory Leo XIII in his Encyclical Letter *Divinum illud* in these words: "Let it suffice to say that, as Christ is the head of the Church, so is the Holy Spirit its soul" [*p. 219*].

If that vital principle by which the whole community of 259 Christians is sustained by its Founder be considered now not in itself, but in the created effects which flow from it, it consists in those heavenly gifts which our Redeemer together with his Spirit bestows on the Church and which he and his Spirit, from whom come supernatural light and holiness, make operative in the Church. The Church, then, no less than each of her holy members can make this thought of the Apostle her own: "It is now no longer I that live, but Christ lives in me" (*Gal. 2:20*) [*p. 220*].

The reason for the name mystical

. . . We desire to make clear why the body of Christ, which 260 is the Church, should be called mystical. This word, used by many early writers, has the sanction of numerous pontifical documents. There are several reasons why it should be used; for by it we may distinguish the body of the Church, which is a society whose head and ruler is Christ, from his physical body, which, born of the Virgin Mother of God, now sits at the right hand of the Father and rests hidden under the Eucharistic veil; as well as from any ordinary body in the natural order, whether physical or moral. This latter distinction is of greater importance in view of modern errors [*p. 221*].

The mystical body compared to a moral body

261   But if we compare the mystical body to what is called a moral body . . . we must notice that the difference between them is not slight, but rather is very considerable and very important. In the moral body, the principle of union is nothing more than the common end, and the common cooperation of all under a social authority for the attainment of that end; whereas in the mystical body, of which We are speaking, this cooperation is supplemented by a distinct internal principle, which exists effectively in the whole organism and in each of its parts, and whose excellence is such, that of itself it is vastly superior to whatever bonds of union may be found in a physical or moral body. This is something, as We said above, not of the natural but of the supernatural order. Essentially it is something infinite, uncreated: the Spirit of God, who, as the Angelic Doctor says, "numerically one and the same, fills and unifies the whole Church" [*p. 222*].

The Church is a perfect society

262   Hence, the proper meaning of this word reminds us that the Church, which should be considered a perfect society in its own right, is not made up of merely moral and juridical elements and principles. It is far superior to all other human societies; it surpasses them as grace surpasses nature, as things immortal are above all those that perish. Such human societies, and especially civil societies, are certainly not to be despised or belittled. But the Church in its entirety is not found within this natural order, any more than the whole of man is encompassed within the organism of our mortal body. The juridical principles, on which also the Church rests and is established, derive from the divine constitution given to it by Christ, and contribute to the attainment of its supernatural end; but what lifts the society of Christians far, far above the whole natural order is the Spirit of the Redeemer, who until the end of time penetrates every part of the Church's being and is active within it. He is the source of every grace and every gift and every miraculous power. Just as our composite mortal body, for all its being a marvelous work of the Creator, falls far short of the eminent dignity of our soul, so the social structure of the Christian community, though eloquent of its

divine architect's wisdom, remains still something inferior, when compared to the spiritual gifts which give it beauty and life, and to their divine source [*p. 222*].

The visibility of the mystical body

From what We have thus far written and explained, Venerable Brothers, it is clear, We think, how grievously they err who arbitrarily picture the Church as something hidden and invisible, as do they also who look upon it as a mere human institution with a certain disciplinary code and external ritual, but lacking power to communicate supernatural life. No, the mystical body of Christ, like Christ the head and exemplar of the Church, "is not entire if in him only the visible human nature is looked at . . . or only the invisible divine nature . . . but he is one through the union of both natures and is in both." The case is the same with his mystical body: The Word of God took unto himself a human nature liable to sufferings, so that he might consecrate in his blood the visible society founded by him and "lead man back to things invisible under a visible rule" [*p. 223*].

263

For this reason We deplore and condemn the pernicious error of those who conjure up from their fancies an imaginary Church, a kind of society that finds its origin and growth in charity, to which they somewhat contemptuously oppose another which they call juridical. To draw such a distinction is utterly futile. For they do not understand that it was for the very same reason, namely, to perpetuate the salutary work of the redemption on this earth, that the divine Redeemer wanted the community of which he was the founder to be established as a society perfect in its own order and possessing all juridical and social elements (*see 202*). And for the attainment of the same goal he wanted that society to be enriched with the heavenly gifts of the consoling Spirit. The eternal Father, indeed, wished it to be the "kingdom of his beloved son" (*Col. 1:13*); but it was to be a real kingdom, in which all believers would make the obeisance of their intellect and will, and humbly and obediently model themselves on him, who for our sake "became obedient to death" (*Phil. 2:8*). There can, then, be no real opposition or conflict between the invisible

264

mission of the Holy Spirit and the juridical commission of ruler and teacher received from Christ. Like body and soul in us, they complement and perfect each other, and have their source in our one Redeemer, who not only said, as he breathed on the apostles: "Receive the Holy Spirit" (*John 20:22*), but also clearly commanded: "As the Father has sent me, I also send you" (*John 20:21*), and again: "He that hears you, hears me" (*Luke 10:16*) [*p. 224*].

265   Now since this social body of Christ has been designed by its Founder to be visible, this cooperation of all its members must also be externally manifest through their profession of the same faith, and their sharing the same sacred rites, through participation in the same Sacrifice and practical observance of the same laws. In addition, it is strictly needful that everyone must be able to see the supreme head, who gives effective direction to what all are doing in a mutually helpful way towards attaining the desired end, that is the vicar on earth of Jesus Christ. As the divine Redeemer sent a Paraclete, the Spirit of Truth, who in his name should govern the Church in an invisible way; similarly he commissioned Peter and his successors to be his personal representatives on earth and to assume the visible government of the Christian community [*p. 227*].

LETTER OF THE HOLY OFFICE TO
ARCHBISHOP CUSHING OF BOSTON, 1949

An unfortunate controversy over the dictum: "Outside the Church there is no salvation" was the occasion of the following letter. The letter, dated August 8, 1949, is important for the explanation it gives of the necessity of the Catholic Church. The Church is necessary for salvation because such is the command of Christ and because the Church is a necessary means for salvation. But since the Church is such a means only by divine institution, not by intrinsic necessity, membership itself in the Church is not required of all men under all circumstances. (The following translation is made from the Latin published in the *American Ecclesiastical Review*, CXXVII [October, 1952], 307–11.)

We are bound to believe by divine and Catholic faith what **266** is contained in the written word of God or in tradition, and is proposed by the Church as a divinely revealed object of belief either in a solemn decree, or in her ordinary, universal teaching (*see 66*).

The infallible dictum which teaches us that outside the **267** Church there is no salvation, is among the truths that the Church has always taught and will always teach.

But this dogma is to be understood as the Church itself **268** understands it. For our Savior did not leave it to private judgment to explain what is contained in the deposit of faith, but to the doctrinal authority of the Church.

The Church teaches, first of all, that there is question here **269** of a very strict command of Jesus Christ. In unmistakable words he gave his apostles the command to teach all nations to keep whatever he had commanded (*see Matt. 28:19 f.*).

Not least among Christ's commands is the one which orders **270** us to be incorporated by baptism into the mystical body of Christ, which is the Church, and to be united to Christ and to his vicar, through whom he himself governs the Church on earth in a visible way.

Therefore, no one who knows that the Church has been di- **271** vinely established by Christ and, nevertheless, refuses to be a subject of the Church or refuses to obey the Roman Pontiff, the vicar of Christ on earth, will be saved.

The Savior did not make it necessary merely as by precept **272** for all nations to enter the Church. He also established the Church as a means of salvation without which no one can enter the kingdom of heavenly glory.

Of those helps to salvation that are ordered to the last end **273** only by divine decree, not by intrinsic necessity, God, in his infinite mercy, willed that such effects of those helps as are necessary to salvation can, in certain circumstances, be obtained when the helps are used only in *desire* or *longing*. We see this clearly stated in the Council of Trent about the sacrament of regeneration and about the sacrament of penance (*see 560, 571*).

274   The same, in due proportion, should be said of the Church insofar as it is a general help to salvation. To gain eternal salvation it is not always required that a person be incorporated *in fact* as a member of the Church, but it is required that he belong to it at least in *desire* and *longing*.

275   It is not always necessary that this desire be explicit as it is with catechumens. When a man is invincibly ignorant, God also accepts an *implicit desire,* so called because it is contained in the good disposition of soul by which a man wants his will to be conformed to God's will.

276   This is clearly taught by the Sovereign Pontiff Pope Pius XII in his dogmatic letter on the mystical body of Christ, dated June 29, 1943 (*see introd. to 239*). In this letter the Sovereign Pontiff clearly distinguishes between those who are *actually* incorporated into the Church as members and those who belong to the Church only in *desire*.

277   In treating of the members who make up the mystical body here on earth, the Sovereign Pontiff says: "Only those are *really* to be included as members of the Church who have been baptized and profess the true faith, and who have not had the misfortune of withdrawing from the body or for grave faults been cut off by legitimate authority" (*see 242*).

278   Towards the end of the same encyclical, when with all his heart he invites to union those who do not pertain to the body of the Catholic Church, the pope mentions those "who unsuspectingly belong to the mystical body of the Redeemer by some kind of *desire* or *longing*." He by no means excludes these men from eternal salvation; but, on the other hand, he does point out that they are in a condition "in which they cannot be secure about their salvation . . . since they lack many great gifts and helps from God, gifts they can enjoy only in the Catholic Church."

279   With these prudent words the pope censures those who exclude from eternal salvation all men who belong to the

Church *only with implicit desire;* and he also censures those who falsely maintain that men can be saved equally as well in any religion (*see 173 ff.; 178*).

It must not be imagined that any desire whatsoever of entering the Church is sufficient for a man to be saved. It is necessary that the desire by which a man is related to the Church be informed with perfect charity. And an *implicit desire* cannot have its effect unless a man has supernatural faith: "For he who comes to God must believe that God exists and is a rewarder to those who seek him" (*Heb. 11:6*). The Council of Trent says: "Faith is the beginning of man's salvation, the foundation and source of all justification, without which it is impossible to please God and to be counted as his sons" (*see 565*). **280**

THE ENCYCLICAL *HUMANI GENERIS*, 1950

In censuring a multiplicity of modern errors (*see introd. to 141*), Pope Pius XII reminds the faithful that they are to hold firmly to the doctrine on the Church which he had taught in the encyclical *Mystici corporis.*

That the mystical body of Christ and the Catholic Church in communion with Rome are one and the same thing, is a doctrine based on revealed truth, and as such was set forth by Us in an encyclical a few years back (*see 239 ff.*); some imagine, nevertheless, that they are not bound to hold it. That we must needs belong to the true Church, if we are to attain everlasting salvation, is a statement which some reduce to an empty formula. Others, again, belittle the reasoning process by which we accept the credentials of the Christian faith. **281**
(2319)

The Triune God

The greatest of the revealed mysteries of Christianity is the mystery of the most Holy Trinity. It exceeds the grasp of human reason; for reason, by its own power, can only know God in the unity of his nature as creator.

To maintain the purity of this lofty doctrine, the Church has in every age frequently been required to insist on the unicity of the divine nature, on the perfect distinction and perfect equality of the Divine Persons, and on the order of origins that exists between them. The Church has not adopted any one set of the various speculations of theologians about the Trinity; but it has not hesitated to censure theological opinions that endangered the purity of the revealed doctrine. For exactitude in Trinitarian terminology the Church has been extremely solicitous, knowing that in a matter of such great difficulty and importance faulty expressions are only a step removed from errors in the faith.

Early heresies about the Trinity began by denying that there are really three distinct Divine Persons in God. These heresies are known as modalism, monarchianism, Sabellianism, and Patripassianism. Though the doctrines of each group varied, they all held that God was one in person as well as in nature and that the different persons were merely different modes or manifestations of the same divine being. Tritheism went to just the opposite extreme; it taught that the three persons were three distinct gods.

Arianism was opposed to Sabellianism. It taught that Christ was really a distinct person from the Father, but that he was a creature. The famous Arian syllogism argues thus: The Second

Person is the Son, therefore posterior to the Father; he is not, therefore, eternal. Consequently, he is a creature. The general tenets of this doctrine were adopted by the Anomoeans and the Eunomians. The Semi-Arians taught that the Son was not a creature, but still that he was not God; he was like God. Macedonianism, finally, taught that the Holy Spirit was not God but a creature like the angels.

LETTER TO DIONYSIUS OF ALEXANDRIA, *cir.* 260

Pope St. Dionysius (259–68) wrote this public doctrinal letter to Bishop Dionysius of Alexandria; he condemns the errors of Sabellius and the tritheist Marcion.

282
(48)
(1) Next, I would do right to speak against those who by their dividing and partitioning the one God into three separate powers and divinities destroy the unity of God, the most sacred teaching of the Church of God. For I have learned that some of those among you who preach and teach the divine word counsel this opinion. These men hold an opinion exactly opposite, I might say, to Sabellius's opinion. For Sabellius's blasphemy is that the Son is the Father, and the Father the Son. These men somehow preach three gods since they divide the sacred unity into three different hypostases completely separate from one another. It is necessary that the divine Word be one with the God of all and that the Holy Spirit remain in God and dwell in him. There is every reason, then, that the divine Trinity be brought together and united in unity, as in one supreme point, that is, the almighty God of all things. The teaching of the foolish Marcion who divides and separates the one God into three principles is a teaching from the devil, not the teaching of those who truly follow Christ and who are content with the teachings of the Savior. These latter clearly understand that the Sacred Scripture teaches the Trinity, but nowhere does the Old or New Testament mention three gods.

283
(51)
(3) It is not necessary, therefore, to divide the wonderful and divine unity into three divinities, and the excellence and vast greatness of God should not be obscured by the word *making*. It is right to believe in God the Father almighty, and

in Christ Jesus his Son, and in the Holy Spirit, and to believe that the Word is one with the God of all. For he says, "I and the Father are one" (*John 10:30*); and, "I am in the Father and the Father in me" (*John 14:10*). This is the way to keep intact the sacred preaching of the divine Trinity and unity.

THE COUNCIL OF ROME, 382

The Tome of Damasus

After the condemnation of Arianism by the definition of the Council of Nicaea (325), controversy soon broke out over the appropriateness of the Nicene term ὁμοούσιος to express the truth that the Son is *consubstantial* with the Father. Western Catholics more readily accepted the term, perhaps, because of Tertullian's expression, *consubstantialis*. Eastern writers, as, for instance, St. Cyril of Alexandria, often used φύσις, οὐσία, and ὑπόστασις indiscriminately. Hence, when the West imposed the term ὁμοούσιος it was accused of Sabellianism.

Around the year 382 a local council met at Rome at which Pope St. Damasus (366–84) presented a collection of the principal Christological and Trinitarian errors of the time—the famous Tome of Damasus. It enumerates and condemns these errors, especially those of the Macedonians. Pope St. Celestine I (422–32) apparently considered these canons law; they may be considered definitions of faith.

(1) We pronounce anathema against those who do not proclaim with complete freedom that He [*the Holy Spirit*] is of one power and substance with the Father and the Son. | 284 (59)

(2) We also anathematize those who follow the error of Sabellius, saying that the Father is the same person as the Son. | 285 (60)

(3) We pronounce anathema against Arius and Eunomius, who with the same ungodliness, though in different words, assert that the Son and the Holy Spirit are creatures. | 286 (61)

(10) If anyone denies that the Father is eternal, that the Son is eternal, and that the Holy Spirit is eternal: he is a heretic. | 287 (68)

(11) If anyone denies that the Son was born of the Father, that is, is of his divine substance: he is a heretic. | 288 (69)

289
(70)
(12) If anyone denies that the Son of God is true God, just as the Father is true God, having all power, knowing all things, and equal to the Father: he is a heretic.

290
(71)
(13) If anyone says that He [*the Son*] made flesh was not in heaven with the Father while he was on earth: he is a heretic.

291
(74)
(16) If anyone denies that the Holy Spirit is truly and properly from the Father, and, like the Son, is of the divine substance and is true God: he is a heretic.

292
(75)
(17) If anyone denies that the Holy Spirit has all power and knows all things, and is everywhere, just as the Father and the Son: he is a heretic.

293
(76)
(18) If anyone says that the Holy Spirit is a creature, or was created by the Son: he is a heretic.

294
(77)
(19) If anyone denies that the Father made all things through the Son and through his Holy Spirit, that is, all things visible and invisible: he is a heretic.

295
(78)
(20) If anyone denies that the Father, Son, and Holy Spirit have one divinity, authority, majesty, power, one glory, dominion, one kingdom, and one will and truth: he is a heretic.

296
(79)
(21) If anyone denies that the three persons, the Father, the Son, and the Holy Spirit, are true persons, equal, eternal, containing all things visible and invisible, that they are omnipotent, judge all things, give life to all things, make all things, and conserve all things: he is a heretic.

297
(80)
(22) If anyone denies that the Holy Spirit must be adored by every creature, just as the Son and the Father: he is a heretic.

298
(82)
(24) But if anyone, while saying that the Father is God and the Son is God and the Holy Spirit is God, makes a division [*in the Trinity*] and says that they [*the Divine Persons*] are gods, and does not say that they are one God, precisely on account of the one divinity and power which we believe and know is possessed by the Father and the Son and the Holy

Spirit; and if he slights the Son or the Holy Spirit in such a way so as to think that only the Father is called God and in this way believes in one God: he is a heretic on all counts and is even a Jew. For the name of gods was given by God to all the angels and the saints; but, for the Father, Son, and Holy Spirit, because of the one same divinity, the name of God and not of gods is indicated and manifested to us in order that we may believe that we are baptized in the Father, Son, and Holy Spirit only, and not in names of the archangels or angels, as heretics or Jews or even foolish pagans believe. [*The first clause of this paragraph is very obscure in the Latin. The translation given has been guided by the sense of the Greek version given by Theodoret* (MG, *LXXXII, 1225A*).]

Therefore this is the salvation of Christians: that believing in the Trinity, that is in the Father, Son, and Holy Spirit, and being baptized in the Trinity, we may unhesitatingly believe that in the Trinity there is only one true divinity and power, majesty and substance.

THE ELEVENTH COUNCIL OF TOLEDO, 675

The following creed was read at the Eleventh Council of Toledo on November 7, 675. It had been prepared by Quiricius, the archbishop of Toledo, president of the provincial council. The seventeen bishops in attendance approved the creed and it was adopted on November 9. This council has not been expressly approved by the pope; consequently, this creed cannot be considered a document of faith in itself, though most of the doctrine summarized in it is part of Catholic faith. The creed is based on creeds of earlier councils, and on the writings of St. Hilary and St. Augustine.

We confess and we believe that the holy and indescribable **299** Trinity, Father, Son, and Holy Spirit is one only God in his **(275)** nature, a single substance, a single nature, a single majesty and power.

We particularly profess that the Father is not born, not created, but is unbegotten. For he, from whom the Son was born and the Holy Spirit proceeded, has origin from no one. He is, therefore, the source and origin of the whole divinity; he is the Father of his own essence and he begot the Son of his indescribable substance in an indescribable way [*variant:*

the Father, indescribable substance indeed, begot the Son of his own substance in an indescribable way]; nevertheless he did not beget a being different from what he himself is. God begot God; light begot light; from him, therefore, is all fatherhood in heaven and on earth (*see Eph. 3:15*).

300
(276)

We also confess that the Son was born of the substance of the Father, before all ages, without beginning, and that he was not created; for the Father did not exist without the Son nor did the Son ever exist without the Father at any period of time. Yet the Father is not from the Son as the Son is from the Father because it is not the Father who was generated by the Son, but rather the Son by the Father. The Son, therefore, is God from the Father; and the Father is God but not from the Son—truly Father of the Son but not God from the Son. But the Son is Son of the Father and God from the Father. However the Son is completely equal to God the Father because his birth has not begun in time and has not ceased. We also believe him to be of one substance with the Father, and he is therefore called ὁμοούσιος with the Father, that is, of the same substance with the Father. For the Greek word ὁμός means *same*, and οὐσία means *substance*, and together they signify *having the same substance*. We must believe that the Son is begotten or born from the womb of the Father, that is, from his very substance and not from nothing or from some other substance. Therefore the Father is eternal and the Son is eternal. Consequently, if he was always Father, he always had a Son of whom he was the Father; and for this reason we confess that the Son was born of the Father without beginning. Nor because of the fact that the Son of God was born of the Father do we call him a small part of a divided nature; rather, we maintain that the perfect Father begot a perfect Son but without any lessening and without any division, because it is characteristic of only the divinity to have a Son not unequal to itself. He is the Son of God by nature not by adoption; and we must believe that God the Father begot him not through his will and not of necessity, for there is no necessity in God nor does the will precede wisdom.

301
(277)

We also believe that the Holy Spirit, the Third Person in the Trinity is God, and that he is one and equal with God the Father and God the Son, of one substance as well as of one nature. However, he is not begotten nor created, but he proceeds from both and is the Spirit of both. We believe that the Holy Spirit is neither unbegotten nor begotten: lest, if we say *unbegotten* we should be asserting two Fathers; and if we said *begotten* we should appear to be preaching two Sons. He is called the Spirit, not only of the Father nor only of the Son but equally of the Father and of the Son. He proceeds not from the Father into the Son nor from the Son to sanctify creatures; but he is shown to have proceeded from both equally, because he is known as the love or the sanctity of both. The Holy Spirit is believed to be sent by the two together as the Son is sent by the Father; but he is not considered inferior to the Father and the Son in the way in which the Son, because of the human nature which he has assumed, testifies that he is inferior to the Father and the Holy Spirit.

This is the way to speak about the Trinity. It must not be called and believed to be triple, but a Trinity. And it cannot correctly be said that there is a Trinity in one God but that the one God is a Trinity. In the relative names of the persons, the Father is referred to the Son, the Son to the Father, and the Holy Spirit is referred to both; however, though the persons are called three in their relations, nevertheless the nature or substance is believed to be one. Nor do we, when we proclaim three persons, also proclaim three substances, but rather one substance and three persons. For the Father is Father not with respect to himself, but with respect to the Son; and the Son is Son not with respect to himself, but in relation to the Father. The Holy Spirit is Spirit not with respect to himself, but in relation to the Father and the Son, because he is called the Spirit of the Father and of the Son. Likewise when we say *God*, there is no relation to another indicated as Father to Son, or Son to Father, or Holy Spirit to Father and Son, but he is called God absolutely. **302** **(278)**

For even if we are asked about the persons individually, we must answer that each is God. Therefore, we say that the Father is God, the Son God, and the Holy Spirit God, and each individually; nevertheless, there are not three gods but one God. Similarly, we say that the Father is omnipotent, the **303** **(279)**

Son omnipotent, and the Holy Spirit omnipotent, and each individually; nevertheless, there are not three omnipotent beings, but one omnipotent being, just as we profess one light and one principle. Therefore, we confess and believe that each person individually is God in the full sense and that all three persons are one God. There belongs to them one, undivided, and equal deity, majesty, and power which is not less in the individual person nor greater in the three persons. For God does not possess less because each person is called God individually, nor does God possess more because all three persons are called one God. Therefore, the Holy Trinity which is the one, true God is not disjoined from number nor is it contained by number.

304
(280)
For number is manifest in the relationship of the persons, but what is numbered in the substance of the divinity does not appear. The persons imply number only inasmuch as they are related one to the other; inasmuch as they are taken by themselves they are without number. For so much does one proper name belong to this Holy Trinity that it cannot be plural in the three persons. Therefore, we believe what is written in the Holy Scriptures: "Great is our Lord, and great is his power: and of his wisdom there is no number" (*Ps. 146:5*). But because we have said that these three persons are one God, we cannot say that the Father is the same as the Son or that he is the Son who is the Father, or that he who is the Holy Spirit is the same as the Father or the Son. For the Son is not the same person as the Father, nor is the Father the same person as the Son, nor is either the Father or the Son the same person as the Holy Spirit; yet the Father is the same being as the Son, the Son is the same being as the Father, and the Father and the Son the same being as the Holy Spirit; that is, one God in nature. For when we say that the Father is not the same as the Son we are referring to the distinction of persons. When, however, we say that the Father is the same as the Son, the Son is the same as the Father, and the Holy Spirit is the same as the Father and the Son, this clearly pertains to the nature or the substance by which God is, because by substance they are one. We distinguish persons; we do not divide the deity.

We acknowledge trinity in the distinction of persons; we **305** profess unity because of the nature or substance. The three **(281)** are one, as a nature, that is, not as person. Nevertheless, these three persons are not to be considered separable, since we believe that no one of them existed or at any time effected anything before the other, after the other, or without the other. For in existence and in operation they are found to be inseparable, because we believe that between the Father who generates and the Son who is generated and the Holy Spirit who proceeds, there never was any interval of time in which the one generating would at any time precede the one generated, or in which the one generated would not be present to the one generating, or in which the Spirit who proceeds might appear to come after the Father and the Son. For this reason we profess and believe that the Trinity is not separable but is distinct. Hence there are said to be three persons, as our predecessors define, in order that they may be known but not that they may be separated. For if we listen to what the Holy Scripture says of Wisdom: "She is the brightness of eternal light" (*Wisd. 7:26*); then, as we see that the brightness inheres inseparably in the light, so we shall confess that the Son cannot be separated from the Father. We do not confuse those three persons of the one inseparable nature, but, on the other hand, we by no means profess that they are separable. This matter the Trinity itself has condescended to reveal to us even in the very names themselves by which it willed the persons to be individually known, not permitting one person to be understood without the other person. For the Father is not known apart from the Son, and the Son is not known apart from the Father. For the very connotation of the personal name forbids the persons to be separated; although the relation does not name the persons at the same time, it does imply them at the same time. No one is able to hear any one of those names without being forced to think of the other. Although these three are one, and the one is three, there remains to each one of the persons his own personal property; for the Father has eternity without birth, the Son has eternity with birth, and the Holy Spirit has procession without birth but from eternity.

The Triune God

THE FOURTH LATERAN COUNCIL, 1215

More than four hundred bishops answered the summons of Innocent III (1198–1216) to the Fourth Lateran Council, the twelfth ecumenical council. In addition to a profession of faith and a definitive statement against the Albigenses and Waldensians, the fathers of the council censured Joachim of Flora (1130–91) for his erroneous tract against Peter Lombard. Joachim asserted that Peter Lombard put a quaternity in God. The council, however, approved Peter Lombard's doctrine and defined the traditional belief in the Triune God.

Chapter 1. The Catholic Faith

A definition against the Albigenses and other heretics

306 (428) We firmly believe and profess without qualification that there is only one true God, eternal, immense, unchangeable, incomprehensible, omnipotent, and indescribable, the Father, the Son, and the Holy Spirit: three persons but one essence and a substance or nature that is wholly simple. The Father is from no one; the Son is from the Father only; and the Holy Spirit is from both the Father and the Son equally. God has no beginning; he always is, and always will be; the Father is the progenitor, the Son is the begotten, the Holy Spirit is proceeding; they are all one substance, equally great, equally all-powerful, equally eternal; they are the one and only principle of all things—Creator of all things visible and invisible, spiritual and corporeal, who, by his almighty power, from the very beginning of time has created both orders of creatures in the same way out of nothing, the spiritual or angelic world and the corporeal or visible universe. And afterwards He formed the creature man, who in a way belongs to both orders, as he is composed of spirit and body. For the devil and the other demons were created by God good according to their nature, but they made themselves evil by their own doing. As for man, his sin was at the prompting of the devil. The Holy Trinity, indivisible according to its essence, and distinct according to its personal properties, first gave this teaching of salvation to the human race through Moses and the prophets and its other servants, according to a well-ordered disposition of time.

The Triune God

Chapter 2. The Error of Abbot Joachim

But we, with the approval of the holy council, believe and profess, with Peter Lombard, that there is a certain one supreme reality, incomprehensible, and beyond description, which truly is the Father, and the Son, and the Holy Spirit. That reality is the three persons taken together and each of them taken singly; and, hence, there is in God only a trinity, not a quaternity; because each of the persons is that reality, namely, the divine substance, essence, or nature. That reality alone is the principle of all things; besides it none other can be found. And that reality does not beget, nor is it begotten, nor does it proceed; but it is the Father who begets, the Son who is begotten, the Holy Spirit who proceeds; thus, there are distinctions between persons, and unity in nature. Although "the Father is one person, the Son is another person, and the Holy Spirit yet another person, still none is a different being." Rather, the very same being which is the Father is also the Son and the Holy Spirit; consequently, according to the orthodox and Catholic faith they are believed to be consubstantial. For the Father in eternally generating the Son gave him his own substance as the Son himself testifies: "What my Father has given me is greater than all" (*see John 10:29*). But it cannot be said that he gave him part of his substance, and retained part for himself, because the substance of the Father is indivisible, since it is altogether simple. Neither can one say that the Father transferred his own substance in generation to the Son, as though he gave it to the Son in such a way that he did not retain it for himself; otherwise he would cease to be a substance. It is clear, therefore, that in being born the Son received the undiminished substance of the Father, and thus the Father and the Son have the same substance; and thus the same reality is the Father, and the Son, and the Holy Spirit who proceeds from both. When, therefore, the Truth prays for his faithful to the Father, he says: "I will that they should be one in us, as we also are one" (*see John 17:22*); this term "one" applied to the faithful means a union of charity in grace; applied to the Divine Persons, it indicates the unity of identity in nature, as the Truth says elsewhere: "You

307
(432)

are to be perfect, even as your heavenly Father is perfect" (*see Matt. 5:48*). In more explicit terms he would have said: "You are to be perfect with the perfection of grace, as your heavenly Father is perfect with perfection of nature." Creator and creature are to be perfect, each in his own way, because between them no similarity can be found so great but that the dissimilarity is even greater.

Therefore, if anyone presumes to defend or approve the opinion or teaching of the above mentioned Joachim in this matter: let everyone silence him as a heretic.

THE SECOND COUNCIL OF LYONS, 1274

This council, the fourteenth ecumenical council, held during the reign of Gregory X (1271–76), contributed an explicit definition about the procession of the Holy Spirit to Trinitarian doctrine. Moreover, in the profession of faith prescribed for Michael Palaeologus (*see introd. to 152*), the council summarizes the Church's doctrine on the Trinity.

Constitution on the Procession of the Holy Spirit

308 (460) With faithful and devout profession we confess that the Holy Spirit proceeds eternally from the Father and the Son, not as from two principles, but as from one; not by two spirations but by one. This has been the profession, preaching, and teaching of the holy Roman Catholic Church, the mother and teacher of all the faithful, up to the present day. This is the unchangeable and true doctrine of the orthodox Fathers and Doctors, both Latin and Greek. But because some, in ignorance of the indisputable truth stated above, have fallen into various errors, we desire to forestall errors of this kind, and, with the approval of the holy council, we condemn and reprobate those who presume to deny that the Holy Spirit proceeds eternally from the Father and the Son, or those who injudiciously dare to assert that the Holy Spirit proceeds from the Father and the Son as from two principles, and not as from one.

Profession of Faith of Michael Palaeologus

309 (461) We believe in the Holy Trinity, Father, Son, and Holy Spirit, in one omnipotent God, and in the whole Godhead in the Trinity: coessential, consubstantial, coeternal, and co-omnipotent; of one will, power, and majesty; the creator of all things created, from whom, in whom, and by whom are all things in heaven and on earth, visible and invisible, corporeal and spiritual. We believe that each individual person in the Trinity is the one, true, complete, and perfect God.

And we believe that the Holy Spirit, completely and perfectly true God, proceeding from the Father and from the Son, is coequal, consubstantial, co-omnipotent, and coeternal with the Father and the Son in all things. We believe that this Holy Trinity is not three gods, but one God, omnipotent, eternal, invisible, and unchanging. **310** **(463)**

THE COUNCIL OF FLORENCE, 1438-45

In its decree for the Monophysitic Jacobites on February 4, 1442 (*see introd. to 164*), the Council of Florence, the seventeenth ecumenical council, laid a firm foundation of orthodox Trinitarian doctrine as the basis for future harmony. The procession of the Holy Spirit from both Father and Son is explicitly mentioned; the identity of the Divine Persons where there is no relative opposition is stressed in the famous formula; the doctrine of circumincession is clearly set forth; the identity of Father and Son as a single principle of the Holy Spirit is compared to the identity of the three Divine Persons as a single principle of creation.

Decree for the Jacobites

The holy Roman Church, founded by the decree of our Lord and Savior firmly believes, professes, and teaches: There is one true God, all-powerful, unchangeable, and eternal, Father, Son, and Holy Spirit, one in essence, but three in persons. The Father is not begotten; the Son is begotten of the Father; the Holy Spirit proceeds from the Father and the Son. The Father is not the Son or the Holy Spirit; the Son is not the Father or the Holy Spirit; the Holy Spirit is not the Father or the Son. Rather, the Father is only the Father; the Son is only the Son; and the Holy Spirit is only the Holy Spirit. The Father alone has, of his own substance, begotten the Son; the Son alone has been begotten of the Father alone; the Holy Spirit alone proceeds both from the Father and equally from the Son. These three persons are one God, not three gods; for the three persons have one substance, **311** **(703)** one essence, one nature, one divinity, one immensity, one eternity. And everything is one where there is no distinction by relative opposition. [*At the Council of Florence, John, a theologian of the Latin fathers, testifies: "According to both the Latin and the Greek Doctors, the only thing that distinguishes the persons in the divine processions is the relation that is called the relation of origin. This relation involves only two elements: a principle and someone proceeding from it." Likewise, the learned Cardinal Bessarion, archbishop of Nicaea and a theologian for the Greek fathers, said: "Everyone knows that the personal names in the Trinity are relative."*]

312
(704)
"Because of this unity, the Father is entirely in the Son and entirely in the Holy Spirit; the Son is entirely in the Father and entirely in the Holy Spirit; the Holy Spirit is entirely in the Father and entirely in the Son. None of the persons precedes any of the others in eternity, nor does any have greater immensity or greater power. From eternity, without beginning, the Son is from the Father; and from eternity and without beginning, the Holy Spirit has proceeded from the Father and the Son." All that the Father is, and all that he has, he does not have from another, but of himself; he is the principle that has no principle. All that the Son is, and all that he has, he has from the Father; he is a principle from a principle. All that the Holy Spirit is and all that he has, he has from the Father and equally from the Son. Yet the Father and the Son are not two principles of the Holy Spirit, but one principle, just as the Father and the Son and the Holy Spirit are not three principles of creation, but one principle.

313
(705)
Therefore, the holy Roman Church condemns, disapproves, anathematizes, and declares to be separated from the body of Christ, which is the Church, all who hold any contrary opinions. Consequently, she condemns Sabellius who unifies the persons and completely does away with the real distinction among them. She condemns the Arians, the Eunomians, the Macedonians who say that only God the Father is true God and classify the Son and the Holy Spirit as creatures. She further condemns all who put any degree or inequality in the Trinity.

The Triune God

THE VATICAN COUNCIL, 1869-70

SCHEMA OF THE DOGMATIC CONSTITUTION ON THE PRINCIPAL MYSTERIES OF THE FAITH

The theologians of the Vatican Council, the twentieth ecumenical council, had prepared a schema of the principal mysteries of the faith as a second part of the Dogmatic Constitution on Catholic Doctrine. **This schema, part of which is given below, was revised, though not finally, by the deputation that prepared it; but it was never adopted by the council in formal session. Although having no official authority, it is included here as a valuable document reflecting Catholic belief.** The errors of Anton Günther (1783–1863) were the occasion of the preparation of the chapters and canons on the Trinity. (The following translation is made from the text given in *Collectio Lacensis*, VII, 553 f., 565.)

Chapter 1. The Holy Trinity

Of all the mysteries that we profess in the light of faith, **314** the supreme mystery is God himself, who is one in essence, three in persons, Father, Son, Holy Spirit. According to the truth of the Catholic faith, the blessed Trinity is one God, because the essence or substance common to the three persons is really and numerically one. For from all eternity the Father generates the Son, not in producing by emanation another essence equal to his own, but in communicating his own simple essence. And in like manner, the Holy Spirit proceeds, not by a multiplication of the essence, but he proceeds by a communication of the same singular essence by one eternal spiration from the Father and the Son as from one principle.

This essence, then, or nature, one in number, truly is the **315** Father, the Son, and the Holy Spirit; it is equally three persons and each of them individually. Thus the persons are really distinct from one another, but in nature or essence, they are one and the same (*see DB 431*).

And since, in God, everything is one where there is no **316** relative opposition (*see 311*), there is one will and one operation with which the most Holy Trinity creates, arranges, and governs everything extrinsic to itself. The Divine Persons do not act extrinsically according to the relations of origin by which they are distinguished, but insofar as they are one unique principle.

Canons on Chapter 1

317 1. If anyone says that there are three essences or substances in God just as there are three persons: let him be anathema.

318 2. If anyone says that the divine substance is one and the same not in number, but in species or in the quality of the three persons: let him be anathema.

319 3. If anyone says that the Trinity is one God, not because of the singleness of the one substance, but because of the equality of three substances of God and because of the relation of the persons to one another: let him be anathema.

320 4. If anyone says that creation or any other extrinsic operation is proper to one divine person in such a way that it is not one and undivided and common to all three persons: let him be anathema.

THE ENCYCLICAL MYSTICI CORPORIS, 1943

In this encyclical, dated June 29, 1943 (*see introd. to 239*), Pope Pius XII (1939–58) includes this declaration of the indwelling of the Holy Spirit in the souls of the just. (This translation is made from the text in *Acta Apostolicae Sedis*, XXXV [1943], 231–32.)

The indwelling of the Holy Spirit

321
(2290) We are well aware that many a veil shrouds this profound truth of our union with the divine Redeemer and in particular of the Holy Spirit's indwelling in souls and impedes our power to understand and explain it. This mystery is enveloped in a darkness, rising out of the mental limitations of those who seek to grasp it. But We know, too, that well-directed and earnest study of this doctrine and the clash of diverse opinions and their discussion, provided love of truth and due submission to the Church be the arbiter, will open rich and bright vistas, by the light of which true progress can be made in these sacred sciences. Hence, We do not censure

those who in various ways and with diverse reasonings strain every effort to understand and to clarify the mystery of this our marvelous union with Christ. But if they do not want to deviate from true doctrine and from the legitimate teaching authority of the Church, they must accept the following general and indisputable principle: to reject every explanation of this mystic union according to which the faithful would in any way so pass beyond the sphere of creatures and sacrilegiously encroach upon the divine, that even a single attribute of the eternal Godhead could be predicated of them as their own. And besides let them hold this as certain truth, that in these mysteries everything must be regarded as common to the most Blessed Trinity, insofar as they have God as supreme efficient cause.

They must likewise take note that there is question here of a hidden mystery which in this earthly exile can never be fully disclosed, and grasped, and expressed in human language. The Divine Persons are said to inhabit inasmuch as they are present to intellectual creatures in a way that transcends human comprehension, and are known and loved by them, yet in a way that is unique, purely supernatural, and in the deepest sanctuary of the soul. If we would approach at least a little towards perceiving this truth, let us not neglect the method highly recommended by the Vatican Council in similar cases (*see* 75). When the council seeks light so as to discern at least partially the hidden things of God, it finds it in comparing these mysteries one with another and with the last end towards which they point. Therefore, Our most wise predecessor Leo XIII of happy memory, speaking of our union with Christ and with the divine Paraclete who dwells within us, and fixing his gaze on that blessed vision through which this mystical union will attain its confirmation and perfection in heaven, says: "This wonderful union, which is properly called indwelling, differs from that by which God embraces and gives joy to the saints only by reason of our earthly state." In that celestial vision it will be granted to the eyes of the human mind strengthened by the light of glory, to contemplate the Father, the Son, and the Holy Spirit in an utterly ineffable

322
(2290)

manner, to be immediately present throughout eternity at the processions of the Divine Persons, and to rejoice with a happiness very much like to that with which the holy and undivided Trinity is happy.

God the Creator and Sanctifier

It is possible to know God's existence from the creatures that he made. It is, moreover, possible to know that creatures were made by God out of nothing. Instead of trusting the discovery of this difficult truth, full of religious import, to merely human inquiry, God has revealed the fact that he alone is the creator of all that is, and the Church has taught this truth authoritatively from its beginning. The goodness of all creatures, not excepting material things, is an evident corollary from their creation by God. Further, the true concept of creation excludes every form of emanationism and pantheism, while it emphasizes the liberality, power, wisdom, and goodness of God, manifested by his free creation of the world in time. These truths are the cornerstones on which men can build lives of Christian optimism and personal responsibility. For that reason the Church has always insisted on them as basic to the revealed religion entrusted to it by God.

Among the things God created, man himself is of greatest importance and interest for man. As questions have arisen in the course of centuries over the nature and origin of man, over his body and soul, and their origin from God, the Church has given authoritative answers to safeguard the deposit of faith.

But it was not enough for the Church to speak merely of man's nature. There are other truths, known only by revelation, that are of supreme importance for man's ultimate destiny: man was created in a state of original justice in which he enjoyed not only the preternatural gifts of fullest control over his emotions—integrity—and of bodily immortality, but also the greatest and most mysterious gift that God could communicate to him—a share in God's own life, making man a child of God by adoption, a true heir with the right to possess God as his eternal inheritance. The original state was lost by the first man's sin, and all of his descendants are therefore born in original sin, deprived of all these gifts. Yet this does not mean that their nature is vitiated; for the original justice was something entirely gratuitous, in no way required for man's perfection. It does mean that man by himself is completely helpless to restore himself to the sonship of God and that, if he is ever to achieve the goal he is destined to reach, he can do so only by receiving the justification won for him by the merits of Christ.

The Creation of the World and of Man

From the beginning of the second century to the end of the fourth century the Church was occupied with Trinitarian and Christological heresies. In combating these errors the Church frequently stated the true notion of God's creative act. The earliest creeds had always included the profession of belief in the "Creator of all things." And so, although there were systems of dualistic philosophy in vogue, Gnosticism, for example, the errors that pertained to God as creator were only indirectly condemned.

One system of religious dualism, Manichaeism, spread through Africa to Spain, exacted from St. Augustine thirty books, and caused the Church much grief. This was the intellectual religion of Manes, a Persian who combined Babylonian myths with Zoroastrian dualism, and disguised the mixture with some Christian trappings. Manichaeism was repeatedly condemned in its various forms. The following documents show the Church's firm stand against all errors of pantheism, emanationism, and dualism and its doctrinal positions on the true

nature of God's creative act, the origin of the world, and the
origin of man.

CANONS OF PROVINCIAL COUNCIL OF CONSTANTINOPLE, 543

A provincial council held at Constantinople under the Patriarch Mennas drew up a series of canons against the Origenists.
These were a group of Palestinian monks who claimed Origen
as the author of their erroneous teachings on the origin of the
soul and the limits of God's creative power. According to the
testimony of Cassiodorus, Pope Vigilius (*cir.* 537–55) seems
to have confirmed these canons.

1. If anyone says or thinks that the souls of men pre-exist, **323**
in the sense that they were previously intelligences and holy (*203*)
powers that had become surfeited with divine contemplation
and had turned to something inferior and therefore had grown
cold in the love of God and for this reason were called in
Greek *psychai*, that is, souls, and were sent down into bodies
for punishment: let him be anathema. [*There is a play on
words in the Greek that neither the Latin nor the English
can carry. The word for souls is ψυχαί and the word ἀποψύχειν
in the passive means to grow cold.*]

8. If anyone says or holds that the power of God is finite **324**
or that he has created as much as he could: let him be (*210*)
anathema.

THE COUNCIL OF BRAGA, 561

In 561 some bishops met in the town of Braga, Spain (now in
Portugal), to condemn once and for all the errors of Priscillian,
a devotee of Manichaeism. Priscillian was responsible for the
spread of these errors through Spain, France, and Northern
Italy. In 400 and in 447, at Toledo, these same errors had been
condemned. At Braga the Manichaeans and Priscillianists are
condemned by name.

5. If anyone believes that human souls or angels are com- **325**
posed of the substance of God, as Manes and Priscillian have (*235*)
said: let him be anathema.

6. If anyone says that human souls had previously sinned **326**
in their heavenly home and because of this they were cast (*236*)

down into human bodies on earth, as Priscillian said: let him be anathema.

827
(237)
7. If anyone says that the devil was not first a good angel made by God, or that his nature was not the work of God, but claims that the devil sprang from the darkness and had no creator at all, rather that he is himself the beginning and substance of evil, as Manes and Priscillian have said: let him be anathema.

828
(238)
8. If anyone believes that the devil made some of the creatures in the world and that thunder, lightning, storms, and droughts are caused by the devil by his own power, as Priscillian has said: let him be anathema.

829
(239)
9. If anyone believes that human souls are linked to some foreordaining sign of destiny, as Priscillian and the pagans have declared: let him be anathema.

[*Variant reading.*] If anyone believes *that souls and human bodies are linked to fateful stars* as Priscillian and the pagans have declared: let him be anathema.

830
(241)
11. If anyone condemns human marriage and says that the procreation of children is something detestable, as Manes and Priscillian have said: let him be anathema.

831
(242)
12. If anyone says that the formation of the human body is the devil's work and that conception in the womb of the mother is caused by the devil, and because of this does not believe in the resurrection of the body, as Manes and Priscillian have said: let him be anathema.

832
(243)
13. If anyone says that the creation of all flesh is not the work of God but of evil spirits, as Priscillian has said: let him be anathema.

THE FOURTH COUNCIL OF CONSTANTINOPLE, 869-70

In 870, under Pope Hadrian II (867–72), the fathers at Constantinople condemned the errors of Photius (*cir.* 815–97). The canon which condemns the error on the nature of man is a definition, in accord with all the Fathers and teachers in the Church, that man has one rational, intellectual soul. (This translation follows the Latin text in Denzinger.)

The Creation of the World and of Man

11. The Old and the New Testament both teach that man has one rational, intellectual soul. All the Fathers and the teachers of the Church emphatically affirm this same opinion in their theological discourses. Nevertheless, there are some men, zealous in the pursuit of evil, who have come to such a state of godlessness that they boldly teach that man has two souls. And with a wisdom that has turned to foolishness (*see I Cor. 1:20*), these men make irrational attempts to confirm their heresy. And so this holy universal council, makes haste to uproot this evil cockle that is germinating an evil doctrine. Indeed, with the winnowing fan of truth in hand, and with the desire to cast all chaff into the unquenchable fire and to show forth the clean threshing floor of Christ (*see Matt. 3:12; Luke 3:17*), this council loudly declares anathema both those who originate and those who propagate this godlessness and all those who hold similar opinions. It defines and promulgates that no one at all may have or keep in any way the doctrine of these authors of godlessness. If anyone presumes to go contrary to this great and holy council: let him be anathema and let him be separated from the faith and the worship of Christians.

The traditional, true doctrine of the Church on God's power, his creative act, and the nature of his creature man can be found in the emphatic condemnations of errors that the Church considered dangerous and also in the various professions of faith that were required from those heretics and schismatics who wished to return to the Church.

THE PROFESSION OF FAITH OF
DURANDUS OF OSCA, 1208

The Waldensians (*see introd. to 150*) were infected with the spirit of Manichaeism and consequently held similar errors. In 1208 Innocent XIII (1198–1216) demanded this profession from Durandus and his companions.

And we also believe in our hearts and proclaim with our lips that the Father, the Son, and the Holy Spirit, the one God whom we are treating of, is the creator, maker, governor, and ruler of all corporeal and spiritual things visible and invisible. We believe that both the Old and the New Testament have one and the same author, God; and he, as has been said,

333
(338)

334
(421)

God the Creator and Sanctifier

remaining in the Trinity, created all things from nothing. We
believe that John the Baptist was sent by God and that he was
holy, just, and filled with the Holy Spirit in the womb of his
mother.

THE FOURTH LATERAN COUNCIL, 1215

Similar to the profession of faith required from the Waldensians
was the profession of faith against Albigensianism (*see introd.
to 306*) in 1215. The Albigenses also held Manichaean and
Gnostic errors on creation and the power of God.

Chapter 1. The Catholic Faith

A definition against the Albigenses and other heretics

335
(428)
We firmly believe and profess without qualification that
there is only one true God, eternal, immense, unchangeable,
incomprehensible, omnipotent, and indescribable, the Father,
the Son, and the Holy Spirit: three persons but one essence
and a substance or nature that is wholly simple. The Father
is from no one; the Son is from the Father only; and the Holy
Spirit is from both the Father and the Son equally. God has
no beginning, he always is, and always will be; the Father is
the progenitor, the Son is being born, the Holy Spirit is proceeding; they are all one substance, equally great, equally all-
powerful, equally eternal; they are the one and only principle
of all things—Creator of all things visible and invisible,
spiritual and corporeal, who, by his almighty power, from the
very beginning of time has created both orders of creatures
in the same way out of nothing, the spiritual or angelic world
and the corporeal or visible universe. And afterwards he
formed the creature man, who in a way belongs to both orders,
as he is composed of spirit and body. For the devil and the
other demons were created by God good according to their
nature, but they made themselves evil by their own doing.
As for man, his sin was at the prompting of the devil. The
Holy Trinity, indivisible according to its essence, and distinct
according to its personal properties, first gave this teaching of
salvation to the human race through Moses and the prophets
and its other servants, according to a well-ordered disposition
of time.

146

The Creation of the World and of Man

THE COUNCIL OF VIENNE, 1311-12

The Council of Vienne, the fifteenth ecumenical council, met to abolish the Knights Templars and to prepare reforms in ecclesiastical matters; it also established three points of Catholic doctrine against Peter John Olivi (1248–98). One of his errors in theology concerned the union of soul and body.

The soul as the form of the body

Furthermore, with the approval of the sacred council mentioned previously, We condemn as erroneous and opposed to Catholic truth every doctrine and opinion that rashly asserts that the substance of the rational, intellectual soul is not truly and by its own nature the form of the human body, or that casts doubt on this matter. And we define that, whoever presumes to assert, defend, or stubbornly hold that the rational or intellectual soul is not of its own nature and essentially the form of the body, is to be considered a heretic. In this way the truth of the authentic faith is known to all and the path of error is blocked.

336
(481)

THE ERRORS OF ECKHART, 1329

John XXII (1316–34) reviewed some propositions of Master Eckhart (1260–1327), a writer in mystical theology. His mysticism led him to inaccurate statements in theology and these were condemned on March 27, 1329. Those given here were condemned as heretical except for proposition 26, which was condemned as temerarious and suspected of heresy.

(1) When he was asked why God did not produce the world sooner, he responded that God was not able to produce the world sooner because a being cannot act before it exists; therefore, as soon as God existed, he created the world.

337
(501)

(2) It may likewise be conceded that the world existed from all eternity.

338
(502)

(3) Likewise, at the same time and once for all, when God existed and when he generated his Son, God, coeternal and coequal to himself in all things, he also created the world.

339
(503)

(26) All creatures are an absolute nothing; I do not say that they are a small thing or that they are anything but that they are an absolute nothing.

340
(526)

147

341
(527)
(1) There is an uncreated something in the soul that cannot be created. This is the intellect. And if the whole soul were of this something it would be uncreated and incapable of being created.

THE ERRORS OF THE ARMENIANS, 1341
Benedict XII (1334-42) was zealous in his concern for the reuniting of the schismatic Armenians. In 1341 he thought it necessary to warn the uniates against many former errors of their Church.

342
(533)
5. Likewise, a certain teacher of the Armenians, called Mechitriz, which means paraclete, again introduced the teaching that the human soul of a son is propagated from the soul of his father, as his body is from the body of his father. He taught also that angels are propagated one from another. He gave as his reason for this that, since a rational, existing human soul, and an angel existing in an intellectual nature are a kind of spiritual light, they propagate other spiritual lights from themselves.

THE COUNCIL OF FLORENCE, 1438-45
In the decree for the Jacobites, February 4, 1442 (*see introd. to 703*), the profession of faith included a clear statement of the doctrine of creation and once more anathematized Manichaean doctrine.

343
(706)
The holy Roman Church firmly believes, professes, and preaches that the one true God, Father, Son, and Holy Spirit, is the creator of all things visible and invisible. When God willed, in his goodness he created all creatures both spiritual and corporeal. These creatures are good because they were made by the Supreme Good, but they are changeable because they were made from nothing. The Church asserts that there is no such thing as a nature of evil, because every nature insofar as it is a nature is good. It professes that one and the same God is the author of the Old and the New Testament, that is, of the Law, of the Prophets, and of the Gospel because the holy men of both Testaments have spoken under the inspiration of the same Holy Spirit. It accepts and reverences their books as here listed. [*There follows the canon of books (see 96).*]

Furthermore, the Church anathematizes the foolish doctrine of the Manichaeans who have set down two first causes, one of visible things and the other of invisible things, and who have said that there is one God of the New Testament and another God of the Old Testament.

344
(707)

THE FIFTH LATERAN COUNCIL, 1512-17

In the eighth session of the Lateran Council, the eighteenth ecumenical council, December 19, 1513, the nature of the human soul was defined against the errors of the Neo-Aristotelians.

We regretfully mention that recently the sower of cockle, the ancient enemy of the human race, has dared to oversow the Lord's field and to give increase to some dangerous errors, which have always been disapproved by the faithful. These errors concern the nature of the rational soul especially—for instance, that the soul is mortal or that there is only one soul for all men. Some audacious philosophers have held that this was the truth, at least according to philosophy. Therefore, We desire to use suitable remedies against this error. And with the approval of this sacred council, We condemn and reject all those who claim that the intellectual soul is mortal or that there is a single soul for all men. We condemn those who raise doubts about this matter. For the soul is not only truly, of its own nature, and essentially the form of the human body, as is stated in the canon of our predecessor Pope Clement V of happy memory, and published in the (general) Council of Vienne (*see 336*), but also it is immortal and, corresponding to the number of bodies into which it is infused, is capable of being multiplied in individuals, is actually multiplied, and must be multiplied. . . .

345
(738)

COLLECTION OF MODERN ERRORS, 1864

Pius IX (1846–78) ordered this collection of the errors of the nineteenth century and had it sent to all the bishops of the world. The collection, called the *Syllabus,* was published on December 8, 1864 (*see introd. to 51*). The first two errors condemned express modern pantheistic tenets.

1. There is no supreme, all-wise, and all-provident Godhead distinct from this universe. God is identical with nature and, consequently, subject to change. God is actually in the

346
(1701)

process of becoming, in man and in the world. All things are God and have the very substance of God himself. God and the world are one and the same thing. In like manner spirit is identical with matter, necessity with liberty, truth with falsity, good with evil, and justice with injustice.

347
(1702)
2. Any action of God upon man and the world must be denied.

THE VATICAN COUNCIL, 1869-70
SCHEMA OF THE DOGMATIC CONSTITUTION ON THE PRINCIPAL MYSTERIES OF THE FAITH

This schema, though prepared for the council, never came up for definition (*see introd. to 314*). **The chapter below is presented as a noteworthy, but not authoritative, statement of the theologians of the council.** (This translation follows the text given in *Collectio Lacensis*, VII, 554a; 565c.)

Chapter 2. The Creation and Nature of Man

348
This is what holy mother Church believes and teaches about the origin and the nature of man as she has learned it from Scripture. God was intent on making man to his own image and likeness. That man might have dominion over the entire earth, God breathed the breath of life into the body that he formed from the dust of the earth. This was the soul, created from nothing, immaterial, incorruptible, immortal, and gifted with intelligence and free will. This rational soul is essentially different from the human body, but it is truly, of its own nature, and essentially the form of that body (*see 336, 345*), so that together with the body it constitutes human nature truly and really one.

349
God blessed Adam, the first man, and his wife, Eve, whom God had formed from a rib of Adam, and said to them, "Multiply and fill the earth" (*Gen. 1:28*). Thus, "from one man he has created the whole human race and made them live all over the face of the earth" (*Acts 17:26*). And this was the reason "Adam called his wife Eve because she was the mother of all the living" (*Gen. 3:20*). Adam himself is said to be the father of the world, the first man formed by God (*see Wisd. 10:1*), for all the men who inhabit the earth de-

scend from him by natural generation. Flesh is born of flesh and God creates a new soul and infuses it into each man. If this teaching of faith is denied, the dogma of the sin that was transmitted to all men by one first parent is weakened as is the dogma of the universal redemption by one mediator, Jesus. And it is against the teaching of the Apostle: "Therefore as from the offense of the one man the result was unto condemnation to all men, so from the justice of the one the result is unto justification of life to all men" (*Rom. 5:18*).

Canons on Chapter 2

1. If anyone says that by nature the soul of man is not different from the body, not spiritual, and not immortal: let him be anathema.   **350**

2. If anyone claims that there is another soul in man, really distinct from his rational soul: let him be anathema.   **351**

3. If anyone says that the nature of man composed of body and spirit is not truly and really one: let him be anathcma.   **352**

4. If anyone says that the entire human race did not take its origin from one original parent, Adam: let him be anathema.   **353**

THE DOGMATIC CONSTITUTION ON THE CATHOLIC FAITH

In the first chapter of the Dogmatic Constitution on the Catholic Faith, dated April 24, 1870 (*see introd. to 58*), the fathers of the Vatican Council, with modern errors in mind, declared the true doctrine on creation and God's creative act and anathematized the opposite errors.

. . . Now, therefore, with the bishops of the whole world being associated with Us and concurring in judgment, assembled for this ecumenical council by Our authority in the Holy Spirit, We have determined to profess and declare the saving doctrine of Christ from this Chair of Peter in view of all men. We do so, relying on the word of God in writing and in tradition, as We have received it from the Catholic Church, religiously guarded and authentically explained. All opposing errors We proscribe and condemn by the authority given to Us by God.   **354 (1781)**

God the Creator and Sanctifier

Chapter 1. God the Creator of All Things

The one living and true God and his distinction from the universe

855
(1782)
The holy, Catholic, apostolic Roman Church believes and professes that there is one true and living God, the creator and lord of heaven and earth. He is all-powerful, eternal, unmeasurable, incomprehensible, and limitless in intellect and will and in every perfection. Since he is one unique spiritual substance, entirely simple and unchangeable, he must be declared really and essentially distinct from the world, perfectly happy in himself and by his very nature, and inexpressibly exalted over all things that exist or can be conceived other than himself (*see 358–61, cans. 1–4*).

The act of creation in itself and in opposition to modern errors, and the result of creation

356
(1783)
In order to manifest his perfection through the benefits which he bestows on creatures—not to intensify his happiness nor to acquire any perfection—this one and only true God, by his goodness and "almighty power" and by a completely free decision, "from the very beginning of time has created both orders of creatures in the same way out of nothing, the spiritual or angelic world and the corporeal or visible universe. And afterwards he formed the creature man, who in a way belongs to both orders, as he is composed of spirit and body" (*see 306; 359, 362, cans. 2 and 5*).

The sequel to creation

357
(1784)
Furthermore, by his providence God watches over and governs all the things that he made, reaching from end to end with might and disposing all things with gentleness (*see Wisd. 8:1*). For "all things are naked and open to his eyes" (*Heb. 4:13*), even those things that are going to occur by the free action of creatures.

Canons on Chapter 1

Against all errors about the existence of a God who is creator

358
(1801)
1. If anyone denies that there is one true God, creator and lord of things visible and invisible: let him be anathema (*see 355*).

Against materialism

2. If anyone dares to assert that nothing exists except matter: let him be anathema (*see* 356).

359
(1802)

Against pantheism

3. If anyone says that God and all things possess one and the same substance and essence: let him be anathema (*see* 355).

360
(1803)

Against particular forms of pantheism

4. If anyone says that finite things, both corporeal and spiritual, or at least spiritual, emanated from the divine substance;

361
(1804)

or that the divine essence becomes all things by a manifestation or evolution of itself;

or, finally, that God is universal or indefinite being, which by determining itself makes up the universe which is diversified into genera, species, and individuals: let him be anathema.

Against both pantheists and materialists

5. If anyone does not admit that the world and everything in it, both spiritual and material, have been produced in their entire substance by God out of nothing (*see* 356);

362
(1805)

Against the followers of Günther

or says that God did not create with a will free from all necessity, but that he created necessarily, just as he necessarily loves himself (*see* 356);

Against the followers of Günther and Hermes

or denies that the world was made for the glory of God: let him be anathema.

A REPLY OF THE BIBLICAL COMMISSION, 1909

On June 30, 1909, the Biblical Commission gave this response concerning the historical character of the first chapters of Genesis. Emphasis is placed on the *literal* sense of the passage, which may not be called into question.

Query III: In particular may one question the literal historical sense when these same chapters [*the first three chapters of Genesis*] treat of facts that touch on fundamental points of the Christian religion? To give some examples, among

363
(2123)

others: the creation of all things accomplished by God in the beginning of time, the special creation of man, the formation of the first woman from the first man, the unity of the human race, the original happiness of our first parents in the state of justice, integrity, and immortality, the command given to man by God as a test of obedience, the transgression of the divine command at the persuasion of the devil in the form of a serpent, the degradation of our first parents from that primeval state of innocence, and the promise of a future redeemer.

Response: The literal historical sense may not be questioned.

THE ENCYCLICAL *HUMANI GENERIS*, 1950

Among the currents of thought that evoked this encyclical from Pope Pius XII (1939–58) on August 12, 1950, were some of the old errors about man's ability to know the existence of God and the freedom of God's creative act. Further, some Catholics had been led by an uncritical acceptance of theories of evolution into new theological errors, that of polygenism, for example.

364
(2317)
No wonder if this spirit of innovation has already borne poisonous fruit in almost every sphere of theology. A doubt is raised, whether the human reason, unaided by God's revelation and by his grace, can really prove the existence of a personal God by inference from the facts of creation. We are told that the world had no beginning; that its creation was a necessary event, owing its origin to an act of liberality which the divine Love could not refuse. So, too, God is no longer credited with an infallible foreknowledge, from all eternity, of our free human acts. All this is contrary to the declarations made by the Council of the Vatican (*see 355 ff.*).

365
(2327)
Thus, the teaching of the Church leaves the doctrine of evolution an open question, as long as it confines its speculations to the development, from other living matter already in existence, of the human body. (That souls are immediately created by God is a view which the Catholic faith imposes on us.) In the present state of scientific and theological opinion, this question may be legitimately canvassed by research, and by discussion between experts on both sides. At the same time, the reasons for and against either view must be weighed

and adjudged with all seriousness, fairness, and restraint; and there must be a readiness on all sides to accept the arbitrament of the Church, as being entrusted by Christ with the right to interpret the Scriptures, and the duty of safeguarding the doctrines of the faith. There are some who take rash advantage of this liberty of debate, by treating the subject as if the whole matter were closed—as if the discoveries hitherto made, and the arguments based on them, were sufficiently certain to prove, beyond doubt, the development of the human body from other living matter already in existence. They forget, too, that there are certain references to the subject in the sources of divine revelation, which call for the greatest caution and prudence in discussing it.

There are other conjectures, about polygenism (as it is called), which leave the faithful no such freedom of choice. Christians cannot lend their support to a theory which involves the existence, after Adam's time, of some earthly race of men, truly so called, who were not descended ultimately from him, or else supposes that Adam was the name given to some group of our primordial ancestors. It does not appear how such views can be reconciled with the doctrine of original sin, as this is guaranteed to us by Scripture and tradition, and proposed to us by the Church. Original sin is the result of a sin committed, in actual historical fact, by an individual man named Adam, and it is a quality native to all of us, only because it has been handed down by descent from him (*see Rom. 5:12–19; 372–75, cans. 1–4*).

366
(2328)

Original Justice and Original Sin

It has been the constant teaching of the Church that God established man in sanctity and justice, and gave him the gifts of integrity and immortality. These gifts were entirely gratuitous on God's part; and when Adam sinned, he lost these gifts for himself and for his posterity. The Pelagian heresy, which exaggerated the natural powers of man, consistently denied the existence of an original supernatural condition (see introd. to 527).

THE SIXTEENTH COUNCIL OF CARTHAGE, 418

In August, 416, the provincial councils of Carthage (sixty-three bishops) and Milevis (sixty bishops) condemned the principal errors of Pelagius and informed Pope St. Innocent I (401–17) of their condemnation. The pope fully agreed with the sentence passed upon Pelagius by the Carthaginian bishops.

Pope St. Zosimus (417–18), Innocent's successor in the papacy, deceived by the ambiguous statements of Pelagius, sent word to the African bishops that Pelagius was absolved from the excommunication. The bishops, knowing Pelagius's deceit, wrote Pope Zosimus that he should hold to the sentence pronounced by Pope Innocent I against Pelagius. Pope Zosimus then wrote the African bishops that he was transmitting all the documents to them for their common consultation. As a result of this letter, on May 1, 418, the African bishops, about two hundred of them, held another council and composed a series of canons against Pelagius (*see also 527–32, cans. 3–8*). They were confirmed by Pope Zosimus.

367
(101)
1. All the bishops who were gathered in the holy Council of the Church of Carthage agreed on this: whoever says that Adam, the first man, was created mortal so that, whether he sinned or not, he would have died a bodily death, that is, he would have departed from the body, not as a punishment for sin but by the necessity of his nature: let him be anathema.

CATALOGUE OF ERRORS ON GRACE AND ORIGINAL SIN, *cir.* 435-42

This document, the famous *Indiculus*, was apparently collected by St. Prosper of Aquitaine some time between 435 and 442. By the year 500 it was universally recognized as containing the traditional Catholic doctrine of the Holy See against Pelagian and Semi-Pelagian errors. The first chapter of the *Indiculus* teaches that after original sin man cannot rise from his fallen state without God's grace.

368
(130)
Chapter 1. All men lost their "natural powers" and their innocence in the sin of Adam. And no one is capable of rising from the depths of this loss by his own free will if the grace

of the merciful God does not lift him up. In this sense Pope
Innocent of happy memory declared and wrote in his letter
to the Council of Carthage: "At one time man fully exploited
his free will when, using his gifts too freely, he fell and sank
into the abyss of sin. And he found no way to rise from those
depths. Deceived by his powers of free choice, he would
have been eternally crushed by his fall, if the coming of Christ
afterwards had not gratuitously lifted him up, and, through
the cleansing of a new regeneration, taken away every sin
of the past in the bath of his baptism."

THE SECOND COUNCIL OF ORANGE, 529

This council was approved by Pope Boniface II (530-32) on
January 25, 531 (*see introd. to 543*). Its main task was to combat Semi-Pelagian errors and to vindicate St. Augustine's
teaching on grace. The following canons have reference to the
true doctrine on the nature of man's original innocence and his
sin.

Original sin

1. If anyone says that it was not the whole man, that is,   **369**
both body and soul, that was "changed for the worse" through   **(174)**
the offense of Adam's sin, but believes that the freedom of the
soul remained untouched and that only the body was made
subject to corruption, he is deceived by the error of Pelagius
and contradicts the words of Scripture: "The soul that sinneth, the same shall die" (*Ezech. 18:20*); and: "Do you not
know that to whom you offer yourselves as slaves for obedience, to him whom you obey you are the slaves?" (*Rom. 6:16*);
and: "By whatever a man is overcome, of that he also becomes
the slave" (*see II Pet. 2:19*).

2. If anyone asserts that Adam's sin was injurious only to   **370**
Adam and not to his descendants, or if he declares that it was **(175)**
only the death of the body which is punishment for sin, and
not the sin, the death of the soul, that passed from one man
to all the human race, he attributes an injustice to God and
contradicts the words of the Apostle: "Through one man sin
entered into the world and through sin death, and thus death
has passed into all men because all have sinned" (*see Rom.
5:12*).

God the Creator and Sanctifier

THE COUNCIL OF TRENT, 1545-63

The Council of Trent, the nineteenth ecumenical council, opened on December 13, 1545, and, although there were two interruptions, it continued through the reigns of five popes until December 4, 1563. It met to provide a Catholic reform and a counter-reform against the Reformers and to declare to the faithful the true Catholic faith (*see introd. to 95*). The following definitions about original sin and its consequences were approved in the fifth session, June 17, 1546.

DECREE ON ORIGINAL SIN

371
(787)
Our Catholic faith, without which it is impossible to please God (*see Heb. 11:6*), must remain in its purity, sound, unshaken, and free from errors. The Christian people must not be carried about with every wind of doctrine (*see Eph. 4:14*). But that serpent of old, the perpetual enemy of the human race, in addition to the many other evils with which he troubles the Church of God in our day, has revived old controversies and started new ones about original sin and its remedy. Therefore, the holy, ecumenical, and general Council of Trent has assembled lawfully in the Holy Spirit. Under the supervision of the same three legates of the Apostolic See, she wishes at this time to turn her attention to recall those who have strayed and to strengthen those who have remained in agreement; and having followed the testimony of Holy Scripture, of the holy Fathers, and of the approved councils, and the judgment and consent of the Church, she determines, professes, and declares the following doctrine on original sin.

372
(788)
1. If anyone does not profess that the first man Adam immediately lost the justice and holiness in which he was constituted when he disobeyed the command of God in the Garden of Paradise; and that, through the offense of this sin, he incurred the wrath and the indignation of God, and consequently incurred the death with which God had previously threatened him and, together with death, bondage in the power of him who from that time had the empire of death (*see Heb. 2:14*), that is, of the devil; "and that it was the whole Adam, both body and soul, who was changed for the worse through the offense of this sin" (*see 369*): let him be anathema

2. "If anyone asserts that Adam's sin was injurious only to Adam and not to his descendants," and that it was for himself alone that he lost the holiness and justice which he had received from God, and not for us also; or that after his defilement by the sin of disobedience, he "transmitted to the whole human race only death" and punishment "of the body but not sin itself which is the death of the soul": let him be anathema. "For he contradicts the words of the Apostle: 'As through one man sin entered into the world and through sin death, and thus death has passed into all men because all have sinned'" (*see Rom. 5:12; 370*).

373
(789)

3. If anyone says that this sin of Adam, which is one by origin, and which is communicated to all men by propagation not by imitation, and which is in all men and proper to each, is taken away either through the powers of human nature or through a remedy other than the merit of the one mediator, our Lord Jesus Christ who reconciled us to God in his blood, having become for us justice, and sanctification, and redemption (*see I Cor. 1:30*); or, if anyone says that, through the sacrament of baptism rightly conferred in the form of the Church, this merit of Christ Jesus is not applied to adults and to infants alike: let him be anathema. Because "there is no other name under heaven given to men by which we must be saved" (*Acts 4:12*). Hence the words: "Behold the lamb of God, behold him who takes away the sins of the world" (*see John 1:29*). And: "All you who have been baptized into Christ, have put on Christ" (*Gal. 3:27*).

374
(790)

4. "If anyone denies that newly born infants are to be baptized," even though they may have been born of baptized parents, "or says that they are indeed baptized for the remission of sins but that they do not contract from Adam any original sin that must be expiated in the bath of regeneration" to obtain eternal life; "and, consequently, that for them the form of baptism—for the remission of sins—is to be understood, not in a true, but in a false sense: let him be anathema. Because the words of the Apostle: 'As through one man sin entered into the world and through sin death, and thus death has passed into all men because all have sinned' (*see Rom. 5:12*), cannot be understood in any other way than as the

375
(791)

Catholic Church everywhere has always understood them. Because of this rule of faith, in accordance with apostolic tradition even infants, who have not yet been able to commit any personal sins, are baptized for the remission of sin in a very true sense, that they may be cleansed by regeneration of what they have contracted by generation." For "unless a man be born again of water and the Holy Spirit, he cannot enter into the kingdom of God" (*John 3:5*).

876
(792)
5. If anyone says that through the grace of our Lord Jesus Christ conferred in baptism the guilt of original sin is not remitted, or even says that not everything having the true and proper nature of sin is taken away but is only brushed over or not imputed: let him be anathema. For God hates nothing in the regenerated because there is no condemnation for those truly buried with Christ by means of baptism into death (*see Rom. 6:4*), who do not walk according to the flesh (*see Rom. 8:1*), but putting off the old man and putting on the new man which was created according to God (*see Eph. 4:22 ff.; Col. 3:9 f.*), are made innocent, without stain, pure, no longer hateful, but beloved sons of God, heirs, indeed, of God and joint heirs with Christ (*see Rom. 8:17*) so that absolutely nothing delays their entrance into heaven. It is the mind of this council and it professes that concupiscence or the tendency to sin remains in the baptized; but since it is left to provide a trial, it has no power to injure those who do not consent and who, by the grace of Christ Jesus, manfully resist. Moreover, those who compete according to the rules will be crowned (*see II Tim. 2:5*). As for this concupiscence, which the Apostle sometimes calls sin (*see Rom. 6:12 ff.*), this holy council declares that the Catholic Church has never understood that it is called sin because there is, in the regenerated, sin in the true and proper sense but only because it is from sin and inclines to sin. If anyone thinks the contrary: let him be anathema.

6. Nevertheless this same holy council declares that it is not its intention to include in this decree on original sin the blessed and immaculate Virgin Mary, Mother of God; but it declares that the constitutions of Pope Sixtus IV of happy

memory are to be observed under the penalties contained in these constitutions; and it renews these penalties here.

CONDEMNED ERRORS OF MICHEL DE BAY, 1567

The very clear pronouncements of the Council of Trent about original justice and original sin did not prevent subtle errors about the supernaturalness of that justice and the effects of that sin from spreading among Catholics.

Michel de Bay (*cir.* 1513–89), professor of theology at Louvain, denied that the gifts of integrity and immortality which man had before the Fall were truly supernatural. In this he agreed with the Pelagians. He claimed that sin destroyed man's natural powers to such an extent that without God's grace he could do nothing but sin. In this he agreed with the Protestants. De Bay's great injury to the Church was his influence on Jansen (*see introd. to* 627). For the historical background of these errors and their condemnation by Pope St. Pius V, October 1, 1567, see the introduction to 608.

21. The elevation of human nature to a participation of the divine nature was due to the integrity of man in his first state and for that reason should be called natural, not supernatural. **377** (*1021*)

26. The integrity found in first creation was not a gratuitous elevation of human nature, but its natural condition. **378** (*1026*)

46. Voluntariness does not pertain to the essence and definition of sin; nor is the question whether every sin must be voluntary one of definition, but of cause and origin. **379** (*1046*)

47. Hence, original sin truly has the essence of sin without any relation or reference to the will from which it took its origin. **380** (*1047*)

48. Original sin is voluntary by reason of the habitual will of an infant, and it holds sway habitually in infants because there is no contrary exercise of choice in the will. **381** (*1048*)

49. And under the sway of this habitual will it happens that an infant who dies without the sacrament of regeneration, when he does obtain the use of reason, actually has hatred for God, blasphemes God, and rejects the law of God. **382** (*1049*)

383
(1055)
55. God could not from the beginning have created man in the state in which he is now born.

384
(1078)
78. The immortality of the first man was not a gift of grace, but his natural condition.

THE VATICAN COUNCIL, 1869-70

SCHEMA OF THE DOGMATIC CONSTITUTION ON THE PRINCIPAL MYSTERIES OF THE FAITH

In the schema that had been prepared (*see introd. to 314*) there was a chapter on the elevation and Fall of man. It was the intention of the council to make a dogmatic pronouncement about this matter, but it did not have sufficient time to do so. **The document is included here, not as having dogmatic authority in itself, but as a noteworthy statement of Catholic doctrine.** (The following translation is made from the text given in *Collectio Lacensis*, VII, 555 ff., 566.)

Chapter 3. The Elevation and Fall of Man

385
Moreover, in this beginning of the human race, the Christian faith sees a great mystery of divine goodness. Man was created in the image of God and, by his very nature, ordained to know, worship, and love God in a way proper to his innate ability. But God, the supreme creator and lord of creation, whose power is not limited by the properties and laws of created nature, in his infinite goodness, willed to raise the human race, in the person of its first parent, to a sublime state superior to man's natural condition. In this state man is made partaker of the divine nature itself (*see II Pet. 1:4*). And so, in addition to the gifts that perfect man's own nature, God poured out the Holy Spirit into man, so that he who is by nature a slave, might become, by the grace of holiness, a son. From then on, man might obey God's commands and perform works of virtue, not with the strength of his unaided nature, but with the charity poured out from heaven, and thus he might merit an eternal inheritance. In addition, God, by his grace, made the flesh fully subject to the spirit, and took away from mortal man the fear of death. For man was certainly mortal because of the condition of his animal body; he was immortal through a gift of the Creator.

Original Justice and Original Sin

God placed man in the happiness of Paradise, as in a fore- **386**
taste of life, and endowed him with free will, but in such a
way that He could rule man with His commands and inspire
fear in him by death. God put before man life and death, and
if he chose life, he was to grow in all virtues and pass to the
kingdom of God. There he would see the God of gods, not as
God can be seen by man's natural powers, but face to face,
as God is in himself. Man would be transformed in God by
this vision, and would drink his fill at the font of divine pleasure.

This is the elevation of man which Catholic teachers, after **387**
the example of the holy Fathers, have correctly called a supernatural elevation. It is supernatural because it transcends both
the powers and the exigency of created nature, and, therefore, is not due to man's merits nor to his natural condition,
but is a purely gratuitous gift of God's goodness.

But man, ungrateful to his Creator and Father, freely vio- **388**
lated God's command, and together with his descendants, he
fell from the supernatural state to which he had been elevated.
He incurred the anger and the wrath of God; he lost holiness
and justice for himself and for us; and defiled by sin, he
handed down to the entire human race not only death and
corporal punishment, but sin, the death of the soul. This sin
of Adam is transmitted to all his children by propagation,
not by imitation; and it constitutes each man in the condition
of a sinner. This is what the Church has always taught, and
what the Council of Trent has defined. With the approval of
the present council, We renew the decrees of the Council of
Trent.

All the faithful must firmly believe and constantly profess **389**
that the Blessed Virgin Mary, the Mother of God, from the
very first instant of her conception, by a singular grace and
privilege of almighty God, and in view of the merits of
Christ, the savior of the human race, was preserved free from
every stain of original sin. This We have declared and defined
in Our apostolic constitution *Ineffabilis Deus*.

Canons on Chapter 3

390   1. If anyone does not profess that the human race, in the person of its first parent, was elevated to a supernatural state: let him be anathema.

391   2. If anyone says that a supernatural order is to be admitted only insofar as whatever does not pertain to the essential perfection of man can be said to be supernatural; and if anyone does not confess that there are divine gifts and institutions which surpass the powers and the exigency of created nature and perfect it beyond its own order: let him be anathema.

392   3. If anyone says that the sanctity and justice, in which man was established before the Fall, were not supernatural, but were of such a nature that man could attain them by living a good life according to his innate natural faculties: let him be anathema.

393   4. If anyone says that original sin is not truly and properly sin in the descendants of Adam unless they approve of original sin by actual consent in sinning: let him be anathema.

394   5. If anyone says that original sin is formally concupiscence or that it is a physical or a substantial disease of human nature; or if he says that the privation of sanctifying grace is not of the essence of original sin: let him be anathema.

THE ENCYCLICAL *HUMANI GENERIS*, 1950

This important encyclical of Pope Pius XII (1939–58), published August 12, 1950, warned the faithful of new errors that threatened Catholic dogma (*see introd. to 141*). Among these errors was an opinion that threatened the very notion of the supernatural.

395
(2318)   . . . Others destroy the gratuitous character of the supernatural order, by suggesting that it would be impossible for God to create rational beings without equipping them for the beatific vision and calling them to it. Not content with that, they throw over the definitions of the Council of Trent by misrepresenting the whole nature of original sin, and indeed of sin in general, considered as an offence against God; the whole nature, too, of satisfaction which Christ offered on our behalf.

The Incarnation and Redemption

After the sin of Adam, man could no longer attain the supernatural end to which he had been ordered by God. It was to redeem men from this condition that the Son of God, the Second Person of the Blessed Trinity, became man himself. By his sacrificial death on the cross, Jesus Christ merited for men their reinstatement as sons of God. Baptized into his mystical body, they are to possess their supernatural goal forever with him, "when he hands over the kingdom to God the Father" (I Cor. 15:24).

After the mystery of the most Holy Trinity, the Incarnation of the Son of God is the greatest mystery of the Christian religion. Because it is so difficult to understand, this mystery has been the subject of innumerable heresies. In opposition to these errors the Church has tirelessly explained the true doctrine about the character and person of Jesus Christ, aware that, in the present order, the salvation of men depends on a correct understanding of who Christ is and on a willing cooperation with the work of salvation that Christ inaugurated.

Because of the Incarnation which united the divine nature with a human nature in his own divine person, Christ was a high priest and mediator between God and man. As priest he offered himself, the victim, in the sacrifice of the cross to atone for men's sins and reconcile them to God. It remains for men to apply to themselves the merits of his sacrifice by their own cooperation with the graces won by Christ.

The same decree of divine Wisdom that willed the Incarnation of the Son of God also closely associated the mother of the

God-man with him in his redemptive work. Hence, Mary was adorned with special privileges of grace to fit her to fill her role as Coredemptress. She was perpetually a virgin; yet she was also not only mother of Christ but in the truest sense Mother of God.

Christ taught men the way to salvation by his words and by the example of his life, a life ruled by love for God and men. Christian piety, therefore, taught by the Church, has honored and imitated the actions of Christ's earthly life. It has also held in special reverence the lives and persons of those who, like Mary, the Mother of God, and the other saints, martyrs, confessors, and virgins, have succeeded most perfectly in reproducing the ways of Christ in their own lives.

The Person of the Redeemer

THE COUNCIL OF ROME, 382

The Tome of Damasus

Though directed principally at Trinitarian errors (*see introd. to 284*), the anathemas of Pope St. Damasus I (366–84) also were directed at related errors in Christology. The sixth canon is against the doctrine of Diodorus of Tarsus who said there was a duality of sonships in Christ, the one natural, the other adoptive; the seventh canon rejects Apollinaris's heresy; the fourteenth canon condemns both Patripassianism (monarchianism) and the older error of Marcion that the Son's human nature was not a true human nature.

396
(64) (6) We anathematize those who say that there are two Sons, one existing before time, another after the assumption of human nature from the Virgin.

397
(65) (7) We anathematize those who say that in the human body [*of Christ*] the Word of God dwelt in place of the rational and intellective human soul; because the very Son and Word of God did not take the place of the rational and intellective soul in his body, but he assumed and preserved a

soul like ours (that is, a rational and intellective soul) but without sin.

(14) If anyone says that in the suffering of the cross it was God who felt the pain and that it was not felt by the body and soul with which Christ the Son of God had clothed himself—the servant's form which he had assumed, in the words of Scripture (*see Phil. 2:7*): such a person is in error.

398
(72)

THE COUNCIL OF EPHESUS, 431

The heresy of Nestorius which posited a double personality, a divine and a human, in Christ, found its greatest opponent in St. Cyril of Alexandria. It was the latter's dogmatic letter to the heresiarch Nestorius that the Council of Ephesus, the third ecumenical council, adopted as an expression of orthodox Catholic belief when it met in its first session on July 22, 431. Since the God-man was one Divine Person, his mother could rightly be called the *Mother of God*. This appellation of the Virgin Mary had become a focal point of the dispute between Nestorius's followers and the Catholics.

For we do not say that the nature of the Word became man by undergoing change; nor that it was transformed into a complete man consisting of soul and body. What we say, rather, is that by uniting to himself in his own person a body animated by a rational soul, the Word has become man in an inexpressible and incomprehensible way and has been called the Son of man; not merely according to will or complacency, but not by merely assuming a person either. And we say that the natures that are brought together into true unity are different; still, from both there is one Christ and Son; not as though the difference between the natures were taken away by their union, but rather both divinity and humanity produce the perfection of our one Lord, Christ and Son, by their inexpressible and mysterious joining into unity. . . . It was not that first an ordinary human being was born of the holy Virgin, and then the Word descended upon that man; but in virtue of the union he is said to have undergone birth according to the flesh from his mother's womb, since he claims as his own birth, the generation of his own flesh. . . . Thus

399
(111a)

The Incarnation and Redemption

[*the holy Fathers of the Church*] have not hesitated to call the holy Virgin *Mother of God.*

ST. CYRIL'S ANATHEMATISMS AGAINST NESTORIUS

The year before the Council of Ephesus, St. Cyril of Alexandria (376–444) had written these famous twelve condemnations of Nestorian errors relating to Christ. No conciliar approval has ever been given to these anathematisms of St. Cyril; but their orthodoxy is incontestable. St. Cyril's terminology so emphasized the unity of person in Christ that the Monophysites were later able to invoke his patronage for their error that Christ had but one nature. The third and fourth canons exemplify the difficulties caused by Cyril's terminology (*see 498*). Still, his insistence on the title *Mother of God* for the Virgin Mary is itself a guarantee of the accuracy of St. Cyril's Christology.

400
(113)
1. If anyone does not profess that Emmanuel is truly God and that the holy Virgin is, therefore, Mother of God (for she gave birth in the flesh to the Word of God made flesh): let him be anathema.

401
(114)
2. If anyone does not profess that the Word of God the Father was hypostatically united to flesh and that Christ is one having his own flesh, that is, one person who is both God and man: let him be anathema.

402
(115)
3. If, in reference to the one Christ, anyone makes a division of the hypostases after the union, joining them in a mere association of dignity, or of authority or of power, and not, rather, in a real physical union: let him be anathema. [*Cyril identifies* φύσις (nature) *and* ὑπόστασις (substance, hypostasis). *He often uses the one for the other, thus showing that he regards them as synonymous.*]

403
(116)
4. If anyone takes the words found in the writings of the Gospels and of the apostles, whether they are said of Christ by the saints or of Christ by himself, and distributes them between two persons or hypostases, attributing some of them as to a man, properly understood in contrast to the Word of God, and the rest to the Word of God the Father exclusively, on the grounds that they are proper to God alone: let him be anathema. [*Sometimes, as in this canon, Cyril gives to* ὑπόστασις *the meaning* person. *Sometimes, too, he uses* φύσις

in the same sense. This ambiguity was not finally removed
from orthodox terminology until the Council of Chalcedon.
Its definition canonized the Western usage according to which
ὑπόστασις was reserved to mean person in contradistinction to
οὐσία or φύσις, which were kept to mean substance or nature
respectively.]

5. If anyone dares to say that Christ is a man bearing God
within him and not, rather, that he is truly God as he is the
only Son of God by nature, inasmuch as the Word was made
flesh and is a sharer like ourselves in flesh and blood (*see
Heb. 2:14*): let him be anathema.

404
(117)

6. If anyone dares to say that the Word of God the Father
is God or Lord over Christ and does not, rather, profess that
He himself is both God and man, because the Word was made
flesh according to the Scriptures (*see John 1:14*): let him be
anathema.

405
(118)

7. If anyone asserts that the man Jesus was actuated by
God the Word, and that he was invested with the glory of the
Only-begotten, as though the man Jesus were someone other
than the Word: let him be anathema.

406
(119)

8. If anyone dares to say that the man assumed ought to be
co-adored with God the Word, and co-glorified and co-named
God, as one person in another (for this is the interpretation
that the constant addition of *co-* will lead to); and does not,
rather, adore Emmanuel with one adoration and apply to him
one doxology, inasmuch as the Word was made flesh (*see John
1:14*): let him be anathema.

407
(120)

9. If anyone says that the one Lord Jesus Christ was glorified by the Spirit as though through the Spirit Jesus exercised
a power not proper to himself, and as though he had received
from Him the ability to act against unclean spirits and to
work miracles among men; and if he does not say, rather,
that the Spirit by which he worked the miracles was his very
own: let him be anathema.

408
(121)

10. The divine Scripture says that Christ became the high
priest and apostle of our confession (*see Heb. 3:1*), and he

409
(122)

offered himself up for us to God the Father in the odor of sweetness (*see Eph. 5:2*). If anyone, therefore, says that it was not the Word of God himself who was born to be our high priest and apostle when he was made flesh (*see John 1:14*) and a man like us, but that, properly speaking, it was another man, distinct from Him, who was born of woman; or if anyone says that He presented His offering for Himself as well and not solely on our behalf (for as He was sinless, He had no need of any offering): let him be anathema.

410
(123) 11. If anyone does not profess that the flesh of the Lord is life-giving and that it belongs to the very Word of God the Father, but professes instead that it belongs to someone other than Him, who was linked with Him by dignity, or to someone who merely had a divine indwelling; and if he does not profess, rather, that this flesh is life-giving, as we declared, because it was made proper to the Word who has power to give life to all things: let him be anathema.

411
(124) 12. If anyone does not profess that the Word of God suffered in the flesh, and was crucified in the flesh, and experienced death in the flesh, and became the first-born from the dead (*see Col. 1:18*), inasmuch as he is, as God, both life and giver of life: let him be anathema.

LETTER TO FLAVIUS, PATRIARCH OF CONSTANTINOPLE, 449

Opposition to Nestorianism and devotion to the terminology of St. Cyril had led a group of Alexandrian partisans, helped by Eutyches (*cir.* 375–*cir.* 454), a politically influential monk in Constantinople, to affirm so complete a union of the divinity and humanity in Christ that after the Incarnation there was but one divine-human nature in Christ. This error was the beginning of Monophysitism. When Eutyches had been condemned by Flavian, bishop of Constantinople, he appealed to Rome for redress. Pope St. Leo the Great (440–61) sent a letter to the bishop of Constantinople expounding "what the Catholic Church universally believes and teaches." The letter, which came to be known as the Tome of Leo, was later accepted by the Council of Chaledon (451) as an accurate expression of the traditional teaching on the two natures and one person of Christ.

(3) Hence, the proper character of each nature was kept inviolate, and together they were united in one person. Thus was lowliness assumed by majesty, weakness by power, mortality by eternity; and a nature that could not be defiled was united to one that could suffer in order to repay the debt attaching to our state. Hence, as was suitable for the alleviation of our distress, one and the same mediator between God and men, himself man, Christ Jesus (*see I Tim.* 2:5), was both mortal and immortal under different aspects. In the full and perfect nature of true man, therefore, the true God was born —perfect in every characteristic proper to us as well as in every one proper to himself.

412
(*143*)

(4) And so the Son of God, descending from his heavenly throne, yet not leaving the glory of the Father, enters into this world's weakness and is generated in a new manner, born with a new birth. He is generated in a new manner: because, though invisible in his divine nature, he has become visible in ours; and, though surpassing comprehension, he has wished to be comprehended; though remaining prior to all time, he has taken on existence in time; and, though Lord of the universe, he has hidden his limitless majesty and assumed the form of a servant. God though he is, subject neither to suffering nor death, he has not disdained to become man, subject to both suffering and the law of death. With a new birth too he has been born: for a virgin undefiled, though experiencing no carnal pleasure, furnished the substance for his human flesh. From his mother, our Lord received his nature, but no guilt. Yet the miraculous manner of our Lord Jesus Christ's birth, born as he was from the womb of a virgin, does not make his nature any different from ours. For the same person is true God and true man; and there is no deception in this unity in which the lowliness of man and the dignity of God are joined. For, as God, he suffers no change because of his condescension, nor as man, is he absorbed by the divine dignity; for each nature performs the functions proper to itself, yet in conjunction with the other nature: the Word does what is proper to the Word, and the humanity what is proper to the humanity. The one shines forth in miracles; the other is the subject of mistreatment. And as the Word does not leave

413
(*144*)

aside the glory that he has, equal to the Father's, neither does the humanity relinquish the nature of our race.

THE COUNCIL OF CHALCEDON, 451

In addition to accepting Leo's Tome, the Council of Chalcedon, the fourth ecumenical council, also issued, at the emperor's insistance, a declaration of faith. It embodied the traditional doctrine in considerable detail and in Leo's terminology. The supreme importance of the Council of Chalcedon in the development of Christology is its crystallization of an unambiguous terminology for expressing the truths of the Incarnation (*see 496–501*).

414
(148)
Following the holy Fathers, therefore, we all with one accord teach the profession of faith in the one identical Son, our Lord Jesus Christ. We declare that he is perfect both in his divinity and in his humanity, truly God and truly man composed of body and rational soul; that he is consubstantial with the Father in his divinity, consubstantial with us in his humanity, like us in every respect except for sin (*see Heb. 4:15*). We declare that in his divinity he was begotten of the Father before time, and in his humanity he was begotten in this last age of Mary the Virgin, the Mother of God, for us and for our salvation. We declare that the one selfsame Christ, only-begotten Son and Lord, must be acknowledged in two natures without any commingling or change or division or separation; that the distinction between the natures is in no way removed by their union but rather that the specific character of each nature is preserved and they are united in one person and one hypostasis. We declare that he is not split or divided into two persons, but that there is one selfsame only-begotten Son, God the Word, the Lord Jesus Christ. This the prophets have taught about him from the beginning; this Jesus Christ himself taught us; this the creed of the Fathers has handed down to us (*see 2, 3*).

As these truths, therefore, have been formulated with all possible accuracy and care, the holy, ecumenical council has ordained that no one may bring forward or put into writing or devise or entertain or teach to others any other faith.

LETTER TO THE SENATE AT CONSTANTINOPLE, 534

After the Council of Chalcedon many Monophysitic bishops remained stubbornly convinced that Chalcedon had denied the faith of Ephesus and of St. Cyril and had accepted a Nestorian position. To reconcile the dissidents with the Catholics, the emperor strove to obtain bilateral recognition of the formula: "One of the Trinity suffered in the flesh" (see 411). The Cyrillian origin of the formula would guarantee its acceptability to the Monophysites; Catholic acceptance of the formula would clear them of any charge of Nestorianism. Pope John II (533–35) wrote the following letter in March, 534, in reply to Justinian's queries about this formula.

Our son the Emperor Justinian has pointed out, as you have learned from the contents of his letter, that disputes have arisen over these three questions: Whether Christ can be said to be one of the Trinity and our God, that is, whether he is one holy person of the three persons of the Holy Trinity? Whether Christ our God suffered in his human nature though in his divinity he was incapable of suffering? . . . Regarding these questions We have been satisfied that the emperor's faith is the Catholic faith and We have certified to it by citations from the prophets, the apostles, and the Fathers. For in the examples given, We clearly show that Christ is one of the Holy Trinity, that is, one holy person of the three persons of the Holy Trinity; in other words, a subsistent being, which the Greeks call a *hypostasis* [*various testimonies are cited: Gen. 3:22; I Cor. 8:6; Nicene Creed; Proclus's letter to the West; etc.*]. As for the truth that God did suffer in his human nature, let Us confirm it likewise by the following citations [*Deut. 28:66; John 14:6; Mal. 3:8; Acts 3:15, 20:28; I Cor. 2:8; St. Cyril's twelfth anathematism; St. Leo's letter to Flavian; etc.*].

415
(201)

THE SECOND COUNCIL OF CONSTANTINOPLE, 553

A further outcome of Justinian's attempt to reconcile the Monophysites with the Catholics was the condemnation of the so-called Three Chapters. This formula was used to describe certain works and doctrines of Theodore of Mopsuestia (cir. 350–cir. 428) and two others, Theodoret of Cyrrhus (cir. 390–cir. 457) and Ibas of Edessa (cir. 380–cir. 457). Theodore had been a prominent bishop and a combatant of Apollinarism and Arianism; but it was claimed by some that his writings unquestionably contain not just the seeds, but the full-blown heresy of Nestorianism. The censures of the council and of the pope attach to opinions contained in citations from a Greek version of the Emperor Justinian. At present a debate is going on whether and how far these Greek translations represent the true thought of the Syriac of Theodore. The outcome of this debate will not change the fact that these citations (whether they represent the true doctrine of Theodore or not) stand condemned.

As anti-Nestorian feeling plus an enthusiastic devotedness to to St. Cyril of Alexandria (and his ambiguous terminology) were important factors in the persistence of Monophysitism, Justinian hoped that the condemnation of the Three Chapters would win from the Monophysites the acceptance of Chalcedon. For these reasons the anathematisms repeatedly belabor the Nestorian errors and their defenders and heap praise on St. Cyril of Alexandria as the champion of orthodoxy (canons 13–14). However, the eighth canon expressly insists, for the benefit of the Monophysites, on the orthodox sense of St. Cyril's famous phrase, "one incarnate nature of the Word of God," which had been used by the Monophysites to support their denial of two natures in Christ (*see also 434 and introd. to 431*). There can be no doubt that the orthodox interpretation of this terminology is justified. It continued to be used, even in the West, for centuries. The provincial council at Rheims (1148), which condemned the errors of Gilbert of Porrée, spoke in the very same sense when it declared: "We believe (and we profess) that the divinity itself—whether one calls it the divine substance or the divine nature—was made incarnate, but in the person of the Son" (*DB 392*).

It was only after endless political maneuvers that Justinian won Pope Vigilius's (537?–55) acceptance in February, 554, of the condemnation issued by the Second Council of Constantinople, the fifth ecumenical council, the previous June, 553. (The text from which the seventh canon is translated is that given in Charles J. Hefele, translated by William R. Clark, *A History of the Councils of the Church*, IV [Edinburgh, 1895], 333–34.)

Anathematisms of the Three Chapters

416
(213)
1. If anyone denies that Father, Son, and Holy Spirit are one nature or substance, one supreme power, a consubstantial Trinity, one Godhead adored in three hypostases or persons: let such a one be anathema. For there is one God and Father, from whom are all things, and one Lord Jesus Christ, through whom are all things, and one Holy Spirit, in whom are all things.

2. If anyone does not profess that there are two births of   **417**
the divine Word—the first before time, timeless, not in body,   **(214)**
from the Father; the other in this last age, when the Word
descended from heaven and took flesh of the holy and glorious
Mother of God and ever-Virgin Mary and was born of her:
let such a one be anathema.

3. If anyone says that the Word of God who worked   **418**
miracles was someone other than the Christ who suffered, or   **(215)**
that the divine Word was joined with the Christ who had
been born of woman, or that He was in him as one person
within another; and does not, rather, say that he who was
made flesh and became man is the one, selfsame Jesus Christ
our Lord, the Word of God, and that both the miracles and
the sufferings which he voluntarily endured in his humanity
are his: let such a one be anathema.

4. If anyone says that the union of the divine Word with   **419**
man was effected through grace, or operation, or equality of   **(216)**
privileges, or through authority, or reference, or position, or
power; or if he says that it was by way of good pleasure as
though the divine Word was pleased with the man, because
He conceived a very high estimation of him, as Theodore
foolishly asserts; or if he says it is by way of homonymic
designation, in virtue of which the Nestorians call the divine
Word Jesus [*Latin version reads "Son" for "Jesus"*] and Christ,
and separately name the man Christ and Son, thus evidently
asserting two persons while pretending to speak of one person, and one Christ, but only by reason of appellation, honor,
dignity, and adoration; and does not, rather, profess that the
union of the divine Word with flesh animated by a rational,
intellectual soul took place by composition, that is, hypostatically, as the holy Fathers taught; and consequently denies
that he who is the Lord Jesus Christ, one of the Holy Trinity,
is one hypostasis: let such a one be anathema. For since *union*
is understood in a number of senses, some, following the
godlessness of Apollinaris and Eutyches and intent upon the
destruction of the component elements, maintain a union by
commingling. Others, who think with Theodore and Nestorius,
and who are delighted in the division, introduce an accidental
union. However, the holy Church of God, rejecting the god-

lessness of either heresy, confesses a union of the divine Word with flesh by composition; that is to say, a hypostatic union. For the union by composition, in the mystery of Christ, preserves the component elements without any commingling, while at the same time it does not admit of any separation.

420
(217)
5. If anyone so understands the "one hypostasis" of our Lord Jesus Christ that it admits of meaning many hypostases and so tries to introduce two hypostases, or two persons, into the mystery of Christ, and speaks of the two persons, which he introduces, as if they were a single person according to dignity, honor, and adoration, as Theodore and Nestorius foolishly wrote; and if he makes the slanderous assertion that the holy Council of Chalcedon used the expression "one hypostasis" in this godless sense, and does not profess, rather, that the Word of God was united to flesh hypostatically and that he, therefore, has but one hypostasis, or person; and that in this sense the holy Council of Chalcedon confessed one hypostasis of our Lord Jesus Christ: let such a one be anathema. For even when the divine Word, one of the Holy Trinity, became flesh, the Holy Trinity did not acquire an additional person, or hypostasis.

421
(218)
6. If anyone says that the glorious, ever-Virgin Mary is not the Mother of God in a true sense, but only by a misuse of language; or that she is Mother of God in a transferred sense as though a mere man were born of her and not the divine Word Incarnate; but that, according to them, the birth of the man is to be attributed to the divine Word because He was joined to the man at his birth; and if he makes the slanderous assertion that it was in this blasphemous sense, thought up by Theodore, that the holy Council of Chalcedon said the Virgin was Mother of God; or if anyone calls her *mother of man* or *mother of Christ* as if Christ were not God, and does not admit that in the proper sense and in all truth she is Mother of God, because the divine Word who was born of the Father before time took flesh of her in this last age, and that the holy Council of Chalcedon also confessed her to be Mother of God in this holy sense: let such a one be anathema.

176

The Person of the Redeemer

7. If anyone, in using the phrase "in two natures," does not profess that the one Jesus Christ our Lord is acknowledged in divinity and humanity, so that by this phrase he indicates the distinction between the natures from which the ineffable union is made without any commingling, without either the Word being transformed into the nature of the humanity nor the humanity changing over into the nature of the Word (for each remains what it is by nature, even after the hypostatic union); but if he takes this phrase as meaning a division into parts within the mystery of Christ, or if, while professing plurality of natures in the one selfsame Jesus, our Lord, the divine Word Incarnate, he does not understand that the elements of which He was composed are separated only in reflective thought, since it is true that their distinction was not destroyed by the union—for He is one from both and is both through One—but instead uses plurality as meaning that the natures are separate and each its own hypostasis: let such a one be anathema.

422
(219)

8. If anyone, though professing that the union was made from two natures, from divinity and humanity, or though saying that there is one incarnate nature of the Word of God, does not understand these expressions in the same sense as the holy Fathers taught, namely, that the hypostatic union of the divine and the human natures resulted in one Christ; but if, instead, he tries in consequence of such expressions to introduce a single nature, or substance, of Christ's divinity and humanity: let such a one be anathema. For when we say that the only-begotten Word was hypostatically united, we do not mean that any commingling of the natures with each other occurred; but, rather, we understand that, with each nature remaining just what it is, the Word was united to humanity. And that is also why Christ, God and man, is one; the selfsame person is consubstantial with the Father in his divinity and consubstantial with us in his humanity; for the Church of God repudiates and condemns those who bring in separation or division just as much as those who bring commingling into the mystery of Christ, a mystery of divine arrangement.

423
(220)

424
(221)
9. If anyone says that Christ is adored in two natures, and thus introduces two adorations, one proper to the divine Word, the other proper to the man; or if, in order to destroy the humanity or to commingle the divinity and the humanity, anyone speaks falsely of a single nature or substance of the natures that have come together, and in this sense adores Christ; but does not rather adore with a single adoration the divine Word Incarnate with his own flesh, according to the tradition in the Church of God from the beginning: let such a one be anathema.

425
(222)
10. If anyone does not profess that our Lord Jesus Christ who was crucified in his humanity is truly God and Lord of glory and one of the Holy Trinity: let such a one be anathema.

426
(223)
11. If anyone does not condemn as heretics Arius, Eunomius, Macedonius, Apollinaris, Nestorius, Eutyches, and Origen, along with their impious writings, and condemn all the other heretics who were condemned by the holy, Catholic, and apostolic Church and by the four holy councils previously named, and condemn those who held or do hold opinions similar to those of the heretics just mentioned and who have remained in their godlessness up till death: let such a one be anathema.

427
(224)
12. If anyone defends the irreverent Theodore of Mopsuestia who said that God the Word is one person, while Christ is another person who was subject to disturbance by the passions of the soul and by the desires of the body, but who was gradually set free from inferior inclinations; and thus being made better through the improvement of his works, and becoming irreproachable by his conduct, he was baptized, though a mere man, in the name of the Father and Son and Holy Spirit; and through the baptism received the grace of the Holy Spirit, and was deemed worthy of adoption; and, as in the case of an imperial image, he is worshiped out of respect for the person of God the Word; and after his Resurrection he has become steadfast in purpose and wholly incapable of sin. Furthermore, the same irreverent Theodore has said that the union of God the Word with Christ is the

same kind as the Apostle describes in the case of man and
wife: "The two shall become one flesh" (*Eph. 5:31*). And in
addition to his other countless blasphemies, he dared to assert that when the Lord breathed on the disciples after his
Resurrection and said, "Receive the Holy Spirit" (*John 20:22*),
he did not give them the Holy Spirit, but breathed on them
merely as a symbol. And as for the confession made by
Thomas when he felt the hands and the side of the Lord after
the Resurrection—Theodore asserted that the words, "My
Lord and my God" (*John 20:28*), were not said by Thomas
about Christ, but that Thomas, struck with admiration over
the miracle of the Resurrection, praised God who had raised
Christ up.

And, worse still, in his explanation of the Acts of the Apostles, this Theodore compares Christ with Plato, Manes, Epi-
curus, and Marcion; and he says that just as each one of
those men devised his own doctrine and caused his own disciples to be called Platonists, Manichaeans, Epicureans, or
Marcionites, so likewise Christ devised his doctrine and
Christians were named after him. If anyone, therefore, defends
this utterly impious man Theodore and his sacrilegious writings in which he puts forth the blasphemies described and
countless others against our great God and Savior Jesus Christ;
and does not instead condemn Theodore and his sacrilegious
writings, together with all who accept them—either by justifying him or claiming that he has set forth orthodox doctrine
—and all who have written to defend him and his sacrilegious
writings, and all who hold similar opinions or who once held
them and remained in such heresy up till death: let such a
one be anathema.

13. If anyone defends the sacrilegious writings of Theodoret
against the true faith, against the first holy Council at Ephesus, and against Blessed Cyril and his twelve anathematisms
(*see 400 ff.*); or if he defends all that Theodoret has written
on behalf of the unrighteous men Theodore and Nestorius
or on behalf of those who hold the same opinions as Theodore
and Nestorius or who accept them together with their godlessness; and if he, therefore, brands as impious those teachers of the Church who hold the hypostatic union of God the

428
(225)

429
(226)

Word; and if he does not condemn the sacrilegious writings described and those who have held or hold like opinions, together with all who have written against the orthodox faith or against Blessed Cyril and his twelve anathematisms and who have died in such impiety: let such a one be anathema.

**430
(227)**

14. If anyone defends the letter, allegedly written by Ibas to the Persian Mari, which denies that God the Word became incarnate of the holy Mother of God and ever-Virgin Mary and became man, but asserts instead that a mere man, whom it terms a temple, was born of her and that God the Word is one person and that the man is someone else; furthermore, it makes the false charge that Blessed Cyril, who proclaimed the orthodox faith of Christians, is heretical and wrote in a vein like that of the unrighteous man Apollinaris; it criticizes the first holy Council at Ephesus as having condemned Nestorius without investigation; and the same sacrilegious letter calls the twelve anathematisms of Blessed Cyril sacrilegious and contrary to the orthodox faith, while it vindicates Theodore and Nestorius together with their godless doctrines and writings. If anyone, therefore, defends this letter, and does not instead condemn it and its defenders, together with those who say that it, or part of it, is right, or those who have written or do write in defense of it or its sacrilegious contents, or who dare, by an appeal to the holy Fathers or to the holy Council of Chalcedon, to vindicate it or the impieties it contains, and who remained in these errors up till death: let such a one be anathema.

THE COUNCIL OF THE LATERAN, 649

Another theologico-political attempt to reconcile Monophysites with orthodox Catholics was the theory advanced by Sergius, patriarch of Constantinople, that in Christ there was only one principle of operation; for example, for his acts of willing, there was only one will. The theory could be perfectly satisfactory to Monophysites, while Catholics might acknowledge the single principle of operation as the divine person, operating through two natures.

Stripped of ambiguity, the theory was but a radical Monophysitism, a new heresy that came to be known as Monothelitism (since it acknowledged only *one will* and one kind of operation in Christ). In 638, an edict of Emperor Heraclius had promulgated the heresy as sound doctrine; in 648 Emperor Constans II reaffirmed the former edict and forbade further discussion. Pope St. Martin I (649–53?) then convoked a council at Rome in 649, which definitively reviewed the entire orthodox Trinitarian and Christological doctrine and rejected every detail of Monothelitism in a series of anathematisms that have the weight of dogmas of faith. St. Cyril's troublesome expression, "one incarnate nature of God the Word," and the term *theandric operation* are given their official and orthodox explanations in canons five and fifteen. (The translation of canon ten omits the editorial suggestion *operator* of DB 263. Canons twelve, thirteen, fourteen, and sixteen are translated from the Greek version in Mansi, X, 1156; except that in the latter part of canon sixteen the missing verb *tribuit* is supplied from the Latin.)

1. If anyone does not profess according to the holy Fathers that the Father and the Son and the Holy Spirit are properly and truly a Trinity in unity and a unity in the Trinity; in other words, that they are one God in three hypostases that are consubstantial and equal in glory; the three possessing one and the same Godhead, nature, substance, supreme power, sovereign dominion, will, and uncreated operation— without beginning, incomprehensible and without change, creating and preserving all things: let such a one be condemned (*see 295–98, 416; DB 81*). **431 (254)**

2. If anyone does not profess according to the holy Fathers that in the proper and true sense the one and only divine Word of the holy, consubstantial, and adorable Trinity, descended from heaven, became incarnate through the Holy Spirit and Mary ever Virgin, and was made man; that in his humanity he was crucified, freely died for us and was buried, and rose on the third day, and ascended into heaven; that he sits at the right hand of the Father and will come again, with the glory he has from his Father and with the body assumed by him and animated as a rational being, in order to judge the living and the dead: let such a one be condemned (*see 1, 397, 418; DB 2*). **(255)**

4. If anyone does not profess according to the holy Fathers that there are in the proper and true sense two births of the **433 (257)**

one and only Jesus Christ, our Lord and our God—the first, before time, eternal, not in body from God the Father; the other, in this last age, in body, from the holy, ever-Virgin Mother of God, Mary; and that the one selfsame Jesus Christ our Lord and God is consubstantial with God the Father according to his divinity and consubstantial with man and his mother according to his humanity; and that he was capable of suffering in his humanity, though incapable of it in his divinity, limited as regards his body, though limitless as regards his Godhead; that he is both created and uncreated, belonging to earth and belonging to heaven, perceptible by sense and by intellect, measurable and immeasurable: in order that the whole man, who had fallen under sin, might be renewed by a complete man who is likewise God: let such a one be condemned (*see 417, 421*).

434
(258)
5. If anyone does not, according to the holy Fathers, profess in the proper and true sense the one incarnate nature of the Word of God, which is to say that our substance, perfect and without diminution, excepting only sin, is in Christ our God: let such a one be condemned (*see 423*).

435
(259)
6. If anyone does not profess according to the holy Fathers that in the proper and true sense the one selfsame Jesus Christ is Lord and God, of two natures and in two natures that are substantially united without any commingling and without any division: let such a one be condemned (*see 414*).

436
(260)
7. If anyone does not profess according to the holy Fathers that in the proper and true sense the substantial distinction of the natures is preserved in him without any commingling and without any division: let such a one be condemned (*see 414*).

437
(261)
8. If anyone does not profess according to the holy Fathers that in the proper and true sense a substantial union of natures without any commingling and without any division is recognized in him: let such a one be condemned (*see 414*).

438
(262)
9. If anyone does not profess according to the holy Fathers that in the proper and true sense the natural specific characters of his divinity and of his humanity were preserved in him

without diminution and without impairment: let such a one be condemned.

10. If anyone does not profess according to the holy Fathers that in the proper and true sense the one selfsame Christ our God has two wills harmoniously united, one divine and one human, inasmuch as he willed our salvation in a natural way through each of his natures: let such a one be condemned. **439** *(263)*

11. If anyone does not profess according to the holy Fathers that in the proper and true sense the one selfsame Christ our God has two operations harmoniously united, one divine and one human, inasmuch as he accomplishes our salvation through each of his natures: let such a one be condemned. **440** *(264)*

12. If anyone professes, according to the accursed heretics, that to both the divinity and the humanity of Christ there belongs one nature, or one will, or one operation, thereby rejecting the profession of the holy Fathers and destroying the plan of salvation of our Savior himself: let such a one be condemned. **441** *(265)*

13. If anyone, following the accursed heretics, adds to what has been devoutly taught by our holy Fathers, namely, that there are two wills and two operations, the divine and the human, essentially preserved in their union in Christ our God, by admitting, contrary to the Fathers' teaching, one will and one operation: let such a one be condemned. **442** *(266)*

14. If anyone, following the accursed heretics, besides denying and rejecting the one will and one operation as it is impiously professed in Christ our God by the heretics themselves, also denies the two wills and the two operations, the divine and the human, which are preserved in their nature in their unity in the same Christ our God and are orthodoxly taught about him by the holy Fathers: let such a one be condemned. **443** *(267)*

15. If anyone, following the wicked heretics, absurdly takes the human-divine operation, which the Greeks call *theandric,* as one operation and does not profess in accord with the holy Fathers that it is twofold, that is, divine and human; **444** *(268)*

or if he professes that the very neologism *divine-human* which has been established designates one operation but does not indicate the wonderful and glorious union of both operations: let such a one be condemned.

445
(269)
16. If anyone, following the accursed heretics in denying the two wills and two operations, a divine and a human, which were essentially preserved in their union in Christ our God and which have been devoutly taught by the holy Fathers, foolishly introduces dissensions and disagreements into the mystery concerning them and therefore does not [attribute] the sayings of the Gospels and of the apostles about the Savior himself to the one selfsame Lord our God Jesus Christ, according to the doctrine of the distinguished Cyril, so as to believe that He is divine in nature and likewise truly man: let such a one be condemned (*see 403*).

THE ELEVENTH COUNCIL OF TOLEDO, 675

This creed from the Eleventh Council of Toledo (*see introd. to 299*) treats the entire mystery of the Incarnation and Redemption in an extended and detailed manner relying, for the most part, on patristic sources.

The Incarnation

446
(282)
Of these three persons we believe that the Son alone assumed a true human nature, a sinless nature, from the holy and immaculate Virgin Mary for the liberation of the human race. He was born from her in a new manner and with a new birth: in a new manner because, though invisible in his divinity, he appears visibly in his humanity; and with a new birth because an undefiled Virgin who did not have intercourse with man was made fruitful by the Holy Spirit and so furnished the substance for his human flesh (*see 413*). This Virgin Birth can neither be fully understood nor can another example of it be pointed out; were it fully understood, it would not be miraculous; were there another example, it would cease to be unique. However, we must not think that, because Mary conceived when the Holy Spirit overshadowed her, this Spirit is therefore the Father of the Son; for thus we would seem to assert that there are two Fathers of the Son—an assertion that is surely wrong.

The Person of the Redeemer

In this miraculous conception Wisdom built for itself a house **447** in that "the Word was made flesh and dwelt among us" (*John* **(283)** *1:14*). However, the Word itself was not turned into flesh and changed in such a way that he ceased to be God because he willed to become man; but <u>the Word was made flesh in such a way that in him there is not merely the Word of God and the human flesh, but there is also a rational, human soul; and this entire being is called God</u> because of the presence of God and also man because of the presence of man. In this Son of God we believe that there are two natures: one of his divinity, the other of his humanity, which the one person of Christ has so united in himself that there can never be any separation either of the divinity from the humanity or of the humanity from the divinity. Hence it is that Christ is perfect God and perfect man, in the unity of one person; and when we say that there are two natures in the Son we do not intend to put two persons in him; for thus there would seem to be a fourth element added to the Trinity—which is utterly false. For God the Word did not assume a human person but a human nature, and with the eternal person of his divinity he united the temporal substance of his humanity.

We likewise believe that Father, Son, and Holy Spirit have **448** one substance; yet we do not say that the Virgin Mary gave **(284)** birth to this one undivided Trinity, but only to the Son who alone assumed our nature into union with his own person. <u>Further, it should be believed that the whole Trinity effected the Incarnation of this Son of God, because the works of the Trinity cannot be divided. Still, it was the Son alone who</u> took a servant's form (*see Phil. 2:7*) <u>unto his one person;</u> not in the unity of the divine nature, but into that which is proper to the Son, not what is common to the three Persons. This form was joined to him in a personal union, that is, in such a way that the Son of God and the Son of man are the one Christ. Furthermore, the same Christ in these two natures consists of three substantial principles: of the Word, which must belong exclusively to God's essence; of a body and of a soul, which belong to his true humanity.

<u>Christ contains in himself, therefore, a twofold substance,</u> **449** <u>that of his own divinity and that of our humanity.</u> However, **(285)**

185

inasmuch as he proceeded eternally from God the Father, he has been born, and nothing more; for inasmuch as he proceeded from the Father, he is not to be considered as creature nor as predestined; but inasmuch as he was born of the Virgin Mary, we must believe that he is not only born but is also a creature and predestined. Yet in his case both the generations were wonderful: for he was born of the Father before time, without any mother; he was born of his mother in this latter age, without any father. As God he produced Mary; as man he was produced by Mary. He himself was both father and son to his mother Mary. As God he is equal to the Father; as man he is less than the Father. Similarly, it must be believed that he is both greater and less than himself; for in the form of God even the Son himself is greater than himself because of the assumed human nature which is excelled by the divine; whereas in the servant's form, he is less than himself, that is, by reason of the human nature which is clearly less than the divine nature. Just as he is clearly less than either the Father or himself because of the assumed human nature, so too he is coequal to the Father according to his divine nature; and he and the Father are greater than the human nature that the person of the Son alone assumed. Again, with regard to the question whether the Son could be both equal to and less than the Holy Spirit, just as he is believed to be in one way equal to the Father and in another to be less than the Father, we answer as follows: According to the form of God he is equal to the Father and the Holy Spirit; according to the servant's form he is less than either Father or Holy Spirit: because neither the Holy Spirit nor God the Father, but the person of the Son alone assumed the human nature according to which he is believed to be less than the former two persons. Further, it is believed that this Son is distinct in his person, but without any separation, from God the Father and the Holy Spirit; but the human nature was taken from man. Moreover, the person is associated with man; but the divine nature or substance is with the Father and the Holy Spirit. Besides, the Son is not sent by the Father only, but it must be believed that he is also sent by the Holy Spirit, because he himself says through the prophet: "And now the Lord has sent me, and his Spirit" (*see Isa.*

48:16). He can also be understood as sent by himself, inasmuch as the action of the whole Trinity is known to be indivisible. This Son who was called the Only-begotten before time, has become the First-born in time: the Only-begotten because of his divine nature; the First-born because of the human nature he assumed.

The Redemption

According to the truth contained in the Gospel, we believe that in the form of his assumed human nature he was conceived without sin, born without sin, and died without sin. He alone was made sin for us (*see II Cor. 5:21*), that is, was made a sacrifice for our sins. Nevertheless, he endured the Passion itself for our offenses without any change in his divine nature; he was sentenced to the death of the cross and suffered true bodily death. And on the third day he came back to life by his own power and arose from the tomb.

450
(286)

THE THIRD COUNCIL OF CONSTANTINOPLE, 680-81

To heal the rift between Constantinople and Rome caused by the Monothelitic heresy, the Emperor Constantine IV prevailed upon Pope Donus (676–78) and his successor Pope St. Agatho (678–81) to send representatives to a general council at Constantinople. The Third Council of Constantinople, the sixth ecumenical council, met to give the final condemnation of Monothelitism and express firm adherence to the faith of Athanasius, Gregory of Nazianzus, Cyril of Alexandria, and Leo the Great. Pope Leo II (682–83) confirmed the acts of the council the following year, 682.

The two wills of Christ

And we likewise proclaim according to the teaching of the holy Fathers that Christ has two volitions or wills, and two natural operations, without division or change, without partition or commingling. And the two natural wills are not opposed (by no means!) as the godless heretics have said; but the human will is compliant, and not opposing or contrary; as a matter of fact it is even obedient to his divine and omnipotent will. For it was necessary for the human will to move itself, but in obedience to the divine will, as the great wisdom of Athanasius has taught; because just as His human nature is said to be and is the human nature of God the Word,

451
(291)

so too the natural will of his human nature is said to be and is God the Word's very own, as he himself says: "I have come down from heaven not to do my own will, but the will of the Father who sent me" (*see John 6:38*). Here he calls the will of his human nature his own will, since the human nature also was his own. For his most holy and innocent body, animated by his soul, was not taken away by being divinized, but stayed true to its own determinate nature. In the same way his human will was not taken away either by being divinized, but is preserved rather, according to the words of Gregory the Theologian [*of Nazianzus*]: "For his will ('his' being understood as referring to the Savior) is not at all opposed to God; it is wholly divinized."

452
(292) Moreover, in our same Lord Jesus Christ, our true God, we glory in proclaiming two natural operations without division or change, without partition or commingling, namely, a divine operation and a human one, as Leo, the teacher in matters relating to God, asserted with utmost clarity: "For each nature performs the functions proper to itself, yet in conjunction with the other nature: the Word does what is proper to the Word, and the humanity what is proper to the humanity" (*see 413*). For we absolutely refuse to admit that there is but one natural operation, that of God and of creature; for thus we would either exalt what is created into the divine nature or else degrade what is uniquely proper to the divine nature to the level of creatures; because we know that both miracles and sufferings belong to one and the same person, according to the different natures of which he consists and in which he has his being, as the marvelous Cyril has said. In every way possible, therefore, we uphold our denial both of commingling and of division and in this concise utterance we may express the entire matter: We believe that one of the Holy Trinity who, after the Incarnation, is our Lord Jesus Christ, is our true God; and we assert that both his natures clearly appear in his one hypostasis. In it throughout the whole ordered conduct of his life he gave evidence of both his miracles and his sufferings, not just in appearance, but in actuality. The difference of natures within the same one person is recognized by the fact that each nature, in conjunction with

the other nature, wills and carries out what is proper to itself. Accordingly, we hold that there are two natural wills and operations concurring in harmony for the salvation of the human race.

LETTER TO THE BISHOPS OF SPAIN AND GALICIA, 793

Just as Monothelitism was a corollary of Monophysitism, adoptionism was a corollary heresy of Nestorianism. Two Spanish bishops of the eighth century began teaching that Mary's son was not the natural but only the adopted Son of God; only the eternally begotten Son was God's natural Son. Nestorius's error of putting two persons in Christ is implicit in this new heresy. The growth of the heresy was checked promptly by the strong repudiation of the error by Pope Hadrian I (772–95) in a letter to the bishops of Spain and Galicia in 793 and by a series of local synods. (Translations follow the text given in Mansi, XIII, 869, and XIII, 844.)

Condemnation of adoptionism

. . . In your irreverence and in your ingratitude for such great favors you do not fear to whisper the vicious suggestion regarding our Redeemer that he is an adoptive Son, as though a mere man, and one subject to all human misfortune, and (a disgraceful thing to say!) that he is a slave. Why are you not afraid, you carping disparagers—hateful to God—to give the name of servant to Him who freed you from servitude to the devil, a servitude that you are trying to submit your traitorous selves to again of your own accord? . . . For although in prophetic type he was termed a servant because of the condition of the servant's form that he received from the Virgin, as the Scripture says: "Hast thou considered my servant Job, that there is none like him in the earth?" (*see Job 1:8*), even so, with St. Gregory we understand that this is meant historically as applied to the holy Job and allegorically as applied to Christ. The fact that Scripture described Him typically as a servant in the person of Job is no reason why we should give Him the name of servant, is it? . . . **453** (310)

THE COUNCIL OF FRIULI, 796

Christ is the natural Son of God

The human and temporal birth was no impediment to that divine, eternal birth; rather, in the one person of Christ **454** (314a)

Jesus there was the true Son of God and the true Son of man. There was not one Son of man and another of God. . . . He was not the putative Son of God, but the true Son; not adopted, but God's own Son, for he was never separated from the Father on account of his assumed human nature. . . . And the reason why we profess that in each nature he is God's own Son and not an adopted Son of God is that, after assuming a human nature, one and the same person is, without any commingling and without any separation, Son of God and Son of man. He is the natural Son of the Father according to his divinity, and natural Son of his mother according to his humanity; but God's own Son in either case . . .

THE FOURTH LATERAN COUNCIL, 1215

The Fourth Lateran Council, the twelfth ecumenical council (*see introd. to 306*), was held under Innocent III (1198–1216). The following statement of traditional Catholic faith in the Incarnation is a part of the council's profession of faith.

455
(429) And finally, the only-begotten Son of God, Jesus Christ, made incarnate by a common action of the Holy Trinity, and conceived by Mary ever Virgin with the cooperation of the Holy Spirit, became a true man composed of a rational soul and human flesh, one person in two natures; and he pointed out the way of life more clearly. According to his divinity, he is immortal and impassible, yet according to his humanity, he became passible and mortal. He also suffered and died on the wood of the cross for the salvation of the human race; he descended into hell; he rose from the dead and ascended into heaven: but he descended with his soul, and he rose in the flesh, and ascended in both together. . . .

THE SECOND COUNCIL OF LYONS, 1274

In the profession of faith proposed to the Emperor Michael Palaeologus at the Second Council of Lyons, the fourteenth ecumenical council, held under Gregory X (1271–76), the section on the Son of God compendiously proposes the orthodox doctrine about Christ in a way that excludes every one of the major Christological errors: Sabellianism, Arianism, Docetism, Apollinarism.

The Person of the Redeemer

We believe in the very Son of God, the Word of God, **456** eternally born of the Father, consubstantial, co-omnipotent, **(462)** and in all things equal to the Father in his divinity, born in time of the Holy Spirit and the ever-Virgin Mary; having a rational soul; having two births, one an eternal birth from the Father, the other a temporal birth from his mother; true God and true man, proper and perfect in both natures. He is not the adopted son, nor an apparent son, but the one and only Son of God, in two natures and of two natures, that is, a divine and a human nature in the singleness of one person. He is impassible and immortal in his divinity, but in his humanity he suffered for us and for our salvation by the true passion of his body. He died, and was buried, and he descended into hell. The third day he rose from the dead by a true resurrection of the body. With the body of his resurrection and with his soul, he ascended into heaven on the fortieth day after the Resurrection. He sits at the right hand of God the Father, and from there he shall come to judge the living and the dead; and he shall render unto everyone according to his works, whether they are good or evil.

THE VATICAN COUNCIL, 1869-70

SCHEMA OF THE DOGMATIC CONSTITUTION ON THE PRINCIPAL MYSTERIES OF THE FAITH

As has been pointed out before (*see introd. to 314*), this Constitution never came before the council for definition. It is presented here as a valuable, though not authoritative, summary of the theology of the Incarnate Word. (This translation is made from the *Collectio Lacensis*, VII, 558 ff., 566.)

Chapter 4. The Mystery of the Incarnation

God foresaw the fall of our race and in the determination **457** of his will, he mercifully decreed to lift up fallen man, to defeat the devil (by whose cunning man had fallen), and to call man back from death to life. Therefore, when the fullness of time had come, he sent his only-begotten Son, born of a woman, to save all who would believe in him from the power of darkness and bring them to the kingdom of this Son of his love. This is the true and genuine faith in the Incarnation, that we believe and profess that our Lord Jesus

Christ is true God and true man; that he is God, begotten of the substance of the Father before time; and that he is man, born in time of the substance of his mother. For the most high and eternal Son of God, who lowered himself for the salvation of the human race, brought us into his glory, but he never ceased to be what he was. Although he was equal to the Father in the form of God, that is, in the nature of God, by his birth of the Virgin Mother he took upon himself the form of a slave, that is, human nature, in such a way that he became a man, with a substance like ours. And thus, in the full and perfect nature of true man, true God was born—perfect in every characteristic proper to us as well as in every one proper to himself. This, then, is the union of human nature with the divine person, a hypostatic union, which the holy councils have defined and the entire Church has believed and preached. God the Word is not one person and the man Jesus another person; rather, one hypostasis or person is God because of his divine nature and man because of the human nature he has assumed.

458   In the Trinity, three distinct persons exist in one nature; but in Christ, on the contrary, one divine person exists in two distinct and different natures. From this everybody should realize that, as the holy Fathers have pointed out, the concept of essence, substance, or nature, is not to be confused with the concept of hypostasis, subsistency, or person. Then they will not say, to the detriment of the most sacred dogmas, that there are always as many persons as there are intellectual natures, or natures conscious of their own existence.

459   Although it was the whole Trinity that effected the Incarnation of the Son of God, because the works of the Trinity cannot be divided, it was the Son alone who took a servant's form unto his one person; not in the unity of the divine nature, but into that which is proper to the Son, not what is common to the three Persons (*see 448*).

460   The Son of God, without leaving the glory of the Father, is born with a new birth and enters into this world's lowliness. Human attributes are truly predicated of God, who is true man; and divine attributes are truly predicated of man, who

The Person of the Redeemer

is true God. Though invisible in his divine nature, he has become visible in ours; though remaining prior to all time, he has taken on existence in time. God though he is, subject neither to suffering nor death, he has not disdained to become man, subject to both suffering and the law of death (*see 413*). This union of properties of each nature in one same person of the Son of God is very clear in the apostolic writings and in the Gospels, and it is handed down and sanctioned by the constant agreement of the Fathers.

Each nature keeps its own proper character without defect, even after the union; for as God he suffers no change because of his condescension, nor, as man, is he absorbed by the divine dignity (*see 413*). Therefore, as there are two natures in Christ, so it must be professed that there are two wills and two operations; however, there is but one who effects our salvation and he is the only-begotten Son of God, who accomplishes divine things by his divine nature and human things by his human nature, yet without commingling or without division of the natures; the form of God shines forth in his miracles, while in the form of a servant he is subject to mistreatment (*see 413*). It is true that Christ shares our flesh and blood, but by no means did he contract the stain of guilt when he took our weak nature; and although he was endowed with true free will, he not only did not sin, but he could not sin. He was not troubled by the passions of the soul or the concupiscences of the flesh, and he did not free himself of these gradually (*see 427, can. 12*), but he was conceived holy of the Holy Spirit in the womb of the most pure Virgin, and he was born holy. **461**

Nevertheless, God so loved the world that he gave his Son, his only-begotten one, as a victim; and for our sake made him as sin who had not known sin. For it was fitting that we should have such a high priest, holy, innocent, undefiled, set apart from sinners and become higher than the heavens (*see Heb. 7:26*). Who through the Holy Spirit offered himself unblemished to God and, by virtue of his own blood he entered once and for all into the Holies, having obtained eternal redemption (*see Heb. 9:11 ff.*). **462**

193

463   Truly, therefore, Christ Jesus is mediator between God and man, one man dying for all; he made satisfaction to the divine justice for us, and he erased the handwriting that was against us. Despoiling principalities and powers, he brought us from our long-standing slavery into the freedom of sons. For if by reason of the one man's offense, death reigned through the one man, much more will they who receive the abundance of the grace, and of the gift of justice reign in life through the one Jesus Christ (*see Rom. 5:17*).

464   The Passion of the Redeemer had this power of making satisfaction for the sins of all men and of meriting for us the grace of justification and inheritance because his human acts had their value according to the dignity of the divine person who worked through the nature he had assumed.

465   Therefore, since we are redeemed not with perishable things, with gold or silver, but with the precious blood of the immaculate, unblemished lamb, let us purify our souls in our obedience to charity (*see I Pet. 1:18 ff.*); and living in the faith of the Son of God, who loved us and gave himself up for us (*see Gal. 2:20*), let us look for the blessed hope and the glorious coming of our great God and Savior, Jesus Christ (*see Titus 2:13*).

466   And in this our age, as deceitful teachers and ungodly men, whom the Apostle predicted would come (*see II Pet. 2:1; Jude 4*), detract more and more from the glory of Him who redeemed them, so much the more zealously should we proclaim his greatness and reverence his majesty. This only-begotten Son of the unbegotten God is the splendor of glory, the figure of his substance, the beginning and the end, through whom and for whom all things were made. Because of the great love with which he loved us, he was delivered up in the servant's form which he has assumed because of our sins; he rose for our justification; and as conqueror of death and of hell, he has ascended above all the heavens and sits at the right hand of the majesty on high, the king of kings and lord of lords. Above every principality and power, the Father has made him heir to the universe so that he might have the primacy over all and be the cause of eternal salvation for those who believed in him and obeyed him. He will come again with great power and majesty to judge the living and the dead; and all those in the tombs will hear the voice of the Son of God and they will come forth. They who have done good works will come forth into the resurrection of life; they who have done evil will rise to their judgment. Then his majesty, his divinity and everlasting power will be revealed and every tongue shall confess that the Lord Jesus Christ is in the glory of God the Father (*see Phil. 2:11*).

Canons on Chapter 4

1. If anyone does not profess that one and the same Jesus Christ our Lord is true man just as he is true God: let him be anathema. **467**

2. If anyone says that the human nature of Christ is not united to God the Word in such a way that the Word subsists in the human nature having made it his own: let him be anathema. **468**

3. If anyone understands the one person of Jesus Christ to contain many persons, or introduces two persons into the mystery of Christ, one divine and one human, joined from conception by an indissoluble bond to make one composite person: let him be anathema. **469**

4. If anyone says that there are necessarily as many persons as there are intellects and wills; or that to deny that there are two persons in Christ is to deny him the perfection of human nature: let him be anathema. **470**

5. If anyone presumes to say that vicarious satisfaction, namely, that of one mediator for all men, is opposed to divine justice: let him be anathema. **471**

6. If anyone does not profess that God the Word by suffering and dying in the flesh he had assumed, could make satisfaction to God for our sins; or that he did truly and properly make this satisfaction and merited grace and glory for us: let him be anathema. **472**

7. If anyone defends the other ungodly doctrines of Apollinaris, Nestorius, Eutyches, or Sergius—condemned in the holy **473**

Councils of Ephesus, Chalcedon, and Constantinople; and if he does not profess the doctrine of the mystery of Christ which was declared by those same councils and by Our predecessors St. Leo and St. Agatho and which was finally confirmed in the ecumenical Council of Florence: let him be anathema.

CONDEMNATION OF THE ERRORS OF THE MODERNISTS, 1907

The modernist Christological errors stem from the basic theories of modernism about the evolutionary growth of dogma and the wholly rationalistic approach that modernism made to history. The result was a complete denial of the Incarnation and the redemptive mission of Christ. The following errors are taken from the collection of errors of the modernists issued July 3, 1907 (*see introd. to 112*) by Pope St. Pius X (1903–14).

474
(2027) 27. The divinity of Jesus Christ is not proved from the Gospels; but it is a dogma that the Christian consciousness deduced from the notion of the Messias.

475
(2028) 28. When Jesus was carrying on his ministry, he did not speak with the intention of teaching that he was the Messias nor were his miracles intended to prove that he was.

476
(2029) 29. It may be conceded that the Christ who appears in the light of history is far inferior to the Christ who is the object of faith.

477
(2030) 30. In all the Gospel texts the title *Son of God* is simply the equivalent of the title *Messias;* but it does not by any means signify that Christ is the true, natural Son of God.

478
(2031) 31. The Christology taught by Paul, John, and the Councils of Nicaea, Ephesus, and Chalcedon is not the doctrine that Jesus taught but one that the Christian consciousness formed about Jesus.

479
(2032) 32. It is impossible to reconcile the obvious meaning of the Gospel texts with the teaching of our theologians about the consciousness and the infallible knowledge of Jesus Christ.

The Person of the Redeemer

33. It is evident to any unprejudiced person either that Jesus taught erroneously about the proximity of the Messianic Coming, or else that a major portion of his teaching contained in the Synoptic Gospels is not authentic.

480
(2033)

34. It is impossible for a critical exegete to attribute unlimited knowledge to Christ, unless he makes a supposition that is inconceivable historically and repugnant to moral sense: namely, that as man Christ had God's knowledge and yet was unwilling to communicate his knowledge of so many things to his disciples and to posterity.

481
(2034)

35. Christ did not always have the consciousness of his Messianic dignity.

482
(2035)

36. The Resurrection of the Savior is not properly a fact of the historical order, but only a fact of the supernatural order that is not and cannot be demonstrated; Christian consciousness derived it gradually from other data.

483
(2036)

37. From the very first, belief in the resurrection of Christ was a belief, not so much in the fact of the Resurrection, as in Christ's immortal life with God.

484
(2037)

38. The teaching on the expiatory death of Christ is not in the Gospels but in Paul only.

485
(2038)

DECREE OF THE HOLY OFFICE, 1918

Catholic piety and theology have always sought to penetrate beyond the fundamental dogmas concerning the constitution of the God-man into the deep recesses of his own psychological experience. Some of these attempts have resulted in theories that unduly restricted the unsurpassed excellence of Christ's human knowledge. On June 5, 1918, the Holy Office felt it necessary to warn against certain propositions as unsafe.

On the knowledge of Christ

This question was proposed by the Sacred Congregation of Seminaries and Universities: Can the following propositions be taught safely?

486
(2183)

I. It is not certain that during his sojourn among men the soul of Christ had the same kind of knowledge that the blessed have, that is, those who have achieved their goal.

197

II. Nor can the opinion be said to be certain which holds that Christ's soul was not ignorant of anything but from the beginning knew in the Word all things past, present, and future, that is, everything that God knows with the knowledge of vision.

488
(2185)

III. The doctrine of certain moderns about a restricted knowledge in Christ's soul should not be any less acceptable in Catholic schools than the opinion of older theologians about a universal knowledge. . . . [*Answer*] They cannot be taught safely.

THE ENCYCLICAL *MISERENTISSIMUS REDEMPTOR*, 1928

In becoming man, Christ joined the whole of mankind closely to himself. This close union demands that men associate themselves closely with Christ in his work of saving mankind. The *objective Redemption* of mankind by Christ's passion and death is a historically completed work. The *subjective Redemption*, or the application of the effects of Christ's sacrifice to all subsequent generations of men, is a work in which men themselves must join. In this richly dogmatic encyclical on the devotion to the Sacred Heart of Jesus, dated May 7, 1928, Pius XI (1922–39) shows what this sharing of Christ's work consists in and why it is necessary. (Of the following excerpts nos. 489–93 are translated from the *Acta Apostolicae Sedis*, XX [1928], 170–72; no. 494, from *ibid.*, p. 174.)

489

The plentiful Redemption of Christ brought us abundant forgiveness for all our sins (*see Col. 2:13*). Nevertheless, owing to the wonderful arrangement of divine Wisdom by which what is lacking in the sufferings of Christ is to be completed in our flesh for his body, which is the Church (*see Col. 1:24*), we are able and, in fact, we ought to join our own acts of praise and satisfaction to those which Christ has presented to God in the name of sinners.

490

However, we must always remember that the entire expiatory value [*of our acts*] depends on the one, bloody sacrifice of Christ, which is uninterruptedly renewed on our altars in an unbloody manner; for "it is one and the same Victim: he who now makes the offering through the ministry of priests and he who then offered himself on the cross; the only difference is in the manner of the offering" (*see 749*).

Therefore, an act of immolation on the part of both priests **491**
and the rest of the faithful must be joined with this most
august Eucharistic Sacrifice so that they too may offer themselves as living victims, holy, and pleasing to God (*see Rom.
12:1*). Indeed, St. Cyprian unhesitatingly asserts that "the
celebration of the Lord's sacrifice does not effect our proper
sanctification, unless our sacrificial offering is in accord with
his passion." Accordingly, the Apostle warns us that "bearing about in our body the dying of Jesus" (*II Cor. 4:10*) and
being buried with Christ and united with him in the likeness
of his death (*see Rom. 6:4 f.*), we ought to crucify our flesh
with its vices and lusts (*see Gal. 5:24*), "escaping from the
corruption of that lust which is in the world" (*II Pet. 1:4*); he
exhorts us that "the life of Jesus be made manifest in our
bodily frame" (*II Cor. 4:10*) and, that as sharers in his eternal
priesthood, we offer "gifts and sacrifices for sins" (*Heb. 5:1*).

For participation in this mysterious priesthood and in the **492**
duty of offering satisfaction and sacrifice is not limited to
those whom our High Priest Jesus Christ uses as his ministers
to offer the clean oblation to the divine Majesty in every
place from the rising of the sun to its very setting (*see Mal.
1:11*); no, it is the duty of the entire Christian family, which
the Prince of the Apostles rightly calls "a chosen race, a royal
priesthood" (*I Pet. 2:9*), to offer expiatory sacrifice (*see Heb.
5:3*) not only for itself but also for the whole human race in
much the same way as every priest and "high priest taken
from among men is appointed for men in the things pertaining to God" (*Heb. 5:1*).

We shall reap a more abundant harvest of mercy and for- **493**
giveness for ourselves and for others to the extent that our
own offering and sacrifice correspond more perfectly to the
sacrifice of our Lord; in other words, to the extent that we
immolate our self-love and our passions and crucify our flesh
with that mystical crucifixion of which the Apostle speaks.
For there is a wonderfully close relationship between Christ
and all the faithful—a relationship like that of the head of
a body to the rest of its members. Moreover, by that mysterious communion of saints, which we acknowledge by our
Catholic faith, all men, as individuals and as nations, are

joined not only in association with one another but also to him "who is the head, Christ; from whom the whole body—fitted together and connected by the aid of every joint, with a view to the operation in due measure of each one of its parts—takes its growth, so as to build itself up in love" (*Eph. 4:15 f.*). This, indeed, is what the mediator between God and man, Christ Jesus, prayed for to his Father when he was approaching death: "I in them and thou in me; that they may be perfected in unity" (*John 17:23*).

494   A further consideration is the truth that Christ's expiatory suffering is renewed and in a way continued and completed in his mystical body, which is the Church. For, to use St. Augustine's words again, "Christ suffered all that he should have suffered; there is now nothing lacking in the measure of his sufferings. His sufferings as head, then, were completed; yet for Christ in his body, sufferings still remained." The Lord Jesus himself mercifully made this truth known when, speaking to Saul who was still breathing threats of slaughter against the disciples (*see Acts 9:1*), he said, "I am Jesus, whom thou art persecuting" (*Acts 9:5*). Obviously he means that, when persecutions are directed against the Church, it is the divine head of the Church himself who is attacked and afflicted. It is entirely proper, then, that Christ who is still suffering in his mystical body should want to have us as his companions in the work of expiation. This is required of us also by our close union with him, since we are "the body of Christ, and individually members of it" (*I Cor. 12:27*), and all the members ought to suffer with the head anything that the head suffers (*see I Cor. 12:26*).

THE ENCYCLICAL MYSTICI CORPORIS, 1943

In the course of this encyclical, dated June 29, 1943, so important for the theology of the Church (*see introd. to 239*), Pope Pius XII (1939–58) touches the question of Christ's knowledge. His doctrine is a strong corroboration of the traditional doctrine of theologians that Christ possessed the beatific vision and with it a knowledge of universal extent. (This translation is made from the text in *Acta Apostolicae Sedis*, XXXV [1943], 230.)

But the knowledge and love of our divine Redeemer, of which we were the object from the first moment of his incarnation, are more than any human intellect or heart can hope to grasp. For hardly was he conceived in the womb of the Mother of God, when he began to enjoy the beatific vision; and in that vision all the members of his mystical body were continually and unceasingly present and he embraced them with his redeeming love.

495
(2289)

THE ENCYCLICAL *SEMPITERNUS REX CHRISTUS*, 1951

To commemorate the fifteenth centenary of the Council of Chalcedon, Pius XII (1939–58) published, on September 8, 1951, this encyclical praising the immortal clarification of Christological doctrine that the council achieved under the leadership of St. Leo the Great. In the course of the encyclical, Pius XII concisely summarizes the problems of terminology that plagued the Church before Chalcedon. Towards the end of the encyclical, the Holy Father uses the occasion to denounce the modern "kenotic theory" of the Incarnation which, completely misunderstanding St. Paul's "He emptied himself, took the nature of a slave, and was made like to men" (*Phil. 2:7*), supposes that in the Incarnation the divinity of Christ was somehow lost by its union with human nature. (This translation is made from the text in *Acta Apostolicae Sedis*, XLIII [1951], 634–38.)

However, each of the two series of those properties and operations is attributed to the one person of the Word; because "one . . . and the same person is . . . truly the Son of God and truly the Son of man." And so he [*Pope St. Leo the Great*] continues: "For each nature performs the functions proper to itself, yet in conjunction with the other nature: the Word does what is proper to the Word, and the humanity what is proper to the humanity" (*see 413*). Here occurs the mention of that well-known communication of the properties, as it is called. Cyril had with good reason defended this communication against Nestorius, by relying on this well-founded axiom: Each of Christ's natures subsists in the single person of the Word, the Word who in his divinity was begotten from the Father before time, and in his humanity was born from Mary in time.

496

This sublime doctrine, drawn from the Gospel, in no way contradicts what had been decreed in the Council of Ephesus. It rejects Eutyches as well as Nestorius . . .

497 The question arises: How is it that the pronouncements of the Council of Chalcedon are so brilliantly effective for defeating error? In Our judgment, the principal reason is that at the council all ambiguity was set aside and the most proper terminology employed. For in Chalcedon's definition of faith, the words *person* and *hypostasis* (πρόσωπον, ὑπόστασις) are taken as synonymous; while the term *nature* (φύσις) has a different meaning and is never used in place of the former words.

498 It is truly regrettable that certain ancient opponents of the Council of Chalcedon, likewise called Monophysites, rejected so clear, so pure, so perfect an expression of faith owing to their misunderstanding of certain terms used by the ancient writers. For although they fought strenuously against the absurd assertion of Eutyches about a commingling of natures in Christ, still they persistently clung to the famous expression, "the one incarnate nature of God the Word." St. Cyril of Alexandria used this expression, taken from St. Athanasius, but his meaning was correct, since he applied the word *nature* to signify the person itself. The fathers at Chalcedon, however, removed from those terms every trace of ambiguity and uncertainty; for bringing the terminology of Trinitarian theology into line with the terminology used in explaining the Incarnation of our Lord, they identified *nature* with *essence* (οὐσία) and *person* with *hypostasis*. They considered that the latter terms ought to be distinguished absolutely from the former two, whereas the dissidents just mentioned identify *nature* with *person*, but not with *essence*. Therefore, according to the more usual and the purest form of expression, we should say that in God there is one nature and three persons; but in Christ, one person and two natures.

499 Likewise entirely opposed to Chalcedon's profession of faith is the erroneous opinion, rather widespread outside the Catholic religion, which imagines that in Christ the divinity of the Word is lost. Called the *"kenotic theory,"* it finds a specious foundation in its shallow misunderstanding of a text of the letter of the Apostle Paul to the Philippians (*see Phil. 2:7*). It is truly a fantastic theory and, like the directly opposite doctrine, Docetism, it makes the whole mystery of the Incarnation and Redemption a lifeless and meaningless illusion. "In the full and perfect nature of true man . . . the true God was born—perfect in every characteristic proper to us as well as in every one proper to himself" (*see 412*). This is the exalted doctrine of Leo the Great.

There is no reason why the human nature of Christ should **500** not be studied more deeply, even according to the viewpoint and method of psychology. Nevertheless, in difficult studies of this kind, there are some who depart from tradition more than they should to build new theories, and who misuse the authoritative definition of the Council of Chalcedon to shore up their own theories.

These persons so extol the state and condition of Christ's **501** human nature that it seems to be considered a sort of independent subject, as though it did not subsist in the person of the Word himself. Yet the Council of Chalcedon, in entire harmony with that of Ephesus, plainly asserts that the two natures of our Redeemer are united "in one person and one hypostasis" (*see 414*); and it forbids putting two individuals in Christ, in such a way that an "assumed man," possessing complete autonomy, would be placed within the Word.

The Mother of God

"To Jesus through Mary" is St. Bernard's succinct statement of the traditional Catholic belief in the important position of Mary in the life of Jesus. It is only as a function of the mystery of Jesus that the mystery of Mary can be studied. Just as the first Eve was associated with the first Adam in the Fall of the human race, so, too, is the second Eve associated with the new Adam in the divine plan of the Redemption. No one who has heard that Jesus came into the world and lived in it can fail

to know what an important part his mother had in his birth or how closely the mysteries of her life blend with the mysteries of his life. Granted the hypostatic union, one can only conclude that Mary is the Mother of God in a true and proper sense and is not surprised that this great dignity of the divine maternity is the foundation of many other prerogatives—her Immaculate Conception, her perpetual virginity, her Assumption, and her being mediatress of all graces.

LETTER TO ANYSIUS, BISHOP OF THESSALONICA, 392

It is a truth of the Catholic faith that Mary kept her state of virginity before, during, and after the birth of Christ. Whenever heretics have assailed this truth, the Church has championed it. In the second half of the fourth century, a certain bishop named Bonoso was denounced to the bishops of Illyricum for having attributed other children besides Jesus to Mary. After they had deprived Bonoso of his episcopal functions, Pope St. Siricius (384–98) writing to Bishop Anysius, of Thessalonica, commended their action against the error.

The virginity of Mary

502
(91)
(3) We surely cannot deny that you were right in correcting the doctrine about children of Mary, and Your Holiness was right in rejecting the idea that any other offspring should come from the same virginal womb from which Christ was born according to the flesh. For the Lord Jesus would not have chosen to be born of a virgin if he had judged that she would be so incontinent as to taint the birthplace of the body of the Lord, the home of the eternal king, with the seed of human intercourse. Anyone who proposes this is merely proposing the unbelief of the Jews saying that Christ could not be born of a virgin. For if they accept the doctrine on the authority of priests that Mary had a number of children, then they will strive with greater effort to destroy the truths of faith.

LETTER TO THE SENATE AT CONSTANTINOPLE, 534

In March, 534, Pope John II (533–35) wrote this letter to the senate at Constantinople clarifying the exact meaning of the Catholic doctrine on the *Mother of God* (*see introd. to 415*).

The Mother of God

Our son the Emperor Justinian has pointed out . . . that
disputes have arisen over these three questions: . . . Whether
Mary ever Virgin, the mother of Christ our God and Lord,
ought to be entitled properly and truly *Mother of God* and
mother of the Word of God who took flesh from her. . . .

503
(*201*)

Furthermore, We teach that the glorious and holy ever-
Virgin Mary is proclaimed, and rightly so, by Catholics to be
properly and truly *Mother of God* and the mother of God the
Word who received his human nature from her. For in the
proper and true sense, he himself did become incarnate in
this last age and condescend to be born of the holy and
glorious Virgin as his mother. Therefore, because the Son
of God in the proper and true sense received his body from
her and was born of her, We profess that she is properly and
truly the mother of God; for God received his body from her
and was born of her. And we say *properly* to exclude the idea
that the Lord Jesus was called God by title of honor or by
favor, according to the absurd opinion of Nestorius; again, we
say *truly* to exclude the idea that he did not receive a true
body from the Virgin but did so only apparently or some other
way, according to the blasphemous assertion of Eutyches.

504
(*202*)

THE COUNCIL OF THE LATERAN, 649

In October, 649, three months after his consecration, Pope
St. Martin I (649–53?) summoned a council to the Lateran
palace in Rome to condemn the Monothelitic heresy (*see
introd. to 431*). The third canon, given below, contains a defense of the true motherhood of Mary and of her perpetual
virginity.

3. If anyone does not profess according to the holy Fathers
that in the proper and true sense the holy, ever-Virgin, immaculate Mary is the *Mother of God*, since in this last age
not with human seed but of the Holy Spirit she properly and
truly conceived the divine Word, who was born of God the
Father before all ages, and gave him birth without any detriment to her virginity, which remained inviolable even after
his birth: let such a one be condemned (*see 421*).

505
(*256*)

The Incarnation and Redemption

THE COUNCIL OF TRENT, 1545-63

The Council of Trent (*see introd. to 371*), in its fifth session on June 17, 1546, expressly stated that it did not intend to include the Blessed Virgin in the decree on original sin (*see 376*). In the sixth session on January 13, 1547, in the twenty-third canon on justification, the council acknowledges the special privilege by which the Blessed Virgin Mary was free from all actual sins.

506
(833)
23. If anyone says that a man once justified cannot sin again, and cannot lose grace, and that therefore the man who falls and sins was never truly justified; or, contrariwise, says that a man once justified can avoid all sins, even venial sins, throughout his entire life without a special privilege of God, as the Church holds in regard to the Blessed Virgin: let him be anathema.

THE CONSTITUTION CUM QUORUNDAM, 1555

Shortly after the Reformation there appeared the beginnings of a rationalistic element that would one day strongly influence Protestant theology. Unitarianism was one of the forerunners of this spirit, denying fundamental revealed truths like the Trinity, the maternity of the Blessed Virgin, and her perpetual virginity. Paul IV (1555–59) condemns the Unitarians for their errors in this constitution dated August 7, 1555, and attests to Mary's virginity before, during, and after the birth of Christ.

507
(993)
. . . With Our apostolic authority we call to account and warn . . . on behalf of the omnipotent God, the Father, the Son, and the Holy Spirit, all those who have asserted or who have believed: . . . that [*the Lord*] was not conceived of the Holy Spirit according to the flesh in the womb of the most Blessed and ever-Virgin Mary, but that his conception in no way differed from the conception of other men, and that he was conceived of the seed of Joseph; or that the same Jesus Christ, our Lord and God, did not submit to the cruel death of the cross to save us from sin and from eternal death and to reconcile us to the Father for everlasting life; or that the same most Blessed Virgin Mary is not the true mother of God and that she did not remain a perfect virgin before, while, and forever after she gave birth.

CONDEMNATION OF THE ERRORS OF
MICHEL DE BAY, 1567

A denial of Mary's sinlessness was one of the many errors of Michel de Bay (*cir.* 1513–89) condemned by Pope St. Pius V (1566–72) (*see introd. to 608*).

73. No one except Christ is without original sin. Therefore, the Blessed Virgin died because of sin contracted from Adam; and all the afflictions that she suffered in this life, like those of other just men, were the punishment of actual or of original sin.

508
(1073)

CONDEMNATION OF JANSENISTIC ERRORS, 1690

The errors of Cornelis Jansen (1585–1638) continued to infect certain theologians even after the strong condemnation of 1653 (*see introd. to 627*). On December 7, 1690, Pope Alexander VIII (1689–91) condemned thirty-one errors that were being spread in Jansenistic writings. The twenty-fourth of these errors denies to Mary her privilege of perfect sinlessness. In the papal document the precise censure to be attached to this error is not determined.

24. The offering of the two young doves which the Blessed Virgin made in the Temple on the day of her purification, the one dove as a holocaust and the other as a sin offering, is sufficient evidence that she was in need of purification, and that her Son (who was offered) was also sullied by the defilement of his mother, according to the words of the Law.

509
(1314)

THE BULL *INEFFABILIS DEUS*, 1854

On December 8, 1854, Pope Pius IX (1846–78) defined that "the most Blessed Virgin Mary . . . was preserved free from all stain of original sin. . . ." This definition did not come as a surprise but was the culmination of long years of preparation. It is interesting to note this historical development:

Pope Sixtus IV (1471–84) gives approval to the feast.

Pope Innocent VIII (1484–92) gives approval to the invocation of Mary under the title of the Immaculate Conception.

At the Council of Trent (1545–63) the fathers did not want the decree on original sin to be understood as including the Blessed Virgin (*see 376*).

In 1567, Pope St. Pius V (1566–72) condemned the proposition of Michel de Bay (*see 508*); during his pontificate the Office of the Immaculate Conception was introduced into the breviary.

Pope Paul V (1605–21) forbade anything contrary to the teaching of Mary's Immaculate Conception to be said in public.

In 1622, Pope Gregory XV (1621–23) forbade any contrary statements to be made in private.

Pope Alexander VII (1655–67) declared that the object of the devotion is the conception of the Blessed Virgin Mary. It is interesting to note that Pope Alexander's statement was incorporated almost verbatim into Pope Pius IX's definition of the dogma.

Pope Clement XI (1700–21) made the feast one of precept in the universal Church.

Proclamation of the dogma of the Immaculate Conception

510
(1641)
For the honor of the holy and undivided Trinity, for the honor and renown of the Virgin Mother of God, for the exaltation of the Catholic faith and the increase of the Christian religion, by the authority of our Lord Jesus Christ, by the authority of the blessed Apostles Peter and Paul, and by Our own authority, We declare, pronounce and define: the doctrine that maintains that the most Blessed Virgin Mary in the first instant of her conception, by a unique grace and privilege of the omnipotent God and in consideration of the merits of Christ Jesus the Savior of the human race, was preserved free from all stain of original sin, is a doctrine revealed by God and therefore must be firmly and constantly held by all the faithful. If, therefore, any shall obstinately maintain a contrary opinion to that which We have defined (God forbid that they do so), let them fully realize that they stand condemned by their own judgment, that they have made shipwreck of their faith, that they have departed from union with the Church. Furthermore, if they dare to express in words or writing or any other way what they believe at heart, by that very action they are subject to the punishments laid down by law.

THE ENCYCLICAL *OCTOBRI MENSE,* 1891

The divine maternity is the foundation for Mary's cooperation in the work of the Redemption. No one ever has or ever will be more intimately and effectively associated with Christ in the objective redemption than his mother. The following documents of Pope Leo XIII (1878–1903) illustrate one of Mary's greatest offices in the work of the subjective redemption, her being mediatress of all graces.

In the encyclical *Octobri mense*, dated September 22, 1891, we are told by Pope Leo XIII that no one can go to the Father except through the Son, and, similarly, no one can go to the Son except through his mother, Mary.

When the eternal Son of God willed to assume the nature of man for the redemption and honor of man, and willed thereby to enter into a sort of mystical marriage with the entire human race, he did not do so before his chosen mother had given her free consent. She was in some way impersonating the human race—as Aquinas truly and beautifully says, "In the Annunciation the consent of the Virgin was awaited in place of that of all human nature." Therefore, we may truly and fittingly affirm, that of the vast treasure of all grace which the Lord has won—since grace and truth have come through Jesus Christ (*see John 1:17*)—nothing at all is given to us, in accordance with God's will, except through Mary. And as no one may go to the great Father except through the Son, in much the same way no one can go to Christ except through his mother.

511
(*1940a*)

THE ENCYCLICAL MAGNAE DEI MATRIS, 1892

Praising the abundance of grace with which God endowed the Virgin Mary, Pope Leo XIII, in the encyclical *Magnae Dei Matris*, dated September 8, 1892, declares that Mary is willing and eager to share her treasure with men. (The translation of this section is made from the text in the *Acta Sanctae Sedis*, XXV [1892–93], 141.)

. . . When we go in prayer to Mary we go to the mother of mercy who loves us so much that whatever our need may be, she, of her own accord, even before we ask her, is always immediately ready to help us, especially to gain eternal life. She gives us grace from the treasure that God has given in full measure right from the beginning to her who was worthy to be his mother. Because of this abundance of grace—which is the most wonderful of the praises of the Virgin—she far excels all men and all the orders of angels and she alone of

512

all creatures is next to Christ: "It is a great thing when any saint has enough grace to save many others; but when a saint has grace sufficient for the salvation of all the men of the world, this is the greatest thing of all; this was the case with Christ and the Blessed Virgin."

THE ENCYCLICAL FIDENTEM, 1896

The title *Mediatress with the Mediator,* that is, with Christ, was ascribed to the Virgin Mary by Pope Leo XIII in the encyclical *Fidentem* of September 20, 1896.

513
(1940a)

It is impossible to think of anyone who has ever done or ever will do as much as she has done in reconciling men with God. For it is she who brought a Savior to men when they were rushing towards eternal ruin. She "in place of all human nature" with her wonderful consent received the message of the mystery of peace brought to earth by an angel. She is the one of whom Jesus is born (*see Matt. 1:16*), his true mother, and for that reason the worthy and most beloved mediatress with the Mediator.

THE ENCYCLICAL AD DIEM ILLUM, 1904

In the encyclical *Ad diem illum,* of February 2, 1904, Pope St. Pius X (1903–14) explains the claim that Mary has to the office of being mediatress of all grace—the union of her will with Christ in suffering.

514
(1978a)

As a result of this union of suffering and willing between Mary and Christ, she "most deservedly merited to be the restorer of the lost world" and therefore the dispenser of all gifts that Jesus has won for us with his death and his blood. . . . Seeing that she is holier than all and more closely united with Christ, and as he has chosen her as his associate for the work of human salvation, she merits for us *congruously* (*de congruo*), as they say, what Christ merited *in strict justice* (*de condigno*), and she is the principal agent in distributing graces.

THE APOSTOLIC LETTER INTER SODALICIA, 1918

The Congregation of the Holy Office, in the decree *Sunt quos amor,* of June 26, 1913, praised the custom of calling Mary *Coredemptress;* and on January 22, 1914, it affixed an indulgence to a prayer in which Mary is called *Coredemptress* of the human race. The role of Mary in Christ's redeeming sacrifice is developed by Pope Benedict XV (1914–22) in his apostolic letter *Inter sodalicia,* March 22, 1918. (See DB 1978a, footnote 2, for the text from which the following translation is made.)

As she suffered and almost died together with her suffering and dying Son, so she surrendered her mother's rights over her Son for the salvation of the human race. And to satisfy the justice of God she sacrificed her Son, as well as she could, so that it may justly be said that she together with Christ has redeemed the human race.   **515**

THE APOSTOLIC LETTER EXPLORATA RES, 1923

It is significant that Pope Pius XI in one of his first Marian pronouncements, the apostolic letter *Explorata res,* February 2, 1923, returns to the point of Mary's share in the Redemption. (See DB 1978a, footnote 2, for the text from which the following translation is made.)

The sorrowful Virgin shared with Jesus Christ the work of the Redemption.   **516**

THE ENCYCLICAL MYSTICI CORPORIS, 1943

In the encyclical *Mystici corporis,* dated June 29, 1943 (*see introd. to 239*), Pope Pius XII (1939–58), concludes his exposition of the important doctrine on the mystical body with a prayer for Mary's intercession for the needs of the Church and of all mankind. In introducing this prayer, he outlines the role played by the Mother of God in the salvation of men and explains how she is spiritually the mother of the members of the mystical body. (This translation is made from the text in *Acta Apostolicae Sedis,* XXXV [1943], 247 f.)

Mary, the mother of the mystical body

Venerable Brothers, may the Virgin Mother of God grant the prayers of Our paternal heart—and they are yours too—and obtain for all a true love of the Church. Her sinless soul was filled with the divine Spirit of Jesus Christ more than all other created souls together; and "in the name of the whole human race" she gave her consent for a "spiritual marriage between the Son of God and human nature." Within   **517** her virginal womb Christ our Lord already bore the exalted title of Head of the Church; in a marvelous birth she brought him forth as source of all supernatural life, and presented him, new born, as prophet, king, and priest to those who were the first of Jews and Gentiles to come to adore him. Her only Son, yielding to a mother's prayer in "Cana of Galilee," performed the miracle by which "his disciples believed in him" (*John 2:2, 11*).

**518
(2291)** Free from all sin, original and personal, always most intimately united with her Son, as another Eve she offered him on Golgotha to the eternal Father for all the children of Adam, sin-stained in his fall; and her mother's rights and mother's love were included in the holocaust. Thus she who corporally was the mother of our head, through the added title of pain and glory became spiritually the mother of all his members. She it was who through her powerful prayers obtained the grace that the Spirit of our divine Redeemer, already given to the Church on the cross, should be bestowed anew through miraculous gifts on the newly founded Church on Pentecost. Bearing with courage and confidence the tremendous burden of her sorrows and desolation, truly the Queen of Martyrs, she more than all the faithful filled up "what is lacking of the sufferings of Christ . . . for his body, which is the Church" (*Col. 1:24*), and she continued to show for the mystical body of Christ, born from the pierced heart of the Savior, the same mother's care and ardent love with which she clasped the infant Jesus to her warm and nourishing breast.

THE BULL *MUNIFICENTISSIMUS DEUS*, 1950

On November 1, 1950, Pope Pius XII (1939–58) defined the Assumption of the Blessed Virgin into heaven as a dogma of faith. Leaving the dispute about whether or not Mary died an open question, the pope responded to the petitions of the bishops and priests and faithful by giving honor to the Blessed Virgin with this solemn definition. The Assumption of the Blessed Virgin, body and soul, into heaven is another of the great privileges conceded to her by God for consenting to be his mother.

Proclamation of the dogma of the Assumption

The universal Church, in which the Spirit of Truth dwells, and which he infallibly guides to perfect knowledge of revealed truths, has shown its faith many times in the course of the centuries. Bishops from all over the world with almost perfect unanimity have petitioned that the truth of the corporeal Assumption of the Blessed Virgin Mary into heaven be defined as a dogma of the divine, Catholic faith. The truth of this dogma is based on Sacred Scripture and is deeply rooted in the hearts of the faithful. It is sanctioned by the worship of the Church from the most ancient times. It is completely consonant with all other revealed truths. It has been explained and proclaimed by the study, the knowledge, and the wisdom of theologians. In consideration of all these reasons, We judge that in God's providence the time has come to proclaim solemnly this wonderful privilege of the Virgin Mary. . . .

519
(2332)

 # 41

We, therefore, after humbly and repeatedly praying to God, and calling upon the light of the Spirit of Truth, for the glory of almighty God, who has shown great and particular love for the Virgin Mary, for the honor of his Son, the king of immortal ages and the conqueror of sin and death, for the increase of the glory of his great mother, for the joy and exultation of the whole Church, by the authority of our Lord Jesus Christ, of the blessed Apostles Peter and Paul, and by Our own authority, do pronounce, declare, and define as a divinely revealed dogma: The Immaculate Mother of God, Mary ever Virgin, after her life on earth, was assumed, body and soul, to the glory of heaven.

520
(2333)

 # 44

The Veneration of the Saints

The large number of saints in heaven who form the ranks of the triumphant Church are so many powerful guardians to aid us in the spiritual combat that is our lot here on earth. From its infancy the Church has encouraged its children to invoke the intercession of the saints, always taking care to point out that there is an essential difference between the worship due to God and the homage paid to the saints. The Church invites and encourages the faithful to honor the persons of the saints by honoring their relics and images. The Church has always insisted, too, that the honor given to the saints, to their relics, and to their images, detracts not at all from God's honor, because by honoring the saints, their relics, and images one honors God, from whom comes all holiness.

THE COUNCIL OF CONSTANCE, 1414-18

The Council of Constance (*see introd. to 158*) proposed a list of questions to be put to the followers of Wyclif and Hus as a test of their orthodoxy. The following question is an indirect testimony to the approved custom of venerating the relics and images of the saints.

521
(679) 29. Likewise, whether he believes and asserts that it is licit for the relics and images of the saints to be venerated by the faithful of Christ.

THE COUNCIL OF TRENT, 1545-63

The second decree of the twenty-fifth session of the Council of Trent dealt with the invocation and the veneration of saints, of their relics, and of their images. Since the opinions and statements of the heretics in this matter were so vacillating, now approving, now condemning the practice, the tactic of the council was not to give an outline of the heretical opinions, nor even the details of the Catholic doctrine on the subject, but rather to enunciate only the chief proofs for the doctrine, and to make a simple statement of what was to be believed. In this they followed the same procedure as that of the Council of Constance (1414-18) in condemning the errors of Wyclif and Hus.

Veneration of saints

522
(984) The holy council orders all bishops and others who have the official charge of teaching to instruct the faithful diligently, in accordance with the practice of the Catholic and apostolic Church from the early years of the Christian religion, and in accordance with the common teaching of the holy Fathers and

the decrees of the sacred councils. First of all they should instruct the faithful carefully concerning the intercession and the invocation of the saints, the honor due to their relics, and the lawful use of images—teaching the faithful that the saints, reigning together with Christ, pray to God for men; it is a good and useful thing to invoke the saints humbly and to have recourse to their prayers and to their efficacious help to obtain favors from God through his Son Jesus Christ our Lord who alone is our redeemer and savior. Moreover, they should teach the faithful that only men of irreligious mentality deny that the saints enjoying eternal happiness in heaven are to be invoked; or claim either that saints do not pray for men or else that calling upon them to pray for us even as individuals is idolatry or is opposed to the word of God and is prejudicial to the honor of the one Mediator of God and men, Jesus Christ (*see I Tim. 2:5*); or say that it is foolish to make supplication by word or by thought to those who are reigning in heaven.

Veneration of relics

Furthermore, the sacred bodies of the holy martyrs and of the other saints living with Christ, which have been living members of Christ and the temple of the Holy Spirit (*see I Cor. 3:16; 6:19; II Cor. 6:16*) and which are destined to be taken up to eternal life and glorified by him, should be venerated by the faithful. Through these relics many benefits are granted to men by God. For this reason, those who say that veneration and honor is not due to the relics of the saints, or that these relics and the other sacred memorials are uselessly honored by the faithful, and that it is futile to visit the shrines of the saints in order to implore their assistance are to be condemned absolutely, just as the Church has already condemned them and even now condemns them.

523
(985)

Veneration of images

Further, the images of Christ, of the Virgin Mother of God, and of other saints are to be kept with honor in places of worship especially; and to them due honor and veneration is to be paid—not because it is believed that there is any divinity or power intrinsic to them for which they are reverenced,

524
(986)

The Incarnation and Redemption

nor because it is from them that something is sought, nor that a blind trust is to be attached to images as it once was by the Gentiles who placed their hope in idols (*see Ps. 134:15 ff.*); but because the honor which is shown to them is referred to the prototypes which they represent. Thus it follows that through these images which we kiss and before which we kneel and uncover our heads, we are adoring Christ and venerating the saints whose likenesses these images bear. That is what is enacted by the decrees of the councils, especially the Second Council of Nicaea, against the opponents of images.

Advice for bishops

525
(987) Indeed, let the bishops diligently teach that accounts of the mysteries of our Redemption, as they are expressed in pictures or in other likenesses, instruct and encourage the people to call to mind habitually and go over the articles of faith. Let them also teach that this great benefit is realized from all sacred images not only because the people are reminded of the favors and of the gifts which were given to them by Christ, but also because through the saints of God miracles and salutary examples are put before the eyes of the faithful, so that they may give thanks to God for them, that they may fashion their lives and their actions in imitation of the saints, and that they may be spurred on to adore and love God and to cultivate piety. If anyone thinks or teaches the contrary to these decrees: let him be anathema.

Correcting abuses

526
(988) However, if any abuses creep into these sacred, salutary observances, the holy council greatly desires that these abuses be completely done away with, so that no dogmatically misleading images be set up, or any which would afford occasion of dangerous error to the simple faithful. But if historical and other narratives of the Holy Scriptures are sometimes portrayed and pictured for the benefit of an unlettered group, let the people be taught that although the Divinity is represented in figures, this is not because it is such as can be seen by bodily eyes or portrayed in color or form. . . .

Grace

Where life is, there is activity. In natural human life three elements can be distinguished: life itself, or vital principle, and this is the soul. Secondly, there are the powers, or faculties, which emanate from the soul; for example, the faculties of intellect, will, and sight. Lastly, there are the acts or operations of these faculties, for example, understanding, willing, and seeing. Analogically the same is true of the supernatural life. There is a vital principle inhering in the substance of the soul, and this is sanctifying grace. Then there are the faculties or powers of this supernatural vital principle, the theological virtues of faith, hope, and charity, together with the gifts of the Holy Spirit. Finally, there are the meritorious actions, done with the help of grace.

God raised the first man to the state of sanctifying grace. This was entirely gratuitous, since man had no claim on it. Adam, head of the human race, sinned grievously and lost that great gift for himself and for all of his posterity. Man was then in the state of fallen nature. He was destined for a supernatural goal, the beatific vision of God; but he had lost the means to attain that end.

Because of his great love for mankind, God became man; he redeemed mankind by his death on the cross; he made it possible for men to regain the life of grace and to become heirs of the kingdom of heaven. Christ's life and work, infinite in goodness, were more than sufficient to restore the human race to God's favor, and to make all men the adopted sons of God. It is by justification that a man becomes a new creature in Christ Jesus, just, holy, a son of God, an heir of eternal life. Now that *the gospel has been promulgated, no one is justified except by the actual reception of baptism, by baptism of desire, or by baptism of blood. Christ said very clearly, "Unless a man be born again of water and the Spirit, he cannot enter into the kingdom of God" (John 3:5).*

An adult must prepare himself and dispose himself for receiving the grace of justification by free, salutary acts. He cannot prepare himself, though, unless he is called and aided by divine help. This gratuitous divine help arouses man and helps him to make acts of faith and hope and love of God, to do penance, to resolve to receive baptism, and to begin a new life by the faithful observance of the commandments. And even after a man has been justified, he still needs divine help to persevere in the justice he has received.

Those divine helps which aid a man to dispose himself for justification, to persevere in justice, to merit eternal life by his good works, are all called actual graces. *Justification, which makes man a new creature, because it endures in the soul, is called* habitual grace, *or* sanctifying grace.

THE SIXTEENTH COUNCIL OF CARTHAGE, 418

Grace, original justice, and justification are so related that errors about one inevitably lead to a false understanding of the others. When the assembly of bishops at Carthage, 418, condemned the Pelagian teaching on original justice (*see introd. to 367*), many of the canons they drew up dealt specifically with grace. Pope St. Zosimus (417–18) confirmed the canons.

527
(103)
3. They have likewise decreed: Whoever says that God's grace, which justifies mankind through our Lord Jesus Christ, has the power only for the remission of those sins already committed, and is not also a help to prevent sins from being committed: let him be anathema.

528
(104)
4. They have likewise decreed: Whoever says that God's grace through Jesus Christ our Lord helps us avoid sin solely because it gives us a very clear knowledge and understanding of the positive and negative commandments, but denies that through this grace there is given to us an ability and a love of

doing what we know should be done: let him be anathema. For since the Apostle says: "Knowledge puffs up, but charity edifies" (*I Cor. 8:1*), it would be very wrong to believe that we have Christ's grace for knowledge, which puffs up, and not for charity, which edifies. Knowledge of what we ought to do and love of doing it are both gifts of God. Thus knowledge working with charity cannot make us puffed up. For it is written of God: "He that teacheth man knowledge" (*Ps. 93:10*); but it is also written: "Love is from God" (*I John 4:7*).

5. They have likewise decreed: Whoever says that the grace of justification was given us so that grace could facilitate our fulfilling what our free will is ordered to do, as if to say that, if grace were not given, it would be possible but not easy to obey God's commandments without that grace: let him be anathema. For the Lord was speaking of the observance of the commandments when he said: "Without me you can do nothing" (*John 15:5*). He did not say: "Without me it will be more difficult for you to do anything." **529** **(105)**

6. They have likewise decreed: Whoever thinks St. John the Apostle's statement—"If we say that we have no sin, we deceive ourselves, and truth is not in us" (*I John 1:8*)—is to be taken in the sense that he is saying we have sin because humility demands us to say so, not because we actually do have sin: let him be anathema. For the apostle continues: "If we acknowledge our sins, He is faithful and just to forgive us our sins and to cleanse us from all iniquity" (*I John 1:9*). Hence it is quite clear that this is said not only from humility but truthfully. For the apostle could have said: "If we say we have no sin we exalt ourselves, and humility is not in us." But since he says: "We deceive ourselves, and truth is not in us," he clearly shows that the person who says he has no sin is not speaking the truth. **530** **(106)**

7. They have likewise decreed: Whoever says that the reason why the saints say, "forgive us our debts" (*Matt. 6:12*) in the Our Father is not that they are requesting this for themselves—for such a request is not necessary for them—but that they are requesting it for others of their people who are debtors; and whoever says that the reason why each of the **531** **(107)**

saints does not say, "forgive me my debts," but "forgive us our debts," is that the just man is understood to make this request for others rather than for himself: let him be anathema. The Apostle James was a holy and a just man when he said, "For in many things we all offend" (*Jas. 3:2*). Why was the word *all* added? Was it not added to express the same idea as is found in the Psalm: "And enter not into judgment with thy servant: for in thy sight no man living shall be justified" (*Ps. 142:2*)? The same idea is found in the prayer of Solomon, the wise man: "For there is no man who sinneth not" (*III Kings 8:46*). And we read in the book of Job: "He sealeth up the hand of all men, that every one may know his works" (*Job 37:7*). Even the holy and just Daniel used the plural form in his prayer when he said, "We have sinned, we have committed iniquity," and when he says the other things that he truly and humbly confesses (*Dan. 9:5, 15*). And lest anyone should think, as some do, that he was not speaking of his own sins, but of those of his people, he said further on: "While . . . I was praying, and confessing my sins and the sins of my people" to the Lord my God (*Dan. 9:20*). He was unwilling to say "our sins"; therefore he said, "my sins and the sins of my people," since he foresaw as a prophet there would be some who would misunderstand him.

532
(108)
8. They have likewise decreed: Whoever says that, when the saints pray the Our Father, they say "forgive us our debts" (*Matt. 6:12*) humbly rather than truthfully: let him be anathema. For who would tolerate the thought of a man praying and lying, not to men but to the Lord himself, since he says with his lips that he wishes to have his debts forgiven, but denies in his heart that he has anything to be forgiven?

CATALOGUE OF PAPAL PRONOUNCEMENTS ON THE DOCTRINE OF GRACE AND ORIGINAL SIN, *cir.* 435-42

This catalogue, the *Indiculus* (*see introd. to 368*), has been considered an authoritative statement of the Roman Church's teaching.

Introduction

533
(129)
Some who pride themselves on having the name of Catholics are, either through malice or inexperience, spending their

time on the condemned propositions of the heretics, and they
have the presumption to contradict very faithful writers. Although these men do not hesitate to heap anathemas upon
Pelagius and Coelestius, still they find fault with our own
teachers for being extremists. They say that they follow and
approve only what, through the ministry of its bishops, the
Holy See of the Apostle St. Peter has taught and approved
against the enemies of the grace of God. For this reason it
has been necessary to make a diligent investigation as to what
judgment the rulers of the Roman Church made about heresy
that arose during their time, and what opinion they thought
should be held about the grace of God against the dangerous
upholders of "free will." We are also attaching some statements of the councils of Africa, which the apostolic bishops
certainly adopted as their own when they gave them their
approval. Therefore, to instruct more fully those who are
doubtful about some point, we promulgate the doctrine of the
Holy Fathers in this brief catalogue. Thus, if a person is not
too contentious, he may see that the conclusion of all these
disputes is contained in the following brief summary, and
that there is no ground left him for asserting the contrary if
only he believes and professes his faith with the Catholics as
follows:

Errors on grace condemned

Chapter 2. Unless he who alone is good grants a partici-   **534**
pation in his being, no one has goodness within himself. This **(131)**
truth is proclaimed by that pontiff [*St. Innocent I*] in the following sentence of the same letter (*see 368*): "For the future,
can we expect anything good from those whose mentality is
such that they think they are the cause of their goodness and
do not take into account him whose grace they obtain each
day, and who hope to accomplish so much without him?"

Chapter 3. No one, not even he who has been renewed by   **535**
the grace of baptism, has sufficient strength to overcome the **(132)**
snares of the devil, and to vanquish the concupiscence of the
flesh, unless he obtains help from God each day to persevere
in a good life. And the truth of this statement is confirmed by
the same pope's teaching in the letter cited above (*see 368,*

534): "For although he redeemed man from his past sins, still, since he knew man could sin again, he had at hand many things whereby he could restore man and set him straight even after man sinned, offering those daily remedies upon which we must rely and trust in our struggle; for by no other means would we be able to overcome our human mistakes."

Approval of the statements of Pope Zosimus

536
(134)
Chapter 5. All the efforts, and all the works and merits of the saints must be attributed to the praise and glory of God, because no one can please God with anything that is not His very own gift. It is the directive authority of Pope Zosimus of happy memory that leads us to this conclusion; for, when writing to the bishops of the whole world, he says: "But We, inspired by God (for all good things must be attributed to the source from which they proceed), have committed the entire matter to the consideration of our brothers and co-bishops." This letter shone with the light of purest truth, and the bishops of Africa held it in such esteem that they wrote the following reply to Zosimus: "We considered the contents of the letter which you made sure was sent to all the provinces —the letter in which you said, 'But We, inspired by God . . .' —as a swift thrust of the naked sword of truth with which you dispatch those who exalt human freedom above God's grace. What have you ever done with greater freedom of choice than to commit this entire matter to our humble consideration? And, nevertheless, with sincerity and wisdom you knew that your decision to commit the matter to us was inspired by God, and you truthfully and courageously proclaimed that it was. Without doubt, you did so because the will is prepared by the Lord (*see Prov. 8:35, Septuagint*), and he himself as a father touches the hearts of his sons with inspirations that they may do good of any sort. For as many as are led by the Spirit of God, they are the sons of God (*see Rom. 8:14*). Thus we do not judge that we are without freedom of choice nor do we entertain any doubt that God's grace plays an even more predominant role in each and every good impulse of man's will."

537
(135)
Chapter 6. God so works in the hearts of men and in free will itself that the holy thought, the gentle counsel, and every

movement of a good will are from God, because it is through
him that we can do any good, and without him we can do
nothing (*see John 15:5*). The same teacher Zosimus instructed
us to acknowledge this truth when, speaking to the bishops
of the world about the assistance of divine grace, he said:
"Is there ever a time when we do not need his help? Therefore, in every action and situation, in every thought and movement, we must pray to him as to our helper and protector. For
whatever human nature presumes to do by itself manifests
pride, since the Apostle warns: 'Our wrestling is not against
flesh and blood, but against the Principalities and the Powers
of this darkness, against the spiritual forces of wickedness on
high' (*see Eph. 6:12*). And as he says on another occasion:
'Unhappy man that I am! Who will deliver me from the body
of this death? The grace of God through Jesus Christ our Lord'
(*see Rom. 7:24 f.*). And again: 'By the grace of God I am what
I am, and his grace in me has not been fruitless; in fact I have
labored more than any of them, yet not I, but the grace of
God with me' " (*I Cor. 15:10*).

Condemnation of Pelagius approved

Chapter 7. We likewise uphold as the personal teaching of
the Apostolic See what was set down in the decrees of the
Council of Carthage and defined in the third chapter: "Whoever says that God's grace, which justifies mankind through
our Lord Jesus Christ, has the power only for the remission
of those sins already committed, and is not also a help to
prevent sins from being committed: let him be anathema" (*see*
527).

538
(136)

We uphold also what was defined in the fourth chapter:
"Whoever says that God's grace through Jesus Christ our Lord
helps us avoid sin solely because it gives us a very clear
knowledge and understanding of the positive and negative
commandments, but denies that through this grace there is
given to us an ability and a love of doing what we know
should be done: let him be anathema. For since the Apostle
says: 'Knowledge puffs up, but charity edifies' (*I Cor. 8:1*),
it would be very wrong to believe that we have Christ's grace
for knowledge, which puffs up, and not for charity, which

539
(137)

edifies. Knowledge of what we ought to do and love of doing it are both gifts of God. Thus knowledge working with charity cannot make us puffed up. For it is written of God: 'He that teacheth man knowledge' (*Ps. 93:10*); but it is also written: 'Love is from God'" (*I John 4:7; see 104*).

540
(138)
We uphold also what was defined in the fifth chapter: "Whoever says that the grace of justification was given us so that grace could facilitate our fulfilling what our free will is ordered to do, as if to say that, if grace were not given, it would be possible but not easy to obey God's commandments without that grace: let him be anathema. For the Lord was speaking of the observance of the commandments when he said: 'Without me you can do nothing' (*John 15:5*). He did not say: 'Without me it will be more difficult for you to do anything.'"

The liturgy and the necessity of grace

541
(139)
Chapter 8. The preceding chapters are the inviolable decrees of the most holy and Apostolic See, the decrees by which our reverend Fathers, suppressing the spread of a dangerous novelty, taught us to attribute to the grace of Christ both the initial impulses of a good will and the increase of praiseworthy efforts as well as final perseverance in them. Besides these decrees, let us also examine the sacred words of the prayers the priests say. Let us examine these sacred words which were handed down from the apostles throughout the world and which are uniformly used in every Catholic church, and thus find in the prayers of the liturgy confirmation for the law of our faith. For when the leaders of the holy people perform the functions of the office entrusted to them, they plead the cause of the human race before the tribunal of divine mercy. And with the whole Church earnestly praying along with them, they beg and they entreat that the faith be given to infidels, that idolators be freed from the errors of their ungodliness, that the veil be removed from the hearts of the Jews so that the light of truth may shine upon them, that heretics may come to their senses and accept the Catholic faith, that schismatics may receive the spirit of charity that restores life, that sinners be given the healing powers of repentance, and, finally, that catechumens may be brought to the sacrament of

regeneration and that the heavenly court of mercy may be opened to them. That these requests from the Lord are not just a matter of form is shown by the actual course of events. For God, indeed, deigns to draw many men from errors of every description—men whom he has rescued from the power of darkness and transferred into the kingdom of his beloved Son (*see Col. 1:13*), and whom he has changed from vessels of wrath into vessels of mercy (*see Rom. 9:22 f.*). And this is felt to be so exclusively a divine operation, that thanksgiving and praise are being constantly given to God, who brings about the enlightenment and correction of such persons.

Chapter 9. . . . By these ecclesiastical norms and these documents derived from divine authority, we are so strengthened with the help of the Lord, that we profess that God is the author of all good desires and deeds, of all efforts and virtues, with which from the beginning of faith man tends to God. And we do not doubt that his grace anticipates every one of man's merits, and that it is through him that we begin both the will and the performance (*see Phil. 2:13*) of any good work. To be sure, free will is not destroyed by this help and strength from God, but it is freed; so that from darkness it is brought to light, from evil to good, from sickness to health, from ignorance to prudence. For such is God's goodness to men that he wills that his gifts be our merits, and that he will grant us an eternal reward for what he has given us. Indeed, God so acts in us that we both will and do what he wills; he does not allow to lie idle in us what he bestowed upon us to be employed, not neglected. And he acts in this manner in us so that we are cooperators with his grace. And if we notice that there is some weakness in us because of our own negligence, we should with all care hasten to him who heals all our diseases and redeems our lives from destruction (*see Ps. 102:3 f.*), and to whom we say each day, "Lead us not into temptation but deliver us from evil" (*Matt. 6:13*).

542
(141)

THE SECOND COUNCIL OF ORANGE, 529

One of the most important councils of the sixth century was the Second Council of Orange, held in southern Gaul. The presiding prelate was Archbishop Caesarius of Arles. The following numbers contain the canons on grace which the prelates signed on July 3, 529, against the Semi-Pelagians, especially against their denial of the necessity of grace for the beginning of faith. On January 25, 531, Pope Boniface II (530–32) confirmed the Second Council of Orange, and since then this part of the controversy against the Semi-Pelagians has been considered closed.

Grace

543
(176)

3. If anyone says that the grace of God can be conferred because of human prayer, but that it is not grace that prompts us to pray, he contradicts the Prophet Isaias or the Apostle who says the same thing: "I was found by those who did not seek me; I appeared openly to those who made no inquiry of me" (*Rom. 10:20; see Isa. 65:1*).

544
(177)

4. If anyone argues that God awaits our will before cleansing us from sin, but does not profess that even the desire to be cleansed is accomplished through the infusion and the interior working of the Holy Spirit, he opposes the Holy Spirit speaking through Solomon: "The will is prepared by the Lord" (*Prov. 8:35, Septuagint*). And he opposes the Apostle's salutary message: "It is God who of his good pleasure works in you both the will and the performance" (*Phil. 2:13*).

545
(178)

5. He is an adversary of the apostolic teaching who says that the increase of faith as well as the beginning of faith and the very desire of faith—by which we believe in Him who justifies the unjustified, and by which we come to the regeneration of sacred baptism—inheres in us naturally and not by a gift of grace. This grace is the inspiration of the Holy Spirit, guiding our will away from infidelity to faith, from godlessness to piety. For St. Paul says: "We are convinced of this, that he who has begun a good work in you will bring it to perfection until the day of Christ Jesus" (*see Phil. 1:6*). And he says: "You have been given the favor on Christ's behalf—not only to believe in him but also to suffer for him" (*see Phil. 1:29*). And again: "By grace you have been saved through faith; and that not from yourselves, for it is the gift of God" (*see Eph. 2:8*). For those who say that it is a natural faith by which we believe in God teach that all those who are separated from the Church of Christ are, in a certain sense, believers.

Grace

6. If anyone says that mercy is divinely conferred upon us **546** when, without God's grace, we believe, will, desire, strive, **(179)** labor, pray, keep watch, study, beg, seek, knock for entrance, but does not profess that it is through the interior infusion and inspiration of the Holy Spirit that we believe, will, or are able to do all these things in the way we ought; or if anyone grants that the help of grace is dependent upon humility or human obedience, and does not grant that it is the very gift of grace that makes us obedient and humble, he contradicts the words of the Apostle: "What hast thou that thou hast not received?" (*I Cor. 4:7*); and: "By the grace of God, I am what I am" (*I Cor. 15:10*).

15. "From the man that God had formed, Adam was **547** changed through his own iniquity, and the change was for **(188)** the worse. From the man that iniquity had formed, the man of faith is changed through the grace of God, and the change is for the better. The former was the change of the first sinner; the latter, as the Psalmist says, is the change of the hand of the Most High" (*see Ps. 76:11*).

The teaching of tradition on grace

And thus, according to the passages of Holy Scripture and **548** according to the explanations of the ancient Fathers, quoted **(199)** above [*i.e., in cans. 1–25*], we, with God's help, must believe and preach the following: The free will of man was made so weak and unsteady through the sin of the first man that, after the Fall, no one could love God as was required, or believe in God, or perform good works for God unless the grace of divine mercy anticipated him. Therefore, we believe that the renowned faith which was given to the just Abel, to Noe, to Abraham, to Isaac and Jacob, and to that vast number of the saints of old, was given through the grace of God and not through natural goodness, which had first been given to Adam. This faith of theirs the Apostle Paul has praised in his preaching. And we know and believe that even after the coming of Christ this grace of faith is not found in the free will of all who desire to be baptized, but is conferred through the generosity of Christ, according to what has already been said and according to what Paul preaches: "You have been given the

favor on Christ's behalf—not only to believe in him, but also
to suffer for him" (*Phil. 1:29*). And also: "God who has begun
a good work in you will bring it to perfection until the day of
our Lord" (*see Phil. 1:6*). And again: "By grace you have been
saved through faith; and that not from yourselves, for it is
the gift of God" (*see Eph. 2:8*). And the Apostle says of himself: "I have obtained mercy that I might be faithful" (*see
I Cor. 7:25; I Tim. 1:13*). He does not say, "because I was
faithful," but he says, "that I might be faithful." And Scripture
says further: "What hast thou that thou hast not received?"
(*I Cor. 4:7*). And again: "Every good gift, and every perfect
gift is from above, coming down from the Father of Lights"
(*see Jas. 1:17*). And again: "No one has anything unless it is
given him from above" (*see John 3:27*). There are innumerable
passages of Sacred Scripture that can be cited to bear witness
to grace, but they have been omitted for the sake of brevity.
And, indeed, more texts would not help a person for whom
these few are not sufficient.

The teaching of tradition on predestination

549
(200) According to Catholic faith we also believe that after grace
has been received through baptism, all the baptized, if they
are willing to labor faithfully, can and ought to accomplish
with Christ's help and cooperation what pertains to the salvation of their souls. We do not believe that some are predestined
to evil by the divine power; and, furthermore, if there are
those who wish to believe in such an enormity, with great
abhorrence we anathematize them. We also believe and profess for our salvation that in every good work it is not that
we make a beginning and afterwards are helped through
God's mercy, but rather, that without any previous good
merits on our part, God himself first inspires us with faith in
him and love of him so that we may faithfully seek the sacrament of baptism, and so that after baptism, with his help, we
may be able to accomplish what is pleasing to him. Therefore, we evidently must believe that the remarkable faith of
the thief whom the Lord called to his home in paradise (*see
Luke 23:43*), the faith of Cornelius the centurion to whom an
angel of the Lord was sent (*see Acts 10:3*), and the faith of

Zacchaeus who merited to receive the Lord himself (*see Luke 19:6*), was not a gift of nature but a gift of God's generosity.

CONDEMNATION OF ERRORS OF MARTIN LUTHER, 1520

Beginning from his open attack on the practice of indulgences in the Church in 1517, Luther had gone on to expound certain fundamental doctrinal errors. He held that nature, entirely corrupted and deprived of moral liberty by sin, is forced to sin. Justification is something completely extrinsic to man and consists in this, that sin is no longer imputed to the sinner but instead the merits of Christ, laid hold of by the faith of confidence alone, are imputed to him. After patient waiting and lengthy consideration, Pope Leo X (1513–21) finally issued the bull *Exsurge Domine* in June, 1520, condemning forty-one errors of Luther. They were taken from Luther's own writings and related to free will, original sin, the sacraments in general, faith, grace, sin, penance, confession, the primacy, etc. As presented in the bull, the individual errors are not given a precise doctrinal censure.

1. It is a heretical, though common, opinion that the sacraments of the New Law give justifying grace to those who place no obstacle in the way. **550** *(741)*

2. To deny that sin remains in a child after baptism is to despise both Paul and Christ alike. **551** *(742)*

3. The tendency to sin hinders a departing soul's entrance into heaven, even though there is no actual sin. **552** *(743)*

31. In every good work the just man sins. **553** *(771)*

32. A good work perfectly performed is a venial sin. **554** *(772)*

36. After sin, free will is a term without meaning; and when it does what is in its power, it sins mortally. **555** *(776)*

THE COUNCIL OF TRENT, 1545-63

One of the most important sessions of the Council of Trent (*see introd. to 95*) was the sixth, which lasted from June 21, 1546, until January 13, 1547. After long debate, much discussion, drafting and redrafting, the decree on justification was finally published.

Grace

DECREE ON JUSTIFICATION

Preface

556
(792a)
Since at this time a certain erroneous teaching about justification is being broadcast with the consequent loss of many souls and serious damage to Church unity, this holy, ecumenical, and general Council of Trent has been lawfully convoked in the Holy Spirit for the praise and glory of the omnipotent God, for the tranquillity of the Church, and for the salvation of souls. Presiding over the council in the name of our most holy father and lord in Christ, Paul III by divine providence pope, are the very reverend lords, John Mary del Monte, bishop of Praeneste; Marcellus, titular priest of Santa Croce in Jerusalem; cardinals of the holy Roman Church, and apostolic legates *de latere*. Under their guidance, this council intends to set forth for all the faithful of Christ the true, sound doctrine of justification, which the "Sun of justice" (*Mal. 4:2*) Jesus Christ, the author and finisher of our faith (*see Heb. 12:2*), has taught, which the apostles have handed down, and which the Catholic Church, under the inspiration of the Holy Spirit, has always preserved. The council gives strict orders that hereafter no one is to presume to believe, preach, or teach anything contrary to what is defined and declared in this decree.

Chapter 1. The Insufficiency of Nature and the Law to Justify Man

557
(793)
First, the holy council declares that, for an honest, unprejudiced understanding of the doctrine of justification, it is necessary to admit that all men had lost innocence in the sin of Adam (*see Rom. 5:12; I Cor. 15:22; 368*). They became unclean (*see Isa. 64:6*). And (according to the word of the Apostle) they "were by nature children of wrath" (*Eph. 2:3*), as the council taught in its decree on original sin. So completely were they slaves of sin (*see Rom. 6:20*) and under the power of the devil and of death, that neither the power of nature for the Gentiles (*see 575, can. 1*) nor the very letter of the Law of Moses for the Jews could bring liberation from that condition. And yet their free will, though weakened and unsteady, was by no means destroyed (*see 579, can. 5*).

Grace

Chapter 2. God's Dispensation and the Mystery of Christ's Coming

And so it came about that, when the glorious fullness of
time had come (*see Eph. 1:4; Gal. 4:4*), the heavenly Father,
"the Father of mercies and the God of all comfort" (*II Cor.
1:3*), sent Jesus Christ his Son to men. Christ had been announced and promised to many holy Fathers before the Law
and during the time of the Law (*see Gen. 49:10, 18*). He was
sent that the Jews, who were under the Law, might be redeemed, and that the Gentiles, who were not pursuing justice,
might secure justice (*see Rom. 9:30*), and that all might receive the adoption of sons (*see Gal. 4:5*). God has set him
forth as a propitiation by his blood through faith for our sins
(*see Rom. 3:25*), not for our sins only, but also for those of
the whole world (*see I John 2:2*).

558
(794)

Chapter 3. Who Are Justified through Christ

But even though Christ did die for all (*see II Cor. 5:15*),
still all do not receive the benefit of his death, but only those
with whom the merit of his Passion is shared. Truly, men
would not have been born without justice except that they
were born children of Adam's seed. For it is because of their
descent from him that in their conception they contract injustice as their own. So likewise they would never have been
justified except through rebirth in Christ (*see 576, can. 2;
584, can. 10*), for this rebirth bestows on them through the
merit of his Passion the grace by which they are justified. For
this benefit the Apostle exhorts us to give thanks always to
the Father "who has made us worthy to share the lot of the
saints in light" (*Col. 1:12*), and who has rescued us from the
power of darkness and transferred us into the kingdom of his
beloved Son, in whom we have redemption and remission of
sins (*see Col. 1:13 f.*).

559
(795)

Chapter 4. A Summary Description of the Justification of a Sinner and the Manner of Justification under the Dispensation of Grace

In the preceding words a description is given of the justification of the unjust. Justification is a passing from the state

560
(796)

in which man *is* born a son of the first Adam, to the state of grace and adoption as sons of God (*see Rom. 8:15*) through the second Adam, Jesus Christ our Savior. After the promulgation of the gospel this passing cannot take place without the water of regeneration (*see 691, can. 5*) or the desire for it, as it is written: "Unless a man be born again of water and the Holy Spirit, he cannot enter into the kingdom of God" (*John 3:5*).

Chapter 5. The Necessity for Adults to Prepare Themselves for Justification and the Origin of This Justification

561
(797)
    Moreover, the holy council declares that in the case of adults justification must begin with God's prevenient grace through Jesus Christ (*see 577, can. 3*). That is, it must begin with God's call, a call which they do not merit. The purpose of this call is that they who are turned away from God by sin may, awakened and assisted by his grace, be disposed to turn to their own justification by freely assenting to and cooperating with that grace (*see 578, can. 4; 579, can. 5*). The result is that, when God touches the heart of man with the illumination of the Holy Spirit, the man who accepts that inspiration certainly does something, since he could reject it; on the other hand, by his own free will, without God's grace, he could not take one step towards justice in God's sight (*see 577, can. 3*). Hence, when it is said in Sacred Scripture, "Turn ye to me, and I will turn to you" (*Zach. 1:3*), we are reminded of our freedom; when we answer, "Convert us, O Lord, to thee, and we shall be converted" (*Lam. 5:21*), we acknowledge that God's grace prepares us.

Chapter 6. The Manner of Preparation

562
(798)
    Adults are disposed for justification in this way (*see 581, can. 7; 583, can. 9*): Awakened and assisted by divine grace, they conceive faith from hearing (*see Rom. 10:17*), and they are freely led to God. They believe that the divine revelation and promises are true (*see 586, can. 12; 588, can. 14*), especially that the unjustified man is justified by God's grace "through the redemption which is in Christ Jesus" (*Rom. 3:24*). Next, they know that they are sinners; and, by turning from a salutary fear of divine justice to a consideration of

God's mercy, they are encouraged to hope, confident that God will be propitious to them for Christ's sake. They begin to love God as the source of all justice and are thereby moved by a sort of hatred and detestation for sin, that is, by the penance that must be done before baptism. Finally, they determine to receive baptism, begin a new life, and keep the divine commandments. This disposition is described in Holy Scripture: "He who comes to God must believe that God exists and is a rewarder to those who seek him" (*Heb. 11:6*); and: "Take courage, son, thy sins are forgiven thee" (*Matt. 9:2; Mark 2:5*); and: "The fear of the Lord driveth out sin" (*Ecclus. 1:27*). "Repent and be baptized every one of you in the name of Jesus Christ for the forgiveness of your sins; and you will receive the gift of the Holy Spirit" (*Acts 2:38*); and: "Go, therefore, and make disciples of all nations, baptizing them in the name of the Father, and of the Son, and of the Holy Spirit, teaching them to observe all that I have commanded you" (*Matt. 28:19*); finally: "Prepare your hearts unto the Lord" (*1 Kings 7:3*).

Chapter 7. The Nature and the Causes of the Justification of a Sinner

Justification itself follows upon this disposition or preparation, and justification is not only the remission of sins (*see 585, can. 11*), but sanctification and renovation of the interior man through the voluntary reception of grace and gifts, whereby a man becomes just instead of unjust and a friend instead of an enemy, that he may be an heir in the hope of life everlasting (*see Titus 3:7*). The causes of this justification are the following: The final cause is the glory of God and of Christ, and life everlasting. The efficient cause is the merciful God, who freely washes and sanctifies (*see 1 Cor. 6:11*) sealing and anointing with the Holy Spirit of the promise, who is the pledge of our inheritance (*see Eph. 1:13 f.*). The meritorious cause is the beloved only-begotten Son of God, our Lord Jesus Christ, who, when we were enemies (*see Rom. 5:10*), by reason of his very great love wherewith he has loved us (*see Eph. 2:4*), merited justification for us by his own most holy Passion on the wood of the cross, and made satisfaction for us to God the Father. The instrumental cause is

563
(799)

the sacrament of baptism, which is the "sacrament of faith"; without faith no one has ever been justified. Finally, the only formal cause is "the justice of God, not the justice by which he is himself just, but the justice by which he makes us just" (*see 584, can. 10; 585, can. 11*), namely, the justice which we have as a gift from him and by which we are renewed in the spirit of our mind. And not only are we considered just, but we are truly said to be just, and we are just, each one of us receiving within himself his own justice, according to the measure the Holy Spirit imparts to each one as he wishes (*see I Cor. 12:11*), and according to the disposition and co-operation of each one.

564
(800)   For although no one can be just unless he is granted a share in the merits of the Passion of our Lord Jesus Christ; still, in the justification of the unjustified that is precisely what happens when, by the merit of the same most holy Passion, the charity of God is poured forth by the Holy Spirit into the hearts (*see Rom. 5:5*) of those who are justified and remains in them (*see 585, can. 11*). Whence in the very act of being justified, at the same time that his sins are remitted, a man receives through Jesus Christ, to whom he is joined, the infused gifts of faith, hope, and charity. For faith without hope and charity neither perfectly unites a man with Christ nor makes him a living member of his body. Therefore it is said most truly that faith without works is dead (*see Jas. 2:17 ff.*) and useless (*see 593, can. 19*), and that in Christ Jesus neither circumcision is of any avail, nor uncircumcision, but faith which works through charity (*see Gal. 5:6; 6:15*). This is the faith that, according to apostolic tradition the catechumens ask of the Church before the reception of the sacrament of baptism when they petition for "the faith that gives eternal life." But faith, without hope and charity, cannot give eternal life. Next the catechumens immediately listen to Christ's words, "If thou wilt enter into life, keep the commandments" (*Matt. 19:17; see 592–94, cans. 18–20*). Accordingly, as soon as they are baptized, the catechumens are commanded to keep brilliant and spotless the true Christian justice they have received, as being the best robe (*see Luke 15:22*) that has been given them by Christ Jesus to replace the one Adam lost for

himself and for us by his disobedience, so that they may wear it before the tribunal of our Lord Jesus Christ and have life everlasting.

Chapter 8. The Correct Meaning of the Statement: The Sinner Is Gratuitously Justified by Faith

But when the Apostle says that man is justified "through faith" (see 583, can. 9) and "freely" (Rom. 3:22, 24), those words must be understood in the sense that the Catholic Church has always continuously held and declared. We may then be said to be justified through faith, in the sense that "faith is the beginning of man's salvation," the foundation and source of all justification, "without which it is impossible to please God" (see Heb. 11:6) and to be counted as his sons. We may be said to be justified freely, in the sense that nothing that precedes justification, neither faith nor works, merits the grace of justification; for "if out of grace, then not in virtue of works; otherwise (as the same Apostle says) grace is no longer grace" (Rom. 11:6).

565
(801)

Chapter 9. Against the Heretical Teaching of Presumptuous Trust

It is necessary to believe that sins are not remitted and have never been remitted except freely by the divine mercy for Christ's sake. Nevertheless, it must not be said that sins are forgiven or have ever been forgiven to anyone who boasts a confidence and a certain knowledge of the forgiveness of his sins and who relies upon this confidence alone. This empty, ungodly confidence (see 586, can. 12) may exist among heretics and schismatics and actually does exist in our times and is preached against the Catholic Church with bitter arguments. Furthermore, it should not be asserted that they who are truly justified must unhesitatingly determine within themselves that they are justified; and that no one is absolved from his sins and justified except one who believes with certainty that he is absolved and justified. Moreover, it should not be asserted that absolution and justification are brought about by this faith alone (see 588, can. 14), as if to say that whoever lacks this faith doubts God's promises and the efficacy of Christ's death and resurrection. For no devout man should entertain

566
(802)

doubts about God's mercy, Christ's merits, and the power and efficacy of the sacraments. Similarly, whoever reflects upon himself, his personal weakness, and his defective disposition may fear and tremble about his own grace (*see 587, can. 13*), since no one can know with the certitude of faith, which cannot admit any error, that he has obtained God's grace.

Chapter 10. The Increase of Justification in One Who Has Been Justified

567
(803)
Therefore, in this way the justified become both friends of God and members of his household (*see John 15:15; Eph. 2:19*), advancing from virtue to virtue (*see Ps. 83:8*), renewed (as the Apostle says) day by day (*see II Cor. 4:16*), that is, by mortifying the members of their flesh (*see Col. 3:5*) and showing them as weapons of justice (*see Rom. 6:13, 19*) unto sanctification by observing the commandments of God and of the Church. When faith works along with their works (*see Jas. 2:22*), the justified increase in the very justice which they have received through the grace of Christ and are justified the more (*see 598, can. 24; 606, can. 32*), as it is written: "He who is just, let him be just still" (*Apoc. 22:11*), and again: "Fear not to be justified even to death" (*Ecclus. 18:22*), and again: "You see that by works a man is justified, and not by faith only" (*Jas. 2:24*). Indeed, the holy Church begs this increase of justice when she prays: "O Lord, give us an increase of faith, hope, and charity."

Chapter 11. The Observance of the Commandments: Its Necessity and Possibility

568
(804)
No one, even though he is justified, should consider himself exempt from keeping the commandments (*see 534, can. 20*). And no one should say that it is impossible for the just man to keep the commandments of God, for that is a rash statement censured with anathema by the Fathers (*see 592, can. 18; 596, can. 22; 549*). "For God does not command the impossible; but when he commands, he cautions you to do what you can, and also to pray for what you cannot do," and he helps you so that you can do it. His commandments are not burdensome (*see I John 5:3*); his yoke is easy and his burden light (*see Matt. 11:30*). For those who are sons of God

love Christ; and those who love him (as he himself testifies) keep his words (*see John 14:23*), and this they can certainly do with God's help. For granted that in this mortal life, however just and holy men be, they sometimes commit at least slight daily sins, which are also called venial sins (*see 506, can. 23*); still, they do not on that account cease to be just. For the just say truthfully and humbly, "Forgive us our debts" (*Matt. 6:12; see 531*). Hence, the just themselves should feel a greater obligation to walk in the way of justice because, now set free from sin and become slaves to God (*see Rom. 6:22*), living temperately and justly and piously (*see Titus 2:12*), they can advance through Christ Jesus, through whom they have had access unto grace (*see Rom. 5:2*). For God "does not abandon" those who have been once justified by his grace, "unless they abandon him first." Therefore, no one should take pride in faith alone (*see 583, can. 9; 593, can. 19; 594, can. 20*), thinking that faith alone makes him an heir and that he will come into the inheritance, even if he does not suffer with Christ that he may also be glorified with him (*see Rom. 8:17*). For even Christ himself (as the Apostle says), "Son though he was, learned obedience from the things that he suffered; and when perfected, he became to all who obey him the cause of eternal salvation" (*Heb. 5:8 f.*). Therefore the Apostle himself admonishes the just when he says: "Do you not know that those who run in a race, all indeed run, but one receives the prize? So run as to obtain it. . . . I therefore so run, as not without a purpose; I so fight, as not beating the air; but I chastise my body and bring it into subjection, lest perhaps after preaching to others I myself should be rejected" (*I Cor. 9:24 ff.*). Moreover, Peter, the Prince of the Apostles, says: "Strive even more by good works to make your calling and election sure. For if you do this, you will not fall into sin at any time" (*II Pet. 1:10*). Hence, it is clear that they are against the correct doctrine of religion when they say that the just man commits a venial sin in everything he does (*see 599, can. 25*), or (what is more intolerable) say that he merits eternal punishment. They also are incorrect who state that the just sin in all their works if, in those works, in order to overcome their sloth and encourage themselves to run the race, they look for an everlasting reward in addition to their primary intention of glorifying God (*see 600, can. 26; 605, can. 31*). For it is written: "I have inclined my heart to do thy justifications forever, for the reward" (*Ps. 118:112*), and in speaking of Moses, the Apostle says that he was looking to the reward (*see Heb. 11:26*).

Chapter 12. Rash Presumption of One's Predestination Must Be Avoided

569
(805)
And no one, so long as he lives in this mortal life, ought to be so presumptuous about the deep mystery of divine predestination as to decide with certainty that he is definitely among the number of the predestined (*see 589, can. 15*), as though it were true that, because he is justified, either he cannot sin again (*see 506, can. 23*), or, if he does sin, he should promise himself certain repentance. For it is impossible, without a special revelation, to know whom God has chosen as his own (*see 590, can. 16*).

Chapter 13. The Gift of Perseverance

570
(806)
The same is to be said of the gift of perseverance (*see 590, can. 16*), about which it is written, "He who has persevered to the end will be saved" (*Matt. 10:22; 24:13*). This gift can be had only from Him who has the power to determine that he who does stand shall stand with perseverance (*see Rom. 14:4*), and who can lift up him who falls. Let no one feel assured of this gift with an absolute certitude, although all ought to have most secure hope in the help of God. For unless men are unfaithful to his grace, God will bring the good work to perfection, just as he began it, working both the will and the performance (*see Phil. 2:13; 596, can. 22*). Yet, let them who think they stand take heed lest they fall (*see I Cor. 10:12*), and let them work out their salvation with fear and trembling (*see Phil. 2:12*) in labors, in sleepless nights, in almsgiving, in prayers and offerings, in fastings, and in chastity (*see II Cor. 6:3 ff.*). Knowing that they are reborn unto the hope of glory (*see I Pet. 1:3*) and not yet unto glory itself, they should be in dread about the battle they must wage with the flesh, the world, and the devil. For in this battle they cannot be the victors unless, with God's grace, they obey the Apostle who says: "We are debtors, not to the flesh, that we should

live according to the flesh. For if you live according to the flesh you will die; but if by the spirit you put to death the deeds of the flesh, you will live" (*Rom. 8:12 f.*).

Chapter 14. *Those Who Sin after Justification and Their Restoration to Grace*

Those who have received the grace of justification but have lost it through sin can be justified again (*see 603, can. 29*) when, awakened by God, they make the effort to regain through the sacrament of penance and by the merit of Christ the grace they have lost. For this is the manner of justification by which those who have fallen into sin are restored. The holy Fathers aptly called this restoration the "second plank after the ship has been wrecked and grace has been lost." For it was for those who had fallen into sin after baptism that Jesus Christ instituted the sacrament of penance with the words: "Receive the Holy Spirit; whose sins you shall forgive, they are forgiven them; and whose sins you shall retain, they are retained" (*John 20:22 f.*). Hence, it must be taught that the repentance of a Christian who has fallen into sin is quite different from repentance at the time of baptism. Repentance after falling into sin includes not only giving up these sins and detesting them, or having "a contrite and humbled heart" (*Ps. 50:19*), but it also includes sacramental confession of those sins, or at least the desire to confess when a suitable occasion offers, and the absolution of a priest. It also includes satisfaction by fasts, almsgiving, prayer, and other devout exercises of the spiritual life. These exercises certainly do not make satisfaction for the eternal punishment, for it is remitted together with the guilt by the sacrament or by the desire of the sacrament. Rather they make satisfaction for the temporal punishment (*see 604, can. 30*) which (as Sacred Scripture teaches), is not always entirely—as is the case in baptism—done away with for those who, ungrateful for the grace of God they have received, have grieved the Holy Spirit (*see Eph. 4:30*), and have not feared to destroy the temple of God (*see I Cor. 3:17*). The following has been written about this type of repentance: "Remember therefore whence thou hast fallen, and repent and do the former works" (*Apoc. 2:5*); and again: "The sorrow that is according to God

571
(807)

produces repentance that surely tends to salvation" (*II Cor. 7:10*); and again: "Repent" (*Matt. 3:2; 4:17*); and: "Bring forth therefore fruit befitting repentance" (*Matt. 3:8*).

Chapter 15. Grace, but Not Faith, Is Lost by Every Mortal Sin

572
(808)
We must also assert, in opposition to some clever men who "by smooth words and flattery deceive the hearts of the simple" (*Rom. 16:18*), that the grace of justification, once received, is lost not only by unbelief, which causes the loss of faith, but also by any other mortal sin, even though faith is not lost. This assertion defends the teaching of divine law that excludes from the kingdom of God not only those without faith, but also those with faith who are fornicators, adulterers, effeminate, sodomites, thieves, covetous, drunkards, evil-tongued, greedy (*see I Cor. 6:9*), and all others who commit mortal sins. These sins separate men from the grace of Christ, and they can be avoided with the help of divine grace.

Chapter 16. The Merit of Good Works As a Result of Justification, and the Nature of Merit

573
(809)
Therefore, with this in mind, justified men, whether they have continuously kept grace once they have received it, or whether they have lost it and recovered it again, should consider these words of the Apostle: "Abound in every good work, knowing that your labor is not in vain in the Lord" (*see I Cor. 15:58*); "for God is not unjust, that he should forget your work and the love that you have shown in his name" (*Heb. 6:10*); and: "Do not lose your confidence, which has a great reward" (*see Heb. 10:35*). And eternal life should therefore be set before those who persevere in good works to the end (*see Matt. 10:22*) and who hope in God. It should be set before them as being the grace that God, through Jesus Christ, has mercifully promised his sons, and "as the reward" which, according to the promise of God himself, must assuredly be given them for their good works and merits (*see 600, can. 26; 606, can. 32*). For this is that crown of justice which the Apostle says is laid up for him after the fight and the race; the crown that will be given him by the just Judge, and not to him alone but to all who love His coming (*see II Tim.*

4:7 f.). Indeed, Christ Jesus himself always gives strength to the justified, just as the head gives strength to the members (*see Eph. 4:15*) and the vine gives strength to the branches (*see John 15:5*). This strength always precedes, accompanies, and follows the good works of the justified and without it the good works cannot be at all pleasing to God or meritorious (*see 576, can. 2*). Since this is true, it is necessary to believe that the justified have everything necessary for them to be regarded as having completely satisfied the divine law for this life by their works, at least those which they have performed in God. And they may be regarded as having likewise truly merited the eternal life they will certainly attain in due time (if they but die in the state of grace) (*see Apoc. 14:13; 606, can. 32*), because Christ our Savior says: "He who drinks of the water that I will give him shall never thirst, but it will become in him a fountain of water, springing up into life everlasting" (*see John 4:13 f.*). Thus, it is not personal effort that makes justice our own, and God's justice is not disregarded or rejected (*see Rom. 10:3*); for, the justice that is said to be ours because it inheres in us is likewise God's justice because he has put it in us through the merit of Christ (*see 584, can. 10; 585, can. 11*).

Christ promises even to the person who gives a drink of cold water to one of his least ones that he shall not be without his reward (*see Matt. 10:42*), and the Apostle says that our present light affliction, which is for the moment, prepares for us an eternal weight of glory that is beyond all measure (*see II Cor. 4:17*). Although in Holy Scripture such high value is placed on good works, nevertheless, a Christian should have no inclination either to rely on himself or to glory in himself instead of in the Lord (*see I Cor. 1:31; II Cor. 10:17*), whose goodness towards all men is such that he wants his gifts to be their merits (*see 141; 606, can. 32*). And since "in many things we all offend" (*Jas. 3:2; see 506, can. 23*), each one ought to keep severity and judgment in view as well as mercy and goodness. Neither should anyone pass judgment on himself, even if he is conscious of no wrong, because the entire life of man should be examined and judged not by human judgment, but by the judgment of God who "will both bring to

574
(*810*)

light the things hidden in darkness and make manifest the counsels of hearts; and then everyone will have his praise from God" (*I Cor. 4:5*), who, as it is written, will render to every man according to his works (*see Rom. 2:6*).

No one can be justified unless he faithfully and unhesitatingly accepts the Catholic doctrine on justification (*see 607, can. 33*). Finally, this holy council has decreed to list the following canons so that all may know not only what they should believe and put into practice, but also what they should shun and avoid.

Canons on Justification

575
(811)
1. If anyone says that, without divine grace through Jesus Christ, man can be justified before God by his own works, whether they were done by his natural powers or by the light of the teaching of the [*Mosaic*] Law: let him be anathema (*see 557 f.*).

576
(812)
2. If anyone says that divine grace is given through Jesus Christ merely to facilitate man's living justly and meriting everlasting life, as if he could accomplish both, although with great difficulty, by his free will without grace: let him be anathema (*see 559, 573*).

577
(813)
3. If anyone says that without the Holy Spirit's prevenient inspiration and without his help man can believe, hope, and love or be repentant as is required if the grace of justification is to be given to him: let him be anathema (*see 561*).

578
(814)
4. If anyone says that the free will of man, moved and awakened by God, in no way cooperates with the awakening call of God by an assent by which man disposes and prepares himself to get the grace of justification; and that man cannot dissent, if he wishes, but, like an object without life, he does nothing at all and is merely passive: let him be anathema (*see 561*).

579
(815)
5. If anyone says that after Adam's sin man's free will was destroyed and lost, or that there is question about a term only, indeed, that the term has no real foundation; and that the fictitious notion was even introduced into the Church by Satan: let him be anathema (*see 557, 561*).

Grace

6. If anyone says that it is not in man's power to make his ways evil, but that God performs the evil works just as he performs the good, not only permissively but also properly and directly, so that Judas's betrayal no less than Paul's vocation was God's own work: let him be anathema.

580
(816)

7. If anyone says that all works performed before justification, regardless of how they were performed, are truly sins or merit God's hatred; or that the more zealously a person strives to dispose himself for grace, the more grievously he sins: let him be anathema (*see 562*).

581
(817)

8. If anyone says that the fear of hell, which makes us turn to the mercy of God in sorrow for sins or which makes us avoid sin, is itself a sin or that it makes sinners worse: let him be anathema (*see 562*).

582
(818)

9. If anyone says that a sinful man is justified by faith alone, meaning that no other cooperation is required to obtain the grace of justification, and that it is not at all necessary that he be prepared and disposed by the action of his will: let him be anathema (*see 562, 565, 568*).

583
(819)

10. If anyone says that men are justified without Christ's justice by which he gained merit for us, or are formally just by the justice of Christ: let him be anathema (*see 559, 563*).

584
(820)

11. If anyone says that men are justified either through the imputation of Christ's justice alone, or through the remission of sins alone, excluding grace and charity which is poured forth in their hearts by the Holy Spirit and inheres in them, or also that the grace which justifies us is only the good will of God: let him be anathema (*see 563 f., 573*).

585
(821)

12. If anyone says that justifying faith is nothing else than confidence that divine Mercy remits sins for Christ's sake, or that it is confidence alone which justifies us: let him be anathema (*see 562, 566*).

586
(822)

13. If anyone says that, to attain the remission of sins, everyone must believe with certainty and without any misgiving because of his own weakness and defective disposition, that his sins are remitted: let him be anathema (*see 566*).

587
(823)

588
(*824*)
14. If anyone says that man is absolved from his sins and justified because he believes with certainty that he is absolved and justified; or that no one is truly justified except him who believes he is justified, and that absolution and justification are effected by this faith alone: let him be anathema (*see 566*).

589
(*825*)
15. If anyone says that a man who has been reborn and justified is bound by faith to believe that he is certainly in the number of the predestined: let him be anathema (*see 569*).

590
(*826*)
16. If anyone says that he has absolute and infallible certitude that he will certainly have the great gift of final perseverance, without having learned this from a special revelation: let him be anathema (*see 569 f.*).

591
(*827*)
17. If anyone says that only those who are predestined to life have the grace of justification, and that all the others who are called, are indeed called, but do not receive grace, inasmuch as they are predestined to evil by the divine power: let him be anathema (*see 549*).

592
(*828*)
18. If anyone says that the commandments of God are impossible to observe even for a man who is justified and in the state of grace: let him be anathema (*see 568*).

593
(*829*)
19. If anyone says that nothing is commanded in the gospel except faith, and that everything else is indifferent, neither prescribed nor prohibited, but free; or that the Ten Commandments do not pertain at all to Christians: let him be anathema (*see 564*).

594
(*830*)
20. If anyone says that a justified man, however perfect he might be, is not bound to observe the commandments of God and of the Church, but is bound only to believe, as if the gospel, apart from the observance of the commandments, were an unconditional and absolute promise of eternal life: let him be anathema (*see 568*).

595
(*831*)
21. If anyone says that God has given Jesus Christ to men as a redeemer in whom they are to trust, but not as a lawgiver whom they are to obey: let him be anathema.

22. If anyone says that without God's special help it is pos- **596** sible for a justified man to persevere in the justice he has re- (*832*) ceived, or says that with God's special help it is impossible: let him be anathema (*see 568, 570*).

23. If anyone says that a man once justified cannot sin **597** again, and cannot lose grace, and that therefore the man who (*833*) falls and sins was never truly justified; or, contrariwise, says that a man once justified can avoid all sins, even venial sins, throughout his entire life without a special privilege of God, as the Church holds in regard to the Blessed Virgin: let him be anathema (*see 569, 574*).

24. If anyone says that justice which has been received is **598** not preserved and even increased before God through good (*834*) works, but that such works are merely the outgrowth and the signs of the reception of justification, not the cause of its in- crease as well: let him be anathema (*see 567*).

25: If anyone says that a just man sins at least venially in **599** every good work, or (what is more intolerable) says that he (*835*) sins mortally, and therefore merits eternal punishment, and that the sole reason why he is not damned is that God does not impute those works unto damnation: let him be anathema (*see 568*).

26. If anyone says that, for good works performed in God, **600** the just ought not to expect and hope for eternal reward (*836*) from God through his mercy and through the merit of Jesus Christ if they persevere to the end in doing good and in ob- serving the divine commandments: let him be anathema (*see 573*).

27. If anyone says that unbelief is the only sin that is mor- **601** tal, or that grace once received can be lost by no other sin, (*837*) regardless of its gravity and enormity, except unbelief: let him be anathema (*see 572*).

28. If anyone says that, when grace is lost through sin, faith **602** is always lost at the same time, or that the faith which does re- (*838*) main is not true faith, granted it is not a living faith; or says that the man who has faith without charity is not a Christian: let him be anathema (*see 572*).

603
(839)
29. If anyone says that the man who falls after baptism cannot rise through God's grace; or that he can indeed recover the justice that has been lost, but by faith alone without the sacrament of penance, according to what the holy Roman and universal Church, instructed by Christ the Lord and his apostles, has always professed, observed, and taught: let him be anathema (*see 571*).

604
(840)
30. If anyone says that, after receiving the grace of justification, the guilt of any repentant sinner is remitted and the debt of eternal punishment is blotted out in such a way that no debt of temporal punishment remains to be paid, either in this life or in purgatory, before the gate to the kingdom of heaven can be opened: let him be anathema (*see 571*).

605
(841)
31. If anyone says that the justified man sins when he performs good works with a view to an eternal reward: let him be anathema (*see 568*).

606
(842)
32. If anyone says that the good works of a justified man are gifts of God to such an extent that they are not also the good merits of the justified man himself; or that, by the good works he performs through the grace of God and the merits of Jesus Christ (of whom he is a living member), the justified man does not truly merit an increase of grace, life everlasting, and, provided that he dies in the state of grace, the attainment of that life everlasting, and even an increase of glory: let him be anathema (*see 567, 573 f.*).

607
(843)
33. If anyone says that this Catholic teaching about justification, stated by the holy council in this present decree, detracts in any degree from the glory of God or from the merits of Jesus Christ our Lord, and does not rather shed light upon the truth of our faith, and ultimately show forth the glory of God and of Jesus Christ: let him be anathema (*see 574*).

CONDEMNATION OF THE ERRORS OF
MICHEL DE BAY, 1567

Michel de Bay (Baius, *cir.* 1513–89), professor of theology at Louvain, began to propose false doctrines in 1551. Fierce opposition was not slow in coming, and in 1560, some theses of de Bay were sent to the faculty at Paris and were condemned.

Grace

When de Bay and his followers raised strenuous protest, Pope Pius IV imposed silence on de Bay. De Bay failed to obey and Pope St. Pius V (1566–72), in the bull *Ex omnibus afflictionibus,* which was not, however, published at that time (1567), put various censures on the theses of de Bay, without mentioning de Bay's name. Then de Bay sent a defense of his teaching to the pope. When the pope had read the defense, he repeated his original condemnation. Although de Bay pretended to submit, he continued spreading his errors. It was then that Pius V's condemnation of de Bay and the bull *Ex omnibus afflictionibus* were published by Gregory XIII in the bull *Provisionis nostrae,* January 29, 1579, and again by Urban VIII in the bull *In eminenti Ecclesiae militantis* in 1641. As presented in St. Pius's bull, the individual errors are not given a precise doctrinal censure.

Against the Protestants Trent had taught that justification is had through gifts of God that become intrinsic to the recipient, but it did not give a precise statement on the supernaturalness of those gifts. When de Bay denied that grace was supernatural and said that it was gratuitous only because the sinner was unworthy of it, St. Pius V, in condemning de Bay's errors, gave the first declarations of the Church on the supernaturalness of grace; that is, on the fact that grace is not due to the exigencies of created nature.

The primitive state of man

21. The exalting of human nature to a participation of the divine nature was due to the integrity of man in his first state and for that reason should be called natural, not supernatural.

608
(*1021*)

55. God could not from the beginning have created man in the condition in which he is now born.

609
(*1055*)

78. The immortality of the first man was not a gift of grace, but his natural state.

610
(*1078*)

Merit

13. Good works performed by the sons of adoption are meritorious, not because they are performed by the spirit of adoption dwelling in the hearts of the sons of God, but only because they conform to the law, and manifest obedience to the law.

611
(*1013*)

Sin

612
(1020)
20. No sin is of its nature venial, but every sin merits eternal punishment.

613
(1050)
50. Evil desires to which reason does not consent and which a man experiences against his will, are forbidden by the commandment: "Thou shalt not covet" (*Exod. 20:17*).

614
(1054)
54. The proposition that God commands nothing that is impossible to man is falsely attributed to Augustine, since it belongs to Pelagius.

615
(1067)
67. In that which a man does from necessity, he sins, even so as to deserve damnation.

616
(1068)
68. Purely negative unbelief is a sin in those to whom Christ has not been preached.

617
(1074)
74. Concupiscence in baptized persons who have fallen back into mortal sin and in whom concupiscence now holds sway, is a sin just as are other bad habits.

Impotence of fallen nature and of free will

618
(1025)
25. All the actions of infidels are sins, and the virtues of philosophers are vices.

619
(1027)
27. Without the help of God's grace, free will can do nothing but sin.

620
(1028)
28. It is a Pelagian error to say that free will can avoid any sin.

The notion of freedom

621
(1039)
39. A voluntary action, even if done from necessity, is still a free action.

622
(1041)
41. In the Scriptures, freedom does not mean freedom from necessity but only freedom from sin.

623
(1066)
66. The only thing opposed to man's natural freedom is violence.

Love and fulfillment of the law

624
(1016)
16. Without charity, obedience to the law is not true obedience.

34. It is meaningless fiction and mockery devised against the Scriptures and the abundant testimonies of the old authors to distinguish a twofold love of God: namely, a natural love whose object is God the author of nature; and a gratuitous love, whose object is God the author of happiness.

625
(1034)

38. All love of a rational creature is either vicious cupidity which has the world as its object, and is forbidden by John, or is the praiseworthy charity which, poured forth in the heart by the Holy Spirit (*see Rom.* 5:5), has God as its object.

626
(1038)

CONDEMNATION OF THE ERRORS OF CORNELIS JANSEN, 1653

Jansenism is a development of Baianism. For Cornelis Jansen, the theology of de Bay represented the exact interpretation of the teaching of St. Augustine. Jansen (1585–1638) was an ardent student of St. Augustine, and his chief aim was to restore to its place of honor the true doctrine of Augustine on grace. He was actively engaged in writing his book on Augustine when he succumbed to an epidemic. Before his death he entrusted his manuscript to his chaplain, and in his will protested that he submitted himself in advance to the decisions of of the Holy See.

Some attempts were made to prevent the printing of the manuscript, but the friends of the dead Jansen were successful in their efforts to bring the famous *Augustinus* to the press. The *Augustinus* met with great success, but the Holy Office condemned the work and prohibited its reading. Urban VIII (1623–44) renewed the condemnation and interdiction in his bull *In eminenti Ecclesiae militantis.* Despite this bull, the work of Jansen continued to spread. Finally, five propositions extracted from the book were submitted to Pope Innocent X (1644–55). After a two years' examination by a commission of cardinals and consultors, in the constitution *Cum occasione,* May 31, 1653, the pope condemned the first four of the following errors as heretical; the fifth error was condemned as false, and if understood to mean that Christ died for the salvation only of the elect, as heretical.

1. There are some of God's commandments that just men cannot observe with the powers they have in their present state, even if they wish and strive to observe them; nor do

627
(1092)

249

men have the grace which would make their observance possible.

628
(1093)
2. In the state of fallen nature internal grace is never resisted.

629
(1094)
3. To merit or demerit in the state of fallen nature it is not necessary for a man to have freedom from necessity, but only freedom from constraint.

630
(1095)
4. The Semi-Pelagians admitted the necessity of internal, preparatory grace for individual acts, even for the beginning of faith; they were heretics for this reason that they wished this grace to be such that the human will could resist it or obey it.

631
(1096)
5. It is Semi-Pelagian to say that Christ died or shed his blood for all men without exception.

CONDEMNATION OF THE ERRORS OF PASQUIER QUESNEL, 1713

The theological errors of Quesnel (1634–1719) are fundamentally only a synthesis of the systems of de Bay and Jansen. His essential theses are based on a confusion between the natural and the supernatural orders. The dogmatic constitution *Unigenitus*, September 8, 1713, in which the errors of Quesnel were condemned, was confirmed by Clement XI (1700–1721) himself in a subsequent bull, *Pastoralis officii*, August 28, 1718, against those who had not accepted it.

Errors concerning the necessity of grace

632
(1351)
1. What is left in the soul that has lost God and his grace except sin and its effects, proud poverty, barren need, that is, the general inability to work, to pray, or to do any good work?

633
(1388)
38. Without the grace of the Savior the sinner is free for nothing but evil.

634
(1389)
39. The will that is not prepared by grace has no light except to go astray, no passion except for self-destruction, no strength except to wound itself, is capable of all evil and incapable of any good.

Grace

40. Without grace we cannot love anything except to our own condemnation.
635 (*1390*)

41. All knowledge of God, even natural knowledge, even among heathen philosophers, can come from God alone; and without grace such knowledge breeds only presumption, vanity, and opposition to God himself instead of adoration, gratitude, and love.
636 (*1391*)

59. The prayer of the wicked is new sin; and what God grants them is a new judgment against them.
637 (*1409*)

Propositions on the two loves

44. There are only two loves that are the sources of desires and deeds. There is the love of God that does everything for God and which God rewards; and there is the love we have for ourselves and for the world, and this love is evil because it does not give God his due.
638 (*1394*)

45. When the love of God no longer reigns in the hearts of sinners, it is inevitable that carnal desire is dominant and vitiates every action.
639 (*1395*)

46. Covetousness or charity determines whether the use of the senses is good or evil.
640 (*1396*)

47. Obedience to the law ought to flow from a source, and this source is charity. When the love of God is the interior principle of obedience to the law, and the glory of God is its end, then its external observance is pure; otherwise, it is nothing but hypocrisy and false justice.
641 (*1397*)

Propositions on the compelling force of divine grace

10. Grace is the work of the hand of the omnipotent God, which nothing can hinder or retard.
642 (*1360*)

11. Grace is nothing more than God's omnipotent will commanding and doing what he commands.
643 (*1361*)

23. God himself has given us the concept of the omnipotent operation of his grace, showing it to us in the operation that produces creatures from nothing and restores life to the dead.
644 (*1373*)

Grace

THE VATICAN COUNCIL, 1869-70
SCHEMA OF THE DOGMATIC CONSTITUTION ON THE PRINCIPAL MYSTERIES OF THE FAITH

The second part of the schema of the Dogmatic Constitution on Catholic Doctrine dealt with the principal mysteries of the faith (*see introd. to 314*). This chapter on grace, with its corresponding canons, is presented as a valuable, though not authoritative, summary of the Catholic doctrine on grace. (This translation is made from the text given in *Collectio Lacensis*, VII, 562–65; 566–67.)

Chapter 5. The Grace of the Redeemer

645   The Catholic Church professes that the grace which is given because of the merits of Christ the Redeemer is of such nature that, not only are we freed through it from the slavery of sin and from the power of the devil, but we are renewed in the spirit of our mind and we regain the justice and sanctity which Adam lost for himself and for us by his sin. This grace does not just repair our natural powers so that, with the help of grace, we can completely conform our habits and our acts to the norm of natural goodness; but it transforms us beyond the limits of nature into the likeness of the heavenly man, that is, Christ, and gives us birth into a new life. For God chose us in Christ Jesus before the foundation of the world and he predestined us to be conformed to the likeness of his Son that he might be the first-born among many brothers. Therefore, the Father gave us this charity that, being born of God, we might receive the name of sons of God and be sons of God. By this adoption as sons, participation in the divine nature was restored to us; it begins now through grace, and will be completed hereafter in glory. We are anointed and made holy by the Son's Spirit whom God has sent into our hearts, and we are made a temple of the divine Majesty in which the most holy Trinity deigns to dwell and to communicate itself to the faithful soul, as Christ our Lord says: "If anyone love me, he will keep my word, and my Father will love him, and we will come to him and make our abode with him" (*John 14:23*).

646   Therefore, it is to be held and professed by all the faithful of Christ that sanctifying grace, by which we are joined to

God, does not consist only in an external favor of God nor is it to be found only in passing acts; but it is a permanent supernatural gift that is infused by God into the soul and inheres there; it is in adults who are made justified, and in infants reborn in baptism. This renovation of man by the Incarnate Word is the mystery hidden from the world. It is the means by which God has more wonderfully restored in the second Adam what he had wonderfully made in the first Adam.

It is regrettable that there are men so blind as to think that **647** the religion of Christ diminishes the dignity of human nature because it is supernatural or that it is prejudicial to liberty or happiness. This divine institution is far from repressing man; rather it elevates him wonderfully. For it frees him from the slavery of sin and prepares him for heavenly glory, adorning and perfecting the properties of nature as it does so. Equally to be avoided is the error of those who, resisting the supernatural ordination of God, argue that man is free to stop within the bounds of nature and to seek for nothing beyond the good of this order. Thus they destroy the necessary connection that the will of God has placed between the two orders, the order which is in nature and that which is above nature. For after the divine Mercy had decreed that man was to be brought to the heavenly kingdom, it made Jesus Christ the way to this kingdom; and there now is no salvation in anyone else. He who does not believe in Christ or who does not keep his commandments will be cast with sinners into darkness where there will be weeping and gnashing of teeth.

Hence it follows that the so-called good life, in which the **648** commandments of God are somehow observed (at least as regards the substance of the works) is far different from the justice and sanctity which lead the one who does these works to the kingdom of heaven. For there is in nature the power for a rational soul to think and do lawful things and this is not blameworthy, but justly and rightly praised. Nevertheless, since these things are done without faith and without grace, none of them has any connection with the godliness that brings a man to eternal life. For what is true of the life of the blessed, namely, that since it is above nature it is a gratuitous gift of God's mercy, is also true of the disposition for that life. Natural powers are not sufficient for any salutary act either in the just to increase their justice or in sinners to dispose them for justification. As our Lord says: "Without me you can do nothing" (*John 15:5*). And the Apostle confirms it: "Not that we are sufficient of ourselves to think anything, as from ourselves, but our sufficiency is from God" (*II Cor. 3:5*). Therefore, it is most truly said that by grace we are not only given the ability to do more easily what we could with difficulty do by our natural powers, but the ability to will and to accomplish what we could not do at all by our natural powers. God it is who of his good pleasure works in us both the will and the performance (*see Phil. 2:13*).

649   These good works which are done with prevenient grace, accompanying grace, and following grace do not merit eternal life without the gift of sanctity by which the just are joined with Christ as members with the head and are associated as sons of God by grace with the natural Son of God. Our Lord tells us: "As the branch cannot bear fruit of itself unless it remain on the vine, so neither can you unless you abide in me" (*John 15:4*). The Apostle says: "But if we are sons, we are heirs with Christ" (*Rom. 8:17*).

650   Those who die in this grace will, with certainty, obtain eternal life, the crown of justice, and just as certainly, they who die deprived of this grace will never arrive at eternal life. For death is the end of our pilgrimage, and shortly after death we stand before the judgment seat of God "so that each one may receive what he has won through the body according to his works, whether good or evil" (*II Cor. 5:10*). And after this mortal life there is no place left for repentance for justification. Therefore, all who die in actual mortal sin are excluded from the kingdom of God and will suffer forever the torments of hell where there is no redemption. Also those who die with only original sin will never have the holy vision of God. The souls of those who die in the charity of God before they have done sufficient penance for their sins of commission or omission, are purified after death with the punishment of purgatory.

Finally, the souls of those who have not incurred any stain **651** of sin after their baptism, or who have committed a sin and have been purified either while they were in the body or after death, are soon taken into heaven and there they clearly see the Triune God and enjoy the divine essence for all eternity (*see 886, 880*).

Therefore, we are warned to do good works while we still have time (*see Gal. 6:10*) because "the night is coming, when no one can work" (*John 9:4*).

Canons on Chapter 5

1. If anyone denies that the order of supernatural grace **652** was restored by Christ the Redeemer: let him be anathema.

2. If anyone says that justification is nothing but the re- **653** mission of sins; or that sanctifying grace is nothing but the favor with which God receives man as pleasing and is prepared to give him the helps of actual grace: let him be anathema.

3. If anyone says that sanctifying grace is not a permanent **654** supernatural gift, inhering in the soul: let him be anathema.

4. If anyone says that a man without grace and faith can **655** be justified before God merely by observing the divine commandments: let him be anathema.

5. If anyone says that the rational nature, without divine **656** grace through Christ Jesus, is capable of doing any good work that disposes for Christian justice and eternal life: let him be anathema.

6. If anyone says that a man can be justified even after **657** death; or if he says that the punishments of the damned in hell will not last forever: let him be anathema.

The Sacraments

When the Word was made flesh and dwelt in our midst, the mysterious, invisible life of God took visible form in this material world of human life. The paradoxical union of the divine with the human, the invisible with the visible, that characterized the Incarnation of the Word, continues in the Church in which the divine person of Christ lives on in mysterious union with the visible, external society, the mystical body, of which he, as man, is the head. The sacramental system of the Church is an extension of this same divine plan. In the seven sacraments Christ communicates the divine life to the members of his Church through visible, external signs which he instituted for this purpose. In themselves the external, perceptible rites of the sacraments are powerless to produce the spiritual effects they signify. It is only by Christ's appointment and by the operation of his power that they can and do effect what they signify. For the same reason, the efficacy of the sacraments is not dependent on the holiness or orthodoxy of their ministers. The early controversies about the need for rebaptizing heretics occasioned clear pronouncements by the Church on this point.

Each of the sacraments confers or increases sanctifying grace. This sanctifying grace is known as sacramental grace inasmuch as it carries with it a right to the supernatural helps necessary and useful for the accomplishment of the purpose of each sacrament. In addition, three of the sacraments, baptism, confirmation, and orders, confer an indelible character which renders their valid repetition impossible.

The Sacraments in General

That there are seven sacraments of the New Law is a truth of Catholic faith. The Church has always taught the existence of the seven sacraments and this teaching had always been universally accepted. It was only in the twelfth century that scholastic theologians began to seek a definition of the nature of a sacrament as such and to be aware that this nature was realized in seven, and only seven, of the Church's rites. From this time, therefore, come the first precise formulations in official Church documents regarding the nature and number of the sacraments in general and the conditions of their administration.

Few heretics of major importance in the history of dogma denied the existence of the sacraments, or contested the number seven, until the Reformers of the sixteenth century. These heretics denied that Christ had instituted any of the sacraments except two, baptism and the Eucharist. They considered that the sacramental signs were not real causes of grace but mere symbols exciting to faith (Luther) or pledges of divine benevolence (Calvin). To meet these fundamental errors the Council of Trent undertook an official presentation of the true doctrine on all of the sacraments in general and each of them in particular.

THE PROFESSION OF FAITH PRESCRIBED FOR DURANDUS OF OSCA AND FOLLOWERS, 1208

In 1208, this profession of faith was proposed by Innocent III (1198–1216) to Durandus of Osca (*see introd. to 150*), a converted Waldensian, and to his followers. Durandus's orthodoxy was no longer in question, but the profession was meant to guarantee the right doctrine in the preaching of the religious society he was founding. The errors included are principally those of the Albigenses and Waldensians. Selections from this profession of faith that pertain to the individual sacraments will be distributed throughout this chapter (*see 685, 713, 853*).

Furthermore, we do not reject the sacraments that are conferred in the Church, in cooperation with the inestimable and invisible power of the Holy Spirit, even though these sacraments be administered by a sinful priest as long as he is recognized by the Church. And we do not disparage ecclesiastical functions and benedictions celebrated by such a one; but we accept them in a kindly manner, as if performed by the most just of men. For the evil life of a bishop or a priest does not invalidate either the baptism of an infant, or the consecration of the Eucharist, or other ecclesiastical duties performed for the faithful.

658
(424)

THE FOURTH COUNCIL OF THE LATERAN, 1215

In the definition of faith against the Albigenses (*see introd. to 151 and 306*) the twelfth ecumenical council included the following doctrine on the sacraments. Not all the sacraments are enumerated here, but the number of the sacraments had not been called into question at this time.

Indeed, there is but one universal Church of the faithful outside which no one at all is saved and in which the priest himself, Jesus Christ, is the victim; his body and blood are truly contained in the Sacrament of the Altar under the species of bread and wine, transubstantiated by the divine power—the bread into his body and the wine into his blood—that, for the enacting of the mystery of unity, we may take from his substance as he himself took from our substance. And no one can consecrate this sacrament except a priest who is rightly ordained according to the Church's powers that Jesus Christ gave to the apostles and to their successors. But the sacrament of baptism (which is performed with water together with the invocation of God and the undivided Trinity; namely, the Father, the Son, and the Holy Spirit) is salutary both for infants and for adults if it is administered correctly by anyone according to the form of the Church. And if after receiving baptism, anyone shall fall into sin, he can always be restored by true contrition. Not only virgins and those who observe continence but also married people who please God by true faith and good works merit to come to eternal happiness.

659
(430)

The Sacraments

THE SECOND COUNCIL OF LYONS, 1274

The great profession of faith of Emperor Michael Palaeologus, subscribed to by his delegates at this Council of Lyons (*see introd. to 152 and 456*), dealt in its latter part with the points of difference between the Latin and Greek Churches in doctrinal matters. The first sentence of this present section on the sacraments seems to mention the sevenfold number of the sacraments as a matter taken for granted by all. It is in the details concerning certain sacraments that the points of difference are touched.

660
(465) Furthermore, the same holy Roman Church holds and teaches that there are seven sacraments of the Church. One is baptism which has been treated above. Another is the sacrament of confirmation which bishops confer by the imposition of hands, anointing those who have been reborn. Then there is penance, the Eucharist, the sacrament of orders, matrimony, and extreme unction which, according to the teaching of St. James, is administered to the sick. The same Roman Church consecrates the sacrament of the Eucharist from unleavened bread, and she holds and teaches that in this sacrament the bread is truly transubstantiated into the body of our Lord Jesus Christ, and the wine into his blood. As regards matrimony, the Church holds that one man may not have more than one wife at the same time, nor is a woman permitted to have more than one husband. When a lawful marriage is dissolved by the death of one of the spouses, the Church teaches that two, three, or even further marriages are successively lawful, provided there is no canonical impediment from any other source.

THE COUNCIL OF CONSTANCE, 1414-18

Although Wyclif and Hus (*see introd. to 158 and 521*) did not deny the existence of seven sacraments, their doctrines concerning their nature and the dispositions required in the minister and recipient of the sacraments was at variance with orthodoxy.

Error of Wyclif

661
(584) 4. If a bishop or a priest is in mortal sin, he does not ordain, he does not consecrate, he does not effect the Sacrifice, and he does not baptize.

The Sacraments in General

22. Likewise, whether he believes that an evil priest who **662** has the correct matter and form and the intention of doing **(672)** what the Church does, truly effects the Sacrifice, truly absolves, truly baptizes, truly confers the other sacraments.

THE COUNCIL OF FLORENCE, 1438-45

After the Council of Florence (*see introd. to 164*) had achieved apparent success in reuniting the Greek with the Latin Church, Pope Eugene IV (1431–47) prolonged the council and continued to work for the reunion of other schismatic groups with Rome. A delegation from the Armenian Church arrived at Florence, and after lengthy conferences reunion was agreed upon. November 22, 1439, the decree *Exultate Deo* on the union, was published. In the decree, along with the Nicene Creed and the definitions of the Councils of Chalcedon and Constantinople, there was an important instruction on the sacraments. This instruction follows St. Thomas's opuscule *De articulis fidei et Ecclesiae sacramentis* very closely and is an authoritative pre-Reformation testimony to the traditional doctrine on the number of the sacraments and to the employment of the terms *matter* and *form* to describe the rites and formulae that constitute the sacraments. It is, however, probably not an infallible definition.

Fifthly, We are putting the true doctrine of the sacraments **663** of the Church into a brief formula as an easier means for **(695)** instructing the Armenians, both those of the present and those of the future. There are seven sacraments of the New Law: they are baptism, confirmation, the Eucharist, penance, extreme unction, holy orders, and matrimony; and they differ greatly from the sacraments of the Old Law. The sacraments of the Old Law did not cause grace but were only a figure of the grace that was to be given through the Passion of Christ; but our sacraments both contain grace and confer it on those who receive the sacraments worthily. The first five of these are ordered to the interior spiritual perfection of the individual; the last two are ordered to the government and to the spread of the whole Church. For by baptism we are spiritually reborn and by confirmation we grow in grace and are strengthened in the faith; being reborn and strengthened, we are nourished with the divine food of the Eucharist.

If, by sin, we become sick in soul, penance spiritually heals us; extreme unction heals us in spirit and in body as well, insofar as it is good for the soul. By holy orders the Church is governed and given spiritual growth; by matrimony she is given bodily growth. All these sacraments are brought to completion by three components; by things as matter, by words as form, and by the person of the minister effecting the sacrament with the intention of doing what the Church does. And if any one of these three is lacking, the sacrament is not effected. Among these sacraments, there are three, baptism, confirmation, and holy orders, which print on the soul an indelible character, that is, a certain spiritual sign distinguishing the recipient from others. Hence, these are not given more than once to one person. The other four do not imprint this character and may be repeated.

THE COUNCIL OF TRENT, 1545-63

Immediately following the Decree on Justification, the Council of Trent (*see introd. to 371*) sets down a list of canons containing the Church's teaching on the sacraments in general; for in the sacraments, justification either begins or is increased or is restored when lost by sin. Luther had reduced the number of the sacraments of the New Law to two instead of seven. The Augsburg Confession declared that the sacraments of extreme unction and confirmation were not instituted by Christ but by the apostles. Luther had taught that faith alone insures the efficacy of the sacraments whatever the intention of the minister or the recipient. Against these and other errors of the Reformers the council put forth the very clear definitions in the following canons.

Prologue to canons on the sacraments in general

664
(843a)
It seemed fitting to treat here of the holy sacraments of the Church so as to complete the salutary doctrine of justification promulgated by the unanimous consent of the fathers in the session immediately preceding. For all true justification either begins through the sacraments, or once begun, increases through them, or when lost is regained through them. Therefore this most holy, ecumenical, and general Council of Trent presided over by the same legates of the Apostolic See, has lawfully assembled in the Holy Spirit to do away with errors and to root out heresies which in this our age are brought

up against the most holy sacraments—heresies once condemned by our Fathers and newly discovered heresies now doing great harm to the purity of the Catholic Church and to the salvation of souls. Following the teaching of the Holy Scriptures, the apostolic traditions, and the agreement of the Fathers and of other councils, the council determined that these present canons should be drawn up and decreed, and the canons that remain for the completion of the work begun, she will, with the help of the Holy Spirit, publish hereafter.

Canons on the Sacraments in General

1. If anyone says that the sacraments of the New Law were not all instituted by Jesus Christ our Lord; or that there are more than seven or fewer than seven—that is, baptism, confirmation, the Eucharist, penance, extreme unction, holy orders, and matrimony; or that any one of these is not truly and properly a sacrament: let him be anathema. **665** (*844*)

2. If anyone says that these same sacraments of the New Law do not differ from the sacraments of the Old Law except in ceremonies and in external rites: let him be anathema. **666** (*845*)

3. If anyone says that these sacraments are equal to one another and that one is not in any way of greater worth than another: let him be anathema. **667** (*846*)

4. If anyone says that the sacraments of the New Law are not necessary for salvation, but that they are superfluous; and that men can, without the sacraments or the desire of them, obtain the grace of justification by faith alone, although it is true that not all the sacraments are necessary for each individual: let him be anathema. **668** (*847*)

5. If anyone says that these sacraments were instituted only for the sake of nourishing the faith: let him be anathema. **669** (*848*)

6. If anyone says that the sacraments of the New Law do not contain the grace that they signify or that they do not confer that grace upon those who do not place any obstacle in the way—as if they were merely external signs of the grace **670** (*849*)

or justice received through faith and insignia, so to speak, of a Christian profession by which men distinguish the faithful from infidels: let him be anathema.

671
(850)
7. If anyone says that, as far as God's part is concerned, grace is not given through these sacraments always and to everybody, even if they receive the sacraments correctly, but only sometimes and to some people: let him be anathema.

672
(851)
8. If anyone says that through the sacraments of the New Law grace is not conferred by the rite itself [*ex opere operato*] but that faith alone in the divine promises is sufficient to obtain grace: let him be anathema.

673
(852)
9. If anyone says that in three sacraments, namely, baptism, confirmation, and holy orders, a character is not imprinted on the soul—that is, a kind of indelible spiritual sign whereby these sacraments cannot be repeated: let him be anathema.

674
(853)
10. If anyone says that all Christians have the power to preach the word and to administer all the sacraments: let him be anathema.

675
(854)
11. If anyone says that the intention, at least that of doing what the Church does, is not required in the ministers when they are effecting and conferring the sacraments: let him be anathema.

676
(855)
12. If anyone says that a minister in the state of mortal sin, though he observes all the essentials that belong to effecting and conferring the sacrament, does not effect or confer the sacrament: let him be anathema.

677
(856)
13. If anyone says that the accepted and approved rites of the Catholic Church that are customarily used in the solemn administration of the sacraments can, without sin, be belittled or omitted by the ministers as they see fit, or that they can be changed into other new rites by any pastor in the Church: let him be anathema.

The twenty-first session of the council on July 16, 1562, is concerned with the sacrament of the Eucharist, but the second chapter is put here because its assertion of the power of the

Church over the administration of the sacraments is pertinent to all the sacraments. This declaration was directed against those who were demanding reception of the Eucharist under the species of wine for the laity (*see introd. to 739*).

Chapter 2. The Power of the Church over the Administration of the Sacrament of the Eucharist

The council furthermore declares that the Church has always had the power to determine or to change things in the administration of the sacraments when it judges that such a procedure would be more useful for those who receive the sacraments or would contribute more to the honor of the sacraments themselves, in accordance with different circumstances and times and places, always keeping the substance of the sacraments the same. It seems that the Apostle referred to this power rather clearly when he said, "Let a man so account us, as servants of Christ and stewards of the mysteries of God" (*I Cor. 4:1*). It is quite evident that he himself used this power not only in many other instances but also in regard to this very sacrament when he laid down certain regulations for its use and said: "The rest I shall set in order when I come" (*I Cor. 11:34*). Holy Mother Church realizes, then, her authority in the administration of the sacraments and although, since the beginnings of the Christian religion, the use of both species may not have been uncommon, as time went on that custom was changed in many places, and now, for just and serious reasons, the Church approves of the custom of communicating under one species and declares that this custom has the force of law. No one may disapprove of it or change it to suit his pleasure without the authority of the Church (*see 743, can. 2*).

678
(931)

THE DECREE LAMENTABILI, 1907

In the reign of Pope St. Pius X (1903–14) the Holy Office issued this decree containing the errors of the modernists (*see introd. to 112*).

39. The opinions on the origin of the sacraments which the fathers of the Council of Trent held and which undoubtedly had an influence on their dogmatic canons are far different from those which are now correctly held by research historians of Christianity.

679
(2039)

The Sacraments

680
(2040)

40. The sacraments owe their origin to the fact that the apostles and their successors interpreted some idea and intention of Christ according to the dictates of the circumstances and the times.

681
(2041)

41. The only purpose of the sacraments is to recall to the minds of men the ever beneficent presence of the Creator.

THE ENCYCLICAL *PASCENDI DOMINICI GREGIS*, 1907

This encyclical of Pope St. Pius X (1903–14) is a detailed exposition and refutation of the errors of the modernists in philosophy and theology. Here the pope condemns the assertion that the sacraments took their origin from a religious impulse or a religious necessity. This assertion of the modernists equivalently reduces the doctrine on the sacraments to the heresy of the Reformers, condemned in the Council of Trent (*see 669, can. 5*).

682
(2089)

. . . Concerning worship of sacred things, not much would have to be said were it not for the fact that the sacraments come under this heading; and here the modernists fall into the gravest errors. They attempt to show that worship results from a twofold impulse or necessity—for, as we have seen, everything in their system is explained by inner impulses or necessities. The first impulse is to attribute some sensible element to religion; the second impulse is to make it known; and this could not be done without some sensible form and sanctifying actions which we call sacraments. For the modernists, the sacraments are mere symbols or signs, though not altogether without power. To explain the nature of this power they compare it to the power of certain phrases, commonly described as catch phrases, that have become vehicles for the spread of great ideas that strike the public mind. What these phrases are to an idea, that the sacraments are to the religious sense—nothing more. The modernists would make their meaning clearer if they were to say that the sacraments are instituted only to foster the faith. This has been condemned by the Council of Trent: "If anyone says that these sacraments were instituted only for the sake of nourishing the faith: let him be anathema" (*see 669, can. 5*).

Baptism

Baptism is the sacrament called the door to the new super-natural life. Through this door men pass from a state of bond-age to the devil and enmity towards God into a state of friend-ship with God by participating his very own life, though in a created way. The Church has always obeyed Christ's com-mand to teach all nations, baptizing them in the name of the Father, and of the Son, and of the Holy Spirit. Baptism is a true sacrament because it was instituted by Christ as an ex-ternal sign for communicating grace to the soul.

The following documents show the constant teaching of the Church concerning the sacrament of baptism.

A LETTER TO THE ARCHBISHOP OF ARLES, 1201

In the letter *Maiores Ecclesiae causas* to Archbishop Humbert, Pope Innocent III (1198–1216), probably answering some difficulties proposed to him by the archbishop, states the doc-trine of the Church on the nature and purpose of the sacrament of baptism, its efficacy, and its necessity even for infants.

For they maintain that it is useless to confer baptism on infants. . . . Our answer is that baptism has taken the place of circumcision. . . . Therefore, as the soul of the circum-cised was not destroyed out of his people (*see Gen. 17:14*), so shall he who is born again of water and the Holy Spirit gain entrance into the kingdom of heaven (*see John 3:5*). . . . Although original sin was remitted through the mystery of circumcision, and the danger of damnation averted, still no one entered the kingdom of heaven, for heaven was closed to everyone until the death of Christ. But through the sacra-ment of baptism made red with the blood of Christ, sin is remitted and entrance is gained to the kingdom of heaven; for Christ's blood has mercifully opened the door of heaven to his faithful. For it would not be fitting that all little chil-dren, so many of whom die each day, perish without having some remedy for salvation provided for them by the merciful

683
(410)

God, who wills that no one perish. . . . The adversaries say that faith or charity and the other virtues are not infused in children since children do not give consent; but the majority do not admit that statement in its absolute sense . . . Some assert that through the power of baptism the guilt in little children is taken away, but grace is not conferred upon them; others say that sin is forgiven and that virtues are infused, and that infants have the virtues as habits (*see 564*), but do not have the use of them until they become adults. . . . We say that a distinction has to be made because there are two types of sin, namely, original and actual. Original sin is contracted without consent whereas actual sin is committed with consent. Therefore, original sin, which is contracted without consent, is forgiven without consent through the power of the sacrament; but actual sin, which is contracted with consent, is by no means forgiven without consent. . . . The punishment for original sin is the loss of the vision of God; the punishment for actual sin is the torment of an everlasting hell.

684
(411) It is contrary to the Christian religion to force someone into accepting and practicing Christianity, if he was always unwilling and thoroughly opposed. Therefore, some make a distinction, and not a foolish one, between unwilling and unwilling, forced and forced. For whoever is violently drawn by fear of punishments and receives the sacrament of baptism to avoid these punishments, such a one, just like the one who comes to the sacraments in bad faith, is imprinted with the character of Christianity; and he, like one who is conditionally though not absolutely willing, is to be forced to the observances of the Christian faith. . . . But one who never consents and is absolutely unwilling receives neither the reality nor the character of the sacrament because express dissent is something more than the absence of any consent. . . . As for those who are asleep and those who are insane, if before becoming insane or before going to sleep, they persisted in their dissent, then they do not receive the character of the sacrament even if they are baptized in such a state, because it is understood that the intention of dissent remains in them; however, the opposite is true if, before they went to sleep, they were

catechumens and had the intention of being baptized. Hence the custom of the Church has been to baptize such people in case of necessity. Therefore, the sacramental rite imprints a character whenever it does not encounter a resisting obstacle of a contrary will.

THE PROFESSION OF FAITH PRESCRIBED FOR DURANDUS OF OSCA AND FOLLOWERS, 1208

(*See introd. to 150 and 658.*)

. . . Therefore, we approve the baptism of infants; we pro-   **685** fess and believe that they gain salvation if, after baptism, they   **(424)** die before committing sin. And we believe that all sins are remitted in baptism, both the original sin that has been contracted and the sins that are committed voluntarily. We judge that confirmation performed by a bishop, that is, the imposition of hands, is holy and that it is to be accepted as a thing to be held in reverence. . . .

THE COUNCIL OF FLORENCE, 1438-45

(*See introd. to 164 and 663.*)

Holy baptism holds the first place among all the sacraments   **686** because it is the door of the spiritual life. By it we are made   **(696)** members of Christ and of his body, the Church. And since through the first man death has come to all men, unless we are reborn of water and of the Holy Spirit, we cannot enter into the kingdom of heaven as the Truth himself tells us (*see John 3:5*). The matter of this sacrament is true and natural water and it is of no importance whether it is cold or warm water. The form is: "I baptize you in the name of the Father, and of the Son, and of the Holy Spirit." Nevertheless, we do not deny that the true sacrament is also effected by these words: "This servant of Christ is baptized in the name of the Father, and of the Son, and of the Holy Spirit"; or: "By my hands this one is baptized in the name of the Father, and of the Son, and of the Holy Spirit." For since the principal cause from which baptism gets its power is the Holy Trinity and the instrumental cause is the minister who performs the external rite of the sacrament, the sacrament is effected if along with the invocation of the Holy Trinity the act performed by the minister

The Sacraments

himself is expressed. The minister of this sacrament is the priest, and it belongs to his office to baptize. However, in the case of necessity not only a priest or a deacon but even a layman, or a woman, or even a pagan and a heretic can baptize provided that they keep the form of the Church and intend to do what the Church does. The effect of this sacrament is the remission of original and actual sin, and also of the punishment that is due to sin. No satisfaction, therefore, is to be enjoined on the baptized for their past sins; and those who die before they commit any sin immediately obtain the kingdom of heaven and the vision of God.

THE COUNCIL OF TRENT, 1545-63

(See introd. to 371 and 664.)

Canons on Baptism

687
(857)
1. If anyone says that the baptism of John had the same power as the baptism of Christ: let him be anathema.

688
(858)
2. If anyone says that true and natural water is not necessary in baptism, and therefore interprets metaphorically the words of our Lord Jesus Christ, "Unless a man be born again of water and the Holy Spirit" *(John 3:5)*: let him be anathema.

689
(859)
3. If anyone says that the Roman Church (which is the mother and teacher of all churches) does not have the true doctrine concerning the sacrament of baptism: let him be anathema.

690
(860)
4. If anyone says that baptism, even that given by heretics in the name of the Father, and of the Son, and of the Holy Spirit, with the intention of doing what the Church does, is not true baptism: let him be anathema.

691
(861)
5. If anyone says that baptism is optional, that is, not necessary for salvation: let him be anathema *(see 560)*.

692
(862)
6. If anyone says that a baptized person cannot lose grace even if he wants to, no matter how much he sins, unless he is unwilling to believe: let him be anathema *(see 572)*.

Baptism

7. If anyone says that through baptism baptized persons become obliged merely to faith alone, and not to keeping the whole law of Christ: let him be anathema (*see 566*).

693
(*863*)

8. If anyone says that baptized persons are freed from all the precepts of holy Church, either those that are contained in the Scriptures or those that are handed down by tradition, so that they are not bound to observe them unless of their own accord they wish to submit themselves to these precepts: let him be anathema.

694
(*864*)

9. If anyone says that the remembrance of the baptism which they have received ought to be so impressed on men that they be brought to understand that all vows taken after baptism are invalid by reason of the promise already made in baptism itself, as if these vows detracted from the faith they professed or from baptism itself: let him be anathema.

695
(*865*)

10. If anyone says that all the sins which are committed after baptism, are remitted or at least made venial by merely recalling and believing in the baptism once received: let him be anathema.

696
(*866*)

11. If anyone says that he who has denied the faith of Christ before infidels must, when he is converted to repentance, receive baptism again even when it was truly and rightly performed: let him be anathema.

697
(*867*)

12. If anyone says that no one is to be baptized except at the age at which Christ was baptized, or at the hour of death: let him be anathema.

698
(*868*)

13. If anyone says that because infants do not make an act of faith, they are not to be numbered among the faithful after they receive baptism and, moreover, that they are to be rebaptized when they come to the use of reason; or if anyone says that it is better to omit the baptism of infants rather than to baptize, merely in the faith of the Church, those who do not believe by an act of their own: let him be anathema.

699
(*869*)

14. If anyone says that when these baptized infants grow up they are to be asked whether they wish to ratify what their

700
(*870*)

sponsors promised in their name at baptism; and if they answer in the negative, they are to be left to their own judgment, and that until they come to their senses, they are not to be forced to a Christian life by any punishment except that of being kept away from the Eucharist and the reception of other sacraments: let him be anathema.

THE DECREE LAMENTABILI, 1907

(Errors of the modernists; see introd. to 112.)

701
(2042)
42. The Christian community brought about the necessity of baptism by adopting it as a necessary rite and joining to it the obligations of the profession of a Christian.

702
(2043)
43. The custom of conferring baptism on infants was a disciplinary evolution and it was one of the reasons why the sacrament resolved itself into two parts, namely, baptism and penance.

Confirmation

Christian tradition has always considered confirmation as a complement to the sacrament of baptism. By baptism one is born into the Christian life; by confirmation one receives the Holy Spirit with his sevenfold gifts and is made a mature and perfect Christian, armed as a soldier of Jesus Christ to fight the spiritual combats on the road to salvation. Like baptism and holy orders, confirmation impresses its peculiar character on the soul. Hence, it can be received only once.

THE PROFESSION OF FAITH PRESCRIBED FOR DURANDUS OF OSCA AND FOLLOWERS, 1208

(See introd. to 658; for testimony on confirmation see last sentence of 685.)

LETTER TO THE CATHOLICOS OF THE ARMENIANS, 1351

On September 29, 1351, Pope Clement VI (1342–52) wrote the letter *Super quibusdam* to Mechitar (Consolator), the *catholicos* or highest bishop of the Armenians. His letter included many questions on the true faith to which the Armenian bishop's affirmative answer would be a profession of faith and an agreement to unity with Rome.

You have given answers that lead us to require of you the following:

First, concerning the consecration of the chrism, do you believe that the chrism cannot rightly and duly be consecrated by a priest who is not a bishop?

703
(571)

Second, do you believe that the sacrament of confirmation cannot ordinarily be administered in virtue of his office by any other than a bishop?

704
(572)

Third, do you believe that the power of conferring the sacrament of confirmation can be given to priests who are not bishops only through the Roman Pontiff who has the fullness of power?

705
(573)

Fourth, do you believe that those anointed with chrism by ordinary priests, who are not bishops and who have not received from the Roman Pontiff some concession or some commission in this matter, are to be anointed again by a bishop or bishops?

706
(574)

THE COUNCIL OF FLORENCE, 1438-45
(*See introd. to 164 and 663.*)

The second sacrament is confirmation. Its matter is chrism blessed by a bishop and made from oil, signifying the purity of a good conscience, and balsam, signifying the sweet odor of a good reputation. The form is: "I sign you with the sign of the cross and I confirm you with the chrism of salvation, in the name of the Father, and of the Son, and of the Holy Spirit." The ordinary minister is the bishop. And, although the simple priest is empowered to perform the other anointings, no one except the bishop should confer this sacrament. For we read that only the apostles, whose office the bishops hold, imparted the Holy Spirit through the imposition of hands. Reading the Acts of the Apostles makes this clear: "Now when the apostles in Jerusalem heard that Samaria had received the word of God, they sent to them Peter and John.

707
(697)

On their arrival they prayed for them, that they might receive the Holy Spirit; for as yet he had not come upon any of them, but they had only been baptized in the name of the Lord Jesus. Then they laid their hands on them and they received the Holy Spirit" (*Acts 8:14 ff.*). In place of that imposition of hands, confirmation is given in the Church. Nevertheless, we read that sometimes through a dispensation of the Apostolic See for a reasonable and very urgent reason a simple priest has administered this sacrament of confirmation with the chrism blessed by a bishop. The effect of this sacrament is that the Holy Spirit is given in it for strength just as he was given to the apostles on Pentecost, in order that the Christian may courageously confess the name of Christ. And therefore, the one to be confirmed is anointed on the forehead, where shame shows itself, lest he be ashamed to confess the name of Christ and especially his cross which was, indeed, according to the Apostle a stumbling block to the Jews and to the Gentiles foolishness (*see I Cor. 1:23*). And for this reason the recipient is signed with the sign of the cross.

THE COUNCIL OF TRENT, 1545-63

(*See introd. to 371 and 664.*)

Canons on Confirmation

708
(871)
1. If anyone says that the confirmation of baptized persons is a useless ceremony and not rather a true and proper sacrament; or that at one time it meant nothing other than a certain catechesis by which those nearing adolescence gave an account of their faith before the Church: let him be anathema.

709
(872)
2. If anyone says that those who attribute some power to the holy chrism of confirmation are offending the Holy Spirit: let him be anathema.

710
(873)
3. If anyone says that the ordinary minister of holy confirmation is not the bishop, but any simple priest: let him be anathema.

THE DECREE LAMENTABILI, 1907

(*Error of the modernists; see introd. to 112.*)

44. There is no proof that the rite of the sacrament of confirmation was used by the apostles: the formal distinction of the two sacraments, baptism and confirmation, does not belong to the history of primitive Christianity.

The Holy Eucharist

When our Lord told the Jews at Capharnaum, "Unless you eat the flesh of the Son of man, and drink his blood, you shall not have life in you" (John 6:54), he referred for the first time to the sacrament of the Holy Eucharist which was to be the center of the life of worship in his Church. The Eucharist is the greatest of the seven sacraments, because it contains the very author of the grace that all the sacraments give. In the Holy Eucharist Christ's redemptive work is re-enacted for men of every age and it produces in them the salutary effects of that redemption. The Eucharist as the Sacrifice of the Mass puts men of every age into vital contact with the life-giving death of Christ on the cross. The Eucharist as a sacrament is a very efficacious means for the faithful who receive Christ's body and blood to grow in the love of God. And under the sacred species of the Eucharist, Christ remains always really present, consoling and invigorating his Church, fulfilling in an altogether special way his promise to be with his Church "all days, even till the consummation of the world" (Matt. 28:20).

The mystery of the Holy Eucharist overpowers the senses. It is not surprising that in the course of time the Church has frequently had to insist on the truth of the Real Presence in the face of heretical errors. Differences of usage in the administration of this sacrament sometimes gave rise to doctrinal errors, like the false belief that Communion under both species was necessary; these too the Church had to condemn. In later times the severest attacks of all came when the Reformers did away with the Mass and the sacrament of the Eucharist.

The Sacraments

THE SIXTH COUNCIL OF ROME, 1079

Berengarius of Tours (999–1088), a nominalist, appealed to
John Scotus Erigena for his heretical doctrine on the Eucharist.
He was condemned in 1050. There followed a series of alter-
nate submissions to the Church and attacks on its decision in his
regard. Gregory VII (1073–85) called him to Rome and made
him sign the following profession of faith in 1079. Though he
again attacked the formula he had signed, he finally died at
peace with the Church.

712
(355)
I, Berengarius, believe interiorly and profess publicly that
the bread and wine, which are placed on the altar, through
the mystery of the sacred prayer and the words of our Redeemer are substantially changed into the true, proper, and
life-giving flesh and blood of our Lord Jesus Christ. After the
consecration it is the true body of Christ, which was born
of the Virgin, and which hung on the cross as an offering
for the salvation of the world, and which sits at the right hand
of the Father. And it is the true blood of Christ which was
poured forth from his side. And Christ is present not merely by
virtue of the sign and the power of the sacrament but in his
proper nature and true substance as is set down in this summary and as I read it and you understand it. This I believe,
and I will not teach any more against this faith. So help me
God and this holy Gospel of God!

THE PROFESSION OF FAITH PRESCRIBED FOR
DURANDUS OF OSCA AND FOLLOWERS, 1208

(See introd. to 658.)

713
(424)
. . . We, with a sincere heart, firmly and unhesitatingly believe and loyally affirm that the Sacrifice, that is, the bread
and the wine [*variant:* that in the sacrament of the Eucharist
those things which before the consecration were bread and
wine], are the true body and the true blood of our Lord Jesus
Christ after the consecration. And in the Sacrifice we believe
that a good priest does nothing more than this and a bad
priest does nothing less; because it is not by the merit of the
one consecrating that the Sacrifice is accomplished, but by the
word of the Creator and by the power of the Holy Spirit.
Hence, we firmly believe and confess that no matter how up-

The Holy Eucharist

right, religious, holy, and prudent someone may be, he cannot and should not consecrate the Eucharist nor perform the Sacrifice of the Altar, unless he is a priest rightly ordained by a bishop who can be seen and can be felt. For this office of sacrifice we believe that three things are necessary: a definite person, that is, a priest properly ordained for that office by a bishop, as we have said above; the solemn words which are expressed by the holy Fathers in the Canon; and a right intention of the one uttering them. And so we firmly believe and profess that whoever believes and maintains that he can perform the Sacrifice of the Eucharist without previously being ordained by a bishop, as we have mentioned, is a heretic, and he shares in the destruction of Core and his accomplices (*see Num. 16*), and is to be excluded from the entire holy Roman Church. We believe that God grants pardon to all truly repentant sinners and we are most glad to join in communion with them. We consider that the anointing of the sick with the consecrated oil is a holy thing.

THE COUNCIL OF CONSTANCE, 1414-18

In the thirteenth session, June 15, 1415, the council published a definition on Communion under one species. In several sessions of the council, some errors of Hus (1369–1415) and Wyclif (1324–84) were condemned. The Bull *Inter cunctas*, February 22, 1418, included these condemnations and some of the questions asked of the heretics (*see introd. to 158 and 521*).

Definition on Communion under one species

In certain sections of the world some men have rashly **714** claimed that Christians ought to receive the holy sacrament **(626)** of the Eucharist under both species, that of bread and of wine. In some places they communicate the laity under both the species of bread and the species of wine. They boldly maintain that the people should communicate after taking their meal, or at other times when they are not fasting, contrary to the Church's praiseworthy custom, approved of with good reason—a custom which they try to condemn as sacrilegious. These are the reasons that lead this present council . . . to declare, decree, and define that although it was after the Supper when Christ instituted this venerable sacrament and although he gave it to his disciples under both species, that of

277

bread and of wine, nevertheless, the praiseworthy authority of the sacred canons and the approved custom of the Church has maintained and now maintains that this sacrament should not be consecrated after supper, and that it is not to be received by the faithful unless they are fasting, except in case of sickness or other necessity, as approved or allowed by law or by the Church. Although in the early Church this sacrament was received by the faithful under both species, still, to avoid certain scandals and dangers, the custom was introduced with good reason, that this sacrament be received under both species by those who consecrate, and by the laity under the species of bread only. For it should be firmly believed, and not doubted in the least that the entire body and blood of Christ are truly contained both under the species of bread and under the species of wine. . . . Therefore, to say that it is sacrilegious or that it is wrong to observe this law or custom, must be considered erroneous. And those who obstinately maintain the opposite of what has been put down should be treated as heretics and severely punished by the bishops or by their officials or by those whose duty it is to investigate heresy.

Questions proposed to the followers of Wyclif and Hus

715
(666)
16. Likewise, whether he believes that after the consecration by the priest there is in the Sacrament of the Altar under the appearance of bread and wine no material bread and wine, but there is the very same Christ who suffered on the cross and sits at the right hand of the Father.

716
(667)
17. Likewise, whether he believes and affirms that after the priest has consecrated, the true flesh and blood of Christ, his soul and divinity, the whole Christ, are present under the species of the bread alone even apart from the species of the wine, and that the same body is present in its entirety and under each of these species taken singly.

THE COUNCIL OF FLORENCE, 1438-45

(See introd. to 663.)

717
(698)
The third sacrament is the Eucharist. The matter of this sacrament is wheat bread and grape wine with a small amount of water to be mixed in before the consecration. Water is

mixed in because, according to the citations of the holy Fathers and Doctors of the Church mentioned before in the discussions, it is believed that our Lord himself instituted this sacrament with wine mixed with water. Furthermore, this is a fitting representation of our Lord's Passion. For as Blessed Alexander, the fifth pope after St. Peter, says: "In the oblation of the mysteries which are offered to the Lord in the solemnity of the Mass, let only bread and wine mixed with water be offered in sacrifice. Not wine only nor water only should be offered in the chalice of the Lord but a mixture of both. For we read that both, that is, blood and water, flowed from the side of Christ." Finally, this is a fitting way to signify the effect of this sacrament, that is, the union of the Christian people with Christ. Water represents the people as the Apocalypse says: "The waters are many peoples" (*see Apoc. 17:15*). And Julius, the second pope after Blessed Sylvester, says: "According to the command of the canons, the Lord's chalice should be offered with wine mixed with water. For we see that the water stands for the people, the wine for the blood of Christ. Thus when wine and water are mixed in the chalice, the people are united with Christ, and the faithful are closely joined to him in whom they believe." Therefore, since the holy Roman Church, which was instructed by the blessed Apostles Peter and Paul, and since all the other churches of the Latins and the Greeks, churches in which there have been brilliant sanctity and learning, have, from the very beginnings of the earliest Church, followed this custom and still follow it, it seems entirely improper for any region whatsoever not to follow this reasonable and universal practice. We therefore decree that the Armenians are to conform to the rest of the Christian world and their priests are to mix a small amount of water with the wine, as has been said, in the offering of the chalice.

The form of the sacrament is the words of the Savior with which he effected this sacrament; for the priest effects this sacrament by speaking in the person of Christ. It is by the power of these words that the substance of bread is changed into the body of Christ, and the substance of wine into his blood. This change takes place in such a way that the whole Christ is present under the species of bread and the whole

Christ is present under the species of wine. Further, the whole Christ is present under any part of the consecrated host or the consecrated wine when separated from the rest.

The effect which this sacrament has in the soul of a person who receives it worthily, is to unite him with Christ. Since it is by grace that a man is incorporated into Christ and united to Christ's members, it follows that those who receive this sacrament worthily, receive an increase of grace. And all the effects which material food and drink have on the life of our body—maintaining and increasing life, restoring health and bringing pleasure—all these effects this sacrament has on our spiritual life. As Pope Urban says, in this sacrament we think of our Savior with gratitude, we are drawn away from evil, we are encouraged to good, and we advance in virtue and in grace.

THE COUNCIL OF TRENT, 1545-63

(See introd. to 664.)

In the thirteenth session on October 11, 1551, under Pope Julius III, the council published its decree on the Holy Eucharist defining the Real Presence, transubstantiation, the reason for Christ's institution of this sacrament, and its excellence. The council also enacted disciplinary decrees with regard to the reverent care and reservation of the sacred species.

DECREE ON THE MOST HOLY EUCHARIST

718
(873a) The holy, ecumenical, and general Council of Trent, lawfully assembled in the Holy Spirit, and presided over by the aforementioned legates and nuncios of the holy Apostolic See, under the special inspiration and guidance of the Holy Spirit, has assembled to set forth the true and long-standing teaching on the faith and the sacraments and to supply a remedy for all the heresies and the other serious evils which now deeply trouble God's Church and divide it into so many different parts. From the beginning it has always been the special desire of the council to uproot completely the cockle of the damnable errors and schisms which in these fateful times of ours an enemy has sown (see Matt. 13:25) in the teaching of faith about the Holy Eucharist and about the use and worship of the Eucharist. In addition to his other

purposes, our Savior left the Eucharist in his Church as a symbol of the unity and love which he desired to unify and unite all Christians. And so this council teaches the true and genuine doctrine about this venerable and divine sacrament of the Eucharist—the doctrine which the Catholic Church has always held and which she will hold until the end of the world, as she learned it from Christ our Lord himself, from his apostles, and from the Holy Spirit, who continually brings all truth to her mind (*see John 14:26*). The council forbids all the faithful of Christ henceforth to believe, teach, or preach anything about the most Holy Eucharist that is different from what is explained and defined in this present decree.

Chapter 1. The Real Presence of Our Lord Jesus Christ in the Most Holy Sacrament of the Eucharist

To begin with, the holy council teaches and openly and straightforwardly professes that in the blessed sacrament of the Holy Eucharist, after the consecration of the bread and wine, our Lord Jesus Christ, true God and man, is truly, really, and substantially contained under the perceptible species of bread and wine (*see 728, can. 1*). It is not contradictory to say that our Savior always sits at the right hand of the Father in heaven according to his natural way of existing and that, nevertheless, in his substance he is sacramentally present in many other places with us. We can hardly find words to express this way of existing; but our reason, guided by faith, can know that it is possible for God, and this we should always believe unhesitatingly. For all our predecessors in the true Church of Christ who treated of this most holy sacrament very clearly professed that our Redeemer instituted this wonderful sacrament at the Last Supper, when, after he had blessed bread and wine, he said in plain, unmistakable words that he was giving them his own body and his own blood. These words are recorded by the Evangelists and afterwards repeated by St. Paul (*see Matt. 26:26 ff.; Mark 14:22 ff.; Luke 22:19 f.; I Cor. 11:23 ff.*). These words have their proper and obvious meaning and were so understood by the Fathers. Consequently, it is indeed an infamy that contentious, evil men should distort these words into fanciful, imaginary figures of

719
(874)

speech that deny the truth about the body and blood of Christ, contrary to the universal understanding of the Church. The Church, the pillar and mainstay of the truth (*see 1 Tim. 3:15*), has detested these satanical falsehoods that evil men have invented, and it accepts with unfailing gratitude this marvelous gift from the hands of Christ.

Chapter 2. The Reason for the Institution of This Most Holy Sacrament

720
(875)
Our Savior, therefore, instituted this sacrament just before leaving this world to go to the Father. He poured out the riches of his divine love for men in this sacrament, making a remembrance of his wonderful works (*see Ps. 110:4*), and he ordered us to receive this sacrament for the preservation of his memory (*see 1 Cor. 11:24*), and to proclaim his death until he should come to judge the world (*see 1 Cor. 11:26*). It was his will that this sacrament be received as the soul's spiritual food (*see Matt. 26:26*), to sustain and build up (*see 732, can. 5*) those who live with his life, as he said, "He who eats me, he also shall live because of me" (*John 6:58*). This sacrament is also to be a remedy to free us from our daily defects and to keep us from mortal sin. It was Christ's will, moreover, that this sacrament be a pledge of our future glory and our everlasting happiness and, likewise, a symbol of that one body of which he is the head (*see 1 Cor. 11:3; Eph. 5:23*). He willed that we, as members of this body, should be united to it by firm bonds of faith, hope, and love, so that we might all say the same thing, and that there might be no dissensions among us (*see 1 Cor. 1:10*).

Chapter 3. The Pre-eminence of the Most Holy Eucharist over the Other Sacraments

721
(876)
In common with the other sacraments, the most holy Eucharist is "a symbol of a sacred thing and a visible form of invisible grace." But the Eucharist also has a unique mark of distinction. The other sacraments do not have the power of sanctifying until someone makes use of them, but in the Eucharist the very author of sanctity is present before the sacrament is used (*see 731, can. 4*). For before the apostles received the Eucharist from the hands of our Lord (*see Matt.*

26:26; *Mark 14:22*), he told them that it was his body that
he was giving them. The Church of God has always believed
that immediately after the consecration the true body and
blood of our Lord, together with his soul and divinity, exist
under the species of bread and wine. His body exists under the
species of bread and his blood under the species of wine according to the import of the words. But his body exists under
the species of wine, his blood under the species of bread, and
his soul under both species in virtue of the natural connection
and concomitance which unite the parts of Christ our Lord,
who has risen from the dead and dies now no more (*see Rom.
6:9*). Moreover, Christ's divinity is present because of its
admirable hypostatic union with his body and soul (*see 728,
can. 1; 730, can. 3*). It is, therefore, perfectly true that just
as much is present under either species as is present under
both. For Christ, whole and entire, exists under the species
of bread and under any part of that species, and similarly the
whole Christ exists under the species of wine and under its
parts (*see 730, can. 3*).

Chapter 4. Transubstantiation

Because Christ our Redeemer said that it was truly his
body that he was offering under the species of bread (*see
Matt. 26:26 ff.; Mark 14:22 ff.; Luke 22:19 f.; I Cor. 11:24 ff.*),
it has always been the conviction of the Church, and this
holy council now again declares that, by the consecration of the
bread and wine a change takes place in which the whole substance of bread is changed into the substance of the body of
Christ our Lord and the whole substance of the wine into the
substance of his blood. This change the holy Catholic Church
fittingly and properly names transubstantiation (*see 729, can.
2*).

722
(877)

Chapter 5. The Worship and Veneration to
Be Shown This Most Holy Sacrament

There can be no doubt, then, that the faithful of Christ, in
accordance with the perpetual custom of the Catholic Church,
venerate this most holy Sacrament with the worship of latria
which is due to the true God (*see 733, can. 6*). Nor is this
Sacrament to be the less adored because it was instituted by

723
(878)

Christ to be received (*see Matt. 26:26 ff.*). For in this Sacrament we believe that the same God is present whom the eternal Father brought into the world, saying of him: "And let all the angels of God adore him" (*Heb. 1:6; see Ps. 96:7*). It is the same God whom the Magi fell down and worshiped (*see Matt. 2:11*) and, finally, the same God whom the apostles adored in Galilee as Scripture says (*see Matt. 28:17*). The holy council furthermore declares that the custom which has grown up in the Church of God of honoring this great and adorable Sacrament with special worship and solemnity on a particular feast day each year, and the custom of carrying the Sacrament in procession through the streets and public places with reverence and respect, are good and very religious customs. For it is most fitting that there be certain set days on which all Christians give unusual and extraordinary indications that they are mindful of their debt of gratitude to the Lord and Redeemer of all for this indescribable and truly divine gift that represents the triumphant victory of his death. And truly, victorious truth should triumph over falsehood and heresy so completely that, in the face of the splendor and joy of the universal Church, the opponents of truth should faint from weakness and defeat, or else they should enter into themselves and return at last to their right senses.

Chapter 6. The Reservation of the Sacrament of the Holy Eucharist and Carrying It to the Sick

724
(879) The custom of reserving the Holy Eucharist in a sacred place is so ancient that it was recognized already in the century of the Council of Nicaea. That the Holy Eucharist should be taken to the sick and that it should be carefully kept in the churches for this purpose is right and very reasonable. Moreover, many councils prescribe this and it is a longstanding custom in the Catholic Church. Consequently, this holy council decrees that this most salutary and necessary custom be retained (*see 734, can. 7*).

Chapter 7. The Preparation One Should Make to Receive the Holy Eucharist Worthily

725
(880) It is not right that anyone should participate in any sacred functions except in a holy manner. Certainly, then, the more

a Christian is aware of the holiness and the divinity of this heavenly Sacrament, the more careful he should be not to receive it without great reverence and sanctity (*see 738, can. 11*), especially since we read in the Apostle the fearful words: "He who eats and drinks unworthily, without distinguishing the body of the Lord, eats and drinks judgment to himself" (*I Cor. 11:29*). Therefore, a person who desires to communicate should recall the Apostle's command: "But let a man prove himself" (*I Cor. 11:28*). The custom of the Church makes it clear that the proof necessary is this: no one who has a mortal sin on his conscience shall dare receive the Holy Eucharist before making a sacramental confession, regardless of how contrite he may think he is. This holy council declares that this custom is to be kept forever by all Christians, including even priests who are bound to celebrate in virtue of their office—provided that they have access to a confessor. If, in case of necessity, a priest should celebrate without having confessed, he should confess as soon as possible.

Chapter 8. The Use of This Wonderful Sacrament

In the use of this sacrament, our Fathers have correctly and with wisdom distinguished three ways of receiving this holy sacrament. They teach that some, such as sinners, receive it only sacramentally. Others receive it only spiritually. These latter, with a living faith which works through charity (*see Gal. 5:6*), receive in desire the heavenly bread put before them and experience profit and benefit from it. The third group receive the sacrament both sacramentally and spiritually (*see 735, can. 8*); they are the ones who prove and prepare themselves beforehand so that clothed in the wedding garment (*see Matt. 22:11 ff.*) they may approach the divine table. In the sacramental reception it has always been the custom in the Church of God that the laity receive Communion from the priests and that priests who are celebrating Mass give Communion to themselves (*see 737, can. 10*). This custom should rightly and deservedly be kept as coming down from apostolic tradition.

726
(881)

Finally with fatherly love the holy council warns and pleads, "through the loving-kindness of our God" (*Luke 1:78*), that

727
(882)

each and every person who counts himself a Christian unite at last with all other Christians in this sign of unity, this bond of love, this symbol of concord. Keeping in mind the great majesty and the most excellent love of our Lord Jesus Christ, who laid down his precious life as the price of our salvation, and who gave us his flesh for our food (*see John 6:48 ff.*), may all Christians have great and strong faith in the sacred mystery of his body and blood; may they worship it with great devotion and pious veneration, so that they can frequently receive their daily bread (*see Matt. 6:11*). May it be true life for their souls and continuous health for their minds. May they be made strong by this bread (*see III Kings 19:8*) for the journey from this miserable exile to their home in heaven. There the veils will be removed and they will partake of the same Bread of Angels (*see Ps. 77:25*) that they now receive under the sacred species.

It is not enough to state the truth without pointing out and refuting errors. Hence, the holy council has decided to add the following canons so that all who know the Catholic teaching may also realize the heresies that they should beware of and avoid.

Canons on the Most Holy Sacrament of the Eucharist

728
(883)
1. If anyone denies that the body and blood, together with the soul and divinity, of our Lord Jesus Christ and, therefore, the whole Christ is truly, really, and substantially contained in the sacrament of the most holy Eucharist, but says that Christ is present in the Sacrament only as in a sign or figure, or by his power: let him be anathema (*see 719, 721*).

729
(884)
2. If anyone says that the substance of bread and wine remains in the holy sacrament of the Eucharist together with the body and blood of our Lord Jesus Christ, and denies that wonderful and extraordinary change of the whole substance of the bread into Christ's body and the whole substance of the wine into his blood while only the species of bread and wine remain, a change which the Catholic Church has most fittingly called transubstantiation: let him be anathema (*see 722*).

730
(885)
3. If anyone denies that in the venerable sacrament of the Eucharist the whole Christ is contained under each species

and under each and every portion of either species when it is divided up: let him be anathema (*see 721*).

4. If anyone says that after the consecration the body and blood of our Lord Jesus Christ are not present in the marvelous sacrament of the Eucharist, but are present only in the use of the sacrament while it is being received, and not before or after, and that the true body of the Lord does not remain in the consecrated hosts or particles that are kept or are left over after Communion: let him be anathema (*see 721*).
731
(*886*)

5. If anyone says that the principal effect of the most holy Eucharist is the forgiveness of sins, or that other effects do not come from the Eucharist: let him be anathema (*see 720*).
732
(*887*)

6. If anyone says that Christ, the only-begotten Son of God, is not to be adored in the holy sacrament of the Eucharist with the worship of latria, including the external worship, and that the Sacrament, therefore, is not to be honored with extraordinary festive celebrations nor solemnly carried from place to place in processions according to the praiseworthy universal rite and custom of the holy Church; or that the Sacrament is not to be publicly exposed for the people's adoration, and that those who adore it are idolators: let him be anathema (*see 723*).
733
(*888*)

7. If anyone says that it is not permissible to keep the sacred Eucharist in a holy place, but that it must necessarily be distributed immediately after the consecration to those who are present; or that it is not permissible to carry the Eucharist respectfully to the sick: let him be anathema (*see 724*).
734
(*889*)

8. If anyone says that Christ present in the Eucharist is only spiritually eaten and not sacramentally and really as well: let him be anathema (*see 726*).
735
(*890*)

9. If anyone denies that each and everyone of Christ's faithful of both sexes, is bound, when he reaches the age of reason, to receive Communion at least every year during the Paschal season according to the command of holy Mother Church: let him be anathema (*see DB 437*).
736
(*891*)

737
(892)
10. If anyone says that it is not permissible for a priest celebrating Mass to give Communion to himself: let him be anathema (*see 726*).

738
(893)
11. If anyone says that faith alone is a sufficient preparation for receiving the sacrament of the most holy Eucharist: let him be anathema. And, lest this great sacrament be received unworthily and thus be received unto death and condemnation, this holy council has determined and decreed that those who have mortal sin on their conscience, no matter how contrite they may think they are, must necessarily make a sacramental confession before receiving, provided that they have access to a confessor. If anyone presumes to teach, or preach, or stubbornly maintain, or defend in public disputation the opposite of this, he is excommunicated by his action (*see 725*).

COMMUNION UNDER BOTH SPECIES AND COMMUNION OF CHILDREN

In the twenty-first session on July 16, 1562, the council proposed this decree to settle once and for all: that Christ did not intend to oblige communion under both species; that this is not necessary for salvation; that the whole Christ is received in the reception of either species; and that little children are not obliged to receive sacramental Communion. The second chapter of this session is given under "The Sacraments in General" (*see 678*).

Chapter 1. The Laity and Clerics Who Are Not Celebrating Are Not Bound by the Divine Law to Receive under Both Species

739
(930)
Therefore, the holy council, guided by the Holy Spirit, who is the Spirit of wisdom and of understanding, the Spirit of counsel and of godliness (*see Isa. 11:2*), and following the custom and the judgment of the Church itself, teaches and declares that the laity and clerics who are not celebrating are not bound by any divine command to receive the sacrament of the Eucharist under both species. And faith leaves no possibility of doubting that Communion under one species is sufficient for their salvation. At the Last Supper, Christ our Lord instituted this adorable Sacrament and gave it to the apostles under the species of bread and wine (*see Matt. 26:26 ff.;*

The Holy Eucharist

Mark 14:22 ff.; Luke 22:19 f.; I Cor. 11:24 ff.). But this manner of institution and of presentation does not prove that all of Christ's faithful are bound by a decree of our Lord to receive under both species (*see 742, can. 1; 743, can. 2*). And it is not right to conclude from the words in the sixth chapter of John that our Lord commands communion under both species (*see 744, can. 3*), regardless of how these words are understood according to the various interpretations of the Fathers and Doctors. Christ said, "Unless you eat the flesh of the Son of man, and drink his blood, you shall not have life in you" (*John 6:54*); but he also said, "If anyone eat of this bread he shall live forever" (*John 6:52*). Again Christ said, "He who eats my flesh and drinks my blood has life everlasting" (*John 6:55*); but he also said, "The bread that I will give is my flesh for the life of the world" (*John 6:52*). Finally, he said, "He who eats my flesh, and drinks my blood, abides in me and I in him" (*John 6:57*); but he also said, "He who eats this bread shall live forever" (*John 6:59*).

Chapter 3. The Whole and Entire Christ and the True Sacrament Is Received under Either Species

As has already been said, our Redeemer instituted this **740** sacrament at the Last Supper and gave it to the apostles under (932) two species. Furthermore, this holy council declares that it must be professed that the whole and entire Christ and the true sacrament is received even under one species alone, and, therefore, as far as the benefits are concerned, those who receive only one species are not deprived of any grace necessary for salvation (*see 744, can. 3*).

Chapter 4. Children Without the Use of Reason Are Not Obliged to Receive Sacramental Communion

Finally, the same holy council teaches that little children **741** who do not have the use of reason are not under any obliga- (933) tion to receive the Eucharist in sacramental communion (*see 745, can. 4*). For they have been regenerated through the bath of baptism (*see Titus 3:5*) and incorporated into Christ, and at their age they cannot lose the grace of the sons of God that they have received. This does not mean that times past are to be condemned because in some places the

289

custom of giving Communion to little children was occasionally practiced. For those holy Fathers had a good reason for their action according to the usages of their times, and it must be unconditionally believed that they did not act that way because it was necessary for salvation.

Canons on Communion under Both Species and on Communion of Little Children

742
(934)
1. If anyone says that each and every one of Christ's faithful ought to receive both species of the most holy sacrament of the Eucharist, because of a command from God or because it is necessary for salvation: let him be anathema (*see 739*).

743
(935)
2. If anyone says that the holy Catholic Church was not led by good reasons to have the laity and the clerics who are not celebrating Mass communicate under the species of bread alone, or that the Church erred in so doing: let him be anathema (*see 678*).

744
(936)
3. If anyone denies that the whole and entire Christ, the source and author of all graces, is received under the species of bread alone, alleging, as some falsely do, that such a reception is not in accord with Christ's institution of the sacrament under both species: let him be anathema (*see 739, 740*).

745
(937)
4. If anyone says that Eucharistic Communion is necessary for little children before they reach the age of reason: let him be anathema (*see 741*).

THE MOST HOLY SACRIFICE OF THE MASS

In the twenty-second session on September 17, 1562, the council proposed the following chapters and canons explaining the nature of the Sacrifice of the Mass. Also the council laid down some disciplinary directives concerning the celebration of the Sacrifice. As is pointed out in Denzinger, the titles of the chapters in this session are not the work of the council; they are, therefore, put in parentheses.

746
(937a)
The holy, ecumenical, and general Council of Trent, lawfully assembled in the Holy Spirit, presided over by the same apostolic legates, has as its purpose to preserve in its purity the ancient, absolute, and completely perfect faith and teaching in the holy Catholic Church about the great mystery of

the Eucharist and to avert heresies and errors. It teaches and lays down, under the inspiration of the Holy Spirit, the following doctrine about the Eucharist as a true and unique sacrifice and declares that this doctrine is to be preached to the faithful.

Chapter 1. (*The Institution of the Most Holy Sacrifice of the Mass*)

As the Apostle Paul testifies, there was no perfection under the former Testament because of the insufficiency of the Levitical priesthood. It was, therefore, necessary (according to the merciful ordination of God the Father) that another priest arise according to the order of Melchisedech (*see Gen. 14:18; Ps. 109:4; Heb. 7:11*), our Lord Jesus Christ, who could perfect all who were to be sanctified (*see Heb. 10:14*) and bring them to fulfillment. He, then, our Lord and our God, was once and for all to offer himself by his death on the altar of the cross to God the Father, to accomplish for them [*ed.:* there] an everlasting redemption. But death was not to end his priesthood (*see Heb. 7:24, 27*). And so, at the Last Supper, on the night on which he was betrayed, in order to leave for his beloved spouse, the Church, a sacrifice (*see 756, can. 1*) that was visible, as the nature of man demands, declaring himself constituted a priest forever according to the order of Melchisedech, he offered his body and blood under the species of bread and wine to God the Father and he gave his body and blood under the same species to the apostles to receive, making them priests of the New Testament at that time. This sacrifice was to re-present the bloody sacrifice which he accomplished on the cross once and for all. It was to perpetuate his memory until the end of the world (*see I Cor. 11:23 ff.*). Its salutary strength was to be applied for the remission of the sins that we daily commit. He ordered the apostles and their successors in the priesthood to offer this sacrifice when he said, "Do this in remembrance of me" (*Luke 22:19; I Cor. 11:24*), as the Catholic Church has always understood and taught (*see 757, can. 2*). For after he celebrated the old Pasch, which the assembly of the children of Israel offered in memory of the passage from Egypt (*see Exod. 12:1 ff.*), Christ instituted a new Pasch. He himself was this new

747
(938)

Pasch, to be offered by the Church through her priests under visible signs, in memory of his departure from this world to the Father when by the shedding of his blood he redeemed us from the power of darkness and transferred us into his kingdom (*see Col. 1:13*).

748
(939)
This is that clean oblation which cannot be defiled by any unworthiness or malice on the part of those who offer it, and which the Lord foretold through Malachi would be offered in all places as a clean oblation to His name, for His name would be great among the Gentiles (*see Mal. 1:11*). The Apostle Paul also refers rather clearly to this oblation in writing to the Corinthians when he says that those who have been defiled by partaking of the table of devils cannot be partakers of the table of the Lord. By *table* he understands *altar* in both cases (*see I Cor. 10:21*). Finally, this is the oblation which was represented by various figures in sacrifices during the time of nature and of the Law (*see Gen. 4:4; 8:20; 12:8; 22; Exod. passim*). For it includes all the good that was signified by those former sacrifices; it is their fulfillment and perfection.

Chapter 2. (*The Visible Sacrifice Is Propitiatory for the Living and the Dead*)

749
(940)
In the divine sacrifice that is offered in the Mass, the same Christ who offered himself once in a bloody manner on the altar of the cross is present and is offered in an unbloody manner. Therefore, the holy council teaches that this sacrifice is truly propitiatory (*see 758, can. 3*), so that if we draw near to God with an upright heart and true faith, with fear and reverence, with sorrow and repentance, through the Mass we may obtain mercy and find grace to help in time of need (*see Heb. 4:16*). For by this oblation the Lord is appeased, he grants grace and the gift of repentance, and he pardons wrongdoings and sins, even grave ones. For it is one and the same victim: he who now makes the offering through the ministry of priests and he who then offered himself on the cross; the only difference is in the manner of the offering. The benefits of this oblation (the bloody one, that is) are received in abundance through this unbloody oblation. By no means, then, does the Sacrifice of the Mass detract from the sacrifice of the

cross (*see 759, can. 4*). Therefore, the Mass may properly be offered according to apostolic tradition for the sins, punishments, satisfaction, and other necessities of the faithful on earth, as well as for those who have died in Christ and are not yet wholly cleansed (*see 758, can. 3*).

Chapter 3. (*Masses in Honor of the Saints*)

And although it is the custom of the Church occasionally to celebrate some Masses in honor and in memory of the saints, the Church teaches that sacrifice is offered not to the saints, but to God alone who has given them their crown (*see 760, can. 5*). Therefore, "the priest does not say: 'I offer this sacrifice to you, Peter and Paul' "; but giving thanks to God for the victories of the saints, the priest implores their help that they may pray for us in heaven, while we remember them on earth.

750
(941)

Chapter 4. (*The Canon of the Mass*)

Holy things must be treated in a holy way and this sacrifice is the most holy of all things. And so, that this sacrifice might be worthily and reverently offered and received, the Catholic Church many centuries ago instituted the sacred Canon. It is free from all error (*see 761, can. 6*) and contains nothing that does not savor strongly of holiness and piety and nothing that does not raise to God the minds of those who offer the Sacrifice. For it is made up from the words of our Lord, from apostolic traditions, and from devout instructions of the holy pontiffs.

751
(942)

Chapter 5. (*The Solemn Ceremonies of the Sacrifice of the Mass*)

Having the nature that he does, man cannot easily meditate on divine things without external helps. For this reason, holy Mother Church has prescribed certain rites for the Mass, some parts to be said in a low tone of voice, some to be said more loudly (*see 764, can. 9*). She also has made use of ceremonies (*see 762, can. 7*) such as sacred blessings, candles, incense, vestments, and other things of like nature which have come down from apostolic teaching and tradition. All of these things are used to point up the majesty of this great sacrifice and to raise the minds of the faithful through these visible

752
(943)

signs of religion and piety to the contemplation of the very exalted things hidden in this sacrifice.

Chapter 6. (*The Mass in Which the Priest Alone Communicates*)

753
(944)
The holy council would desire that in every Mass the faithful who are present communicate not only in spiritual desire, but by a sacramental reception of the Eucharist, so that they might receive greater benefits from this most holy sacrifice. Nevertheless, if such is not always the case, the council does not on that account condemn the Masses in which the priest alone communicates sacramentally as private and illicit (*see 763, can. 8*). Rather, it approves of them and endorses them since such Masses are to be considered truly public Masses, partly because the people communicate spiritually at such Masses, and partly because they are celebrated by a public minister of the Church, not for himself alone, but for all the faithful who pertain to the body of Christ.

Chapter 7. (*Water Is to Be Mixed with the Wine Offered in the Chalice*)

754
(945)
Next, the holy council reminds priests that they have been commanded by the Church to mix water in the wine offered in the chalice (*see 764, can. 9*) because it is believed that Christ did this and also because water came out of his side together with his blood (*see John 19:34*), and mixing water and wine recalls that mystery. And since in the Apocalypse of St. John "waters" are called "peoples" (*see Apoc. 17:1, 15*), this is a symbol of the union of the faithful with Christ their head.

Chapter 8. (*Mass Should Not Be Celebrated in the Vernacular Indiscriminately; the Mysteries of the Mass Are to Be Explained to the People*)

755
(946)
Although the Mass contains much instruction for the faithful, the Fathers did not think that it should be celebrated in the vernacular indiscriminately (*see 764, can. 9*). Therefore, in all churches in all places the ancient rite approved by the holy Roman Church, the mother and teacher of all churches, is to be observed. But lest the sheep of Christ go unfed, lest

the little ones ask for bread and there be no one to break it for them (*see Lam. 4:4*), the holy council orders that pastors and all who have the care of souls are to explain some of the things that are read at Mass. They themselves or their representatives are to do this frequently during the celebration of Mass. Among other things they are to explain something about the mystery of this most holy sacrifice, especially on Sundays and on feast days.

Canons on the Most Holy Sacrifice of the Mass

1. If anyone says that in the Mass a true and proper sacrifice is not offered to God or that the sacrificial offering consists merely in the fact that Christ is given to us to eat: let him be anathema (*see 747*). **756** (948)

2. If anyone says that by the words, "Do this in remembrance of me" (*Luke 22:19; I Cor. 11:24*), Christ did not make the apostles priests, or that he did not decree that they and other priests should offer his body and blood: let him be anathema (*see 747*). **757** (949)

3. If anyone says that the Sacrifice of the Mass is merely an offering of praise and of thanksgiving, or that it is a simple memorial of the sacrifice offered on the cross, and not propitiatory, or that it benefits only those who communicate; and that it should not be offered for the living and the dead, for sins, punishments, satisfaction, and other necessities: let him be anathema (*see 749*). **758** (950)

4. If anyone says that the Sacrifice of the Mass constitutes a blasphemy to the sacred sacrifice that Christ offered on the cross, or that the Mass detracts from that sacrifice: let him be anathema (*see 749*). **759** (951)

5. If anyone says that it is a deception to celebrate Masses in honor of the saints and to ask their intercession with God, according to the mind of the Church: let him be anathema (*see 750*). **760** (952)

6. If anyone says that there are errors in the Canon of the Mass and that it should therefore be done away with: let him be anathema (*see 751*). **761** (953)

762
(954)
7. If anyone says that the ceremonies, vestments, and external signs which the Catholic Church uses in the celebration of its Masses are the source of godlessness rather than helps to piety: let him be anathema (*see 752*).

763
(955)
8. If anyone says that Masses in which the priest alone communicates sacramentally, are illicit and should be done away with: let him be anathema (*see 754*).

764
(956)
9. If anyone says that the rite of the Roman Church prescribing that a part of the Canon and the words of consecration be recited in a low tone of voice, should be condemned; or that Mass should be celebrated only in the vernacular; or that water should not be mixed with the wine offered in the chalice since that would be contrary to Christ's decree: let him be anathema (*see 752, 754 f.*).

THE ENCYCLICAL MEDIATOR DEI, 1947

November 20, 1947, brought a corollary to the encyclical *Mystici corporis*. In that encyclical the intimate union of Christ with his members and of the members with one another had been explained. The present encyclical, *Mediator Dei*, which clarifies the prayer and worship in that mystical body, makes a fitting conclusion to the doctrine on the sacrament of the Eucharist and the Sacrifice of the Mass.

765
(2297)
Together with the Church, therefore, its divine founder is present in every liturgical function; Christ is present in the august Sacrifice of the Altar both in the person of his minister and above all under the Eucharistic species. He is present in the sacraments by reason of the force which he pours into them which makes them ready instruments of sanctification. He is present, finally, in the prayer of praise and petition we direct to God, as it is written: "Where there are two or three gathered together in my name, there am I in the midst of them" (*Matt. 18:20*). . . .

Hence, the liturgical year devotedly fostered and accompanied by the Church is not a cold and lifeless representation of the events of the past, or a simple and bare record of a former age. It is rather Christ himself who is ever living in his Church. Here he continues that most merciful journey which he lovingly began in his mortal life, going about doing good with the design of bringing men to know his mysteries and to live by them. These mysteries are ever present and active, not in a vague and uncertain way as some modern writers hold, but in the way that Catholic doctrine teaches us. According to the Doctors of the Church, they are shining examples of Christian perfection, as well as sources of divine grace, because of the merit and prayers of Christ; they still influence us because each mystery brings its own special grace for our salvation.

The close tie between the ascetical life and liturgical devotion

In the spiritual life, consequently, there can be no difference or conflict between the action of God, who pours forth his grace into men's hearts to perpetuate the work of the Redemption, and the tireless collaboration of man, who must not nullify the gift of God. And neither can the efficacy of the external administration of the sacraments, which comes from the rite itself [*ex opere operato*], conflict with the meritorious action of their ministers or recipients, which we call the agent's action [*opus operantis*]. Similarly, no conflict exists between public prayer and prayers in private, between morality and contemplation of celestial things, between the ascetical life and liturgical devotion. Finally there is no conflict between the jurisdiction and teaching office of the ecclesiastical hierarchy and the specifically priestly power exercised in the sacred ministry. **766** **(2299)**

Considering their special designation to perform the liturgical functions of the Holy Sacrifice and Divine Office, the Church has serious reasons for prescribing that the ministers it assigns to the service of the sanctuary and members of religious institutes devote themselves at certain times to mental prayer, to examination of conscience, and to various other spiritual exercises; for also these persons are in a special manner meant to have a share in the functions of the sacrificial liturgy and in uttering the divine praises. Unquestionably, liturgical prayer, being the public supplication of the illustrious spouse of Christ, is superior in excellence to private prayers. But this superior worth does not at all imply that there is conflict or incompatibility between these two kinds of prayer. For since they are both animated by the same spirit, together they form a perfect union: "Christ is all things and in all" (*Col. 3:11*). Both tend to the same objective: "until Christ is formed" in us (*see Gal. 4:19*).

The participation of the faithful in the priesthood of Christ

767
(2300)
It is therefore desirable . . . that all the faithful should be aware that to participate in the Eucharistic Sacrifice is a serious duty and their supreme dignity. . . .

The fact, however, that the faithful participate in the Eucharistic Sacrifice, does not mean that they also have the power of a priest. It is very necessary that you make this quite clear to your flocks.

For there are today . . . those who are dangerously near falling into errors long since condemned. For they teach that in the New Testament the word *priesthood* means only that priesthood which applies to all who have been baptized. And they hold that the command by which Christ gave the power to his apostles at the Last Supper to do what he himself had done belongs directly to the entire Church of the believers, and that from them, but only gradually, the hierarchical priesthood has come into being. Hence they assert that the people have the true priestly power, whereas the priest acts only in virtue of an office delegated to him by the community. Therefore, they regard the Eucharistic Sacrifice as a "concelebration," in the literal meaning of that term, and think it is more proper that priests should "concelebrate" with people present rather than offer the sacrifice privately with no people present.

768
(2300)
It is not necessary to explain how captious errors of this sort completely contradict the truths We have just stated above, when treating of the place of the priest in the mystical body of Jesus Christ. But we think it is necessary to repeat that the priest acts for the people only because he bears the person of Jesus Christ, who is head of all his members and offers himself in their stead. The priest, therefore, goes to the altar as the minister of Christ, inferior to Christ but superior to the people. The people, on the other hand, since they do not in any way take the place of the divine Redeemer and are not a mediator between themselves and God, cannot possess the power of the priest in any way.

These things are known with the certitude of faith. However, it must also be said that the faithful do offer the divine victim, though in a different way.

This has already been stated in the clearest terms by some of Our predecessors and some Doctors of the Church. Thus Innocent III of immortal memory says: "Sacrifice is offered not only by priests but by all the faithful as well. For what the priests accomplish in a special way in virtue of their office, that the faithful do in a general way by desire." We wish to mention at least one of St. Robert Bellarmine's many statements on this subject. "The sacrifice is principally offered in the person of Christ. The oblation that follows the Consecration, is an action bearing witness that the whole Church is in agreement with the oblation made by Christ, and offers it together with him."

Furthermore the rites and the prayers of the Eucharistic Sacrifice clearly show that the oblation of the victim is made by the priests together with the people . . .

**769
(2300)**

Nor is it surprising that the faithful should be raised to this dignity. For by the waters of baptism, Christians are made members of Christ, the priest, within the mystical body in a way common to all, and by the "character" which is imprinted on their souls, they are destined to give worship to God. Thus they participate, according to their state, in the priesthood of Christ. . . .

But there is also a more profound reason why all Christians, especially those who are present at Mass, are said to offer the sacrifice.

To prevent a dangerous error from arising, it is necessary in this important subject to give an exact definition of the meaning of the word *offer*. The unbloody sacrifice by which Christ is made present upon the altar in the state of a victim through the words of consecration, is performed by the priest and by him alone as bearing the person of Christ, and not as taking the place of the faithful. But by the very fact that he brings the divine victim to the altar, the priest offers the same victim as an oblation to God the Father for the glory of the Blessed Trinity and for the good of the whole Church. Now it is in this offering, in this limited sense of the word, that the faithful have a share according to their ability, and that in two ways; namely, they offer the sacrifice through the hands of the priest and, to a certain extent, they offer it together with him. It is by reason of this participation that the offering made by the people is a part of liturgical worship.

770
(2300)
That Christians offer the sacrifice through the hands of the priest is evident from the fact that the minister at the altar is taking Christ's place as head and is offering sacrifice in the name of all the members. This is the reason why the entire Church may truly be said to make an offering of the victim through Christ. The people are said to offer sacrifice together with the priest not because the members of the Church perform the visible liturgical rite, as the priest does, who alone is divinely appointed for this function, but because they unite their prayers of praise, petition, expiation, and thanksgiving to the prayers and intention of the priest, and of the high priest himself, so that in the offering of the victim and in the external rite of the priest their prayers may be brought to the Father. The external rite of sacrifice must by its very nature represent the internal worship. Now the Sacrifice of the New Law signifies that supreme worship by which the principal offerer who is Christ, and all the members of the mystical body in union with Christ and through him, pay to God the honor and reverence due to him.

THE ALLOCUTION MAGNIFICATE DOMINUM, 1954

When Pope Pius XII (1939–58) proclaimed the feast of the Queenship of Mary on November 1, 1954, he addressed the allocution *Magnificate Dominum* to an assemblage of hundreds of cardinals, bishops, and clergymen gathered from the entire world. In speaking of the sacred priesthood, the pope took occasion to correct an erroneous opinion on the nature of the act of hearing or of celebrating Mass and to warn against misunderstanding of the "priesthood" possessed by the faithful. (The translation is made from the text of the allocution in *L'Osservatore Romano* for November 4, 1954.)

771
. . . The assertion that not only laymen, but sometimes even some theologians and priests are making and disseminating today, must be rejected as an erroneous opinion. The assertion is that the celebration of one Mass which one hundred

priests attend with religious reverence is the same as one hundred Masses celebrated by one hundred priests. Such is not the case. As regards the offering of the Eucharistic Sacrifice, there are as many actions of the High Priest Christ as there are priests celebrating, not as many as there are priests who piously hear the Mass of a bishop or a holy priest who celebrates. For these priests who are present at Mass do not in any way take the place of Christ offering sacrifice. Rather, they are comparable to the faithful of the laity who are present at Mass.

It certainly cannot be denied, nor can there be any doubt that the faithful have a certain "priesthood"; and this priesthood should not be esteemed lightly or minimized. . . . But whatever the true and complete meaning of this estimable title and reality may be, it must be firmly held that this common "priesthood" of all the faithful, profound and mysterious as it is, differs not merely in degree, but in essence, from the priesthood properly and truly so called. This latter resides in the power of taking the place of the High Priest Christ and enacting the sacrifice of Christ himself.

Penance

The work of leading men to salvation is not finished when they are baptized into the life of grace in the Church. It happens that by personal sin men lose the justification they received in baptism. To enable his Church to put these sinners back on the road to salvation, Christ entrusted the Church with the power to forgive, in the sacrament of penance, the sins committed after baptism.

By Christ's will and institution the sacrament of penance is administered in a judicial procedure. The penitent confesses his sins to the duly authorized priest (who is the only minister of this sacrament). Acting as judge, the priest ascertains the gravity of the sins committed and whether the penitent is properly sorry. If the penitent is worthy, the priest gives him absolution and enjoins a suitable penance. This sacrament of heal-

ing and forgiveness restores the life of grace to those who have lost it, or increases it in those who already live in grace; it wipes out the debt of eternal punishment due to mortal sins and removes at least part of the temporal punishment due to either mortal or venial sins; to all it gives strength against future falls into sin.

In the history of the Church there has been a gradual development in the practice regarding the administration of this sacrament. Though the changes were noteworthy, they were all changes in accidentals. It was only with Wyclif and Hus and the Reformers that heresies arose with regard to almost every detail of this sacrament and evoked the clear definitions of the traditional doctrine from the Councils of Constance, Florence, and Trent.

THE COUNCIL OF CONSTANCE, 1414-18

(See introd. to 158 and 521.)

Error of Wyclif

772
(587)
7. If a person is sufficiently contrite, all external confession is superfluous and useless for him.

Questions proposed for the followers of Wyclif and Hus

773
(670)
20. Likewise, whether he believes that in order to be saved a Christian has the obligation, over and above heartfelt contrition, of confessing to a priest, when a qualified one is available; and only to a priest, not to a lay person or persons, no matter how good and devout the latter may be.

774
(671)
21. Likewise, whether he believes that the priest, in the cases over which he has jurisdiction, can absolve a sinner who has confessed and is contrite, and can impose a penance on him.

775
(675)
25. Likewise, whether he believes that the jurisdictional authority of pope, archbishop, and bishop to loose and to bind is greater than the authority of a mere priest, even if he has the care of souls.

Penance

THE COUNCIL OF FLORENCE, 1438-45

(*See introd. to 663.*)

The fourth sacrament is penance. The quasi-matter of this sacrament is made up of the penitent's acts, which are divided into three elements. The first of these is contrition of heart, for which sorrow for the sin committed and the intention to sin no more are required. The second element is oral confession, for which it is required that the sinner confess to the priest all the sins he remembers. The third element is the penance for his sins, which is determined by the judgment of the priest; it is generally performed through prayer, fasting, or almsgiving. The form of this sacrament is the words of absolution that the priest pronounces when he says: "I absolve you" etc. And the minister of this sacrament is a priest who has authority to absolve, either as ordinary or as delegated from a superior. The effect of this sacrament is absolution from sins.

776
(699)

CONDEMNATION OF ERRORS OF MARTIN LUTHER, 1520

The following errors were condemned by Pope Leo X in the bull *Exsurge Domine* on June 15, 1520 (*see introd. to 550*).

5. There is no foundation either in Sacred Scripture or in the ancient holy Christian doctors for the teaching that there are three parts of penance: contrition, confession, and satisfaction.

777
(745)

6. The kind of contrition that is engendered by the recollection, consideration, and detestation of sins, as a person reviews all his years with a bitter heart (*see Isa. 38:15*), meditating on the seriousness of his sins, their number and heinousness, the loss of eternal happiness, and the eternal damnation incurred—this kind of contrition makes one a hypocrite, makes him, in fact, a worse sinner.

778
(746)

7. This is a very true maxim, one more excellent than all the previous teaching about the kinds of contrition: "To do no evil in the future is an excellent penance; the best penance is a new life."

779
(747)

780
(748)   8. By no means may a person presume to confess venial sins, or even all mortal sins, because it is impossible to know all one's mortal sins. That is why only public mortal sins were confessed in the primitive Church.

781
(749)   9. When we desire to confess everything honestly, we are equivalently desiring to leave nothing for God's mercy to pardon.

782
(750)   10. No man's sins are remitted unless he is confident that they are remitted when the priest remits them; moreover, the sin would remain unless he were confident of its remission. For the remission of sin and the gift of grace are not sufficient; it is also necessary to have confidence that the sin is remitted.

783
(751)   11. Your confidence in being absolved should be based in no way on your contrition, but on Christ's words, "Whatever thou shalt loose" etc. (*Matt. 16:19*). Hence, I say, have confidence, if you have obtained the absolution of a priest, and strongly trust that you are absolved, and you will truly be absolved, whatever the case may be with regard to contrition.

784
(752)   12. On the impossible supposition that a person making his confession would not be contrite, or that the priest would give absolution not seriously but in jest, nevertheless, the person confessing would most truly be absolved, if he had confidence that he was absolved.

785
(753)   13. In the sacrament of penance and in the remission of sin, the pope or a bishop does no more than the lowliest priest; moreover, where there is no priest, any Christian, even if it were a woman or a child, does as much.

786
(754)   14. No one is obliged to tell the priest that he is contrite, and the priest should not ask.

THE COUNCIL OF TRENT, 1545-63
(*See introd. to 664 and 371.*)

In the fourteenth session of the council on November 25, 1551, the doctrine on penance was set down in great detail because of the particularly violent attacks on this sacrament by the Reformers.

THE DOCTRINE ON THE SACRAMENT OF PENANCE

The most holy, ecumenical, and general Council of Trent, legitimately assembled in the Holy Spirit, presided over by the same legate and nuncios of the holy Apostolic See, necessarily had a lengthy discussion about the sacrament of penance in the decree on justification (*see 571, 603*), because of the close relationship of the subject matter. Nevertheless, because there are so many different errors concerning this sacrament at the present time, the common good demands a more exact and a more complete definition. Thus, under the protection of the Holy Spirit, all the errors will be detected and refuted, and Catholic truth will appear in its clarity and splendor. This is the truth which the holy council now proposes to all Christians and which must be preserved forever.

787
(893a)

Chapter 1. The Necessity and the Institution of the Sacrament of Penance

If all the regenerated had enough gratitude to God to keep forever the justice received in baptism by his grace and goodness, there would have been no need to institute any other sacrament than baptism for the remission of sins (*see 801, can. 2*). But since God is rich in mercy (*see Eph. 2:4*) and knows our frail structure (*see Ps. 102:14*), he has also prepared a remedy of life for those who, after baptism, have given themselves over to the slavery of sin and to the power of the devil. This remedy is the sacrament of penance (*see 800, can. 1*), and through it the benefit of Christ's death is applied to those who have fallen after baptism. At all times all men who were stained by mortal sin have needed penance to obtain grace and justice. It was equally necessary likewise for those who would ask to be purified by the sacrament of baptism so that they might cast off and correct their wickedness and show their detestation of so great an offense against God by their hatred of sin and by the true sorrow of their soul. Therefore the prophet says: "Be converted and do penance for all your iniquities: and iniquity shall not be your ruin" (*Ezech. 18:30*). And our Lord also said: "Unless you repent, you will all perish in the same manner" (*Luke 13:3*). And Peter, the Prince of the Apostles, likewise recommends penance to sinners who are preparing themselves for baptism, "Repent and be baptized

788
(894)

every one of you" (*Acts 2:38*). However, penance was not a sacrament before the coming of Christ, and even after his coming it is not a sacrament for anyone who has not been baptized. But our Lord instituted the sacrament of penance notably on the occasion when, after his resurrection, he breathed upon his disciples, saying: "Receive the Holy Spirit; whose sins you shall forgive, they are forgiven them; and whose sins you shall retain, they are retained" (*John 20:22 f.*). The universal agreement of the Fathers has always understood that by such a striking action and by such clear words the power of remitting and of retaining sins, and of reconciling the faithful who have fallen after baptism (*see 802, can. 3*) was communicated to the apostles and to their legitimate successors; and with good reason the Catholic Church denounced and condemned as heretical the Novatians, who in the past obstinately denied the power of remitting sins. Therefore, this holy council accepts and approves the true meaning of the words of our Lord. And it condemns the false interpretation of those who attack the institution of the sacrament by distorting those words and referring them to the preaching of the word of God and to the announcing of the gospel of Christ.

Chapter 2. The Difference Between the Sacraments of Penance and Baptism

789
(895)

Moreover, this sacrament is recognized as differing from baptism in many ways. For besides the fact that the matter and form making up the essence of the sacrament are very different, it is certainly clear that the minister of baptism does not have to be a judge; for the Church does not pass judgment on anyone who has not already entered her ranks through the gate of baptism. The Apostle says, "For what have I to do with judging those outside?" (*I Cor. 5:12.*) The situation is different with regard to the members of the household of the faith whom Christ our Lord has made members of his body once and for all by the water of baptism (*see I Cor. 12:13*). For it was his will that, if they should defile themselves with sin after baptism, they would not then be cleansed by receiving baptism again, since this is not allowed in the Catholic Church for any reason whatever; but that they would stand accused before this tribunal of penance in order that the judgment of the priests might set them free, and not once only, but as often as they turn from the sins they have committed to the tribunal in true repentance. Moreover, the effect of baptism is different from that of penance. For putting on Christ in baptism (*see Gal. 3:27*) we become an entirely new creature in him and receive the complete remission of all our sins. But by the sacrament of penance we are by no means able to arrive at that new and spotless life without much weeping and labor, as divine justice demands. Thus the holy Fathers rightly spoke of penance as "a kind of difficult baptism." And this sacrament of penance is necessary for salvation for those who have fallen after baptism, just as baptism itself is necessary for salvation for those not yet regenerated (*see 805, can. 6*).

Chapter 3. The Parts and the Effect of Penance

The holy council teaches, moreover, that the form of the **790** sacrament of penance, which principally contains the power of (*896*) the sacrament, is in those words of the minister: "I absolve you" etc. In accordance with a custom of the holy Church, certain prayers have commendably been added to those words of the minister. However, these added prayers do not pertain in any way to the essence of the form, and they are not necessary for the administration of the sacrament. The quasi-matter of this sacrament is the acts of the penitent, namely, contrition, confession, and satisfaction (*see 803, can. 4*). Inasmuch as these acts are demanded of the penitent according to God's arrangement for the integrity of the sacrament and for the complete and perfect remission of sins, they are, for that reason, called the parts of penance. The complete effect of this sacrament, so far as its full efficaciousness is concerned, is reconciliation with God, which, in devout men who receive the sacrament with devotion, is sometimes followed by peace and serenity of conscience joined to a great consolation of soul. In teaching this doctrine about the parts and the effect of this sacrament, the holy council also condemns the opinion of those who argue that a terror-stricken conscience and faith are the parts of penance (*see 803, can. 4*).

Chapter 4. Contrition

791
(897)
Contrition, which ranks first among these acts of the penitent, is a deep sorrow and detestation for sin committed, with a resolution of sinning no more. Moreover, this spirit of contrition has always been necessary to obtain the forgiveness of sin, and thus, in the case of a man who has fallen after baptism, it is certainly a preparation for the remission of sins, if it be accompanied by trust in the divine mercy and a firm desire of fulfilling the other conditions necessary to receive the sacrament properly. Therefore, this holy council declares that this contrition implies not only abandoning sin and determining to lead a new life and beginning to do so, but also hating one's past life, according to the words: "Cast away from you all your transgressions, by which you have transgressed, and make to yourselves a new heart, and a new spirit" (*Ezech. 18:31*). And surely, if one considers these cries of the saints: "Against thee alone have I sinned, and have done evil before thee" (*Ps. 50:6*); "I am wearied with my sighs, every night my bed is drenched with my tears" (*Ps. 6:7*); "I will recount to thee all my years in the bitterness of my soul" (*Isa. 38:15*), and similar passages, he will easily understand that they spring from a very strong hatred of their past life and from a hearty detestation of sin.

792
(898)
Moreover, the holy council teaches that, although it does sometimes happen that this contrition is made perfect through charity and reconciles man to God before this sacrament is actually received, nevertheless the reconciliation must not be attributed to contrition exclusive of the desire for the sacrament included in the contrition. Imperfect contrition is called attrition (*see 804, can. 5*), since it is usually conceived either from a consideration of the malice of sin or from the fear of hell and its punishments. But the holy council declares that if this imperfect contrition excludes the will to sin, and hopes for pardon, it does not make a man a hypocrite or a greater sinner, but is a gift of God and an inspiration of the Holy Spirit, not, indeed, as already dwelling in the soul, but as merely giving an impulse that helps the penitent make his way towards justice. And although attrition without the sacrament of penance cannot by itself lead the sinner to justifica-

tion, still it disposes him for the attainment of God's grace in the sacrament of penance. For the Ninivites profited from this fear which the terrifying preaching of Jonas inspired in them; they did penance and obtained mercy from the Lord (*see Jonas 3*). Therefore, it is a calumniation of Catholic writers when some falsely accuse them of teaching that the sacrament of penance confers grace when there is no good disposition on the part of those who receive the sacrament—a teaching that the Catholic Church has never taught or held. These calumniators also teach that contrition is forced and extorted, and that it is not voluntary or free (*see 804, can. 5*).

Chapter 5. Confession

From the explanation of the institution of the sacrament of **793** penance already given, the universal Church has always un- **(899)** derstood that integral confession of sins was likewise prescribed by our Lord (*see Jas. 5:16; I John 1:9; Luke 17:14*), and that by divine law this integral confession is necessary for all those who have fallen after baptism (*see 806, can. 7*). For our Lord Jesus Christ, as he was about to ascend from earth to heaven, left priests to be his vicars (*see Matt. 16:19; 18:18; John 20:23*), as rulers and judges to whose authority Christians are to submit all mortal sins that they have fallen into. In accordance with the power of the keys, the priests are to pronounce sentence of forgiveness or retention of the sins. Now it is clear that if priests did not know the case, they could not exercise this judgment, nor could they observe equity in imposing penances if the penitents declared their sins in a general way only, instead of specifically and particularly. Therefore, the conclusion is that penitents must recount in confession all the mortal sins they are conscious of after a thorough examination, even if they be most hidden sins and committed against the last two commandments only (*see Exod. 20:17; Matt. 5:28*); for these sins sometimes wound the soul more grievously and are more dangerous than those sins which are committed openly. As regards venial sins, which do not exclude us from God's grace and into which we fall rather frequently, it is proper and advantageous to mention them and implies no presumption (*see 806, can. 7*), as is clear from the practice of devout men. Nevertheless, they can be left unsaid without any sin, and they can be atoned for in many other ways. But since all mortal sins, even mortal sins of thought, make men children of wrath (*see Eph. 2:3*) and enemies of God, it is necessary to beg God's pardon for all of them in a candid and humble confession. Thus, when Christians make an effort to confess all the sins that they remember, they undoubtedly lay them all before the divine Mercy for forgiveness (*see 806, can. 7*). But those who act otherwise and knowingly hide some sins, present nothing to be remitted by the divine Goodness through the priest. "For if a sick man is ashamed to show the physician his wound, the physician cannot treat something he is ignorant of." Moreover, it follows that even those circumstances which change the species of the sin (*see 806, can. 7*) must be mentioned in confession because if these circumstances are omitted, the penitents cannot confess their sins entirely, the judges do not know the sins, and it is impossible for them to judge properly of the gravity of the sins and impose on the penitents the penance they ought to impose. It is therefore contrary to reason to teach that these circumstances have been devised by men who had nothing better to do, and that the only circumstance that has to be confessed is this: namely, a sin against one's brother.

794
(900) Further, it is wicked to say that confession prescribed in this manner is impossible (*see 807, can. 8*), or to call confession a torturing of consciences. For it is clear that all the Church demands from each penitent is that he examine himself rather carefully and look into the innermost recesses of his conscience, and that he confess those sins by which he remembers having mortally offended his Lord and God. But the other sins, which he does not remember after a thorough examination, are considered as included in a general way in that same confession. It is for these sins that we pray sincerely with the prophet: "From my secret sins cleanse me, O Lord" (*Ps. 18:13*). The difficulty and the shame of confessing one's sins could seem heavy indeed, if it were not lightened by many wonderful advantages and consolations which most assuredly are conferred in absolution on all those who approach this sacrament worthily.

Chapter 6. The Minister of the Sacrament

But with regard to the minister of this sacrament the holy council declares that the teachings which dangerously extend the office of the keys to all men without exception, even to those who are not bishops and priests, are false and completely foreign to the truth of the gospel (*see 809, can. 10*). Those who teach such doctrines think that the words of our Lord: "Whatever you bind on earth shall be bound also in heaven; and whatever you loose on earth shall be loosed also in heaven" (*Matt. 18:18*), and "Whose sins you shall forgive, they are forgiven them; and whose sins you shall retain, they are retained" (*John 20:23*), are, in contradiction to the institution of this sacrament, addressed to all the faithful without distinction or discrimination, with the result that each individual has the power of remitting sins—public sins by a reprimand, if the person reprimanded acquiesces, secret sins by voluntary confession to anyone. The council likewise teaches that even priests who are in mortal sin exercise the office of remitting sins as the ministers of Christ by the power of the Holy Spirit conferred on them when they were ordained, and that those who say that sinful priests do not have this power judge falsely. But although the absolution of the priest is the granting of a gift that is not his own, nevertheless, it is not merely a simple ministry that consists in announcing the gospel or of declaring that the sins are remitted; but it is like a judicial act whereby the sentence is pronounced by the priest as a judge (*see 808, can. 9*). And therefore, the penitent ought not so flatter himself about his faith as to think that by his faith alone he is truly absolved in God's sight, even if there is no contrition, or if the priest has no intention of acting seriously and of truly absolving. For faith without penance does not give any remission of sins, and a person would be very negligent about his salvation if he realized that a priest was absolving him in jest and did not earnestly look for another priest who has a serious intention.

795
(902)

Chapter 7. The Reservation of Cases

Since, therefore, the very nature and idea of a trial demands that the sentence be pronounced over one's own subjects, the Church of God has always been convinced, and this council

796
(903)

asserts that the conviction is perfectly true, that the absolution which a priest gives to a person over whom he has neither ordinary nor delegated jurisdiction must be of no value. But to our most holy Fathers it seemed of sovereign importance for the discipline of Christians that some of the more barbarous and grievous sins should be absolved only by priests of higher rank and not by just any priest. Therefore, by reason of the supreme power that was entrusted to them in the Church, the sovereign pontiffs could reserve to their own special judgment some of the more serious cases of sins. And there should be no doubt that, since all things that are from God are well ordered, all bishops in their own dioceses may do the same thing, but with a view to improvement and not to crush spirits (*see II Cor. 13:10*), by reason of the authority given them over their subjects, an authority greater than that given to other lesser priests. They may do so especially with regard to those cases to which a censure of excommunication is attached. It is in accord with divine authority that this reservation of sins is valid not only in external discipline but also before God (*see 810, can. 11*). However, this same Church of God has always devoutly upheld that there is no reservation at the hour of death, lest this reservation be the occasion of anyone's damnation; and therefore any priest can absolve any penitent from all sins and censures. Outside the hour of death, since priests have no authority in reserved cases, let them strive merely to persuade the penitents to go to higher and legitimate judges to receive the benefit of absolution.

Chapter 8. The Necessity and Benefit of Satisfaction

797
(904)
Finally, as regards satisfaction:—Satisfaction has always been recommended by our Fathers to the Christian people. Yet of all the parts of penance, it has been singled out for bitter attack particularly in our times under pretext of great piety by men who have a semblance of piety but disown its power (*see II Tim. 3:5*). The holy council declares that it is altogether false and contrary to the word of God to say that our Lord never remits guilt without condoning all punishment (*see 811, can. 12; 814, can. 15*). There are clear and telling examples in Sacred Scripture (*see Gen. 3:16 ff.; Num. 12:14 f.; 20:11 f.; II Kings 12:13 f.*), apart from divine tradition, to refute

this error completely. The plan of divine justice would seem to demand that those who have fallen in ignorance before their baptism be restored to grace in a way different from those who, after they have once been freed from sin and slavery to the devil and have received the gift of the Holy Spirit, have not been afraid to destroy knowingly the temple of God (*see I Cor. 3:17*) and to grieve the Holy Spirit (*see Eph. 4:30*). It is in accord with divine mercy that sins should not be forgiven us without any satisfaction, lest we find an occasion (*see Rom. 7:8*) to regard sins lightly, and, offending and insulting the Holy Spirit (*see Heb. 10:29*), fall into more serious sins, treasuring up to ourselves wrath on the day of wrath (*see Rom. 2:5; Jas. 5:3*). There is no doubt that these satisfactions deter from sin, and act like a bridle on penitents, making them more cautious and watchful in the future. They heal the effects of sins by acts of the contrary virtues and do away with evil habits acquired in a bad life. The Church of God has always been of the opinion that there is no more sure way to avert the threatening punishments of God than for men to make use of these works of penance with true sorrow of soul (*see Matt. 3:2, 8; 4:17; 11:21*). In addition, in making satisfaction for our sins, we are made like to Christ Jesus, who has satisfied for our sins (*see Rom. 5:10; I John 2:1 f.*), and from whom is all our capability (*see II Cor. 3:5*). We also have the certain pledge that if we suffer with him we shall also be glorified with him (*see Rom. 8:17*). The satisfaction which we make for our sins is not such that it is not made through Christ Jesus. For of ourselves we cannot do anything as our own, but with the help of him who strengthens us we can do all things (*see Phil. 4:13*). A man has nothing in which he can take pride; but all our pride is in Christ (*see I Cor. 1:31; II Cor. 10:17; Gal. 6:14*), in whom we live, in whom we move (*see Acts 17:28*), in whom we make satisfaction, bringing forth fruits worthy of repentance (*see Luke 3:8*), which have all their value from Christ, are offered to the Father by Christ, and are accepted by the Father through Christ (*see 812–13, cans. 13–14*).

Therefore, in the measure that the spirit of prudence suggests, the priests of the Lord ought to enjoin salutary and   **798**
  (905)

suitable penances, proportioned alike to the kind of sins and to the ability of the penitents. For if they should wink at sins and deal too indulgently with the penitents, and impose very light works for very serious sins, they would become partners in other men's sins (*see I Tim. 5:22*). But let them bear in mind that the satisfaction they impose is not only to preserve the new life and to heal infirmity, but also to inflict reparatory punishment for past sins. For the ancient Fathers believed and taught that the keys of the priests were granted not only to loose, but also to bind (*see Matt. 16:19; 18:18; John 20:23; 814, can. 15*). They did not for that reason think that the sacrament of penance was a tribunal of wrath or of punishment; just as no Catholic has ever felt that the value of the merit and satisfaction of Jesus Christ our Lord has been in any way lessened or diminished by our satisfaction. Because the Reformers understand satisfaction in this way, they teach that the best penance is a new life, and thus they suppress the entire efficacy and usefulness of satisfaction (*see 812, can. 13*).

Chapter 9. Expiatory Works

799
(906)
Moreover, the council teaches that the generosity of the divine bounty is so great that we can make satisfaction in God's sight through Jesus Christ, not only by the penances that we voluntarily undertake to make up for sin, or by those that the priest decides to impose proportionate to the gravity of the sin, but also (and this is a greater proof of love) by patiently bearing the temporal punishments sent by God (*see 812, can. 13*).

Canons on the Sacrament of Penance

800
(911)
1. If anyone says that in the Catholic Church penance is not truly and properly a sacrament instituted by Christ our Lord to reconcile the faithful with God himself as often as they fall into sin after baptism: let him be anathema (*see 788*).

801
(912)
2. If anyone, failing to distinguish between the sacraments, says that the sacrament of baptism as such is the sacrament of penance, as though they were not two distinct sacraments, and that for this reason penance is not correctly called "the second plank after shipwreck": let him be anathema (*see 788*).

3. If anyone says that these words of the Lord our Savior: "Receive the Holy Spirit; whose sins you shall forgive, they are forgiven them; and whose sins you shall retain, they are retained" (*John 20:22 f.*), ought not to be understood as referring to the power of remitting and of retaining sins in the sacrament of penance as the Catholic Church has always understood them from the beginning; and if anyone, to disprove the institution of this sacrament, twists the meaning of those words and refers them to the Church's authority to preach the gospel: let him be anathema (*see 788*).

802
(913)

4. If anyone denies that, for the entire and perfect remission of sins there are three acts required of the penitent as the quasi-matter of the sacrament of penance, namely: contrition, confession, and satisfaction, which are called the three parts of penance; or if anyone says that there are only two parts to penance, namely the terrors of a conscience stricken by the realization of sin, and the faith derived from the gospel or from absolution, by which each one believes that his personal sins are remitted through Christ: let him be anathema (*see 790*).

803
(914)

5. If anyone says that the contrition which is engendered by the examination, consideration, and detestation of sins, as a person reviews all his years in bitterness of soul (*see Isa. 38:15*), meditating on the seriousness of his sins, their number and heinousness, the loss of eternal happiness and the eternal damnation incurred, and so proposes to lead a better life, is not a true and very beneficial sorrow and does not prepare a person for the reception of grace, but that it makes a man a hypocrite and a greater sinner; and finally, that it is a forced sorrow, and not free and voluntary: let him be anathema (*see 792, 778*).

804
(915)

6. If anyone says that sacramental confession was not instituted by divine law or that it is not necessary for salvation according to the same law, or if anyone says that the method which the Catholic Church has always observed from the very beginning, and still observes, of confessing secretly to the priest alone is foreign to the institution and command of Christ, and that it is of human origin: let him be anathema (*see 793 f.*).

805
(916)

806
(917)
7. If anyone says that, to obtain remission of sins in the sacrament of penance, it is not necessary according to divine law to confess each and every mortal sin that is remembered after proper and diligent examination, even secret sins, and sins against the last two commandments, and those circumstances which change the species of a sin; but says that such confession is only useful for instructing and consoling the penitent, and that it was formerly observed only for the purpose of imposing the canonical penance; or if anyone says that those who make an effort to confess all their sins wish to leave nothing to the forgiveness of the divine Mercy; or, finally, that it is not permissible to confess venial sins: let him be anathema (*see 793; DB 901*).

807
(918)
8. If anyone says that the confession of all sins, as the Church practices it, is impossible, and that it is a human tradition that religious men ought to abolish; or if he denies that each and every one of Christ's faithful of both sexes is bound to confess once a year according to the regulation of the great Lateran Council, and says, consequently, that Christ's faithful should be discouraged from confessing during the Lenten season: let him be anathema (*see 794; DB 901*).

808
(919)
9. If anyone says that the sacramental absolution of the priest is not a judicial act, but is the mere ministry of pronouncing and declaring that the sins of the person confessing are remitted, provided only that he believes himself absolved, even if the priest gives absolution in jest and without a serious intention [*reading* etiamsi *for* aut; *see DB 919, note*]; or if anyone says that the confession of the penitent is not required so that the priest can absolve him: let him be anathema (*see* 795).

809
(920)
10. If anyone says that priests who are in the state of mortal sin do not have the power of binding and loosing; or that priests are not the only ministers of absolution, but that to each and everyone of Christ's faithful it was said: "Whatever you bind on earth shall be bound also in heaven; and whatever you loose on earth shall be loosed also in heaven" (*Matt. 18:18*), and "Whose sins you shall forgive, they are forgiven

them; and whose sins you shall retain, they are retained" (*John 20:23*); and that in virtue of these words anyone can absolve sins—public sins by correction alone, if the person corrected acquiesces, secret sins by voluntary confession: let him be anathema (*see 795*).

11. If anyone says that bishops have no right to reserve cases to themselves except where there is question of external discipline, and that the reservation of cases, therefore, does not prevent a priest from validly absolving from reserved cases: let him be anathema (*see 796*). 810 (921)

12. If anyone says that God always remits all the punishment at the same time that he remits the sin, and that the satisfaction of penitents is nothing else than the faith by which they realize that Christ has made satisfaction for them: let him be anathema (*see 797*). 811 (922)

13. If anyone says that satisfaction for the temporal punishment due to sins cannot be made to God through the merits of Christ either by the penances sent from God and patiently endured or by those imposed by the priest, nor by penances voluntarily undertaken, such as fasts, prayers, almsgiving, or other works of piety; and that, consequently, the best penance is merely a new life: let him be anathema (*see 797 ff.*). 812 (923)

14. If anyone says that the satisfaction by which penitents atone for their sins through Jesus Christ is not worship of God, but is a human tradition that obscures the doctrine of grace, the true worship of God, and the benefit of Christ's death itself: let him be anathema (*see 798*). 813 (924)

15. If anyone says that the keys have been given to the Church only to loose and not to bind, and that for this reason when priests impose penances on those who confess, they go against the purposes of the power of the keys and against the institution of Christ; and if anyone says that it is false to assert that, after the eternal punishment is taken away by the power of the keys, temporal punishment normally remains to be expiated: let him be anathema (*see 797*). 814 (925)

CONDEMNATION OF THE ERRORS OF
THE MODERNISTS, 1907

(*See introd. to 112.*)

815
(2046)

46. In the early Church there was no concept of reconciling a Christian sinner by the authority of the Church, but the Church became accustomed to such an idea only gradually. Furthermore, even after penance was acknowledged as an institution of the Church, it was not called a sacrament, because it was regarded as a disgraceful sacrament.

816
(2047)

47. The words of our Lord: "Receive the Holy Spirit; whose sins you shall forgive, they are forgiven them; and whose sins you shall retain, they are retained" (*John 20:22 f.*), have no reference whatever to the sacrament of penance, in spite of what the fathers decreed at Trent.

Indulgences

In the sacrament of penance, sins are forgiven. By indulgences, sins are not forgiven, but temporal punishment due to sin is remitted. Thus, the Church's power of binding and loosing is exercised not only in the sacrament of penance but also in the granting of indulgences. For this reason, and because indulgences as granted in the Church today are historically an outgrowth of the practice of remitting a part or the whole of a sacramental penance, the Church's pronouncements on indulgences are here joined with those on the sacrament of penance.

The sacrament of penance does not usually remove all temporal punishment to which the sinner is liable for his mortal or venial sins. This temporal punishment can be remitted by the Church through indulgences. The remission is not granted by absolution, as in the sacrament of penance; it is attached to the fulfillment of certain conditions such as the performance of good works, or the recitation of specified prayers. Three truths form the doctrinal basis for the practice of indulgences. First, the Church has the power of binding and loosing, conferred on it by Christ (see Matt. 16:19; 18:18). *Second, the satisfactory value of the works of Christ and the saints forms a superabundant treasury. Third, the communion of saints in Christ makes it possible for the Church to apply this treasury to the faithful, both living and dead.*

THE BULL UNIGENITUS DEI FILIUS, 1343

Clement VI (1342–52) published this bull for the Holy Year or the year of jubilee, proclaiming rich indulgences for the faithful for the complete or partial remission of the temporal punishment due to sin. Three doctrinal points are emphasized: the satisfaction of Christ, the willingness of the Church to enrich the faithful from its treasures, and the infinite store of merit won by Christ and his Blessed Mother and the saints.

The only-begotten Son of God, who has become for us God-given wisdom, and justice, and sanctification, and redemption (*see I Cor. 1:30*), not "by virtue of blood of goats and calves, but by virtue of his own blood, has entered once and for all into the Holies, having obtained eternal redemption" (*Heb. 9:12*). He redeemed us not with perishable things, with silver and gold, but with his own precious blood, the blood of the lamb without blemish and without spot (*see I Pet. 1:18 f.*). He was the innocent oblation on the altar of the cross and it was not a scant drop of his blood that he shed (though because of the union with the Word, this would have been sufficient for the salvation of the entire human race), but it is well known that he poured out his blood generously, like a stream, so that from the soles of his feet to the top of his head no soundness was found in him (*see Isa. 1:6*). This merciful shedding of his blood was not to be empty, meaningless, or superfluous, but was to gain a great treasure for the Church militant. Thus, our good Father has willed to enrich his children, so that there may be an infinite treasure for men; those who use it become the friends of God (*see Wisd. 7:14*). **817** **(550)**

This treasure . . . [*Christ*] has committed to the care of St. Peter, who holds the keys of heaven, and to his successors, His own vicars on earth, who are to distribute it for the good **818** **(551)** of the faithful. And they are to apply it with compassion for a proper and reasonable cause, for the benefit of those who are truly sorry and who have confessed, at times for the complete remission of the temporal punishment due to sin, at times for the partial remission, sometimes in a general grant, sometimes to individuals, as they judge pleasing to God.

819
(552) It is also known that the merits of the Mother of God and of all the elect, from the first just man until the last, add something to the store of this treasure. There is no reason to fear about exhausting or decreasing these merits, because, as has been said, the merits of Christ are infinite, and because, in proportion to the number of men who are drawn to justice by the application of these merits, the store of the merits increases.

THE COUNCIL OF CONSTANCE, 1414-18
(See introd. to 128 and 521.)

Questions proposed for the followers of Wyclif and Hus

820
(676) 26. Likewise, whether he believes that, for a just and holy reason, the pope can grant indulgences for the remission of sins to all Christians who are truly contrite and have confessed, especially to those who make pilgrimages to the holy places and to those contributing to them.

821
(677) 27. And whether he believes that by reason of this sort of grant those who visit the churches and those who contribute to them can gain indulgences of this kind.

CONDEMNATION OF ERRORS OF MARTIN LUTHER, 1520
(See introd. to 550.)

822
(757) 17. The treasures of the Church, from which the pope grants indulgences, are not the merits of Christ and of the saints.

823
(758) 18. Indulgences are pious deceptions set for the faithful and are dispensations from doing good works; they belong to the class of things which are permitted but which are not useful.

19. Indulgences, for those who truly gain them, have no power to remit the debt of punishment incurred before divine justice by actual sins. **824 (759)**

20. Those who believe that indulgences are salutary and useful for spiritual profit are misled. **825 (760)**

21. Indulgences are necessary only for public crimes, and they are rightly granted only to the hard of heart and to those who will brook no delay. **826 (761)**

22. Indulgences are neither necessary nor useful for six groups of men, namely: the dead and the dying, the sick, those who are legitimately prevented, those who have not committed serious sins, those who have committed serious sins but not public ones, those who perform the better works. **827 (762)**

THE COUNCIL OF TRENT, 1545-63

In the twenty-fifth session on December 4, 1563, the council defined that the power to grant indulgences was given to the Church by Christ and that the use of them is most salutary.

DECREE ON INDULGENCES

Christ gave the power of granting indulgences to the Church, and since the Church has, even in ancient times, made use of this divinely given power (*see Matt. 16:19; 18:18*), the holy council teaches and commands that the usage of indulgences—a usage most beneficial to Christians and approved by the authority of the holy councils—should be kept up in the Church; and it anathematizes those who say that indulgences are useless, or that the Church does not have the power of granting them. **828 (989)**

Extreme Unction

The Church is solicitous for the preservation and growth of the life of grace in all the faithful throughout their lives. Those whom illness has brought to the danger of death are the object of a special concern. Christ instituted a special sacrament of fortification and healing, with which the Church consoles those children on the threshold of eternity.

Just as confirmation is a complement to baptism, so too extreme unction is a complement to the sacrament of penance. Although it is normally a sacrament of the living, which presupposes the state of grace in the recipient, extreme unction can itself forgive even mortal sins. This would occur when extreme unction is received in good faith by one who has attrition but is not aware of his state of mortal sin or, if he is, is for good reasons unable to confess his sin. But beyond this, extreme unction further purifies the soul with an increase of grace, strengthens it for the sufferings and temptations of its last agony, and prepares it proximately for entry into heavenly beatitude. There is a secondary effect, proper to the sacrament but conditional. This is the bodily healing of the person who is ill.

As with confirmation, early heresies relating to extreme unction were not many. In early Church documents we find evidences for the existence of the sacrament and the rites used in its administration; only in the middle ages and at the time of the Reformation does the Church find it necessary to formulate dogmatic decrees on the existence and nature of this sacrament.

LETTER TO DECENTIUS, BISHOP OF GUBBIO, 416

Decentius had written to Pope St. Innocent I (401–17) to inquire about several points of doctrine on the sacraments. Innocent's reply, dated March 19, 416, included the following testimony on the minister of extreme unction.

The minister of extreme unction

829
(99)
(8) Since your love prompts you to seek advice on this as on other matters, my son Celestine the deacon also mentioned in his letter that Your Excellency had put up for discussion the text in the epistle of St. James the Apostle: "If anyone among you is sick, let him call the presbyters, and let them pray over him, anointing him with oil in the name of the Lord. And the prayer of faith will save the sick man, and the Lord will restore him, and if he has sinned, He will forgive him" (*see Jas. 5:14 f.*). There is no doubt that this ought

to be understood of the faithful who are sick and who can be anointed with the holy oil of chrism which is prepared by a bishop. It is not just priests but all as Christians who may be anointed with this oil when it is necessary for themselves or their families. However, it seems to Us that an idle point is raised when doubt is expressed in the case of a bishop about something that is certainly permitted to priests. For the very reason that it was assigned to priests is that bishops are burdened with other business and are not able to go to all the sick. However, if a bishop is able or thinks someone worthy of a visit from him, then he, whose duty it is to prepare the chrism, can without any hesitation bless and anoint the sick with chrism. But the chrism cannot be poured on those doing penance because this is one of the sacraments. How is it conceivable that one sacrament can be granted to a person to whom the rest of the sacraments are denied?

THE COUNCIL OF FLORENCE, 1438-45
(*See introd. to 164 and 663.*)

The fifth sacrament is extreme unction. Its matter is olive oil blessed by a bishop. This sacrament should not be given except to the sick whose death is feared. The anointing should be done on these parts: on the eyes because of sight, on the ears because of hearing, on the nose because of smelling, on the mouth because of taste or speech, on the hands because of touch, on the feet because of walking, on the reins because of the pleasure that prevails there. The form of this sacrament is: "May the Lord, through this holy anointing and through his loving mercy, forgive you for whatever you have been guilty of through sight" etc. The form is the same for anointing the other members. The minister of this sacrament is the priest. The effect of the sacrament is the healing of the soul, and also of the body, but only inasmuch as this is beneficial. St. James the Apostle says of this sacrament: "Is anyone among you sick? Let him bring in the presbyters of the Church, and let them pray over him, anointing him with oil in the name of the Lord. And the prayer of faith will save the sick man, and the Lord will raise him up, and if he be in sins, they shall be forgiven him" (*Jas. 5:14 f.*).

830
(700)

The Sacraments

THE COUNCIL OF TRENT, 1545-63
(*See introd. to 371 and 664.*)

On November 25, 1551, the fourteenth session of the Council of Trent, the same session that treated of the sacrament of penance, approved the following chapters on the last anointing. The sacrament of extreme unction is the culmination both of the sacrament of penance and of the whole life of penance.

831
(907)
It seemed good to this holy council to add to the preceding doctrine on penance, the following things concerning the sacrament of extreme unction, because the fathers considered this sacrament a culmination not only of penance but of the whole Christian life which itself ought to be a continual penance. First of all the council declares and teaches about the constitution of this sacrament that our merciful Redeemer willed that his servants should always be provided with salutary safeguards against all weapons of all enemies. Accordingly, he prepared great helps in the other sacraments to enable Christians to keep themselves throughout their lives untouched by any serious spiritual harm, and likewise he protected them at the end of life with the invincible strength of the sacrament of extreme unction (*see 835, can. 1*). For even if our adversary seeks occasions throughout the whole of life and goes about that he may devour our souls in any way he is able (*see I Pet. 5:8*), there is no time at which he is more vehemently intent on using all the forces of his cunning to destroy us completely and, if possible, to disturb our trust in the divine Mercy, than when he sees the end of life approaching us.

Chapter 1. The Institution of the Sacrament of Extreme Unction

832
(908)
This holy anointing of the sick was instituted by Christ our Lord as a true and proper sacrament of the New Testament. It is implied in Mark's Gospel (*see Mark 6:13*), and it is commended to the faithful and promulgated by the Apostle James, the brother of the Lord (*see 835, can. 1*): "Is anyone among you sick? Let him bring in the presbyters of the Church, and let them pray over him, anointing him with oil in the name of the Lord. And the prayer of faith will save the sick man,

and the Lord will raise him up, and, if he be in sins, they shall be forgiven him" (*Jas. 5:14 f.*). In these words, as the Church has learned from the apostolic tradition transmitted to her, he teaches the matter, the form, the proper minister, and the effects of this salutary sacrament. For the Church has understood that the matter is oil, blessed by a bishop; for the anointing very fittingly represents the grace of the Holy Spirit which anoints the soul of the sick person in an invisible manner. The following words are the form: "By this anointing" etc.

Chapter 2. The Effects of This Sacrament

Furthermore, the complete effect of this sacrament is explained in the words: "And the prayer of faith will save the sick man, and the Lord will raise him up, and if he be in sins, they shall be forgiven him" (*Jas. 5:15*). For this effect is the grace of the Holy Spirit, whose anointing takes away sins, if there are any still to be expiated, and removes the traces of sin: and it comforts and strengthens the soul of the sick person (*see 836, can. 2*). It gives him great confidence in the divine mercy. Encouraged by this, the sick man more easily bears the inconvenience and trials of his illness and more easily resists the temptations of the devil who lies in wait for his heel (*see Gen. 3:15*). This anointing occasionally restores health to the body if health would be of advantage to the salvation of the soul.

833
(909)

Chapter 3. The Minister of This Sacrament and the Time That It Ought To Be Administered

The directives as to who should be the recipients and the ministers of this sacrament are clearly taught in the words quoted above. They indicate that the proper ministers of this sacrament are the presbyters of the Church (*see 838, can. 4*). This does not refer to the older men nor to the more influential men in the community but to the bishops or the priests duly ordained by the bishops through the laying on of hands of the presbyterate (*see I Tim. 4:14; 838, can. 4*). It is also prescribed that this anointing is to be used on the sick, especially on those who are so dangerously ill that they are thought to be departing this life. Hence the name, the sacrament of the

834
(910)

departing. If, however, the sick recover after they have been anointed, they can again receive the help of this sacrament when their life is again in similar danger. On no account, then, should any attention be paid to those who contradict the clear and unmistakable teaching of the Apostle James (*see Jas. 5:14*) and say that this anointing is either a human invention or else a rite handed down from the Fathers, but without any command of God or promise of grace (*see 835, can. 1*). No attention should be paid to those who say that this anointing has now lost its efficacy, as if it were a grace for healing only in the early Church. No attention should be paid to those who say that the rite and the usage observed by the holy Roman Church in administering this sacrament are contrary to the teaching of the Apostle James and should, therefore, be changed. And, finally, no attention should be paid to those who say that the faithful can, without sin, disregard this sacrament (*see 837, can. 3*). All these claims are in open contradiction to the obvious words of this great apostle. For in performing this anointing, the Roman Church, the mother and teacher of all other churches, is following exactly what St. James prescribed as regards the substance of this sacrament. Disregard, then, of so great a sacrament necessarily involves serious sin and offense to the Holy Spirit.

These, then, are the profession and the teaching of this holy, ecumenical council on the sacraments of penance and extreme unction; the council proposes them for the firm belief of all Christians. She teaches that the following canons are to be kept in their integrity and condemns forever and anathematizes those who maintain the contrary.

Canons on Extreme Unction

835
(926)   1. If anyone says that extreme unction is not truly and properly a sacrament instituted by Christ our Lord (*see Mark 6:13*) and promulgated by the Apostle St. James (*see Jas. 5:14*), but that it is merely a rite handed down from the Fathers, or a human invention: let him be anathema (*see 831 ff.*).

836
(927)   2. If anyone says that the holy anointing of the sick does not confer grace, does not forgive sins, or does not comfort

the sick, but that it no longer has efficacy, as if it were a grace for healing only in times past: let him be anathema (*see 833*).

3. If anyone says that the rite and usage of extreme unction as practiced by the holy Roman Church are contrary to the teaching of the Apostle St. James and should, therefore, be changed, and that this sacrament can, without sin, be disregarded by Christians: let him be anathema (*see 834*).

837
(928)

4. If anyone says that the "presbyters of the Church" who St. James says should be called in to anoint the person who is sick, are not priests ordained by the bishop, but the older men of any community, and that the proper minister of extreme unction is, consequently, not the priest alone: let him be anathema (*see 834*).

838
(929)

Holy Orders

Christ's work of redeeming mankind by his sacrifice on the cross presupposed his own priesthood. This priesthood Christ possessed in all its fullness by the very fact of his Incarnation, for the whole meaning of the Incarnation was to constitute Christ a perfect mediator between God and man, destined to offer a sacrifice of redemption.

That same sacrifice was to be offered repeatedly in the Church in the Sacrifice of the Mass. For this continuation of his own sacrifice, Christ appointed men to share in his own priesthood. The fullest sharing was given to the apostles and their successors the bishops, for these alone have the power to transmit their priestly character to others. Priests possess the same power as the bishops with regard to the offering of sacrifice—the principal function of the priesthood—while deacons have the office of cooperating with the priests in the liturgy of the sacrifice. The lower orders, instituted by the Church, are specified each by its particular relation to the principal priestly function of offering sacrifice. The power of ordaining others is the exclusive prerogative of bishops. For the episcopate, the priesthood, and the diaconate, the imposition of hands by the ordaining bishop has been the indispensable rite from apostolic times.

The sacrament of orders is a social sacrament which has for its purpose not merely the sanctification of the recipient but also the sanctification of the rest of the Church through the powers this sacrament confers. Since it is wholly divine in origin and impresses an indelible character on its recipient, the sacrament of orders definitively places the bishops and priests in a position of higher rank than the laity. In the Middle Ages there appeared for the first time heretics who taught that the priestly powers originated not with God but with the members of the Church themselves. This error would make of the priesthood a human institution. More recently an opposite error gained some currency because of an exaggerated emphasis on, and an unwarranted enlargement of, the concept of the priesthood of the laity. Several sections of Pope Pius XII's Mediator Dei (see 765–71) are concerned with the refutation of this error.

THE COUNCIL OF FLORENCE, 1438-45
(See introd. to 663.)

As has been noted, this Decree for the Armenians of the Council of Florence is probably not an infallible definition with regard to the sacraments. Hardly any theologians today would admit the doctrine that St. Thomas held on the matter and form of orders; yet it is this doctrine that the council follows closely in this instruction. This portion of the document, therefore, has considerable historical interest and is not without dogmatic significance.

839
(701) The sixth sacrament is holy orders. Its matter is that which is handed over in the conferring of the order: the priesthood, for example, is conferred by the presentation of the chalice containing the wine and the paten holding the bread; the diaconate by the giving of the book of the Gospels; the subdiaconate by the handing over of an empty chalice covered with an empty paten; and likewise for the other orders, by the consignation of the things which pertain to the functions

of their office. The form of the order of priesthood is this: "Receive the power of offering sacrifice in the Church for the living and the dead in the name of the Father and of the Son and of the Holy Spirit." And so of the form of the other orders as is contained in detail in the Roman Pontifical. The ordinary minister of this sacrament is the bishop. The effect of the sacrament is an increase of grace so that one may be a suitable minister.

THE COUNCIL OF TRENT, 1545-63

(See introd. to 664.)

In the twenty-third session on July 15, 1563, the council set down the true teaching of the Church on the sacrament of holy orders: that it is a sacrament; that it imprints an indelible character or seal signing the soul of a priest forever. The chapter titles are not the work of the fathers of the council. We are following the Denzinger text by putting these titles in parentheses.

Chapter 1. (The Institution of the Priesthood of the New Law)

In conformity with God's decree, sacrifice and priesthood are so related that both exist in every law. Therefore, in the New Testament, since the Catholic Church has received the holy and visible sacrifice of the Eucharist according to the institution of the Lord, it is likewise necessary to acknowledge that there is in the Church a new, visible, and external priesthood (see 844, can. 1), into which the old priesthood was changed (see Heb. 7:12 ff.). Moreover, Sacred Scripture makes it clear and the tradition of the Catholic Church has always taught that this priesthood was instituted by the same Lord our Savior (see 846, can. 3), and that the power of consecrating, offering, and administering his body and blood, and likewise the power of remitting and of retaining sins, was given to the apostles and to their successors in the priesthood.

840
(957)

Chapter 2. (The Seven Orders)

The ministry of so sacred a priesthood is a divine arrangement, and it was therefore fitting that in the perfectly ordered disposition of the Church there be several different grades of ministers to insure that the ministry be exercised more worthily

841
(958)

The Sacraments

and with greater reverence (*see Matt. 16:19; Luke 22:19; John 20:22 f.*). These orders are to assist the priesthood, and they are arranged in such a way that those who are already set apart by the clerical tonsure are to pass through minor to major orders (*see 845, can. 2*). For Sacred Scripture makes explicit mention not only of priests, but of deacons as well (*see Acts 6:5; I Tim. 3:8 ff.; Phil. 1:1*) and teaches with most solemn words what is to be chiefly attended to when ordaining them. And from the very beginning of the Church, the names of the following grades and the ministries proper to each one, namely: subdeacon, acolyte, exorcist, lector, and porter, are known to have been in use, although they were not of the same rank. For in the writings of the Fathers and of the sacred councils, in which we very frequently read about the other lower orders, the subdeaconate is regarded as a major order.

Chapter 3. (*Orders Is a Sacrament*)

842 (959) Since it is very clear from the testimony of Sacred Scripture, from apostolic tradition, and from the unanimous agreement of the Fathers, that grace is conferred through holy ordination, which is effected by words and external signs, no one should doubt that orders is truly and properly one of the seven sacraments of holy Church (*see 846, can. 3*). For the Apostle says: "I admonish thee to stir up the grace of God which is in thee by the laying on of my hands. For God has not given us the spirit of fear, but of power and of love and of prudence" (*II Tim. 1:6 f.; see I Tim. 4:14*).

Chapter 4. (*The Ecclesiastical Hierarchy and Ordination*)

843 (960) Moreover, in the sacrament of orders, just as in baptism and in confirmation, a character is imprinted (*see 847, can. 4*) which can neither be blotted out nor taken away. Therefore, this holy council rightly condemns the opinion of those who say that the priests of the New Testament have merely temporary power, and that once they have been duly ordained they can become laymen again, if they do not exercise the ministry of the word of God (*see 844, can. 1*). But if anyone says that all Christians without exception are priests of the New Testament or are endowed with equal spiritual power, it is apparent that he upsets the ecclesiastical hierarchy (*see 849, can. 6*), which is like an army in battle array (*see Cant. 6:3*), as much as if, contrary to Paul's teaching, all were apostles, all prophets, all evangelists, all pastors and teachers (*see I Cor. 12:29; Eph. 4:11*). Therefore the holy council declares that, besides the other ecclesiastical grades, the bishops, who have succeeded the apostles, belong in a special way to the hierarchical order; and placed (as the Apostle says) by the Holy Spirit to rule the Church of God (*see Acts 20:28*) they are superior to priests, and can confer the sacrament of confirmation, can ordain ministers for the Church, and they have the power to perform many other functions that those of an inferior grade cannot (*see 850, can. 7*). Moreover, the holy council declares that in the ordination of bishops, of priests, and of other grades, the consent, call, or authority, neither of the people nor of any secular power or public authority is necessary to the extent that without it the ordination is invalid. Rather it decrees that all those who have been called and appointed merely by the people or by the secular power or ruler, and thus undertake to exercise these ministries, and that all those who arrogate these ministries to themselves on their own authority, are not ministers of the Church but should be considered as thieves and robbers who have not entered through the door (*see John 10:1; 851, can. 8*).

Canons on Holy Orders

1. If anyone says that there is not a visible and external priesthood in the New Testament, or that there is no power of consecrating and offering the body and blood of the Lord, and of remitting and of retaining sins, but says that there is only the office and simple ministry of preaching the gospel, or says that those who do not preach are not priests at all: let him be anathema (*see 840, 843*).

844 (961)

2. If anyone denies that in the Catholic Church, besides the priesthood, there are other orders, both major and minor, through which one must pass, as through certain steps, towards the priesthood: let him be anathema (*see 841*).

845 (962)

3. If anyone says that orders or holy ordination is not truly and properly a sacrament instituted by Christ our Lord, or

846 (963)

that it is a kind of human invention thought up by men inexperienced in ecclesiastical matters, or that it is only a kind of rite of choosing ministers of the word of God and the sacraments: let him be anathema (*see 840, 842*).

847
(964)

4. If anyone says that by holy ordination the Holy Spirit is not given and thus it is useless for bishops to say, "Receive the Holy Spirit"; or if anyone says that no character is imprinted by ordination; or that he who was once a priest can become a layman again: let him be anathema (*see 673*).

848
(965)

5. If anyone says that the sacred anointing which the Church uses at holy ordination not only is not required, but is despicable and harmful, just like the other ceremonies: let him be anathema (*see 677*).

849
(966)

6. If anyone says that in the Catholic Church there is no divinely instituted hierarchy consisting of bishops, priests, and ministers: let him be anathema (*see 843*).

850
(967)

7. If anyone says that bishops are not superior to priests, or that they do not have power to confirm and ordain, or says that the power they do have is common both to them and to priests; or says that the orders conferred by them are void without the consent and call of the people or of the secular power; or says that those who have not been rightly ordained by ecclesiastical and canonical power and have not been sent, but come from some other source, are lawful ministers of the word and of the sacraments: let him be anathema (*see 843*).

851
(968)

8. If anyone says that bishops chosen by the authority of the Roman Pontiff are not legitimate and true bishops but a human invention: let him be anathema (*see 843*).

THE APOSTOLIC CONSTITUTION
SACRAMENTUM ORDINIS, 1947

In the ancient Church there is no sign of any handing over of instruments as a rite in the ordination to the diaconate and priesthood. In the Middle Ages, however, this rite was universally observed by the bishops of the Western Church in ordinations to the diaconate and priesthood and was considered by many theologians as necessary for validity. This dif-

Holy Orders

ference in practice between the ancient and the later Church, between the Western and the Eastern Church, gave rise to lively theological debates over the matter and form of this sacrament. Without giving any decision on the speculative questions involved, Pope Pius XII (1939–58) has definitively settled for the future that the presentation of the instruments is not necessary for the validity of these orders. Further, he determines, in the constitution *Sacramentum ordinis,* November 30, 1947, the matter and form for the diaconate, priesthood, and episcopate. (The translation of this selection was made from the *Acta Apostolicae Sedis,* XL [1948], 6.)

1. . . . In the course of centuries the Church did not and could not substitute other sacraments in place of those instituted by Christ our Lord. The reason is that the seven sacraments of the New Law were all instituted by Jesus Christ our Lord, as the Council of Trent teaches [*see 665*], and the Church has no authority over the "substance of the sacraments," that is, over the elements that Christ our Lord himself, according to the testimony of the sources of divine revelation, determined should be kept in the sacramental sign. . . .

3. . . . [*After referring to the ceremonies used in ordinations and recalling the Roman Church's acknowledgment of the validity of the Greek ordination rite, the pontiff speaks as follows.*] The conclusion from this is that for the substance and validity of this sacrament the handing over of the instruments [*traditio instrumentorum*] is not required by the will of our Lord Jesus Christ himself, even according to the mind of the Council of Florence. Nevertheless, if at any time the handing over of instruments was an added requirement for validity because of the will and prescription of the Church, everyone is aware that what the Church itself has established, it also has the power to change and abrogate.

4. Therefore, after praying for heavenly light, We, with Our supreme apostolic authority and with certain knowledge, declare and, as far as it is necessary, decree and make provision: the matter of the holy orders of diaconate, priesthood, and episcopate, is the imposition of hands and that alone; and the form (likewise the only form) is the words determining the application of this matter, which words signify in a

852
(3001)

333

univocal sense the sacramental effects—the power of order and the grace of the Holy Spirit—and which are understood and used by the Church in this sense. Hence it is that We should declare and, to remove all controversies and preclude anxieties of conscience, We do declare with Our apostolic authority and determine (even if there ever was any different legitimate prescription) that the handing over of the instruments [*traditio instrumentorum*], at least in the future, is not necessary for the validity of the holy orders of diaconate, priesthood, and episcopate.

Matrimony

The Church's concern for the safeguarding of the supernatural life in its members is particularly evident in the second social sacrament, the sacrament of matrimony. Family environment has a great influence on the religious development of the members of the family. At the basis of family life stands the natural institution of matrimony. This institution has been raised by Christ to the high dignity of a grace-giving sacrament. Through this sacrament husband and wife not only receive an increase of grace for themselves, but they also receive supernatural helps to enable them to perform well all the duties that the married state imposes upon them. Christian matrimony has a great and sublime mystical signification: it represents the most perfect union of Christ with his Church (see Eph. 5:32).

The man and the woman who enter the marriage contract are themselves the ministers of the sacrament; the priest is present merely as an official witness. The matter of the sacrament is the words or their equivalent in signs inasmuch as they express the mutual giving of the perpetual and exclusive rights over the body. The form of the sacrament is these same words or their equivalent inasmuch as they express the mutual acceptance of the rights over the body.

Matrimony

THE PROFESSION OF FAITH PRESCRIBED FOR DURANDUS OF OSCA AND FOLLOWERS, 1208

(See introd. to 658.)

. . . With the Apostle *(see I Cor. 7)* we do not say that marriage is not to be contracted; but we strictly forbid that those that are contracted in the correct way be broken. That a man and his wife can gain salvation we believe and profess; and we do not condemn a second marriage or even subsequent marriages.

853
(424)

THE COUNCIL OF FLORENCE, 1438-45

(See introd. to 663.)

The seventh is the sacrament of matrimony which is a sign of the close union of Christ and the Church according to the words of the Apostle: "This is a great mystery—I mean in reference to Christ and to the Church" *(Eph. 5:32)*. The efficient cause of matrimony is mutual consent, ordinarily expressed through words and having reference to the present. Three blessings are ascribed to matrimony. The first is the procreation and education of children for the worship of God. The second is the fidelity that each of the spouses must observe towards the other. The third is the indissolubility of matrimony—indissoluble because it signifies the indivisible union of Christ with the Church. Although a separation from bed may be permitted by reason of marital infidelity, nevertheless it is not permitted to contract another matrimony since the bond of a marriage lawfully contracted is perpetual.

854
(702)

THE COUNCIL OF TRENT, 1545-63

(See introd. to 664.)

In the twenty-fourth session on November 11, 1563, the council vindicated the constant teaching of the Church that matrimony is a true and proper sacrament. The council also defined the right of the Church to legislate for marriages of the baptized.

The first parent of the human race, under the inspiration of the Divine Spirit, proclaimed the perpetual and indissoluble bond of matrimony when he said, "This now is bone of my

855
(969)

bones, and flesh of my flesh. . . . Wherefore a man shall leave father and mother, and cleave to his wife: and they shall be two in one flesh" (*Gen. 2:23 f.; see Eph. 5:31*).

Christ our Lord taught more clearly that only two persons are joined and united by this marriage bond. He referred to the final words of the quotation above as words spoken by God and said: "Therefore now they are no longer two, but one flesh" (*Matt. 19:6*); and immediately after this, with the words, "What therefore God has joined together, let no man put asunder" (*Matt. 19:6; Mark 10:9*), he confirmed the stability of that same bond which had been declared by Adam so long before.

Moreover, Christ himself, who instituted the holy sacraments and brought them to perfection, merited for us by his passion the grace that brings natural love to perfection, and strengthens the indissoluble unity, and sanctifies the spouses. The Apostle Paul intimates this when he says: "Husbands, love your wives, just as Christ also loved the Church, and delivered himself up for her" (*Eph. 5:25*); and he immediately adds: "This is a great mystery—I mean in reference to Christ and to the Church" (*Eph. 5:32*).

856 (970) Therefore, since matrimony under the law of the gospel is, because of the grace given through Christ, superior to the marriage unions of earlier times, our holy Fathers, the councils, and the tradition of the universal Church have always rightly taught that matrimony should be included among the sacraments of the New Law. Contrary to this teaching, evil, foolish men of our day, not only entertain wrong notions about this holy sacrament but, in their usual way, under pretext of the gospel, they give freedom to the flesh and, in their words and their writings, they spread—not without great harm to Christians—many ideas that are foreign to the understanding of the Catholic Church and to a long-approved custom dating back to apostolic times. Wishing to stop such folly, this holy, ecumenical council has decided that the more egregious errors and heresies of these schismatics must be done away with, lest more be contaminated by their evil disease; and it declares the following anathemas against these heretics and their errors.

Matrimony

Canons on Matrimony

1. If anyone says that matrimony is not truly and properly one of the seven sacraments of the law of the gospel, and says that it was not instituted by Christ but introduced into the Church by men, and that it does not confer grace: let him be anathema (*see 855 f.*).

857
(971)

2. If anyone says that Christians are permitted to have several wives simultaneously, and that such a practice is not forbidden by any divine law (*see Matt. 19:4–9*): let him be anathema (*see 855*).

858
(972)

3. If anyone says that only those grades of consanguinity and affinity which are mentioned in Leviticus (*see 18:6 ff.*) can be an impediment to entering into marriage and that only those grades can invalidate the contract; and that the Church does not have the power of dispensation over some of these grades or the power to determine more grades as impedient or diriment impediments: let him be anathema.

859
(973)

4. If anyone says that the Church did not have the power to determine diriment impediments to marriage (*see Matt. 16:19*) or that she has erred in determining them: let him be anathema.

860
(974)

5. If anyone says that the marriage bond can be dissolved by reason of heresy, domestic incompatibility, or willful desertion by one of the parties: let him be anathema.

861
(975)

6. If anyone says that the solemn religious profession of one of the spouses does not dissolve a true marriage which has not been consummated: let him be anathema.

862
(976)

7. If anyone says that the Church is in error when it has taught and does teach according to the doctrine of the Gospels and apostles (*see Mark 10; I Cor. 7*) that the marriage bond cannot be dissolved because of adultery on the part of either the husband or the wife; and that neither party, not even the innocent one who gave no cause for the adultery, can contract another marriage while the other party is still living; and that adultery is committed both by the husband who dismisses his adulterous wife and marries again and

863
(977)

The Sacraments

by the wife who dismisses her adulterous husband and marries again: let him be anathema.

864
(978)
8. If anyone says that the Church is in error when she decides that for many reasons husband and wife may separate from bed and board or from cohabitation for a definite period of time or even indefinitely: let him be anathema.

865
(979)
9. If anyone says that clerics in sacred orders or regular clergy who have made solemn profession of chastity can contract marriage, and that the contract is valid, despite the law of the Church and their vow; and that the opposite opinion is nothing but a condemnation of marriage; or if anyone says that all those who feel that they do not have the gift of chastity (even if they vowed it) can contract marriage: let him be anathema. For God does not deny that gift to those who petition it in a correct manner nor does he permit us to be tempted beyond our strength (*see I Cor. 10:13*).

866
(980)
10. If anyone says that the marriage state is to be preferred to the state of virginity or of celibacy and that it is not better and holier to remain in virginity or celibacy than to be joined in marriage (*see Matt. 19:11 f.; I Cor. 7:25 f., 38, 40*): let him be anathema.

867
(981)
11. If anyone says that the prohibition of solemn nuptial ceremonies at certain times of the year is an arbitrary superstition with pagan origins; or if anyone condemns the blessings and the other ceremonies that the Church uses in the solemn nuptials: let him be anathema.

868
(982)
12. If anyone says that marriage cases are not under the jurisdiction of ecclesiastical judges: let him be anathema.

THE ENCYCLICAL ARCANUM DIVINAE SAPIENTIAE, 1880
Pope Leo XIII (1878–1903) repeated the teaching of the Council of Trent on the sacrament of matrimony. The pope stressed the fact that the marriage contract and the sacrament cannot be separated. This encyclical was dated February 10, 1880.

869
(1853)
The teachings of our holy Fathers, the councils, and the tradition of the universal Church must be traced back to the

teaching apostles (*see 856*): namely, that Christ our Lord raised matrimony to the dignity of a sacrament. They teach, too, that Christ brought it about that husband and wife, sheltered and strengthened by the heavenly grace which his merits produced, may attain sanctity in the marriage itself. And in their union, a union marvelously conformed to the pattern of his own mystical marriage with the Church, Christ brought to perfection a love that is natural (*see 855*); and, by the bond of divine charity, he made a stronger union of the naturally indivisible society of husband and wife. . . .

And let no one be influenced by that distinction so highly vaunted by the Royalists who separate the nuptial contract from the sacrament, with the intention of committing the contract to the power and judgment of the civil authority, reserving to the Church the sacramental aspects. As a matter of fact, such a distinction—more truthfully a sundering—cannot be approved of, since it is certain that in Christian marriage the contract cannot be separated from the sacrament. And therefore it is impossible for the contract to be genuine and lawful, unless it is at the same time a sacrament. For Christ the Lord enhanced matrimony with the dignity of a sacrament. But matrimony is the actual contract, provided it is made according to law. A further consideration is that as a consequence matrimony is a sacrament because it is a sacred sign and produces grace, and reflects the mystical marriage of Christ with the Church. The image and likeness of this marriage are found in the bond of the perfect union which joins together a man and a woman, and this is nothing more than matrimony itself. Thus it is evident that among Christians every marriage is by its very nature and essence a sacrament. And nothing is more repugnant to the truth than to say that the sacrament is a kind of embellishment of the contract, or a property extrinsic to and flowing from it, and that the sacrament can be distinguished and separated from the contract by the will of man.

870
(1854)

THE ENCYCLICAL *CASTI CONNUBII*, 1930

On December 31, 1930, this encyclical letter was issued by Pope Pius XI (1922–39). To combat errors of his time, Pope Pius stressed the nature of the sacrament of matrimony, and pointed out the fact that the primary purpose of the contract always was and always will be the procreation of children, and under no circumstances should the primary end be made subordinate to other good but secondary purposes.

871
(2225)

First of all, let this remain the unchanged and unshakable foundation: Matrimony was neither established nor restored by man but by God. It has been protected, strengthened, and elevated not by the laws of men, but by those of God, the author of human nature, and of Christ who restored that same nature. Consequently, these laws cannot be changed according to men's pleasure, nor by any agreement of the spouses themselves that is contrary to these laws. This is the teaching of Sacred Scripture (*see Gen. 1:27 f.; 2:22 f.; Matt. 19:3 ff.; Eph. 5:23 ff.*); this is the constant, universal tradition of the Church; this is the solemn definition of the holy Council of Trent, which in the words of Sacred Scripture teaches and reasserts that the permanent and indissoluble bond of matrimony, its unity and strength, have their origin in God.

Matrimony is a divine institution, but this does not rule out the very noble part that the human will plays in it. For each marriage, a wedding of one man and one woman, cannot exist without the free consent of each spouse. This free act of the will by which each party gives and receives the marriage right is necessary to make a true marriage, and nothing can be substituted for it by any human power. But this liberty only serves to make clear whether or not the parties truly wish to enter the matrimonial state and that with a given person. The nature of matrimony itself is entirely removed from man's liberty, so that, if a person once contracts matrimony, he is subject to its God-given laws and its essential properties. For as the Angelic Doctor wrote of fidelity and procreation, "These are such necessary effects of the marriage contract that if anything contrary to them were expressed in the matrimonial consent, it would not be a true matrimony."

In marriage, therefore, there is a union and a close association of minds which are wedded in a union more important and more intimate than the physical union. This union does not come from any fleeting emotion or interior feeling but from a deliberate and firm decision of the will. And under

God's design a sacred and inviolable bond arises from this wedding of souls.

The particular and unique nature of this contract makes marriage something entirely different from the union which brutes enter under the sheer, blind instinct of nature without reason or free choice, and entirely different from the promiscuous unions that men enter without any true and proper agreement of wills and that give no right to family life.

Hence it is clear that lawful authority has the right and is bound in duty to curb, prevent, and punish indecent unions, which are contrary to reason and nature. Nevertheless, since there is question of a right of human nature itself, the warning given to all by Our predecessor of happy memory Leo XIII is no less clear: "In the choice of a state of life, there can be no doubt that everyone has the power and the freedom to choose one of two courses: either to follow the counsel of Jesus Christ about virginity, or to bind himself with the marriage bond. No man-made law can take away the natural and fundamental right of men to marry, nor can it in any way delimit the principal purpose of marriage, originally established by God's authority: 'Increase and multiply'" (*Gen. 1:28*).

873 (2229)

In addition, Christian parents must realize that they are called not merely to propagate and preserve the human race on earth, nor even to procreate men who worship the true God in just any way, but to give children to the Church of God, to procreate fellow citizens of the saints and members of God's household (*see Eph. 2:19*), so that the number of worshipers of God and of our Savior may be constantly increased. Even though Christian parents are in the state of grace themselves they cannot transmit this grace to their children; in fact, natural generation of life has become a way of death, the way by which original sin passes to children. Yet these parents do, in a way, share in the original state of matrimony in Paradise, since it is their privilege to offer their child to the Church, that she, the fruitful mother of the sons of God, may regenerate the child to supernatural justice with the waters of baptism, making him a living member of Christ,

872 (2226)

The Sacraments

a sharer in immortal life, and an heir to the eternal glory which we all desire with our whole heart. . . .

874
(2231)
The second good of matrimony . . . mentioned by Augustine is fidelity, which is the mutual faithfulness of the spouses in fulfilling the marital contract so that what is due exclusively to one's partner in accordance with this divinely ratified contract, is not denied to one's partner, nor rendered to anyone else. And even to one's own spouse permission may not be given for a thing that is contrary to God's rights and laws, opposed to true marital fidelity, and therefore always illicit.

This fidelity, then, demands above all an absolute unity of marriage such as the Creator established in the marriage of our first parents. He willed that this be a marriage of only one man and one woman. It is true that God, the supreme lawgiver, temporarily relaxed this ancient law to a certain extent. But, beyond any possibility of doubt, the law of the gospel restored the former perfect unity again and abrogated all dispensation. The words of Christ and the Church's consistent teaching and practice make this very clear (*see 855*). . . .

875
(2234)
But the crowning perfection of all these great benefits is realized in that good of Christian marriage which, in the words of St. Augustine, We have called its sacred symbolism (*sacramentum*). This indicates the indissolubility of the bond and Christ's raising and consecrating the contract to be an efficacious sign of grace.

As for the first point, Christ himself emphasized the indissoluble stability of the marriage bond when he said: "What God has joined together, let no man put asunder" (*Matt. 19:6*); and "Everyone who puts away his wife and marries another commits adultery; and he who marries a woman who has been put away from her husband commits adultery" (*Luke 16:18*).

St. Augustine clearly places what he calls the "good of the sacred symbolism" in this indissolubility. "By the use of the term *sacred symbolism* [it is meant] that the marriage union may not be put asunder, and that neither the man nor the woman, if either spouse be put away, may marry another, even to procreate children."

This stability yields to an occasional rare exception, as in certain natural marriages only between infidels, or if between Christians, in marriages that are sacramental, not yet consummated. This exception, however, is not determined by men's will, nor any merely human power, but according to a divine law which the Church of Christ alone preserves and interprets. Never, though, for any reason whatsoever, can this sort of possibility occur for a sacramental, consummated Christian marriage. For such a marriage, as it realizes the fullness of the marriage bond, has, by the will of God, supreme stability and indissolubility, and may never be undone by man's power.

If we wish, in all reverence, to look for the reason behind God's will . . . we shall easily find it in the mystical meaning of Christian marriage which is fully verified in a consummated marriage between two of the faithful. As the Apostle points out in his letter to the Ephesians (which we have been referring to from the beginning), a Christian marriage is compared to the perfect union between Christ and the Church: "This is a great mystery—I mean in reference to Christ and to the Church" (*Eph.* 5:32). This union surely can never be dissolved as long as Christ has life and as long as his Church has life through him. . . .

Besides this indissoluble stability, other and even more sublime benefits are contained in this good of the sacred symbolism (*sacramentum*), and they are well expressed in the word *sacrament*. For to Christians the word *sacrament* is not an empty, meaningless term. Christ our Lord "who instituted the sacraments and brought them to perfection" has raised marriage between his faithful to be a true and genuine sacrament of the New Law. Thus he has, in all truth, made it the sign and the source of the special interior grace "which brings natural love in marriage to perfection, strengthens the indissoluble unity, and sanctifies the spouses" (*see* 855).

Since Christ has made the valid matrimonial consent between the faithful a sign of grace, the essence of the sacrament is so perfectly identified with Christian marriage that there can be no true marriage between baptized persons "that is not at the same time a sacrament."

876
(2236)

877
(2237)

Therefore, when the faithful give their sincere matrimonial consent, they open up for themselves a vast treasure of sacramental grace from which they may draw the supernatural strength to fulfill the duties of their state with fidelity, holiness, and perseverance until they die.

If men do not place any obstacle, this sacrament increases for them the permanent source of their supernatural life, sanctifying grace; and it gives them special additional gifts, good inspirations, and seeds of grace, at the same time augmenting and perfecting their natural faculties. Thus husband and wife can have more than an abstract appreciation of all that pertains to the goals and duties of their married state; they can have an internal realization, a firm conviction, an efficacious will, and an actual accomplishment of it. Finally, this sacrament gives them the right to ask for and receive the help of actual grace as often as they need it to fulfill the duties of their state.

The Last Things

The other chapters in this book treat of the nature of God himself, of the origin of creatures from God, of the road that man must travel to return to God, and of the helps that God has given man to help him along the way. This final chapter includes the documents of the Church that teach what Catholics are to believe about the end of man's journey, about the last things.

The portion of dogmatic theology dealing with this matter is often called eschatology, *from Greek words meaning knowledge of the last things. Theology considers the last things primarily as affecting man, secondarily as affecting the entire universe.*

Two events await each man: death and judgment. That judgment will determine who are to go to hell, who are to go to heaven immediately, who are to be purified in purgatory. So for man these are the last things: death and judgment, purgatory, heaven, and hell.

CANONS OF THE PROVINCIAL COUNCIL OF CONSTANTINOPLE, 543

Pope Vigilius (*cir.* 537–55) may have approved the canons against Origen from which the following canon is taken (*see introd. to 323*).

9. If anyone says or holds that the punishment of devils and wicked men is temporary and will eventually cease, that is to say, that devils or the ungodly will be completely restored to their original state: let him be anathema.

878
(211)

The Last Things

THE ELEVENTH COUNCIL OF TOLEDO, 675

The creed of the council was presented to the bishops by the metropolitan, Quiricius, on November 7, 675, and adopted by them (*see introd. to 299*).

879
(287)
Thus, according to the model of our Head, we profess that there is a true bodily resurrection for all the dead. And we do not believe that we shall rise in a body of air or in any different kind of body (as some have foolishly thought); but we shall rise in this very body in which we now live and are and move. After giving this example of his holy Resurrection, our Lord and Savior ascended and took possession of the home of his Father from which in his divine nature he had never departed. There he sits at the Father's right hand; till the end of time he is awaited as the judge of all the living and the dead. From there he shall come with the holy angels and the saints to pass judgment and to pay to each person the reward due him, according to each one's behavior, good or bad, while he was in the body (*see II Cor. 5:10*). We believe that the holy Catholic Church, which he purchased at the price of his own blood, will reign with him forever. Safe in the heart of this mother, we believe in and profess one baptism for the remission of all sins. By this faith we truly believe in the resurrection of the dead, and we look forward to the joys of the world to come. One thing only we must pray and beg for; it is that, when the Son completes his work of judgment and delivers the kingdom to God the Father (*see I Cor. 15:24*), he may make us sharers in his kingdom, so that, in virtue of the faith by which we have adhered to him, we may reign with him forever. This is a statement of the faith we profess. This faith destroys the doctrine of all heretics; it purifies the hearts of the faithful; it is the way to ascend to God gloriously forever and ever. Amen.

LETTER TO THE ARCHBISHOP OF ARLES, 1201

Innocent III (1198–1216) wrote this letter, *Majores Ecclesiae causas*, to Humbert, archbishop of Arles, explaining the traditional doctrine of the Church on the nature of the sacrament of baptism and its effects (*see introd. to 683*). One sentence pertinent to the destiny of those who die without baptism or with actual sin on their souls is included here.

. . . The punishment for original sin is the loss of the vision of God; but the punishment for actual sin is the torment of an everlasting hell.

880
(*410*)

THE FOURTH LATERAN COUNCIL, 1215

The crowning point of Innocent III's pontificate (1198–1216) was the convocation of this council, the twelfth ecumenical council, in November, 1215. One of the most important works of the council was to condemn the Albigensian heresy. Among the many errors of the Albigenses was that of metempsychosis, the transmigration of souls. Because of their doctrine that matter was intrinsically evil, the Albigenses had false notions about the resurrection of the body and life after death.

. . . He [*Christ*] will come at the end of the world; he will judge the living and the dead; and he will reward all, both the lost and the elect, according to their works. And all these will rise with their own bodies which they now have so that they may receive according to their works, whether good or bad; the wicked, a perpetual punishment with the devil; the good, eternal glory with Christ.

881
(*429*)

LETTER TO THE BISHOP OF TUSCULUM, 1254

On March 6, 1254, Pope Innocent IV (1243–54) sent the following letter to the apostolic delegate in Greece.

23. Finally, in the Gospel the Truth declares that whoever speaks blasphemy against the Holy Spirit, it will not be forgiven him, either in this world or in the world to come (*see Matt. 12:32*). By this it is to be understood that certain faults are pardoned in this life, and certain others in the life to come, and the Apostle says that "the fire will assay the quality of everyone's work," and "if his work burns he will lose his reward, but himself will be saved, yet so as through fire" (*I Cor. 3:13, 15*). And it is said that the Greeks themselves unhesitatingly believe and maintain that the souls of those who do not perform a penance which they have received, or the souls of those who die free from mortal sins but with even the slightest venial sins, are purified after death and can be helped by the prayers of the Church. Since the Greeks say that their Doctors have not given them a definite and proper name for the place of such purification, We, following the

882
(*456*)

tradition and authority of the holy Fathers, call that place purgatory; and it is Our will that the Greeks use that name in the future. For sins are truly purified by that temporal fire— not grievous or capital sins which have not first been remitted by penance, but small and slight sins which remain a burden after death, if they have not been pardoned during life. [*The translation follows Mansi's reading where* non *appears in the last clause of this selection. See XXIII, 582.*]

883
(457)
24. But if anyone dies unrepentant in the state of mortal sin, he will undoubtedly be tormented forever in the fires of an everlasting hell.

25. However, the souls of little children who die after being baptized, and likewise the souls of adults who die in the state of grace and are not detained by sin nor obligated to make satisfaction for sin, pass immediately into the everlasting home.

THE SECOND COUNCIL OF LYONS, 1274
A brief account of the historical background of this council is given in the chapter on the Church (*see introd. to 152*).

884
(464)
We believe that the holy, Catholic, and apostolic Church is the one and true Church. In this Church there is one holy baptism and the true remission of all sins. We believe in the resurrection of the body which we now have and in life everlasting. We believe that for both the New and the Old Testament, for the Law, the Prophets, and the Apostles, there is one author, almighty God our Lord. This is the true Catholic faith; this is the faith that the holy Roman Church believes and teaches in the above articles. Because of various errors which have been brought up, sometimes in ignorance, sometimes in malice, the Church asserts and preaches that those who fall into sin after their baptism are not to be rebaptized, but are to receive forgiveness of their sins through true penance. If those who are truly penitent die in charity before they have done sufficient penance for their sins of omission and commission, their souls are cleansed after death in purgatorial or cleansing punishments, as Frater John has explained for us. The suffrages of the faithful on earth can be of great help in relieving these punishments, as, for instance,

the Sacrifice of the Mass, prayers, almsgiving, and other religious deeds which, in the manner of the Church, the faithful are accustomed to offer for others of the faithful. The souls of those who have not committed any sin at all after they received holy baptism, and the souls of those who have committed sin, but have been cleansed, either while they were in the body or afterwards, as mentioned above, are promptly taken up into heaven. The souls of those who die in mortal sin or with only original sin soon go down into hell, but there they receive different punishments. The same holy Roman Church firmly believes and steadfastly teaches that on the day of judgment all men appear before the judgment seat of Christ with their own bodies, to give an account of their deeds (*see Rom. 14:10 f.*).

THE COUNCIL OF VIENNE, 1311-12

Pope Clement V (1305–14) opened the Council of Vienne, the fifteenth ecumenical council, on October 6, 1311. The most important reason for the council was to decide the case of the Knights Templars. Another reason was to reform morals; and when treating of this reform, the council condemned the following error of the Beghards and Beguines.

(5) Every intellectual nature is in itself naturally happy, **885** and the soul does not need the light of glory to elevate it to **(475)** see God and to enjoy God in blessedness.

THE CONSTITUTION *BENEDICTUS DEUS*, 1336

The constitution *Benedictus Deus*—the famous *Constitutio Benedictina*—was issued by Pope Benedict XII (1334-42) on January 29, 1336. It marked the end of a long controversy by giving the Church's doctrine on the beatific vision.

By this constitution which is to remain in force forever, We, **886** with Our apostolic authority, make the following definition: **(530)** In the usual providence of God the souls of all the saints who departed from this world before the Passion of our Lord Jesus Christ, and also those of the holy apostles, martyrs, confessors, virgins, and others of the faithful who died after receiving the holy baptism of Christ—provided that they had no need of purification at the time of their death, or will not have such need when they die at some future time; or else, if they did then have or will have some need of purification, after they have been purified after death—all these souls, soon after their death and, in the case of those needing it, after the purification We have mentioned, have been, are, and will be in heaven, in the kingdom of heaven and the celestial paradise with Christ, joined to the company of the holy angels. This holds true, after the Ascension of our Lord and Savior Jesus Christ into heaven, even before these souls take up their bodies again and before the general judgment. We define that since the passion and death of the Lord Jesus Christ, they have seen and do see the divine essence with an intuitive and even face-to-face vision, without the interposition of any creature in the function of object seen; rather, the divine essence immediately manifests itself to them plainly, clearly, openly. The same thing is true of the souls of children who have been reborn with the baptism of Christ, and of those still to be baptized after they shall have been baptized, when they die before attaining the use of free will. We also define that those who see the divine essence in this way take great joy from it, and that because of this vision and enjoyment the souls of those who have already died are truly blessed and possess life and eternal rest. We define, further, that the souls of those who will hereafter die, will see the same divine essence and will enjoy it before the general judgment. We define that this vision of the divine essence and the enjoyment of it do away with the acts of faith and hope in those souls, insofar as faith and hope are theological virtues in the proper sense. And We define that after this intuitive and face-to-face vision has or will have begun for those souls, the same vision and enjoyment remains continuously without any interruption or abolition of the vision and enjoyment and will remain up till the final judgment and from then on forever.

887
(531)
Moreover, We define that, according to the general decree of God, the souls of those who die in actual mortal sin go down into hell soon after their death, and there suffer the pains of hell. Nevertheless, on the Day of Judgment, all men will appear with their bodies before the tribunal of Christ to render an account of their personal deeds, that "each one

The Last Things

may receive what he has won through the body, according to his works, whether good or evil" (*II Cor. 5:10*).

LETTER TO THE CATHOLICOS OF THE ARMENIANS, 1351
This selection is taken from the letter written by Pope Clement VI (1342–52) under date of September 29, 1351 (*see introd. to 703*).

We ask: Have you believed and do you now believe that there is a purgatory and that it is the destination of the souls of those who die in grace but have not yet made satisfaction for their sins by complete penance? We likewise ask: Have you believed and do you now believe that they are punished by fire for a time, and that after they are purified, even before the Day of Judgment, they attain eternal happiness which consists in the love of God and face-to-face vision? **888** **(570s)**

THE COUNCIL OF FLORENCE (1438-45)
In its decree for the Greeks, the Council of Florence (*see introd. to 94 and 164*) repeated practically verbatim the doctrine about the last things contained in the profession of faith of Michael Palaeologus (*see 884 and introd. to 152*). The one sentence quoted below, however, adds a significant determination regarding the object of the beatific vision and its perfection in different souls.

. . . The souls of those who have not committed any sin at all after they received baptism, and the souls of those who have committed sin, but have been cleansed either while in the body or afterwards, . . . are promptly taken up into heaven and see clearly the Triune God himself, just as he is, some more perfectly than others according to their respective merits. **889** **(693)**

THE COUNCIL OF TRENT, 1545-63
The fathers assembled at Trent were well aware of the errors of the Reformers with regard to purgatory. The question of purgatory had been introduced in 1547, but circumstances and the order of discussions delayed its examination until the very end of the council. The following decree was issued in 1563. Calling upon Scripture and tradition, the council affirmed the existence of purgatory and the value of suffrages for the souls

in purgatory, especially the value of the Holy Sacrifice of the Mass.

DECREE ON PURGATORY

890
(983)
The Catholic Church, by the teaching of the Holy Spirit, in accordance with Sacred Scripture and the ancient tradition of the Fathers, has taught in the holy councils, and most recently in this ecumenical council, that there is a purgatory (*see 604, can. 30*), and that the souls detained there are helped by the prayers of the faithful, and especially by the acceptable Sacrifice of the Altar (*see 749; 758, can. 3*). Therefore, this holy council commands the bishops to be diligently on guard that the true doctrine about purgatory, the doctrine handed down from the holy Fathers and the sacred councils, be preached everywhere, and that Christians be instructed in it, believe it, and adhere to it. But let the more difficult and subtle controversies, which neither edify nor generally cause any increase of piety (*see I Tim. 1:4*), be omitted from the ordinary sermons to the poorly instructed. Likewise, they should not permit anything that is uncertain or anything that appears to be false to be treated in popular or learned publications. And they should forbid as scandalous and injurious to the faithful whatever is characterized by a kind of curiosity and superstition, or is prompted by motives of dishonorable gain. . . .

THE VATICAN COUNCIL, 1869-70

SCHEMA OF THE DOGMATIC CONSTITUTION ON THE PRINCIPAL MYSTERIES OF THE FAITH

In the schema of the Dogmatic Constitution on the Principal Mysteries of the Faith (*see introd. to 314*), a summary statement of the Church's doctrine on the last things is given near the end of the chapter on grace and in the sixth corresponding canon. It is presented here as a very significant, though not authoritative, document. (This translation is made from the text given in *Collectio Lacensis*, VII, 564-65, 567.)

891
Those who die in this grace will, with certainty, obtain eternal life, the crown of justice, and just as certainly, they who die deprived of this grace will never arrive at eternal

life. For death is the end of our pilgrimage, and shortly after death we stand before the judgment seat of God "so that each one may receive what he has won through the body according to his works, whether good or evil" (*II Cor. 5:10*). And after this mortal life there is no place left for repentance for justification. Therefore, all who die in actual mortal sin are excluded from the kingdom of God and will suffer forever the torments of hell where there is no redemption. Also those who die with only original sin will never have the holy vision of God. The souls of those who die in the charity of God before they have done sufficient penance for their sins of commission or omission, are purified after death with the punishment of purgatory.

Finally, the souls of those who have not incurred any stain of sin after their baptism, or who have committed a sin and have been purified either while they were in the body or after death, are soon taken into heaven and there they clearly see the Triune God and enjoy the divine essence for all eternity (*see 886, 880*).   **892**

Canon

6. If anyone says that a man can be justified even after death; or if he says that the punishments of the damned in hell will not last forever: let him be anathema.   **893**

CONDEMNATION OF ROSMINI-SERBATI'S ONTOLOGISM, 1887

Forty propositions of Antonio Rosmini-Serbati (1797–1855) were condemned by the Holy Office, December 14, 1887 (*see introd. to 86*). The following two errors have reference to the object of the beatific vision.

39. The traces of wisdom and goodness that are reflected in creatures are necessary for those who are in heaven; for, gathered together in the eternal exemplar, those traces are the part of God which can be seen by those in heaven; and they provide the theme for the praises which the blessed sing to God for eternity.   **894 (1929)**

40. Since it is impossible for God, even by the light of glory, to give himself completely to finite beings, he could   **895 (1930)**

not have revealed and given himself to those in heaven unless he did so in a way adapted to their finite intellects. That is to say, God manifests himself to them insofar as he is related to them as their creator, provider, redeemer, sanctifier.

Topical Index

[*References are to marginal numbers.*]

Revelation, Faith, and Reason

Topical Index

Tradition and Holy Scripture

Revelation is contained in Sacred Scripture 94 f. 99 101
and in tradition 9 66 90-93 95 99.

Catholic and apostolic tradition is expressed in the writings of the Fathers 88-92 100
in the ecumenical councils 14 91 f. 429 f.
in the universal and constant agreement of Catholic theologians 180
in the ordinary teaching of the Church throughout the world 66 180 266.

The books of the Old and New Testament 94 96 99 101
are, with all their parts, to be accepted as sacred and canonical 96 99.

They have God as their author 94 f. 99 101 109 f. 116-18 334 884
since they are inspired by the Holy Spirit 94 109 f.

The books of Sacred Scripture are free from error 95 99 118 129 f.
are to be interpreted according to the unanimous agreement of the Fathers and the sense of the Church 9 98 100 103
and are to be judged and interpreted according to sound exegetical principles 89 98 102-11 113-15 119 128-38.

The old Latin Vulgate is an authentic version of these books 97 99 133.

The Church

The Church is a society instituted by Christ 88 191 f. 201-5 234-36 239 f. 250 264.

It forms one mystical body with Christ as its head 153 190 194 f. 239 f. 242 244-51 253-56 260 f. 270 281 313 494
and the Holy Spirit as its soul 192 257-59.

Its end is the salvation of all men 197 201 224 272-74.

The Church is a visible society 193 f. 197 201 203 240 263-65
which is supernatural 192 f. 261 f.
with an immutable organic structure 197 200 235 241 249
and recognizable by certain properties 67 f. 181 193 f. 226.

The Church is
one 3 5 150-53 177 181 194 223-25 229 240 884
holy 1 3 153 181 191 195 884
Catholic 1-3 5 150 153 181 191 884
apostolic 3 5 150 153 181 191 884
perpetual 67 f. 191 197 201 224 234 f.
necessary for salvation 5-7 13 f. 150 f. 153 f. 165 173-76 178 185-88 195 f. 223-25 267-81.

The non-baptized do not belong to the body of the Church 242 277 f. 789.

The Church has the right and duty of guarding and teaching the revealed doctrine 78-80 82 88 98 176 268

Topical Index

and in this function is infallible 77 f. 80 90 168 198 219 226 f.

The pope has this same right and duty 152 216

and is infallible in matters of faith and morals 14 145 147-49 168 216 f. 219 f. 533

when he speaks ex cathedra 219 f.

The ecumenical councils approved by the pope also possess infallibility 13 f. 91 f. 169 429 f.

The Church exercises its infallible teaching authority either in solemn definitions or in its universal ordinary teaching 66 180 198 f.

The Church's teaching must be accepted even in matters not expressly defined 85 180 f. 199 266

by philosophers and by philos-

ophy as well 50 78 176 f. 179 f.

The Church is independent of the civil power 183 f. 192 222.

Christ promised to St. Peter the primacy of jurisdiction over the whole Church and He conferred it upon him 152 171 201-3 237 250.

The Roman Pontiff is the successor of St. Peter 13 146 152-54 166 178 204-6 212-17

and the vicar of Christ 13 159 164 166 206 265.

The Roman Pontiff possesses the primacy of jurisdiction over the whole Church 14 143-46 149 152 f. 164 166 171 206-11 214 f. 229 f. 237 f. 252.

This primacy of jurisdiction is of divine right 152 164 205 f. 211

and is ordinary and immediate over all 211.

The Triune God

There is one personal God 1-4 6 8 306 309-11 314 317 334 355 358.

Human reason can know God's existence with certitude 15 32 46 58 60 88

and can demonstrate it 46 88 364.

Men have no natural immediate knowledge of God 35 38 86 885.

God is simple 306 355

changeless 306 310 f. 346 355 361 431

uncreated 6

eternal 6 306 310 f. 355 431

incomprehensible 306 355 431.

God's attributes are not really distinct from his nature nor from each other 507.

In the one God there are three Di-

vine Persons 2 4 6 283 f. 298 f. 302-7 309 311-14 334 415 f. 431 458 507.

The three Persons are consubstantial 3 284 291 299 301-7 309 311-15 319 416 431

coequal, coeternal, co-omnipotent 6 287 289 292 295 f. 300-303 306 309-13 431.

They are inseparable 305

one principle of all external operation 294 305 f. 312 314 320 334 431 448 459.

But they are really distinct from one another 6 305 311 f.

yet each is wholly in every other one 312.

The Father is not made, nor created, nor generated, nor proceeding 6 299

357

but is a principle without principle 306 311 f.

The Son is true God 2-4 6 283-86 295 f. 298 300 309 f. 414 507 f.

consubstantial with the Father 2-4 300 456 f.

not created 3 f. 6 286

but generated from the substance of the Father 2-4 8 288 299 f. 305 307 311 f. 314 456 f.

eternally 314 417.

He is the natural, not the adoptive Son 300.

The Holy Spirit is true God 2 4 6 283-86 291 299 301-5 309 f.

neither generated, nor created 6 301

but proceeding from the Father and the Son 3 8 301 306 308 310 f. 314

as from one principle 312 314.

God the Creator and Sanctifier

THE CREATION OF THE WORLD AND OF MAN

The triune God created the world 296 306 309 334

out of nothing 306 334 343 356 362

from the beginning of time 306 356 363

and acting freely merely because of his goodness 343 356 362 364.

Creation is falsely explained by the Origenists 323

the Priscillians and Manichaeans 327 f. 332

Eckhart 337-39

pantheists 346 360-62

emanationists 325 361.

It is not the result of dual principles, the good and the evil 2 f. 8 154 306 309 327 334 343 f. 356 358.

God the Creator is infinitely intelligent 355

knowing all things 357

even free future acts of creatures 357 364.

God governs and protects all his creatures with his providence 334 357 431

and only permits sin 580.

Man consists of soul and body 306 336 348 350 356.

The human soul is created by God 341 348 365

immediately 348 365

not through generation 342

and has no pre-existence 323 326.

In each man there is one soul 333 345 351

which is intellectual 333 345 348 351 414 419 455

and united to the body truly, properly, and essentially as its form 336 345 348

enjoying liberty 369 536 f. 555 557 561 619-21 629 f. 642.

The first man was Adam 349 363 367

who was made by the special action of God 348 363 365.

Topical Index

The Incarnation and Redemption

THE PERSON OF THE REDEEMER

which are without division 414
435-37
and without separation or commingling 414 422 435-37 454
461 498.
Each nature has its own proper
characteristics 398 412 438 457
461 496
and its own powers of knowing
and willing 439 441-43 499.
Christ has two natural operations
413 440-45 451 f. 461
and two concordant wills 451 461
but the term *theandric operation*
must be rightly understood
444.
The natures are united hypostatically 4 399 402 f. 414 419-23
429 437 452 455-58 468 f. 721
in a strictly mysterious way 45
not by confusion nor by moral
union nor by activity 399 402
419
nor by mere denomination 419
nor by conversion of one into the
other 7.
In Christ there is but one person 412
418-20 445 454 f. 469 f. 721
who is both God and man 4 399
418-25 433 435.
Consequently the predication of
properties and operations is
reciprocal 403 408 411 415
425 427 460 496.
Christ is to be adored in his divinity
and his humanity with one
adoration 407 424 427.
Christ is the only Son of God 396
the natural Son 412
not an adoptive Son 453 f. 456

and he has an eternal and a temporal birth 417 433 449 454
456.
Christ was holy and entirely sinless
4 397 409 414 427 434 450
461 f.
Christ's human soul enjoyed the
beatific vision 255 486 495.
He suffered freely in his Passion
418 432.
He worked miracles 17 64 72 418
and made prophecies 64.
Men could not be saved by their
own effort 557 575
but only by the merits of Christ
374 559 573 584
who is their Redeemer 457 558
595 645 f. 712 719 722 817
831
and Savior 445 457 560 573 647
719 f. 802.
Christ became man for our salvation
2-4 7 197 455 457 645 f.
and died to repair the harm done
to human nature by the sin of
Adam 374 558 564.
Christ satisfied by his Passion for all
men and the sins of the whole
world 374 395 409-11 450 456
463 f. 472 490 558 f. 563 573
584 631 817.
His satisfaction is infinite 817 819.
The death of Christ was a true sacrifice 409 747 749 759.
Christ is the mediator of God and
of men 374 412 463 471 493
and as man he is priest 151 409
462 491 f. 747 749.
Christ is present in every liturgical
function of the Church 765.

THE MOTHER OF GOD

Mary the Mother of Christ is in the
proper and true sense *Mother
of God* 399 f. 413 417 421 433
502 505 507.

She was a virgin 4 400 413 417
432 f. 446 455 f. 502 507
and always remained a virgin 417
502 505 507.

She was conceived without original sin 376 389 505 508 510

and remained free from all sin 506 508 f.

surpassing all other saints in holiness 512 514 517.

She is the Mediatress of all graces 511-14

and coredemptress with Christ 514-16.

She has been gloriously assumed into heaven, body and soul 519 f.

Mary is the mother of the mystical body 517 f.

THE VENERATION OF THE SAINTS

It is praiseworthy to venerate the saints 522 750 760.

The worship of images is allowed 12 521 523

and so is the veneration of relics 12 521 523.

This kind of worship is relative worship 524.

Grace

Justification is not something external 376 527 551 563 584 f. 646 653.

Justification is an internal sanctification and renovation 376 559 f. 563 f. 573 646 653 877

making man a friend of God 563
an adopted son of God 558 560 645
an heir of eternal life 563 873
a partaker of the divine nature 254 608 645

and is accompanied by infusion of faith, hope, and charity 564 683.

Justification is not merited by man's actions 374 543-46 548 561-63 565 575 577

but rests on the merits of Christ 374 507 527 558 f. 564 573 584 645 652

and an adult can and should prepare himself for it 561 f. 575 578 581 583 587 791 804.

Faith is the foundation and root of justification 63 67 280 545 565

but alone is not sufficient 562 564-66 583 586 f. 603 668 672 783 f. 795 803 811.

Actual grace is a supernatural help of God 527-29 535 f. 544-48 561-63 576

illuminating the intellect and inspiring the will 65 537 539 561

and is distinguished as exciting and helping grace 546 549 561 f. 571 577 f.

antecedent, concomitant, and subsequent grace 573 649

incipient and perfecting grace 570

prevenient grace 544 561 577 649

operating grace 561 577 792
elevating grace 368.

Grace is necessary for every salutary act 534-38 541-46 548 f. 557 575-77 596 648 655 f.

but without grace man's acts are not necessarily sinful 555 619 632 648.

Topical Index

THE INFUSED VIRTUES

The Sacraments

THE SACRAMENTS IN GENERAL

There are seven sacraments of the New Law 10 660 663 665

  instituted by Christ 10 665 679 f. 855 f. 877

  not merely to nourish faith 669 681 f.

  nor as mere signs of justification received 670

  but as means of grace 668 670-72

  which are symbols of something holy, and visible forms of invisible grace 721 877.

They consist of the right matter and form 662 f. 789 842

  placed by a minister with the intention of doing what the Church does 662 f. 675 690.

The Church cannot change the substance of the sacraments 678 852.

The sacraments confer grace 10 550 663 668 670 f. 681 683 by the performance of the rite (*ex opere operato*) 672 766

  in those who place no obstacle in the way 550 670 f. 684.

Three sacraments imprint a character and cannot be received more than once 10 663 673 684 843.

The sacraments can be validly conferred by the proper minister for each, even though he is a sinner 658 661 f. 676 795 809

  even though he is a heretic 690

  but not by any Christian whatever 227 674 850.

The minister must have a right intention 662 f. 675 784.

The sacraments are necessary for salvation either in themselves or in desire; but not all the sacraments are necessary for everybody 10 668.

BAPTISM

Baptism is the first sacrament 659 f. 686

  and the sacrament of regeneration 686 741.

The remote matter of baptism is natural water 659 686 688.

The form of baptism is in certain words 298 659 686 690.

The effects of baptism are

  removal of original sin 190 368 376 683 685 f. 789

  removal of personal sin 190 368 685 f. 789

  remission of temporal punishment 376 571 651 686 797 884

  conferring of grace 190 368 376 563 741

  uniting the baptized with Christ 190 195 242 245 270 374 686 741 769 789 873

  receiving the baptized into the Church 190 221 270 277 686 694 700

  imprinting a character 663 673 684 843.

All men must receive baptism 273 560 563 686 691 701 789

  at least in desire 273 560.

Baptism can be received only once 10 663 673 697 699 789 884.

Topical Index

The minister of baptism is ordinarily a priest 686 but in case of necessity anyone may baptize provided he has the proper intention 662 686 690.

CONFIRMATION

Confirmation is a true sacrament 660 663 685 707 f. 711.

The remote matter of this sacrament is holy chrism 707 709.

The form is in certain words 707.

The effects of confirmation are to confer the Holy Spirit for strength 663 707 and to imprint a character 10 663 673 843.

Confirmation can be received only once 663 673.

The ordinary minister is the bishop 660 685 704 707 710 843 850.

The extraordinary minister is a priest with special faculties 705-7.

The subject of confirmation is any baptized person 660 708.

THE HOLY EUCHARIST

Christ is really present in the Eucharist 11 659 f. 712 f. 715 717 719-23 728-31 735 765 and the whole Christ under either species 11 714 716 f. 721 730 744 and this presence is brought about by transubstantiation 11 659 f. 712 f. 717 722 729.

The Eucharist is a true sacrament 659 f. 663 714 f. 717 whose matter is wheat bread and grape wine 717 and whose form is in the words of Christ 713 717 721 747.

Only a rightly ordained priest having a right intention can validly consecrate 658 f. 713.

The Eucharist is to be worshipped with the worship of latria 723 733.

In Holy Communion, the whole Christ is received under either species 11 714 721 740 744.

They who have the use of reason must receive Holy Communion during Easter time 736.

The effects of Holy Communion are the remission of sin 720 732 union with Christ and an increase of grace 717 remission of venial sins and temporal punishment 720 732 preservation from mortal sin 720 perseverance in good 727 and a pledge of eternal life 720.

THE HOLY SACRIFICE OF THE MASS

The Mass is a true sacrifice 11 491 659 746-53 756-59 840 853 884 instituted by Christ at the Last Supper 747 757 840 and it re-presents the sacrifice of the cross and applies its merits 490 747 749.

The sacrifice does not consist in Holy Communion only 756.

In the Mass, Christ is the victim 659 713 747 749 but the manner of offering differs from that of the cross 749 and Christ is also the principal offerer 659 749 768-70

Topical Index

through the ministry of priests 492 713 749.

There are as many actions of the High Priest Christ as there are priests celebrating 771.

The common "priesthood" of all the faithful differs in essence from the priesthood properly so called 767 f. 771.

The effects of the Mass are
to worship God 758
to give thanks 758
to beg pardon and to make petition 11 493 749 758.

PENANCE

Penance is a true sacrament 571 660 663 713 776 788 f. 800-803 815

distinct from baptism 788 f. 791

and was instituted by Christ 571 788 800 802

in the form of a judgment 789 793 795 808 816.

The form of this sacrament is a judicial sentence through the words of the priest 571 776 789 f. 795 808.

The matter, quasi-matter, or parts of this sacrament are acts of the penitent 774 776 f. 790 803.

Contrition, which includes detestation of sin and a resolve not to sin in the future, 779 791

is necessary for absolution 776 783 f. 791 f.

and can be either perfect 792 or imperfect 792 804.

Confession is necessary by divine law 776 793 805 f.

at least in desire 571 792.

The confession should be external and oral 772 776

and integral 793 806.

A penance should be imposed 774 776 793 797-99 814.

The effects of this sacrament are
the remission of sins committed after baptism 604 659 774 776 788-90 800 884

the remission of eternal punishment 571 604

but not always the remission of all the temporal punishment 571 604 811 814 882.

The minister of this sacrament is
not a layman 773 785

but only a priest 571 795 809 840

who should have the power of jurisdiction 774-76 796 808 810.

A person must confess his sins at least once a year 807.

INDULGENCES

Indulgences have salutary and useful effects 12 823 828

and remit temporal punishment due to sin 818 824

through the application of the treasures of the Church 817-19 822

and have been in use from ancient times 828.

Topical Index

The Last Things

Death is the punishment for sin 363 367 370 388 557.

Some souls enter into heaven immediately after death 686 883 f. 886 889 892.

The state of grace is required for entrance into heaven 564 573 606 891.

Beatitude consists in the immediate, intuitive, face-to-face vision of God and its enjoyment 886 888 f. 892.

The beatific vision is brought about by means of the light of glory 885

is uninterrupted 886

is eternal 7 67 881 884 886

is the reward of good works 165 573 600 606

admits of different degrees 606 889.

Some souls are detained in purgatory 12 604 882 888 890 f.

The existence of purgatory is shown in Scripture 882.

Purgatory consists in the satisfactory punishments which the souls undergo 604 884 886 888 890 f.

The souls in purgatory are helped by the living with suffrages, satisfactory works, and almsgiving 12 882 884 890

and especially by the Sacrifice of the Mass 890.

Those who die in original sin or in grave personal sin immediately go down into hell 165 884 887 891

where they suffer the loss of the vision of God 880 891.

Those who have done evil also suffer the pain of sense 7 165 880 f. 883.

The punishment of hell is eternal 7 165 650 657 878 880 f. 883 893.

The souls of the children in limbo who die without baptism do not suffer the punishment of fire 880 884.

At the end of the world there will be a resurrection of the dead 1 3 5 7 f. 331.

The resurrection will affect all 7 466 879 881 884

even the damned 887.

All will rise with their own bodies 7 881 884

which will not be purely spiritual 879.

There will be a general judgment 2 f. 8 887.

Christ will be the judge 3 f. 7 432 456 466 879 884

and He will render to everyone according to his works 456 879 881 887.

The Ecumenical Councils
of the Church

1.	325	The First Council of Nicaea	Treated especially of the consubstantiality of the Word, against the Arians.
2.	381	The First Council of Constantinople	Treated of the divinity of the Holy Spirit, against the Macedonians.
3.	431	The Council of Ephesus	Defined that there is one person in Christ, against Nestorius; taught that Mary is truly Mother of God (θεοτόκος); dealt with problems of grace, against Pelagius.
4.	451	The Council of Chalcedon	Treated of the distinction of the two natures in Christ, against the Monophysitic Eutyches.
5.	553	The Second Council of Constantinople	Dealt with Origenism and with the Three Chapters.
6.	680–81	The Third Council of Constantinople	Defined the two wills in Christ, against the Monothelites.
7.	787	The Second Council of Nicaea	Dealt with the veneration of images, against the Iconoclasts.
8.	869–70	The Fourth Council of Constantinople	Dealt with the norm of faith and the deposition of Photius.

The Ecumenical Councils of the Church

9.	1123	The First Lateran Council	Treated of lay investiture, discipline, and morals.
10.	1139	The Second Lateran Council	Treated of matters of discipline and morals.
11.	1179	The Third Lateran Council	Dealt with the Albigenses.
12.	1215	The Fourth Lateran Council	Dealt with the Waldensians, the Albigenses, and Abbot Joachim; treated of matters of discipline and morals.
13.	1245	The First Council of Lyons	Treated of matters of discipline.
14.	1274	The Second Council of Lyons	Treated of union with the Greeks.
15.	1311–12	The Council of Vienne	Dealt with Peter John Olivi, the Beghards and the Beguines, and the suppression of the Knights Templar.
16.	1414–18	The Council of Constance	Dealt with the errors of Wyclif and Hus, and the Great Western Schism.
17.	1438–45	The Council of Florence	Effected a short-lived union with the Eastern Churches.
18.	1512–17	The Fifth Lateran Council	Dealt with Church reform and with the neo-Aristotelians.
19.	1545–63	The Council of Trent	Defined the Church's teaching against the Reformers; treated of matters of discipline and reform.
20.	1869–70	The Vatican Council	Treated of the faith and the Church against the rationalists, semi-rationalists, and Gallicans.

Table of Reference to Denzinger's
Enchiridion Symbolorum

In the table on the following pages, when the number of a selection in *The Church Teaches* is given as corresponding to the number of a selection in Denzinger's *Enchiridion symbolorum*, this means that at least part of the *Enchiridion* document is here translated in the number given.

Sometimes one number of the *Enchiridion* is divided among several numbers of *The Church Teaches*.

DB	TCT	DB	TCT	DB	TCT	DB	TCT
6	1	75	292	112	146	137	539
13	4	76	293	113	400	138	540
14	5	77	294	114	401	139	541
39	6	78	295	115	402	141	542
40	7	79	296	116	403	143	412
48	282	80	297	117	404	144	413
51	283	82	298	118	405	148	414
54	2	86	3	119	406	171	147
57a	143	91	502	120	407	172	148
59	284	99	829	121	408	174	369
60	285	100	144	122	409	175	370
61	286	101	367	123	410	176	543
64	396	103	527	124	411	177	544
65	397	104	528	129	533	178	545
68	287	105	529	130	368	179	546
69	288	106	530	131	534	188	547
70	289	107	531	132	535	199	548
71	290	108	532	134	536	200	549
72	398	110	145	135	537	201	{ 415
74	291	111a	399	136	538		503

DB = Denzinger's *Enchiridion symbolorum*
TCT = *The Church Teaches*

Table of Reference

DB	TCT	DB	TCT	DB	TCT	DB	TCT
202	504	263	439	428 { 306	573	705
203	323	264	440	428 { 335	574	706
210	324	265	441	429 { 455	584	661
211	878	266	442	429 { 881	587	772
212	91	267	443	430 { 151	588	158
213	416	268	444	430 { 659	617	159
214	417	269	445	432	307	626	714
215	418	270	92	456	882	629	160
216	419	275	299	457	883	631	161
217	420	276	300	460	308	632	162
218	421	277	301	461	309	636	163
219	422	278	302	462	456	666	715
220	423	279	303	463	310	667	716
221	424	280	304	464	884	670	773
222	425	281	305	465	660	671	774
223	426	282	446	466	152	672	662
224	427	283	447	468	153	675	775
225	428	284	448	469	154	676	820
226	429	285	449	475	885	677	821
227	430	286	450	481	336	679	521
235	325	287	879	496	155	693	889
236	326	291	451	497	156	694	164
237	327	292	452	498	157	695	663
238	328	308	93	501	337	696	686
239	329	310	453	502	338	697	707
241	330	314a	454	503	339	698	717
242	331	338	333	526	340	699	776
243	332	351	149	527	341	700	830
254	431	355	712	530	886	701	839
255	432	410 { 683	531	887	702	854
256	505	410 { 880	533	342	703	311
257	433	411	684	550	817	704	312
258	434	421	334	551	818	705	313
259	435	423	150	552	819	706 { 94
260	436	424 { 658	570s	888	706 { 343
261	437	424 { 685	571	703	707	344
262	438	424 { 713	572	704	714	165
		424 { 853			738	345

DB = Denzinger's *Enchiridion symbolorum*
TCT = *The Church Teaches*

Table of Reference

DB	TCT	DB	TCT	DB	TCT	DB	TCT
741	550	793	557	830	594	865	695
742	551	794	558	831	595	866	696
743	552	795	559	832	596	867	697
745	777	796	560	833 { 506		868	698
746	778	797	561	833 { 597		869	699
747	779	798	562	834	598	870	700
748	780	799	563	835	599	871	708
749	781	800	564	836	600	872	709
750	782	801	565	837	601	873	710
751	783	802	566	838	602	873a	718
752	784	803	567	839	603	874	719
753	785	804	568	840	604	875	720
754	786	805	569	841	605	876	721
757	822	806	570	842	606	877	722
758	823	807	571	843	607	878	723
759	824	808	572	843a	664	879	724
760	825	809	573	844	665	880	725
761	826	810	574	845	666	881	726
762	827	811	575	846	667	882	727
765	166	812	576	847	668	883	728
766	167	813	577	848	669	884	729
767	168	814	578	849	670	885	730
768	169	815	579	850	671	886	731
771	553	816	580	851	672	887	732
772	554	817	581	852	673	888	733
776	555	818	582	853	674	889	734
783	95	819	583	854	675	890	735
784	96	820	584	855	676	891	736
785	97	821	585	856	677	892	737
786	98	822	586	857	687	893	738
787	371	823	587	858	688	893a	787
788	372	824	588	859	689	894	788
789	373	825	589	860	690	895	789
790	374	826	590	861	691	896	790
791	375	827	591	862	692	897	791
792	376	828	592	863	693	898	792
792a	556	829	593	864	694	899	793

DB = Denzinger's *Enchiridion symbolorum*
TCT = *The Church Teaches*

Table of Reference

DB	TCT	DB	TCT	DB	TCT	DB	TCT
900	794	937a	746	975	861	1047	380
902	795	938	747	976	862	1048	381
903	796	939	748	977	863	1049	382
904	797	940	749	978	864	1050	613
905	798	941	750	979	865	1054	614
906	799	942	751	980	866	1055 {	383
907	831	943	752	981	867		609
908	832	944	753	982	868	1066	623
909	833	945	754	983	890	1067	615
910	834	946	755	984	522	1068	616
911	800	948	756	985	523	1073	508
912	801	949	757	986	524	1074	617
913	802	950	758	987	525	1078 {	384
914	803	951	759	988	526		610
915	804	952	760	989	828	1091	170
916	805	953	761	993	507	1092	627
917	806	954	762	994	8	1093	628
918	807	955	763	995	9	1094	629
919	808	956	764	996	10	1095	630
920	809	957	840	997	11	1096	631
921	810	958	841	998	12	1314	509
922	811	959	842	999	13	1351	632
923	812	960	843	1000	14	1360	642
924	813	961	844	1013	611	1361	643
925	814	962	845	1016	624	1373	644
926	835	963	846	1020	612	1388	633
927	836	964	847	1021 {	377	1389	634
928	837	965	848		608	1390	635
929	838	966	849	1025	618	1391	636
930	739	967	850	1026	378	1394	638
931	678	968	851	1027	619	1395	639
932	740	969	855	1028	620	1396	640
933	741	970	856	1034	625	1397	641
934	742	971	857	1038	626	1409	637
935	743	972	858	1039	621	1503	171
936	744	973	859	1041	622	1515	172
937	745	974	860	1046	379	1622	15

DB = Denzinger's *Enchiridion symbolorum*
TCT = *The Church Teaches*

DB	TCT	DB	TCT	DB	TCT	DB	TCT
1623	16	1673	49	1794	68	1831	211
1624	17	1674	50	1795	75	1832	212
1625	18	1675	176	1796	76	1833	213
1626	19	1676	177	1797	77	1834	214
1627	20	1677	178	1798	78	1835	215
1634	21	1682	179	1799	79	1836	216
1635	22	1683	180	1800	80	1837	217
1636	23	1686	181	1801	358	1838	218
1637	24	1696	182	1802	359	1839	219
1638	25	1697	183	1803	360	1840	220
1639	26	1698	184	1804	361	1853	869
1641	510	1701	346	1805	362	1854	870
1642	27	1702	347	1806	60	1891	86
1643	28	1703	51	1807	61	1895	87
1644	29	1704	52	1808	62	1929	894
1645	30	1705	53	1809	101	1930	895
1646	173	1706	54	1810	69	1936a	221
1647	174	1707	55	1811	70	1936b	222
1648	175	1708	56	1812	71	1940a	{ 511
1649	31	1709	57	1813	72	1940a	{ 513
1650	32	1715	185	1814	73	1943	102
1651	33	1716	186	1815	74	1944	103
1652	34	1717	187	1816	81	1945	104
1659	35	1718	188	1817	82	1946	105
1660	36	1781	354	1818	83	1947	106
1661	37	1782	355	1819	84	1949	107
1662	38	1783	356	1820	85	1950	108
1663	39	1784	357	1821	201	1951	109
1664	40	1785	58	1822	202	1952	110
1665	41	1786	59	1823	203	1953	111
1666	42	1787	99	1824	204	1954	223
1667	43	1788	100	1825	205	1955	224
1668	44	1789	63	1826	206	1956	225
1669	45	1790	64	1827	207	1957	226
1670	46	1791	65	1828	208	1958	227
1671	47	1792	66	1829	209	1959	228
1672	48	1793	67	1830	210	1960	229

DB = Denzinger's *Enchiridion symbolorum*
TCT = *The Church Teaches*

Table of Reference

DB	TCT	DB	TCT	DB	TCT	DB	TCT
1961	230	2029	476	2123	363	2292	133
1962	231	2030	477	2145	88	2293 {	134
1978a	514	2031	478	2146	89		135
2001	112	2032	479	2147	90	2294 {	136
2002	113	2033	480	2183	486		137
2003	114	2034	481	2184	487		138
2004	115	2035	482	2185	488	2297	765
2006	232	2036	483	2186	129	2299	766
2007	233	2037	484	2187	130	2300 {	767
2009	116	2038	485	2225	871		768
2010	117	2039	679	2226	872		769
2011	118	2040	680	2229	873		770
2012	119	2041	681	2231	874		771
2013	120	2042	701	2234	875	2301	852
2014	121	2043	702	2236	876	2302	140
2015	122	2044	711	2237	877	2317	364
2016	123	2046	815	2286	242	2318	395
2017	124	2047	816	2287	252	2319	281
2018	125	2052	234	2288 {	258	2327	365
2019	126	2053	235		257	2328	366
2023	127	2054	236	2289	495	2329	141
2024	128	2055	237	2290 {	321	2330	142
2027	474	2056	238		322	2332	519
2028	475	2089	682	2291	518	2333	520

DB = Denzinger's *Enchiridion symbolorum*
TCT = *The Church Teaches*

General Index

General Index

Baptism (*continued*)

character imprinted by, 663, 673, 684, 843

Council of Florence on, 686

Council of Trent on, 687-700

error of Luther about, 551

errors of the modernists about, 701 f.

first of the sacraments, 686

form of, 298, 659, 686, 690

grace conferred by, 190, 368, 376, 563, 741

incorporation into the mystical body by, 190, 195, 242, 245, 270, 277, 374, 686, 741, 769, 789, 873

of infants, 375, 659, 683, 685, 699 f., 702

infusion of virtues in, 564, 683

instrumental cause of, 686

intention in, 684, 686, 690

matter of, 659, 686, 688

membership in the Church by, 190, 221, 270, 277, 686, 694, 700

minister of, 686, 690

necessity of, 273, 560, 563, 683, 686, 691, 701, 789

not metaphorical, 688

obligations imposed by, 693 f., 700

original sin remitted by, 190, 368, 376, 683, 685 f., 789

principal cause of, 686

punishment remitted by, 376, 571, 651, 686, 797, 884

repetition of, 10, 663, 673, 697, 699, 789, 884

of St. John, 687

time for reception of, 698

vows valid after, 695

Barcos, de, Martin, 79

Bautain, Louis: rejection of fideism, 12 f., 15-20

Bay, de, Michel, 249 f.: error about the Mother of God, 207, 508; errors about grace, 246, 608-26; errors about original justice, 161, 377 f., 383 f.; errors

Bay, de, Michel (*continued*)

about original sin, 161, 379-82

Beatific vision (*see also* TI: The Last Things, 367)

in Christ, 255, 486, 495

degrees in, 606, 889

errors of Rosmini-Serbati about, 894 f.

eternity of, 886

light of glory necessary for, 885

nature of, 386, 395, 886

object of, 386, 886, 888 f., 892

reward of good works, 165, 573, 600, 606

Beghards, 349

Beguines, 349

Benedict XII (pope): *Benedictus Deus,* on the last things, 349, 886 f.; on creation, 148, 342

Benedict XV (pope): *Inter sodalicia,* on the Mother of God, 210, 515; *Spiritus Paraclitus,* on Scripture, 55, 129 f.

Benedictus Deus by Benedict XII: on the last things, 349, 886 f.

Berengarius (of Tours), profession of faith for, 276, 712

Bernard, St., 203

Bessarion, 311

Biblical Commission: letter to Suhard, on *Genesis,* 64, 140; reply on creation, 153, 363

Bishops: jurisdiction of, 208, 229-31, 252; as successors of the apostles, 90, 201, 208, 231, 843, 849

Bishops of Spain and Galicia, letter of Hadrian I to: on Jesus Christ, 189, 453

Blessed Virgin Mary (*see also* TI: The Mother of God, 360 f.)

Assumption of, 519 f.

coredemptress, 514-16

Council of Constantinople (II) on, 421

Council of Ephesus on, 167, 399

Council of the Lateran (649) on, 205, 505

Council of Trent on, 206, 506

378

General Index

General Index

Confirmation (*continued*)
consecration of chrism for, 703
Council of Florence on, 707
Council of Trent on, 708-10
distinct from baptism, 711
effects of, 10, 663, 673, 707, 843
form of, 707
matter of, 703, 707, 709
minister of, 660, 685, 704-7, 710, 843, 850
subject of, 660, 708
true sacrament, 660, 663, 685, 707 f., 711

Constance, Council of
on the Church, 76, 158-63
on the Eucharist, 277, 714-16
on indulgences, 820 f.
on penance, 772-75
on the sacraments, 260, 661 f.
on veneration of the saints, 214, 521

Constans II (emperor), 181

Constantine IV (emperor), 187

Constantinople, II Council of: on Jesus Christ, 173, 416-30; on tradition, 91

Constantinople, III Council of: on Jesus Christ, 187, 451 f.

Constantinople, IV Council of: on the Church, 213; on creation, 144, 333

Constantinople, letter of John II to senate at: on Jesus Christ, 172, 415; on the Mother of God, 204, 503 f.

Constantinople, Provincial Council of: on creation, 143, 323 f.; on hell, 345, 878

Constitutio Benedictina, 349, 886 f.

Consubstantiality of the Son of God, 2-4, 300, 414, 432 f., 456 f.; *see also* Son of God

Contrition; see Penance

Coredemptress, 514-16

Councils, ecumenical: infallibility of, 14, 91 f., 169, 429 f.; list of, 368 f. (Individual councils are indexed by name.); Roman Pontiff superior to, 210;

Councils, ecumenical (*continued*)
tradition expressed in, 14, 91 f., 429 f., 739

Creation (*see also* TI: Creation of the World and of Man, 358)
beginning of time with, 306, 356, 363
Council of the Vatican on, 348-62
error of Mechitriz about, 342
errors of Eckhart about, 337-41
errors of the Manichaeans about, 325-28, 331 f., 344
errors of the ontologists about, 40 f.
errors of the Origenists about, 323 f.
errors of the pantheists about, 346 f., 360-62
errors of the Priscillianists about, 325-28, 331 f.
errors of Rosmini-Serbati about, 40 f.
freedom of God in, 343, 356, 362, 364
God the author of, 1-4, 8, 94, 294, 306, 309, 334, 344 f., 355-62
purpose of, 356, 362
single good principle in, 94, 154, 306, 309, 327, 331 f., 343 f., 356, 358

Creed
Apostles', 1, 1
Athanasian (*Quicumque*), 4, 6 f.
of IV Council of the Lateran, 6
of II Council of Lyons, 6
of XI Council of Toledo, 6
of the Council of Trent, 6, 8-14
of Epiphanius, 3, 4 f.
Nicene, 1, 2
Niceno-Constantinopolitan, 2, 3

Criticism, higher, 105

Crucifixion of Jesus Christ; *see* Jesus Christ

Cum occasione by Innocent X: on Jansenism, 249, 627-31

Cum quorundam by Paul IV: on the Mother of God, 206, 507

General Index

Eucharist (*continued*)
Council of Rome (VI) on, 712
Council of Trent on, 718-38
forgiveness of sins by, 732
form of, 713, 717, 721
institution of, 719, 740
matter of, 717, 754, 764
minister of, 658 f., 713
power of the Church over, 678
pre-eminence of, 721
purpose of, 720
reservation of, 724, 734
sacrifice of; *see* The Mass
transubstantiation in, 11, 659 f.,
712 f., 717, 722, 729
true sacrament, 659 f., 663, 714,
717
union with Christ through, 717
unleavened bread in, 660
worship of, 723, 733
Eugene IV (pope), *261*
Eunomians, *124,* 426
Eunomius: error about the Trinity,
286, 313
Eusebius, *1, 68*
Eutyches, 147, 426, 473, 497:
errors about Jesus Christ, *170;*
error about the Mother of God,
504
Evil: cause of (*see* Creation;
Devil); permitted by God, 580
Evolution of man, 365 f., *see also*
Soul, human; Body, human
Ex omnibus afflictionibus by St.
Pius V: on grace, *246,* 608-26
Exegesis; *see* Sacred Scripture
Explorata res by Pius XI: on the
Mother of God, *211,* 516
Exsurge Domine by Leo X: on
errors of Luther, 229, 550-55;
on penance, *303,* 777-86
Extreme unction (*see also* TI: Ex-
treme Unction, *366*)
body affected by 663, 830, 833
complement of penance, 831
Council of Florence on, 830
Council of Trent on, 831-38
form of, 830, 832
grace conferred by, 833, 836

Extreme unction (*continued*)
institution of, 832
matter of, 713, 829 f., 832
minister of, 829 f., 832, 834, 838
obligation of receiving, 834, 837
St. James on, 660, 829 f., 832,
834 f., 837
sins remitted by, 833, 836
subject of, 829 f., 832, 834
true sacrament, 660, 663, 713,
829-37
Exultate Deo: on the sacraments,
261, 663

Faith (*see also* Reason; Revelation;
TI: Revelation, Faith, and
Reason, *355;* TI: The Infused
Virtues, *362*)
capacity of reason for knowing,
20, 24, 26, 33, 46
certainty of, 25-27, 30
definition of, 63
errors of Frohschammer on, 42-50
the foundation of justification,
63, 67, 280, 545, 565
free assent of, 63, 65, 69, 73
gratuitousness of, 15, 29 f., 33,
63, 65, 68, 73, 545, 548 f.
history in agreement with, 89
infused in justification, 564, 683
intellectual character of, 24-26,
63, 65, 70, 73, 75, 88, 562
lost by infidelity, 243, 572, 602
motive of, 24-26, 63 f., 68, 70 f.,
74, 88
necessity of, 6 f., 26, 29 f., 65, 67,
562-66, 648, 655
not blind assent, 18, 24, 64 f., 71,
88
object of, 66, 75, 180, 266
obligation to accept, 24, 26, 63,
67-69
philosophy and, 21, 45 f., 50,
176 f.
reason in accord with, 22, 31, 54,
64, 71, 77-79, 82, 89, 106, 127
reason prior to, 19, 33
replaced by the Beatific Vision,
886

Faith (*continued*)
revelation prior to, 15, 32, 70
supernaturalness of, 63, 70, 75,
545, 548 f.
suspending assent to, 68, 74
theological virtue, 63, 886
Fall of man; *see* Original sin
Fatalism, 32
Father, First Person of the Trinity:
consubstantiality of, 2-4, 8,
284, 291, 299-307, 309-15,
319, 416, 431-33, 456 f.; distinct person, 6, 285, 305, 311-
13, 315; source of all fatherhood, 299; without origin, 6,
299 f., 306, 311 f.; *see also* TI:
The Triune God, *357 f.*
Fathers (of the Church): authority
in Scripture, 9, 98, 100, 103;
teachers of tradition, 88-92
Fideism, Bautain's rejection of, *12,*
15-20
Fidentem by Leo XIII: on the
Mother of God, *210, 513*
Filioque, 72
Flavius, letter of St. Leo the Great
to: on Jesus Christ, *170,* 412 f.
Florence, Council of, 206, 215,
473
and the Apostles' Creed, *1*
on baptism, 686
on the Church, 77, 164 f.
on confirmation, 707
on creation, *148,* 343 f.
on the Eucharist, 717
on extreme unction, 830
on holy orders, *328,* 839
on the last things, *351,* 889
on matrimony, 854
on penance, 776
on the sacraments, *261,* 663
on tradition, *43,* 94
on the Trinity, *135,* 311-13
Freedom: of man's will, 32, 369,
536 f., 555, 557, 561, 579, 619-
23, 629 f., 633, 642: rationalistic, 42-50, 176 f.; required
for sin, 615; *see also* Grace,
freedom under

Free will, error of Luther about,
555
Freedom of Science by Frohschammer, *21*
Friuli, Council of: on Jesus Christ,
454
Frohschammer, James, *13, 20, 42-
50, 81*

Genesis, 140-42, 363
Gilbert of Porrée on Jesus Christ,
174
Gioberti, Vincenzio, *19*
Gnosticism, *146*
God (*see also* The Triune God; TI:
The Triune God, *357 f.*)
Creator; *see* Creation
eternity of, 6, 287, 296, 300, 306,
309-13, 355, 431
existence known by natural reason, 15, 20, 32, 46, 48, 58, 60,
75, 88, 364, 636
immensity of, 6, 306, 355
immutability of, 2, 306, 310 f.,
346, 355, 431
incomprehensibility of, 306, 355,
431
knowledge in, 64, 355, 357, 364
natural knowledge about, 15, 20,
32, 46, 48, 58, 60, 88: errors of
Ontologists about, 35-39, 86 f.
omnipotence of, 1-4, 6, 8, 64,
286, 289, 292, 295 f., 306, 309-
13, 324, 431
simplicity of, 306, 355
unicity of, 1-4, 6, 8, 306, 309-11,
314, 317, 334, 355, 358
Good works: errors of Luther
about, 553 f.; man's natural
capacity for, 553-55, 581, 599,
619 f., 632-37, 648
Gospel of St. John, historicity of,
123-25
Gospels: historicity of, 120 f.; integrity of, 122; *see also* Scripture
Grace (*see also* Justification; TI:
Grace, *361 f.*)

General Index

Grace (*continued*)
adoptive sonship through, 558, 560, 645
antecedent, concomitant, and subsequent, 573, 649
conferred *ex opere operato* by the sacraments, 672
conferred by the sacraments, 10, 550, 663, 668, 670-72, 682 f., 721, 877
contained in the sacraments, 663, 670
Council of Carthage (XVI) on, 527-32
Council of Orange (II) on, 543-49
Council of Trent on, 556-607
Council of the Vatican on, 252, 645-57
description of sanctifying, 646 f., 653 f.
elevating, 368
errors of de Bay about, 608-26
errors of Jansen about, 627-31
errors of Luther about, 550-55
errors of Quesnel about, 632-44
exciting and helping, 546, 549, 561 f., 571, 577 f.
freedom under, 65, 386, 536, 542, 549, 561 f., 578, 580, 628 f., 630, 642-44, 647
illumination and inspiration by, 65, 537, 539, 544, 546, 561
incipient and perfecting, 570
Indiculus on, 533-42
loss of, 243, 569-72, 597, 601 f., 692
necessary to avoid sin, 529, 535, 540, 576
necessary for salutary acts, 534-37, 541-46, 548 f., 557, 575-77, 596, 648 f., 655 f.
operating, 561, 577 f., 792
prevenient, 544, 561, 577, 649
supernatural help, 527-29, 535 f., 538, 544-48, 561 f., 576
Gravissimas inter by Pius IX: on faith and reason, 20, 42-50
Greeks, Decree for the, 77, 164

Gregory the Great, St.: on the Roman Pontiff, 208
Gregory of Nazianzus, St., 187, 452
Gregory VII (pope), 276
Gregory X (pope), 134, 190: on the Church, 72
Gregory XII (pope), 76
Gregory XIII (pope): *Provisionis nostrae*, on de Bay, 247
Gregory XV (pope): and the Immaculate Conception, 208
Gregory XVI (pope), 12
Günther, Anton, 13, 137: error about creation, 362

Hadrian I (pope): letter to bishops of Spain and Galicia, on Jesus Christ, 189
Hadrian II (pope), 144
Heaven: Council of Florence on, 351, 889; grace and entrance into, 564, 573, 606, 891; immediate entrance into, 686, 883 f., 886, 889, 892; *see also* TI: The Last Things, 367
Hell (*see also* TI: The Last Things, 367)
Council of the Lateran (IV) on, 347, 881
eternity of, 7, 165, 650, 657, 878, 880 f., 883, 891, 893
immediate entrance into, 165, 884, 887, 891
Provincial Council of Constantinople on, 345, 878
punishments in, 7, 165, 880 f., 883, 891
salutary fear of, 562, 582
Heraclius (emperor), 181
Hermes, 27: error about creation, 362; errors about faith, 73 f.
Hilary, St., 127
History, faith in agreement with, 89
Holy Eucharist; *see* The Eucharist
Holy Office, the
on the beatific vision, 894 f.
on the Church, 79, 107, 170, 232-38

385

Holy Office (*continued*)
on Jesus Christ, *197*, 486-88
letter to Cushing, on the Church, *118*, 266-80
letter to the English bishops, on the Church, *84*, 181
on ontologism, *35*, 86 f.
on the sacraments, *265*, 679-82
on Scripture, *52*, 112-28
Sunt quos amor, on the Mother of God, *210*
Holy orders (*see also* TI: Holy Orders, *366*)
ceremonies of, 848
character imprinted by, 10, 663, 673, 843, 847
Council of Florence on, *328*, 839
Council of Trent on, 840-51
effects of, 795, 839, 842, 847, 852
form of, 839, 842, 847, 852
grades of, 841, 845, 849 f.
institution of, 757, 840, 846
matter of, 834, 839, 842, 852
minister of, 713, 839, 843, 850
true sacrament, 660, 663, 839, 842-44, 846
Holy Spirit (*see also* TI: The Triune God, *357 f.*)
adoration of, 297
consubstantiality with the Father and the Son, 284, 291, 299, 301-7, 309-15, 319, 416, 431 f.
distinct person, 6, 305, 311-13, 315
eternity of, 5 f., 287, 296, 306, 309-12
indwelling of, 4, 321 f., 385, 611, 792, 797
inspiration of Scripture by, 94, 99, 109 f., 129
procession of, 3 f., 6, 8, 291, 301, 305-7, 308, 310-12, 314
soul of the mystical body, 257-59
true God, 2, 4, 6, 283 f., 286, 291, 299, 301-5, 309 f.
Holy Trinity; *see* The Triune God
Hope: infused in justification, 564; justification and, 556; loss of,

Hope (*continued*)
243; as a motive for action, 568, 605; replaced by the beatific vision, 886; *see also* TI: The Infused Virtues, *362*
Hormisdas, St. (pope): on the Roman Pontiff, *69*, 147 f.
Houtin, 53
Human race, origin of, 349, 353, 363, 366
Humani generis by Pius XII: on the Church, *121*, 281; on creation, *154*, 364-66; on original sin, *164*, 395; on Scripture, *65*, 141 f.
Humbert (cardinal), *71*
Humbert (archbishop), letter of Pius III to: on baptism, *267*, 683 f.
Hus, John, *78*: errors about the Church, *76*, 160-63; questions for followers: about veneration of relics, *214*; about the minister of the sacraments, 662; about the Eucharist, 277, 715 f.; about penance, 773-75; about indulgences, 820 f.
Hypostatic union in Christ: existence of, 4, 7, 399, 401-7, 409-11, 414, 419-23, 429, 437, 448, 452, 455-58, 468 f., 721; perfection of natures in, 398 f., 412-14, 422, 434-38, 445, 447, 449, 454-57, 461, 467, 496, 498; *see also* Jesus Christ

Ibas of Edessa, *173*, 430
Images, veneration of, 12, 521, 524 f.
Immaculate Conception, 376, 389, 505: Council of Trent and, *207*, 376; definition of, 510; error of de Bay about, 508; history of dogma of, *207 f.; see also* Blessed Virgin Mary
Immortality of Adam, 363, 367, 370, 372, 384 f., 388, 557
Incarnation: efficient cause of, 448,

General Index

Incarnation (*continued*)
455, 459; errors of the modernists on, 474-85; purpose of, 2-4, 7, 197, 374, 455, 457, 558, 564, 645 f.; *see also* Jesus Christ; Hypostatic union; TI: The Person of the Redeemer, *359 f.*

Index, Congregation of the, *18, 20, 35,* 43

Indiculus: on grace, *220,* 533-42; on original sin, *156,* 368

Indifferentism: collection of modern errors on, *86,* 185-88; *see also* The Church, necessity of

Indulgences (*see also* TI: Indulgences, *365*)
Council of Constance on, 820 f.
Council of Trent on, *321,* 828
errors of Luther about, 822-27
not dispensation from good works, 823
power of the Church over, 828
power of the Pope over, 818, 820-22
remission of temperal punishment, 818, 824
treasury of, 818 f., 822
usefulness of, 12, 823, 825-28

In eminenti Ecclesiae militantis by Urban VII, *247, 249*

Ineffabilis Deus by Pius IX, *389:* on the Immaculate Conception, *207,* 510

Infallibility; *see* The Church; Roman Pontiff; Councils

Infants, baptism of, 375, 659, 683, 685, 699 f., 702

Infidelity, negative, 616

Infused virtues, 564, 585, 683; *see also* TI: The Infused Virtues, *362*

Injunctum nobis by Pius IV, *6,* 8-14

Innocent I, St. (pope), *156,* 368, 534: letter to the African bishops, on the Roman Pontiff, *68,* 144; letter to Decentius, on extreme unction, *322,* 829

Innocent III (pope): *Majores Ecclesiae causas:* on the punishment of sin, *346,* 880; on the sacraments, *267,* 683 f.; *see also* Durandus of Osca

Innocent IV (pope): letter to bishop of Tusculum, on purgatory, *347,* 882 f.

Innocent VIII (pope): and the Immaculate Conception, *207*

Innocent X (pope): on the Church, *79, 170; Cum occasione,* on Jansenism, *249,* 627-31

Inquisition, the Congregation of, *19*

Inspiration; *see* Scripture, inspiration of

Integrity (preternatural gift): of Adam, 363, 378, 385; gratuitousness of, 377 f., 383, 385; *see also* Original justice; Original sin

Inter cunctas, 277

Inter sodalicia by Benedict XV: on the Mother of God, *210,* 515

Introduction to Philosophy by Frohschammer, *21*

Jacobites, Decree for the: on the Church, 77, 165: on creation, *148,* 343; on Scripture, *43,* 94; on the Trinity, 135, *311-13*

Jansen, Cornelis, *79, 161, 250:* errors about grace, *249,* 627-31; errors about the Mother of God, *207,* 509

Jerome, St., 129, 131

Jesus Christ (*see also* Son of God; TI: The Person of the Redeemer, *359 f.*)
adoration of, 407, 424, 427
ascension into heaven, 1-4, 7 f.
beatific vision in, 255, 486, 495
birth of, 1, 4, 399 f., 413, 417, 433, 446, 448 f., 454, 456 f.
Council of Chalcedon on, 414
Council of Constantinople (II) on, 416-30

General Index

General Index

John II (*continued*)
 at Constantinople, on Jesus
  Christ, *172;* on the Mother of
  God, *204*
John XXII (pope): *Licet juxta doc-*
  trinam, 76; on creation, *147*
John Chrysostom, St.: on Sacred
  Scripture, 137
John of Jandun, *75 f.,* 155-57
John the Baptist, 334, 687
Judgment; *see* TI: The Last Things,
  367
Judgment, general, 1-5, 7 f., 432,
  456, 466, 879, 881, 884, 886 f.:
  Council of Lyons (II) on, 884
Julius, St. (pope): letter to the
  Orientals, on the Roman See,
  68, 143
Justification (*see also* TI: Grace,
  361 f.)
 causes of, 563
 Council of Trent on, 556-607
 description of, 560
 faith the foundation of, 63, 67,
  280, 545, 565
 faith alone insufficient for, 562,
  564-66, 583, 586-88, 603, 668,
  672, 783 f., 795, 803, 811
 gratuitousness of, 374, 543-46,
  548, 561-63, 565, 575, 577
 increase of, 567, 598, 606, 663,
  717
 infusion of virtues in, 564, 585,
  683
 internal sanctification and renovation, 376, 559 f., 563 f., 573,
  645 f., 653 f., 877
 the Law of Moses and, 557 f.,
  575
 merit after, 567, 573 f., 576, 598,
  600, 605 f., 611, 650
 perseverance in, 569 f., 589 f.,
  596 f.
 preparation for, 561 f., 577 f.,
  581, 583, 791, 804
 restoration of, 571, 603 f., 659
 sins truly removed by, 376, 527,
  551, 563, 584 f., 645 f., 653

Justification (*continued*)
 uncertainty of, 566, 587 f.
Justinian (emperor), 69, *173 f.,*
  415, 503

Kenotic theory, 499
Knights Templars, *147*
Knowledge
 in the beatific vision, 886, 888 f.,
  892
 in Christ, 255, 479, 481, 486-88,
  495
 in God, 355, 357, 364
 God known by natural, 15, 20,
  32, 46, 48, 58, 60, 75, 88, 364,
  636
 in ontologism, 35-41
 supernatural distinct from natural, 21-23, 27, 30, 45-50, 52,
  58, 62, 70, 75, 79
Knowledge of God: errors of the
  Beghards and Beguines about,
  885; errors of the ontologists
  about, 35-39, 86 f.; errors of
  Rosmini-Serbati about, 40 f.,
  86 f.; impossibility of natural
  immediate, 35-39, 86 f.

Laity, priesthood of, 492, 767-71,
  843
Lamennais, de, *13, 18*
Lamentabili by Pius X, 89: on baptism, 701 f.; on the Church,
  107, 232-38; on confirmation,
  711; on Jesus Christ, 474-85; on
  penance, 815 f.; on the sacraments, *265,* 678-81; on tradition and Scripture, *52,* 112-28
Last things; *see* TI: The Last
  Things, *367*
Lateran, Council of (649): on
  Jesus Christ, *180,* 431-45; on
  the Mother of God, *205,* 505;
  on tradition, 92
Lateran, IV Council of
 on the Church, 72, 151
 on creation, *146,* 335

389

General Index

Lateran, IV Council of (*continued*)
Creed of, *6*
on Jesus Christ, *190*, 455
on the last things, *347*, 881
on the sacraments, *259*, 659
on the Trinity, *132*, 306 f.
Lateran, V Council of: on the human soul, *149*, 345
Law of Moses and justification, 557 f., *575*
Le Roy, *53*
Leo the Great, St., *148*, *187*, *201*, *473*, *496*, *499*: letter to Flavius, on Jesus Christ, *170*, 412 f.; Tome of, *170*, 412 f.
Leo II (pope), *187*
Leo IX, St. (pope): letter to Caerularius, on the Church, *71*
Leo X (pope): *Exsurge Domine:* on the Church, *78*, 166-69; on the errors of Luther, *229*, 550-55; on penance, *303*, 777-86
Leo XIII (pope), *19*, *36*, *48*, *58*, *129*, *240*, *258*, 322, *872*
Arcanum divinae sapientiae, on matrimony, *338*, 869 f.
Fidentem, on the Mother of God, *210*, 513
Magnae Dei Matris, on the Mother of God, *209*, 512
Octobri mense, on the Mother of God, *209*, 511
Providentissimus Deus, on Scripture, *48*, 102-11
Sapientiae Christianae, on the Church, *102*, 221 f.
Satis Cognitum, on the Church, *103*, 223-31
Lex orandi, lex credendi, 135, *541*
Licet juxta doctrinam by John XXII: on the Church, *76*, 155-57
Life, eternal; *see* TI: The Last Things, *867*
Light of glory: necessity of, 885; *see also* Beatific vision
Literal meaning of Scripture, *134*
Literary types in Scripture, 137 f., 140-42

Liturgy: Christ's presence in, **765**; in ascetical life, 766
Loisy, *53*
Lombard, Peter: on the Trinity, *132*, 307
Louis of Bavaria, *76*
Louvain, University of, *19*, *161*, **246**
Love; *see* Charity
Lumen gloriae, necessity of, 885
Luther, Martin, errors of,
on baptism, 229, 551
on the Church, *78*, 166-69
on free will, 229, 555
on good works, 229, 553 f.
on indulgences, 822-27
on penance, *303*, 777-86
on the sacraments, 229, 258, 262, 550
on sin, 229, 551-55
Lyons, II Council of, *214*
on the Church, *72*, 152
creed of, *6*
on Jesus Christ, *190*, 456
on the last things, 884
on the sacraments, *260*, 660
on the Trinity, *134*, 308-10

Macedonians, *124 f.*, 313, 426
Magnae Dei Matris by Leo XIII: on the Mother of God, *209*, 512
Magnificate Dominum by Pius XII: on the Mass, *300*, 771
Majores Ecclesiae causas by Innocent III: on the punishment of sin, *346*, 880; on the sacraments, *267*, 683 f.
Malebranche, *19*
Man
composed of body and soul, **306**, 336, 348, 350, 356
creation of, 348-53; *see also* Soul; Body
liberty of, 32, 369, 536 f., **555**, 557, 561, 579, 619-23, 629 f., 633, 642; *see also* Grace, freedom under
supernatural destiny of, 45, **59**,

General Index

Milan, synod of, *1*

Miracles: criterion of revelation, 17, 25, 64, 72, 88, 475; historicity of, 55, 72

Miserentissimus Redemptor by Pius XI: on the Redemption, *198*, 489-94

Modalism, *123*

Modernism, oath against, *36*, 88-90

Modernists

 errors about the Church, *107*, 232-38

 errors about dogma, 88-90

 errors about the Incarnation, 474-85

 errors about penance, 815 f.

 errors about the sacraments, 679-82

 errors about tradition and Scripture, *52*, 112-28

Monarchianism, *123*

Monophysitism, *168, 170, 173 f., 180*, 498

Monothelitism, *180, 187*

Mortal sin; *see* Sin, mortal

Mother of God; *see* Blessed Virgin Mary; TI: The Mother of God, *360 f.*

Munich, Congress of, *83*

Munich, letter to archbishop of: on rationalism, *20*, 42-50

Munich, University of, *20*, 43

Munificentissimus Deus by Pius XII: on the Assumption, *212*, 519 f.

Mysteries: canon defining existence of, 81; conditions for understanding, 75 f.; limits of reason in investigating, 22 f., 27, 30, 44-50, 52, 55, 57, 75 f.; reality of, 21

Mystical body (*see also* The Church) Head of, 153, 172, 190, 195, 240, 242, 245-56, 260, 270, 494

 membership in; *see* Baptism

 Mother of, 517 f.

 origin of, 244

 reason for name, 260

 in Scripture, 239 f.

Mystical body (*continued*)

 Soul of, 257-59

 sufferings of, 494

 visibility of, 263-65

Mystici corporis by Pius XII: on the Church, *107*, 239-65, 276-79; on the Holy Spirit, *138*, 321 f.; on knowledge in Christ, *200*, 495; on the Mother of God, *211*, 517 f.

Myths, 55, 142

Naturalism, *25, 32, 34*

Neo-Aristotelians: errors about the human soul, *149*, 345

Nestorianism, *173 f., 189*, 419

Nestorius, 147, 426, 429 f., 473, 496 f.: error about Jesus Christ, *167 f.*, 399-411; error about the Mother of God, 504

Nicaea, I Council of, *125*, 147, 478

Nicaea, II Council of, 524: on tradition, 93

Nicene Creed, *1, 2*

Niceno-Constantinopolitan Creed, *2, 3*

Notes of the Church, 67 f., 181, 193 f.; *see also* Church: one, holy, Catholic, apostolic

Number in the Trinity, 304

Oath against modernism by Pius X, *36*, 88-90

Occam, *76, 78*

Octobri mense by Leo XIII: on the Mother of God, *208*, 511

Old Law, sacraments of, *663, 666*

Olivi, Peter John: error about the human soul, *147*, 336

Ontologism, description of, *19*

Ontologism of Rosmini-Serbati, *36*, 86 f., *353*, 894 f.

Ontologists: errors about creation, 40 f.; errors about knowledge of God, 35-39, 86 f.

Orange, II Council of: on grace, *225*, 543-49; on original sin, *157*, 369 f.

General Index

Pius XI (pope) (*continued*)
the Redemption, *198*, 489-94;
Explorata res, on the Mother
of God, *211*, **516**
Pius XII (pope)
Divino afflante Spiritu, on Scripture, *57*, 131-39
Humani generis: on the Church,
121, **281**; on creation, *154*,
364-66; on Scripture, *65*, 141 f.;
on the supernatural order, *164*,
395
and letter to Suhard, on Scripture, *64*, 140
Magnificate Dominum, on the
Mass, *300*, 771
Mediator Dei, on the Eucharist,
296, 765-70
Munificentissimus Deus, on the
Assumption, *212*, 519 f.
Mystici corporis: on the Church,
107, 239-65, 276-79; on the
Holy Spirit, *138*, **321** f.; on
knowledge in Christ, *200*, **495**;
on the Mother of God, *211*,
517 f.
Sacramentum ordinis, on holy
orders, *332*, 852
Sempiternus Rex Christus, on
Jesus Christ, *201*, 496-501
Polygenism, 366; *see also* Human
race, origin of
Pope; *see* Roman Pontiff
Praestantia by Pius X, 53
Predestination, **196**, 549, 569, 580,
589, 591
Predication of properties and operations in Christ, 403, 408, 411,
415, 425, 427, 460, 496
Priesthood (*see also* Holy orders)
of Christ, 151, 409, 462, 491 f.,
659, 747, 749, 771
episcopacy superior to, 843, 850
form of, 839, 842, 847, 852
institution of, 747, 757, 840, 846
of the laity, 492, 767-71, 843
matter of, 834, 839, 842, 852
in the Old and New Law, 747,
840

Priesthood (*continued*)
powers conferred in, 767-71, 840,
844
Primacy; *see* Roman Pontiff
Priscillianists: errors about creation,
143, 325-28, 331 f.; errors
about the human soul, 325 f.,
329
Professions of faith, *1-9; see also*
Creeds
Progressionists, 62
Prophecies: criterion of revelation,
25, 64, 88; historicity of, *55*
Prosper of Aquitaine, St., *156*
Providence, 334, 346 f., 357, 431
Providentissimus Deus by Leo XIII,
58, 134: on Scripture, *48*, 102-
11
Provisionis nostrae by Gregory XIII,
247
Punishment, eternal; *see* Hell
Purgatory (*see also* TI: The Last
Things, *367*)
assistance of souls in, **12**, 882,
884, 890
Council of Lyons (II) on, 884
Council of Trent on, 890
determination of name for, 882
existence of, **12**, 604, 650, 882,
884, 886, 888, 890 f.
proved in Scripture, 882

Quanta cura by Pius IX: on the
Church, *85*, 182-84
Quanto conficiamur moerore by
Pius IX: on the Church, *82*,
178
Quaternity in God, rejection of, **307**
Quesnel, Pasquier, errors about
grace, *250*, 632-44
Quicumque (Creed), *4*, 6 f.
Quidort (John of Paris), 73
Qui pluribus by Pius IX: on faith
and reason, *13*, 21-26
Quiricius, *6*, *127*, *346*

Rationalism, 21-30, 34, 42-57
Reason, human (*see also* Revela-

General Index

Reason, human (*continued*)
tion; Faith; TI: Revelation, Faith, and Reason, 355)
errors of Frohschammer about, 42-50
faith in agreement with, 22, 31, 54, 64, 71, 77-79, 82
knowledge of revelation by, 20, 24, 26, 33, 46
limitations of, 27-30, 44 f., 47, 49, 51-53, 56 f., 62, 69, 76, 79-82
prior to faith, 19, 33
weakened by original sin, 20, 28 f., 46
Redemption: objective and subjective, *198;* universality of, 463 f., 471, 558 f., 631, 712; *see also* Jesus Christ
Reformers: and the Church, 182, 207; and original sin, *158,* 371-76; and penance, 798; and the sacraments, *262;* and Scripture, *44*
Relations in the Trinity, 302, 304 f., 311, 316, 319
Relics, veneration of, 12, 521, 523
Religion; *see* Revelation
Reprobates as members of the Church, 160 f.
Resurrection of Christ, 1-4, 7 f., 450, 456, 483 f.: historicity of, 18, 483 f.
Resurrection of the human body (*see also* TI: The Last Things, *367*)
Council of Lyons (II) on, 884
Council of Toledo (XI) on, 879
fact of, 1, 3, 5, 7 f., 331, 466, 879, 881, 884, 887
one's own body restored in, 7, 879, 881, 884
qualities of the body in, 879
universality of, 466, 879, 881, 884, 887
Revelation (*see also* Faith; Reason; TI: Revelation, Faith, and Reason, 355)
Bautain and, 15-20
capacity of reason for knowing,

Revelation (*continued*)
20, 24, 26, 33, 46, 76, 79 f.
errors of the modernists about, 88-90
errors of the traditionalists about, 21-26
fact of, 48, 58, 75
faith subsequent to, 15, 32
God the author of, 25 f., 48, 58, 95, 99, 129, 306; *see also* Scripture, God the author of
immutability of, 23, 53, 80, 83, 88, 91, 148, 236
Mosaic, 16, 20
necessity of, 29, 54, 59, 61 f., 75
obligation to accept, 24, 26, 63, 67 f.
philosophy and, 21, 45 f., 50, 176 f.
proofs for divine origin of, 16-18, 25 f., 64, 67, 71 f., 88, 475
Rheims, Council of, *174*
Richard (cardinal), 52
Roess, *12*
Roman Church, primacy of, 13, 143-45, 152 f., 207, 238
Roman Pontiff
authority of, 149, 154, 156-58, 164, 168, 171, 208-11, 230, 252, 271
head of the Church, 164, 171, 210, 215, 229-31
infallibility of, 14, 145, 147-49, 152, 168, 212-20, 533
primacy of, 14, 143-46, 152 f., 164, 166, 171, 181, 184, 204, 206 f., 212, 214 f., 229 f., 252
successor of St. Peter, 13, 144, 146, 152-54, 164, 166, 171, 178, 204-6, 212-17
vicar of Christ, 13, 155, 159, 164, 166, 171, 206, 214 f., 250 f., 265, 272
Roman See, primacy of, 143, 164, 181
Rome, Council of (382): on Jesus Christ, *166,* 396-98; on Scripture, *44;* on the Trinity, *125,* 284-98

General Index

General Index

Sunt quos amor by the Holy Office: on the Mother of God, *210*

Supernatural mode of revelation, *58* f., *62*

Supernatural order (*see also* TI: Original Justice and Original Sin, *359*)
definition of, 387
destiny of man in, *45*, *59*, 385 f., *395*, 886
enumeration of gifts in, 385
gratuitousness of, 377 f., 383-85, 387, 390-92, 395, 647
man's fall from; *see* Original sin
ordination of natural order to, 647

Super quibusdam by Clement VI: on the sacraments, *272*, 703-6

Swords, the theory of two, *154*

Syllabus; *see* Collection of modern errors

Synoptic Gospels, authenticity of, *480*

Tertullian, 23, *125*

Theandric operation, *181*, 444

Theodore of Mopsuestia, *173*, 419 f., 427-30

Theodoret of Cyrrhus, *173*, 429

Theology, philosophy distinct from, 27, 46, 56

Thomas Aquinas
on the head of the Mystical Body, 254
and holy orders, 328
on matrimony, 871
method of, 34
and the power of the Church, 73
on Scripture, 137

Three Chapters, *173*, 416-30

Timothy (Aelurus), *147*

Toledo, XI Council of: on the Incarnation, *184*, 446-49; introduction to the Creed of, *6*; on the Redemption, *184*, 450; on the Resurrection, *346*, 879; on the Trinity, *127*, 299-305

Tome of Damasus: on Jesus Christ, *166*, 396-98; on the Trinity, *125*, 284-98

Tome of Leo, *170*, 412 f.

Tradition (*see also* TI: Tradition and Holy Scripture, *356*)
errors of the modernists about, 112-28
existence of unwritten, 93, 95, 99
expressed in the Church's *magisterium*, 66, 180, 266
expressed in the councils, 14, 91 f., 429 f.
source of revelation, 9, 66, 90-93, 95, 99
taught by the Fathers, 88-92

Traditionalism, *18*

Transmigration of souls, *347*

Trent, Council of
on baptism, 687-700
on communion, *288*, 739-45
on confirmation, 708-10
Creed of, *6*, 8-14
on the Eucharist, *280*, 718-38
on extreme unction, *324*, 831-38
on holy orders, *329*, 840-51
and the Immaculate Conception, 207
on indulgences, *321*, 828
on justification, *229*, 556-607
on the Mass, *290*, 746-64
on matrimony, *335*, 855-68
on the Mother of God, *206*, **506**
on original sin, *158*, 371-76
on penance, *304*, 787-814
on purgatory, *351*, 890
on the sacraments, *262*, 664-78
on tradition and Scripture, *44*, 95-98
on veneration of saints, *214*, 522-26

Tritheism, *123*

Triune God (*see also* TI: The Triune God, *357* f.)
circumincession in, 312
consubstantiality of persons in, 2-4, 299, 301-7, 309-15, 319, 431-33, 456 f.
Council of Lyons (II) on, 308-10
Council of Rome (382) on, 284-98
Council of the Vatican on, 314-20

General Index

Triune God (*continued*)
Decree for the Jacobites on, 311-13
distinct persons in, 6, 305, 311-13, 315, 458
error of Arius about, 286, 313
error of Eunomius about, 286, 313
error of Joachim about, 307
error of Sabellius about, 285, 313
errors of Günther about, 137
existence of, 2-4, 6, 8, 283 f., 298 f., 302-7, 309, 311-15, 334, 415 f., 431, 458, 507
indwelling of, 322, 645
inseparability of persons in, 305
number in, 304
operations common to, 294, 305 f., 312, 314, 316, 320, 334, 431, 448
Peter Lombard on, 307
relations in, 302, 304 f., 311, 316, 319
unity of, 282 f., 295 f., 298 f., 302-5, 307, 309-11, 314-19, 416, 431
Tusculum, letter of Innocent IV to the bishop of: on purgatory, 347, 882 f.
Tyrrell, 53

Ubaghs, Gerhard, 19
Unam sanctam by Boniface VIII: on the Church, 73, 153 f., 250
Unigenitus Dei Filius by Clement VI: on indulgences, 319, 817-19
Unitarianism, 206
Universals in ontologism, 37
Urban VIII (pope): *In eminenti Ecclesiae militantis*, 247, 249

Vatican, Council of
on the Church, 86, 94, 189-220
on creation in general, 151, 354-62
on the creation of man, 150, 348-53

Vatican, Council of (*continued*)
on faith, 26, 63-74
on the elevation of man, 162, 385-94
on faith and reason, 26, 75-85
on grace, 252, 645-57
on the Incarnation, 191, 457-73
on the last things, 352, 891-93
on revelation, 26, 58-62
on tradition and Scripture, 46, 99-101
on the Trinity, 137, 314-20
Veneration of the saints; *see* Saints
Venial sin, punishment of, 882; *see also* Purgatory
Vicar of Christ; *see* Roman Pontiff
Vienne, Council of, 345: on creation, 147, 336; on the last things, 349, 885
Vigilius (pope), 143, 174, 345
Virginity of the Blessed Virgin, 1, 3 f., 8, 400, 413, 417, 432, 446, 455 f., 502, 505, 507
Virginity preferred to matrimony, 866
Virtues infused in baptism, 564, 585, 683
Vision, beatific; *see* Beatific vision
Voluntariness in sin, 379-82
Vosté, J. M., 64
Vows valid after baptism, 695
Vulgate, authenticity of, 44, 97, 99, 133

Waldes, Peter, 72
Waldensians, 132, 145 f., 258
Wyclif, 214: error about the sacraments, 661; errors about the Church, 76, 78, 158 f.; errors about penance, 772-75; questions for followers: about the Eucharist, 277, 715 f.; about indulgences, 820 f.; about the sacraments, 661; about the veneration of relics, 214, 521

Zoroastrianism, 142
Zosimus, St. (pope), 156, 218

400